Remaking Citizenship in Multicultural Europe

Citizenship, Gender and Diversity

Series Editors: **Beatrice Halsaa,** University of Oslo, Norway, **Sasha Roseneil,** Birkbeck College, University of London, UK and **Sevil Sümer,** Uni Rokkan Centre, University of Bergen, Norway

Titles in the series include:

Beatrice Halsaa, Sasha Roseneil, Sevil Sümer (*editors*)
REMAKING CITIZENSHIP IN MULTICULTURAL EUROPE
Women's Movements, Gender and Diversity

Line Nyhagen Predelli and Beatrice Halsaa. With Cecilie Thun, Kim Perren and Adriana Sandu.
MAJORITY–MINORITY RELATIONS IN CONTEMPORARY WOMEN'S MOVEMENTS
Strategic Sisterhood

Forthcoming titles:

Sasha Roseneil (*editor*)
BEYOND CITIZENSHIP?
Feminism and the Transformation of Belonging

Ana Cristina Santos
SOCIAL MOVEMENTS AND SEXUAL CITIZENSHIP IN SOUTHERN EUROPE
Enacting Activism

Citizenship, Gender and Diversity
Series Standing Order ISBN 978–0–230–28054–0   Hardback
                            978–0–230–28055–7   Paperback
(outside North America only)

You can receive future titles in this series as they are published by placing a standing order. Please contact your bookseller or, in case of difficulty, write to us at the address below with your name and address, the title of the series and the ISBN quoted above.

Customer Services Department, Macmillan Distribution Ltd, Houndmills, Basingstoke, Hampshire RG21 6XS, England

Remaking Citizenship in Multicultural Europe

Women's Movements, Gender and Diversity

Edited by

Beatrice Halsaa
Centre for Gender Research, University of Oslo, Norway

Sasha Roseneil
Birkbeck College, University of London, UK

and

Sevil Sümer
Uni Rokkan Centre, University of Bergen, Norway

First published 2012 by
PALGRAVE MACMILLAN

Palgrave Macmillan in the UK is an imprint of Macmillan Publishers Limited,
registered in England, company number 785998, of Houndmills,
Basingstoke,
Hampshire RG21 6XS.

Palgrave Macmillan in the US is a division of St Martin's Press LLC,
175 Fifth Avenue, New York, NY 10010.

Palgrave Macmillan is the global academic imprint of the above companies
and has companies and representatives throughout the world.

Palgrave® and Macmillan® are registered trademarks in the United States,
the United Kingdom, Europe and other countries

ISBN: 978–0–230–27628–4

This book is printed on paper suitable for recycling and made from fully
managed and sustained forest sources. Logging, pulping and manufacturing
processes are expected to conform to the environmental regulations of the
country of origin.

A catalogue record for this book is available from the British Library.

A catalog record for this book is available from the Library of Congress.

10 9 8 7 6 5 4 3 2 1
21 20 19 18 17 16 15 14 13 12

Printed and bound in the United States of America

Contents

Tables and Figures

Tables

Figures

Acknowledgements

This book emerged out of the FEMCIT project, a transnational, multidisciplinary feminist research project that ran from 2007 to 2011. Many people contributed to the collective work of FEMCIT.

Firstly, we thank everyone who was part of the FEMCIT project. We start by acknowledging Tone Hellesund, the first Scientific Coordinator of FEMCIT, whose enthusiasm, vision and belief that we might secure funding for a large European project about women's movements kick-started it all. We also especially thank Siren Høgtun, the Administrative Coordinator, who managed the complex administrative and financial aspects of the project, and Solveig Bergman, who was the other member, with us, of the 'Project Office', responsible for the scientific direction and management of FEMCIT. We owe a big 'thank you' to the Steering Committee – Nicky Le Feuvre, Line Nyhagen Predelli, Joyce Outshoorn and Monica Threlfall – for their meticulous work and good humour throughout the project. We thank all the partners in the project, who were also involved from the beginning: Anne-Jorunn Berg, Hilda Rømer Christensen, Drude Dahlerup, Małgorzata Fuszara, Hana Hašková, Teresa Kulawik, Sabine Strasser and Celia Valiente. And last, but certainly not least, the researchers who joined FEMCIT to work on particular sub-projects: Jenny Bredull, Saloua Chaker, Isabel Crowhurst, Susanne Dodillet, Radka Dudová, Rune Ervik, Lenita Freidenvall, Michala Hvidt, Berit Gullikstad, madeleine kennedy-macfoy, Anna Krajewska, Beata Laciak, Karin S. Lindelöf, Elisabet Ljunggren, Esmeranda Manful, Milka Metso, Dorota Orłowska, Ana Prata, Kateřina Pulkrábková, Esther Quintero, Minna Rantalaiho, Trine Rogg Korsvik, Anne Rudolf, Adriana Sandu, Ana Cristina Santos, Minna Seikkula, Mariya Stoilova, Cecilie Thun, Zuzana Uhde and Joanne Wilson. We note, in particular, the work of Jenny Bredull in the preparation of this book, and thank her for her patience and attention to detail. It has been one of the great privileges of our academic lives to have worked with this extraordinary group of feminist researchers.

We thank the FEMCIT advisory board – Myra Marx Ferree, Keiko Funabashi, Jeff Hearn, Gail Lewis, Gretchen Ritter and Chunghee Sarah Soh – for their thoughtful engagement with the project. Eiman Hussein, Diana Mulinari, Belinda Pyke, Joanna Regulska, Birte Siim, Myria Vassiliadou and Alison Woodward also offered us invaluable critical commentaries on our work at various points in the project, and Yeşim Arat, Rosie Cox, Hana Havelková, Joni Lovenduski, Baukje Prins and Lynne Segal provided inspiration and intellectual refreshment as speakers at our internal meetings.

We acknowledge the financial support of the European Union 6th Framework (project number: 028746), and, in particular, the advice and encouragement we received from our last project officer at the European Commission, Simona Ardovino. We also acknowledge the generosity of the Norwegian Research Council (project number: 184386/V10), which further supported our research and related activities.

Each of the institutional partners in FEMCIT – the universities and research institutes in which we all work – provided the context for the research, and numerous administrators and financial officers carried out the crucial background work that kept the research going: Uni Rokkan Centre and the University of Bergen, as the coordinating institution; Birkbeck, University of London, the University of Oslo, Leiden University, University of Toulouse–Le Mirail the Academy of Science of the Czech Republic and Warsaw University for hosting FEMCIT conferences, meetings and PhD Schools; and the Nordic Gender Institute (NIKK), Carlos III University of Madrid, Loughborough University, University of Stockholm, Södertörn University College, University of Copenhagen, University of Vienna, London Metropolitan University and the University of Leeds, as the other partner institutions.

We would also like to recognize the support and encouragement we have received from our own academic communities, the colleagues and friends with whom we talked about the FEMCIT project over the years. Not attempting to name them all does not mean that we don't know who they are!

FEMCIT was an exciting, engrossing and, at times, all-consuming enterprise, and we especially owe thanks to those closest to us: Margaretha Nicolaysen, Nina Wakeford, Selma S. Mutlu and Alev Sümer.

Finally, we acknowledge the vital contribution to FEMCIT and to this book of the women and men – the women's movement activists and the 'ordinary' people, politicians and policy-makers – whose experiences and practices of remaking citizenship are the subject of this book.

Beatrice Halsaa,
Sasha Roseneil and
Sevil Sümer

Contributors

Solveig Bergman is a sociologist who is currently attached to the Centre for Gender Research at the University of Oslo. Between 2003 and 2011 she was Director of NIKK (Nordic Gender Institute in Oslo), Norway. Before that she worked as researcher and lecturer in sociology and women's studies at Åbo Akademi University, Finland. Her publications have focused on women's movements in the Nordic countries and Germany, gender and politics, and collective mobilization and claims-making around child care. She has participated in several Nordic and international research and policy-oriented projects and networks.

Isabel Crowhurst is Lecturer in Sociology and Criminology in the School of Social Science, Kingston University, London, UK. Her research on gender, sexuality and migration focuses on practices and regulation of intimacy and commercial sex. She is currently working on a collaborative project on the regulation of prostitution in contemporary Europe, and completing a monograph titled *Regulating Migrant Prostitution*.

Drude Dahlerup is Professor of Political Science and leader of the Women in Politics Research Centre (WIP) at Stockholm University, Sweden. She has published extensively on women in politics, women's movements and feminist theory. Her edited book *Women, Quotas and Politics* (2006) is the first global analysis of gender quotas in politics. Together with Monique Leyenaar she is currently editing a book titled *Breaking Male Dominance in Old Democracies* (forthcoming). She has worked for UNDP and IPU (Inter-Parliamentary Union) as a consultant on women's political empowerment and gender quota systems in Sierra Leone, Cambodia and Tunisia. Together with International IDEA (The International Institute for Democracy and Electoral Assistance) and IPU she runs the global web site on quotas: www.quotaproject.org.

Radka Dudová is Senior Researcher in the Institute of Sociology of the Academy of Sciences of the Czech Republic. Between 2008 and 2010 she worked as postdoctoral researcher at Department of Political Sciences, Leiden University, the Netherlands. She is the author of the books *Otcovství po rozchodu rodičovského páru* [Fatherhood after the Parents' Separation] (2008) and *Interrupce v České republice: zápas o ženská těla* [Abortion in the Czech Republic: A Struggle for Women's Bodies] (2012).

Rune Ervik is Senior Researcher at Uni Rokkan Centre, Uni Research, Bergen, Norway. His main research interest is comparative welfare state studies. He is co-author (with Nanna Kildal and Even Nilssen) of *The Role of International*

Organizations in Social Policy. Ideas, Actors and Impact (2009), and is currently leading a project on ageing policies in Europe.

Lenita Freidenvall is Senior Lecturer in Political Science in the Department of Political Science, Stockholm University, Sweden and Co-Director of the Women in Politics Research Centre. She specializes in political representation, candidate selection and gender quotas. Her published works include *Vägen till Varannan damernas* [Towards 'Half for the Ladies'] (2006), 'Quotas as a Fast Track to Equal Representation of Women', *International Feminist Journal of Politics* (2005) with Drude Dahlerup, and 'Judging Gender Quotas: Predictions and Results', *Policy & Politics* (2010) with Drude Dahlerup. She is co-editor of *Politik och Kritik: En feministisk guide till statsvetenskap* [Politics and Critique: A Feminist Guide to Political Science] (2011) with Maria Jansson and *Bortom Rösträtten* [Beyond Suffrage] (2011) with Josefin Rönnbäck, and is currently working on a project on the Arab Spring and women's political representation.

Małgorzata Fuszara is a sociologist and Professor at the Institute of Applied Social Sciences, Warsaw University, Poland, where she teaches the sociology of law and gender studies. She is an International Associate of the Oxford Centre for Family Law and Family Policy and a member of the editorial board of *Signs* and the *European Journal of Women's Studies*. She is the author of *Everyday Conflicts and Celebratory Justice, Family in Court*, and *Women in Politics;* editor of *Women in Poland in Turn of the Century. New Gender Contract?* and *New Men*; and co-author of *Cooperation or Conflict? State, EU and Women*.

Beatrice Halsaa is Professor in Gender Studies at the Centre for Gender Research, University of Oslo, Norway. She has worked on women's political participation and gender equality policy at a local and national level, academic feminism and the mobilization and organizing of women's movements for many years. She is co-author of *Majority–Minority Relations in Contemporary Women's Movements. Strategic Sisterhood* (2012) with Line Nyhagen Predelli, and has co-edited *Rettferdighet* [Justice] (2010) with Anne Hellum, and *Crossing Borders. Re-Mapping Women's Movements at the Turn of the 21st Century* (2004) with Hilda Rømer Christensen and Aino Saarinen.

Hana Hašková is a sociologist and Senior Researcher at the Institute of Sociology of the Academy of Sciences of the Czech Republic and teaches at Charles University, Prague. Her research focuses on the sociology of gender, reproduction and intimate lives, and discourses and practices of care. She is a co-founder of the interdisciplinary peer-reviewed journal *Gender, rovné příležitosti, výzkum* which has contributed to the development of gender studies in Czech society. She has led research projects on childbirth practices, childlessness and changes in family and partnership forms. She is author of *Fenomén bezdětnosti* [The Phenomenon of Childlessness] (2009) and co-editor of *Women and Social Citizenship in Czech Society* (2009). In 2010 she received the Otto Wichterle Prize for young scientists.

Tone Hellesund is an ethnologist, university librarian and senior researcher at the Stein Rokkan Centre for Social Studies, University of Bergen, Norway. She has worked on historical and contemporary transformations of intimacies and sexualities. She is the author of *Kapitler fra singellivets historie* [Chapters from the History of Single Life] (2003) and *Identitet på liv og død. Marginalitet, homoseksualitet og selvmord* [Identities for Life and Death: Marginality, Homosexuality and Suicide] (2008).

madeleine kennedy-macfoy is a sociologist and postdoctoral research fellow at the Centre for Gender Research, University of Oslo, Norway. Her doctoral research was a qualitative study of perceptions and experiences of 'citizenship' amongst minoritized young people living and attending school in marginalized parts of suburban Paris and inner city London. madeleine's thesis builds on and expands understandings of the relationship between diaspora and citizenship in these two metropolitan centres. Her postdoctoral research extended this work into the field of women's movements, focusing on the contributions of minoritized women's organizations to the remaking of gendered citizenship in European contexts.

Anna Krajewska is a sociologist and lawyer and Assistant Professor at the Institute of Applied Social Sciences, University of Warsaw, Poland. She also collaborates with the Institute of Public Affairs. Her interests lie with the sociology of law and the sociology of gender. She is author of *Consumer Disputes and Their Resolution* (2009) and a number of articles about gender.

Teresa Kulawik is Professor of Gender Studies at Södertörn University in Stockholm, Sweden. She holds a PhD in Political Science from the Free University Berlin, Germany. She is a specialist in comparative gender studies and has published extensively on welfare state formation in Sweden and Germany. Her current research examines the intersections between body politics, feminism, citizenship and cultures of public knowledge. Recent publications include 'Body Politics, Biomedicine and Gender in Sweden: A Study within a Discursive Institutionalist Approach' (forthcoming, *Critical Policy Studies*), 'The Politics of Human Embryo Research in Poland' (chapter in *Exploring Central and Eastern Europe's Biotechnology Landscape*, Robbins and Huzair (eds.), 2011) and 'Feminist Discursive Institutionalism', *Gender & Politics* (2009).

Nicky Le Feuvre is Full Professor of Sociology at the Social Science Institute of the University of Lausanne, Switzerland, where she leads several research projects on gender and the labour market, with a particular focus on the transformation of gender inequalities across the life-course. She has published widely on the feminization of professions (doctors, lawyers, academics, domestic workers) in a cross-national comparative perspective. She is co-editor of *Le sexe de la mondialisation: Genre, classe, race et nouvelle division du travail* [The Sex of Globalisation: Gender, Class, Race and the New Division of Labour] (2010) and is currently working on the employment experiences of male and female seniors (50 years+) in France and Switzerland.

Milka Metso is a junior researcher in Sociology and Women's Studies at the University of Toulouse–Le Mirail, France. She has done research on 'Economic citizenship' within the FEMCIT project where she was responsible for the Finnish part of the research as well as for carrying out the French field-work. She has also studied at Leeds Metropolitan University (UK) and at the University of California, Berkeley, USA. Her research interests are inequalities in professional life, gender and changes in the national gender contracts. She has previously worked on several French research projects, as well as for two European research projects 'Women Career Family Friendly: Reinforcing and Reproducing Good Practices of Reconciliation between Family Life and Qualified Women's Work in Three EU Countries' and 'Changing Knowledge and Disciplinary Boundaries through Integrative Research Methods in the Social Sciences and Humanities' (5th PCRD). She also works as equality advisor outside academia.

Line Nyhagen Predelli is Senior Lecturer in Sociology in the Department of Social Sciences, Loughborough University, UK. A sociologist and political scientist, her research deals with issues of gender, religion, migration and ethnic relations, citizenship, political participation and social movements. Her book *Majority–Minority Relations in Contemporary Women's Movements. Strategic Sisterhood* (co-authored with Beatrice Halsaa), which examines women's movements in Norway, Spain and the United Kingdom, will be published in 2012. She is author of *Issues of Gender, Race, and Class in the Norwegian Missionary Society in Nineteenth Century Norway and Madagascar* (2003).

Joyce Outshoorn is Professor Emeritus of Women's Studies at the Faculty of Social and Behavioural Sciences, University of Leiden, The Netherlands, and has a longstanding research interest in women's movements, women's equality policy and body politics, notably abortion and prostitution. She is editor of *The Politics of Prostitution* (2004) and co-editor of *Changing State Feminism* (2007) with Johanna Kantola. Her work has been published in the *Public Administration Review, Social Politics, Acta Politica,* the *Journal of Comparative Public Policy* and the *European Journal of Women's Studies*.

Ana Prata is Assistant Professor in Sociology at the Department of Sociology, California State University Northridge, USA, and Visiting Fellow at the University of Leiden, The Netherlands. She has published research on European women's movements, abortion, democratization, gender and sexuality, and sex trafficking. Her recent publications include papers for *Women's Studies International Forum*, the *Journal of Women's History,* and the *Journal of the Portuguese Women's Studies Association* (*Ex aequo,* forthcoming). She is currently involved in a longitudinal study of women's organizing in democratic Portugal (1974–2010).

Kateřina Pulkrábková graduated from the Faculty of Social Sciences at Charles University, Prague, Czech Republic with a Master's degree in Sociology (specializing in biographic sociology). Her diploma thesis 'The View of Non-Profit Organizations on the Institution of Foster Parenting' was awarded the Eduard Beneš prize. Her general research interests are in the institutional arrangements of family and in family dynamics. The primary focus of her work on FEMCIT was on Roma minorities. She has taught at Charles University since 2006.

Minna Rantalaiho is a clinical child protection social worker in Salo, southwest Finland. Her research interests are in welfare and well-being from gender and child perspectives; she has published a range of articles and reports in this area. Besides working as a practitioner, she is currently completing a research report on children's everyday experiences of economic inequality.

Sasha Roseneil is Professor of Sociology and Social Theory, and Director of the Birkbeck Institute for Social Research at Birkbeck, University of London, UK. She is also Professor of Sociology in the Centre for Gender Research at the University of Oslo, Norway. She is the author of *Disarming Patriarchy* (1995), and *Common Women, Uncommon Practices: The Queer Feminisms of Greenham* (2000). She is editor or co-editor of *Stirring It: Challenges for Feminism* (1994), *Practising Identities* (1999), *Consuming Cultures* (1999), *Globalization and Social Movements* (2000), *Social Research after the Cultural Turn* (2012), and special issues of *Citizenship Studies* (2000), *Feminist Theory* (2001, 2003), *Current Sociology* (2004) and *Social Politics* (2004).

Ana Cristina Santos holds a PhD in Gender Studies from the University of Leeds, UK, and a Master's degree in Sociology from the University of Coimbra, Portugal. She is a senior researcher at the Centre for Social Studies, University of Coimbra, and Honorary Research Fellow at the Birkbeck Institute for Social Research, University of London. She has been involved in a number of research projects exploring issues of gender, sexual and reproductive rights, citizenship and human rights. She has recently received funding to work on a new project on disabled women and intimate citizenship. She is currently writing her next book entitled *Social Movements and Sexual Citizenship in Southern Europe* (2012).

Mariya Stoilova is a research fellow at Birkbeck, University of London, UK. She has research interests in intimacy and sexuality, gender relations and social movements in Eastern Europe, and biographical-narrative research methods. She is the author of 'Post-Socialist Gender Transformations and Women's Experiences of Employment', *Journal of Organizational Change Management* (2010) and of a book chapter, 'Heteronormativity, Intimate Citizenship and the Regulation of Same-Sex Sexualities in Bulgaria' (2010, with Sasha Roseneil).

Sabine Strasser is Professor of Social and Cultural Anthropology at the University of Vienna, Austria. Her research interests include migration, transnational relations, the politics of diversity and multiculturalism, and Islam in Turkey and Europe. She is author of *Bewegte Zugehörigkeiten. Nationale Spannungen, transnationale Praktiken und transversale Politik* [Moving Affiliations. National Tensions, Transnational Practices and Transversal Politics] (2009) and co-editor of *Multikulturalismus queer gelesen* [Multiculturalism Read Queer. Forced Marriage and Same-Sex Marriage in Plural Societies] (2010).

Sevil Sümer is a sociologist and Senior Researcher at Uni Rokkan Centre, and Senior Lecturer at the Department of Sociology, University of Bergen, Norway. She is a member of the Gender Equality Commission of the Norwegian Ministry of Children, Equality and Social Inclusion (2010–12). Her research has focused on the issues of gender, work, family, work-family reconciliation and social policy. She has participated in various international research projects on gender, parenthood and employment. She is the author of 'Becoming Working Mothers: Reconciling Work and Family at Three Particular Workplaces in Norway, the UK and Portugal' (*Community, Work & Family*, 2008) and *European Gender Regimes and Policies: Comparative Perspectives* (2009).

Monica Threlfall is Reader in European Politics at London Metropolitan University, UK. In addition to the broad field of gender politics, she has researched democratization theory, the Spanish Socialist Party and women's movement, electoral systems, EU social policy-making and integration, and the Council of Europe's Social Charter. She is lead author of *Gendering Spanish Democracy* (2005). More recent articles include: 'The Purpose of Electoral Reform for Westminster', *Political Quarterly* (2010), 'Reassessing the Role of Civil Society Organisations in the Transition to Democracy in Spain', *Democratization* (2008), 'Explaining Gender Parity Representation in Spain: the Internal Dynamics of Parties', *West European Politics* (2007), and 'The Social Dimension of the European Union: Innovative Ways of Advancing Integration', *Global Social Policy* (2007).

Cecilie Thun is a PhD candidate in Political Science at the University of Oslo, Norway. Her fields of research are citizenship and feminism, women's movements, and gender/ethnicity/religion. Her publications include: '"Norwegian Women Got Gender Equality through Their Mothers' Milk, But Anti-Racism Is Another Story": An Analysis of Power and Resistance in

Norwegian Feminist Discourse', *NORA* (2012), 'Inclusive Women's Organisations in Denmark and Norway?', *Kvinder, Køn og Forskning* (2010) with Helene Pristed Nielsen.

Zuzana Uhde is Junior Researcher in the Gender & Sociology Department at the Institute of Sociology of the Academy of Sciences of the Czech Republic and specializes in social and critical feminist theory, including global justice scholarship and transnational care practices. She is the editor-in-chief of the academic journal *Gender, rovné příležitosti, výzkum,* and editor of the Czech collection of Iris M. Young's work *Proti útlaku a nadvládě* [Against Oppression and Domination] (2010) in addition to authoring a number of articles on the 'distorted emancipation of women' and the concept of care.

Celia Valiente is Associate Professor of Sociology in the Department of Political Science and Sociology, Universidad Carlos III de Madrid, Spain. Her main research interests are gender equality policies and the women's movement in Spain from a comparative perspective. She has published articles in *Gender & Society*, the *European Journal of Political Research*, *Politics & Gender*, and *South European Society & Politics*.

1
Remaking Citizenship in Multicultural Europe: Women's Movements, Gender and Diversity

Sasha Roseneil, Beatrice Halsaa and Sevil Sümer

How has citizenship been challenged and transformed by the collective action of women in recent decades? What difference have women's movements made to the laws, policies and everyday lived experiences of citizenship? How might feminist practice and feminist theory combine to better grasp the gendered and racialized complexities of citizenship in an increasingly multicultural, diverse and unequal Europe? How can we assess the current state of citizenship in Europe from the perspective of women, particularly minoritized women? And is citizenship really a useful concept for feminist politics anyway?

At a time when many are once more hoping that collective action by citizens might change the world for the better, this book turns our gaze on the difference that collective action by *women* has made to the landscape of contemporary citizenship. Over the past 40 years, women's movements have radically transformed many of the laws and policies, and the public and personal practices of everyday life, that constitute our experiences of social and political inclusion and belonging. Inspired by feminist practice and theory, the book offers an expanded conceptualization of citizenship that is rooted in the challenges posed by women's movements to all aspects of life – political, social, economic, cultural, bodily and intimate. It traces the ways in which women's movements have been remaking citizenship in multicultural Europe, highlighting some of the most significant shifts that might be attributed to them. But, attending also to the vicissitudes and complexities of struggles for full, gender-fair citizenship, it argues that there is still much to be achieved, particularly for women from minoritized and racialized groups. Citizenship may be a political and scholarly buzzword, but citizenship also serves as a real 'passport' to rights and recognition, inclusion and belonging. The effects of citizenship affect us all.

Drawing on the findings of FEMCIT: Gendered Citizenship in Multicultural Europe, a multidisciplinary, cross-national research project, *Remaking*

Citizenship is more than an edited collection of papers.[1] The book is the product of an intensive period of collaboration between a large group of feminist scholars in which we have tried to grasp the legacies of recent mobilizations by women. From a range of disciplinary and theoretical perspectives, the contributors share a concern to explore the relationship between women's movements and citizenship across the diverse and multicultural terrains of Europe.[2] Casting our gaze back over the movements that have developed since the 1960s (and recognizing their continuity with earlier feminist mobilizations), we focus on the 'bottom-up', agentic processes by which citizenship has been remade through the posing of explicit political claims and demands, and by means of the, more or less explicit, cultural challenges and discursive reconfigurings enacted by women's movements. This involves moving beyond an understanding of women's movements as dissident (Sparks, 1997) forms of resistance, to analysing and assessing their generative role in the remaking of the social and political world. Of course we are not the first to attempt to do this: we draw and build upon an expansive literature on women's movements and the history of feminism,[3] and a vibrant body of feminist scholarship on citizenship.[4] However, there has been surprisingly little work that has systematically examined the legacies and impacts of contemporary women's movements across different national contexts, that pays careful attention to processes of racialization and minoritization, or that has worked with a conceptualization of citizenship that embraces the redefinition and expansion of the notion that these movements have undertaken.

Our analyses of the remaking of citizenship through the claims, demands, and cultural and discursive practices of women's movements, and of the waves made by these movements – their ripples, resonances and reverberations – are historically and spatially situated. Above all, this book has been written in the context of the critiques of white, majority ethnic feminist politics articulated by black and minoritized/ racialized women[5] and by postcolonial and critical race theory.[6] We foreground attention to the claims and experiences of women from minoritized and racialized groups, to processes of minoritization and racialization within women's movements and across the social formation, and to the often contested relations between 'majority' and 'minoritized' women's groups.[7]

The trans-European political contexts of our research are also salient. Funded, and inevitably shaped in a myriad of ways, by the European Union, the FEMCIT project has been carried out during a period of rapid 'Europeanization' – in the wake of the widening and deepening of the European Union through the accession of former Soviet bloc states, the Lisbon Treaty's strengthening of the idea of European citizenship, and the establishment of the EU Charter of Fundamental Rights. That our feminist project about gendered citizenship and women's movements in multicultural Europe secured EU funding is related to the institutionalization of gender equality at the transnational level, as well as to political concerns about democratic legitimacy and social cohesion in Europe. In other words, our research into the impacts of women's movements on gendered citizenship has itself been facilitated by the movement of feminist concerns through the European policy and research machine.[8]

We also conducted our research against the global backdrop of intensifying economic crisis, the ongoing 'war on terror', and an often fierce, and highly gendered, debate about multiculturalism, across an increasingly diverse Europe in which more and more people have roots in, and links to, more than one nation-state. The 13 countries[9] of eastern, western, northern and southern Europe that feature in our analyses have very different histories of multiculture:[10] histories of colonialism and its legacies, of immigration and emigration, of long-settled minority ethnic groups, of religious minorities, indigenous minorities, and displaced, diasporic and travelling peoples, and of sexual minorities. In this context, our cross-national, comparative approach always recognizes that the 'differences that matter' (Ahmed, 1998) vary between countries, and have changed over time.

Reconceptualizing citizenship

Building on the body of feminist scholarship on citizenship that has proliferated in recent years, the book works with an expanded critical conceptualization of citizenship. If citizenship in the Marshallian tradition refers, as a normative ideal, to 'full membership of a community' (Marshall, 1950), it is, in practice, about rights, responsibilities and legal status, *and* it is about participation, identity and belonging in relation to the state and civil society (Lister, 2007; Lister et al., 2007; Abraham et al., 2010). But, vitally, the study of citizenship must also be concerned with their opposites – the absence of rights, the derogation of responsibility and the lack of capacity to exercise responsibility and agency, legal non-personhood, non-participation and exclusion, and subjective experiences of outsider-status and non-belonging. Citizenship is always constituted in relation to its outside – those who lack the status of citizen, and hence the 'passport' to a multitude of rights, at times including the very recognition of personhood. Thus, we address both the promise of citizenship – what it might be, according to the transformative, inclusive imaginings and desires of women's movements – and its contemporary instantiations, which fall short of the ideals of those who would remake citizenship.

We are particularly concerned with *lived* citizenship – with what citizenship actually means in people's lives and how our lives as citizens are affected by our social and material circumstances (Hall and Williamson, 1999:2). Our interests are in *practices* of citizenship – of women's movement activists, of politicians, policy- and law-makers, and of 'ordinary people' in their everyday lives – and we attend to both vertical and horizontal aspects of citizenship (Siim, 2000; Yuval-Davis, 2008) – relationships between states and citizens, denizens, and non-citizens, and between citizens (and denizens and non-citizens), including relations within women's movements.[11] Understanding citizenship as an expansive field of practice that encompasses social and political arrangements and contestations, public policies and everyday life, we address the central domains of struggle of (mainly) post-1960s women's movements, and embrace the feminist move to recognize the fundamental entanglement of the public and the personal. So, alongside chapters discussing the more familiar *political and social* dimensions of citizenship, there are chapters engaging with *intimate* citizenship, *economic* citizenship and *bodily* citizenship.

Designing the FEMCIT research project around empirical investigations of six 'dimensions of citizenship' – political, social, economic, multicultural, bodily and intimate – was both a theoretically informed and a practical decision. It allowed us to establish discrete sub-projects that would develop their own studies of particular issues of citizenship across several countries, according to the expertise and interests of the research partners (see Appendix I). And it expressed our commitment to a feminist, multidimensional and multidisciplinary understanding of citizenship that does not prioritize the traditional domain of institutionalized politics (as political science approaches to citizenship might), or the realm of social rights and social protection (as social policy approaches might), or the economic sphere (as political economy approaches might). Yet, we emphasize that these 'dimensions of citizenship' are never empirically separable; definitions and delineations of each dimension are contestable, the boundaries between them fuzzy.[12] And although we carried out dedicated studies of 'multicultural citizenship' (kennedy-macfoy, this volume; Nyhagen Predelli and Halsaa, 2012), a concern with the multicultural runs through each study, as it runs through each chapter in the book.

Researching women's movements, their impacts and resonances

This book, and the FEMCIT project from which it emerges, have been driven in large part by the desire to better understand the difference that women's movements, in all their diversity, have made to conditions of citizenship, to the possibilities of women's full inclusion, recognition and participation in social, political and cultural life in contemporary Europe. Our focus is primarily on the feminist orientated elements of women's movements, those that confront and seek to transform dominant gendered power relations. But we include, under the umbrella term 'women's movements', a broad variety of organizations and groups: those that are explicitly feminist, and those 'just' acting for women's rights and interests; those that are formally constituted and those that are informally organized; unfunded, activist-based groups and publicly/charitably funded non-governmental organizations with paid workers. In order to encompass women's mobilization under a variety of political regimes (communism, right-wing dictatorship, liberal and social democracy), we include both autonomous feminist and women's groups, and semi-autonomous women's groups and organizations. Recognizing that fields of social movement action are overlapping, and that the struggles of oppressed and minoritized groups are not neatly divided into empirically distinct 'movements', we also include gender-mixed organizations in some of the studies, in order to attend to the concerns and experiences of minoritized and racialized women who organize in mixed groups, and to consider issues of same-sex sexuality in the research on intimate citizenship (Threlfall et al., this volume; Roseneil et al., this volume)

Working from the 'bottom-up', and taking the claims and demands of women's movements as our central concern, the book explores struggles for social, political and cultural inclusion, for redistribution and recognition, for autonomy and self-determination, through the lenses of intimate, economic, social, bodily and political citizenship. Chapters focus on a selection of issues that women's movements have identified as central to their projects of social change:

- the organization of intimate life – partnership, parenting, gender and sexual identities and practices, and gender and sexual violence;
- gender inequalities and women's experiences in paid work, particularly in the elder care sector;
- the arrangement of child care and parental leave;
- the autonomy of women's bodies – abortion and prostitution;
- the political representation of women, and particularly women from minoritized groups, and the political agency of women politicians; and
- the broad social, political and cultural 'citizenship experiences', as well as the understandings and strategic mobilizations of the notion of citizenship, of women's movement activists from both majority and minoritized/racialized groups.

Our research draws on historical institutionalist and discursive approaches from political science and comparative policy analysis, and qualitative approaches from sociology and psychosocial studies. The scope of the FEMCIT project called for new empirical research on the issues we identified as particularly significant case studies (see Appendix I), and contributors used a wide range of methods to carry out these case studies.[13] We carried out discursive, thematic and content analysis of public policy documents, parliamentary debates and women's movement publications – journals, magazines, newsletters, declarations and manifestos. We conducted focus group discussions and preference ranking exercises with ordinary citizens, non-citizens and activists; key informant and expert interviews with politicians and policy-makers, activists, organizers and workers in women movement (broadly defined) groups and organizations. And we engaged in participant observation within women's movement organizations, and in-depth biographical and biographical-narrative interpretative interviews with elder care workers and people living outside conventional families, respectively. The chapters each present and discuss the particular methods used in more detail.

Each study discussed in the book is cross-national, with the countries selected primarily according to a 'most different' comparative research design, based on their differing welfare and gender regimes, or political/religious histories, although also with an element of pragmatism, according to the national location, expertise and linguistic competence of the lead researchers. In terms of geography, from northern Europe, the Nordic social democratic welfare states, Finland, Norway and Sweden are included; from southern Europe, relatively recently democratized, former right-wing dictatorships, Portugal and Spain; from western Europe, Belgium, France, Netherlands and the United Kingdom; and from eastern Europe, democratized former Communist regimes, Bulgaria, Czech Republic, Poland and FYR Macedonia. Building our research thus, around comparative, cross-national studies, runs the risk of methodological nationalism (see Strasser, this volume). We are certainly aware that whilst citizenship is inherently bound up with the nation-state (even in its transnational EU form), and whilst many of the policies and laws in which we are interested are nationally bounded, the lived lives of the people we studied, and the women's movements and feminist ideas with which we are concerned, flow across borders. The book seeks to hold in tension a recognition of the on-going salience of nation-states, national citizenship and national contexts, with an understanding of the increasingly transnational character of social, cultural and political life. In fact, the process of carrying out research in 13 European countries has underlined how the national specificities of women's movement histories and the significant differences in the archival resources and academic literatures on these movements are related to wider gendered political and social histories, and to the economic wealth of national societies and the ways in which such wealth is distributed and concentrated (see Le Feuvre et al., this volume). But it has also emphasized the importance of a comparative lens in making national specificities visible. In an academic world ever more dominated by Anglophone literatures, and particularly by paradigms developed in the United States, attention to differences between European nation-states and societies becomes more important.[14] Moreover, carrying out cross-national research has drawn attention to the discrepancy between the supranational political valency of the concept of citizenship and its untranslatability into some national languages (see Nyhagen Predelli, Halsaa and Thun, this volume).

Our interest in the difference that women's movements have made is expressed in the full title of the original project – *Gendered Citizenship in Multicultural Europe: The Impact of Contemporary Women's Movements*. In seeking to understand their 'impact', we explore the ways that women's movements' claims and demands, ideas and beliefs, and interventions and actions have contributed to changes in law and policy. We examine how they have been incorporated by states and institutions of civil society, and we analyse how they have infused and transformed everyday practices, cultural understandings and subjectivities. We attempt to trace pathways of influence, to identify the echoes and resonance of the movements, as they reverberate across the social formation, and within the differing political opportunity structures offered by diverse gender and welfare regimes. We also attend to the multifarious ways in which women's movements *have not* yet realized their goals, the ways in which full gender-fair citizenship is still, as yet, an aspiration. And we note both that feminist gains always face the possibility of modification and reversal,[15] and that feminist claims might be co-opted by non-feminist actors and transmuted into policies and practices that serve other political ends, or that twist, distort or radically diverge from the intentions of movement activists.[16]

Indeed, we must emphasize that isolating the influence and effects of women's movements on citizenship is a challenging, if not impossible, task. [17] First, there is the problem, already signalled above, of definition – of determining the boundaries of the 'women's movements' whose impact we wish to analyse. Women's movements operate on a wider terrain of non-institutionalized political action. Their aims, strategies and actions often overlap and intersect with those of other social movements – most notably for our research, lesbian and gay movements (see Roseneil et al., this volume) and mixed gender anti-racist and minority rights movements – and all are embedded in, and contribute to, wider cultural shifts and value change.

Second, there is the problem of the complex and rapidly shifting landscapes within which women's movements operate. We need to consider the role played in the transformation of citizenship by many processes of social, political, economic and cultural change that are themselves associated with the emergence and success of women's movements. Particularly important are the processes of individualization and de-traditionalization (Beck and Beck-Gernsheim, 1995; Beck, 2002; Giddens, 1992) that are reshaping the worlds of work, welfare and intimacy, and that paradoxically both encompass and are in tension with many of the changes in gender, sexuality and social organization sought and produced by post-1960s women's movements.

In the sphere of macro-politics, processes of democratization (the end of right-wing dictatorships and the fall of communism) and Europeanization (enacted by transnational institutions such as the European Union and the Council of Europe, and by social actors such as the European Social Forum and the European Women's Lobby) have been vital forces shaping both women's movements and citizenship. As human rights, anti-discrimination and gender and sexual equality politics have become part of the legal and policy fabric of Europe – institutionalized, judicialized and 'mainstreamed' – identifying ' women's movements' as distinctive, bounded, non-state actors on the political stage becomes more difficult. With the fundamental shifts in modes of governance that have seen the down-sizing and displacement of 'public' and welfare state activities and the expansion of the third sector (Rose and Miller, 1992; Kooiman, 2000; Newman and Clarke, 2009), women's movements have been facing reconfigured states that present constantly changing opportunities for collaboration and incorporation (Banaszak, Beckwith and Rucht, 2003). The globalizing forces of world markets and institutions, the power of neo-liberalism, as ideology and practice, and the increasing convergence of welfare policy in this context, particularly the emergence of the social investment model of welfare (Jenson, 2009), are all powerful factors in the transformation of economic and social citizenship for women in Europe.[18] And processes of post-colonialization, the intensification of mobility and migration, particularly for women, and the changing meanings of national belonging in 'super-diverse' (Vertovec, 2007) contexts are central aspects of the remaking of citizenship, shaping the lives of all who live in Europe.

For the past 40 years, women's movements have been part and parcel of these processes of social change, both contributing and responding to them. We certainly do not claim to do justice to the complex, recursive entanglements of all of these processes of social change with women's movements and with citizenship, but we see this book as making a contribution to their analysis, and we encourage readers to read more of the work of the FEMCIT project (see Appendix III).

The chapters

The chapters that follow this introduction together contribute to the development of a critical, multidimensional analysis of the state of gendered citizenship in multicultural Europe, and to tracing some of the many ways in which women's movements have been remaking citizenship – as a concept, as law, policy and state practice, and as everyday lived experience.

In Chapter 2, *Rethinking Citizenship in Multicultural Europe*, Sabine Strasser prepares the way for the empirical chapters that follow by offering an overview of recent key debates about citizenship. Rooting her discussion firmly in the context of contemporary Europe, she stages a critical encounter with feminist, multicultural and transnational approaches to citizenship. She shows how a supposedly universal concept of citizenship has been extended and reconfigured as a result of feminist, multicultural and transnational societal transformations, and through activist, political and scholarly debates. Feminists have argued for the need to engender the concept of citizenship and have highlighted the centrality of the public/private dichotomy to traditional notions of citizenship. They have drawn attention to the double-edged nature of citizenship which both includes and excludes, emancipates and disciplines, is struggled for 'from below', and enforced 'from above'. Strasser sets out some of the most important new feminist ways of thinking about citizenship – developed in particular by Ruth Lister, and taken further in the FEMCIT project and in this book – that focus on the lived experiences of citizenship as rights (and responsibilities), belonging and participation. She goes on to discuss the recent fate of multiculturalist policies and the fierce public contestations about multiculturalism that have taken place in Europe over the past decade. In particular, she grapples with the question of cultural essentialism as it arises in public and feminist-theoretical debates about multiculturalism and multicultural citizenship, and with the ways in which questions of gender and sexual equality and autonomy emerge in these discussions. The third strand of thinking that has been reshaping the conceptualization of citizenship in scholarly literatures is concerned with processes of transnationalization, the emergence of new forms of global connectedness, and the questions this raises for nation-state-based notions of citizenship. This, Strasser argues, challenges the methodological nationalism that frames much research on citizenship (including, perhaps, this book), and she proposes a feminist conceptualization of transnational citizenship, drawing on the work of Nira Yuval-Davis and Pnina Werbner, that is attentive to the cultural multiplicity of everyday border-crossing practices.

In this concern with the centrality of questions of culture to the theorization of contemporary practices of gendered citizenship, Strasser's distinctive perspective as an anthropologist emerges, and is carried forward in a discussion of the issue of forced marriage. Forced marriage has been the subject of considerable controversy across Europe during the past decade, one of the prime exemplars of the state of public debate and cultural anxiety about gender equality, cultural diversity, transnational migration and citizenship. Strasser argues that the European Union's 2003 directive on family reunification, and the actions of a number of member states to introduce a minimum age of between 21 and 24 for family reunification of third-country nationals does not punish actual incidents of forced marriage, but rather pre-emptively 'protects', and thereby prevents, young people from exercising intimate citizenship rights. The promotion of gender equality is transmuted into the control of immigration, discrimination against third-country nationals, and the violation of intimate citizenship rights. Strasser concludes by advocating a 'critical relativist' approach as a way through these contemporary citizenship contestations. This would involve attending to the complex realities of those who are 'inside' the cultural groups targeted by policies such as those on forced marriage, and at the same time engaging with the perspectives of 'outsiders', subjecting both to critical scrutiny.

After Strasser's engagement with the troubled question of forced marriage, Chapter 3, *Remaking Intimate Citizenship in Multicultural Europe*, offers an extended discussion of intimate citizenship. Sasha Roseneil, Isabel

Crowhurst, Tone Hellesund, Ana Cristina Santos and Mariya Stoilova contribute to the theoretical conceptualization of the quintessentially feminist notion of intimate citizenship, through a study of experiences of inclusion and exclusion, recognition and misrecognition, freedom and oppression in intimate life. Expanding the FEMCIT project's focus on women's movements to encompass lesbian and gay movements, they seek to tease out the influences of both movements on everyday experiences and subjective understandings of intimate citizenship in four European countries: Norway, the UK, Portugal and Bulgaria. The methods they employed include an historical study of the claims and demands of these movements in relation to intimate life and intimate citizenship; a critical analysis of law and policy concerning intimate life; and a biographical-narrative study of the everyday experiences of intimate citizenship of people living outside conventional nuclear families and couples. The sample was designed to be able to comment on ongoing gendered processes of transformation in intimate life, particularly processes of individualization, as experienced by members of both majority and minoritized groups in the four countries.

Roseneil et al. first identify four main areas of intimate citizenship claim-making by women's and lesbian and gay movements – around issues of partnership; reproductive rights and parenting; sexual and gender identities and practices; and gender and sexual violence – and point to the differing salience of these issues across the four countries studied. They then present an analysis which seeks to assess the impact of these intimate citizenship claims and demands, and their institutionalization through law and policy, on the life stories of their interviewees. The authors point to notable differences between the four countries studied: Norway, the country where women's and lesbian and gay movements have been most effective in securing integration into state institutions and policy, appears to show the strongest evidence of their impact on people's lives, followed by the UK, Portugal and then Bulgaria. Almost all of the women and most of the lesbians and gay men interviewed showed evidence of the impact of the movements in their accounts of their intimate lives, whilst the heterosexual men were less likely to have been affected.

Then, through a complex and detailed analysis of the biographical-narrative interviews, Roseneil et al. identify and present, through short exemplary case studies, five main narratives of intimate citizenship articulated by their interviewees: narratives of self-realization and authenticity; narratives of struggle; narratives of un-fulfilment or failure; conventional narratives; and narratives of oppression. Their chapter concludes with a discussion of some of the many failures of full intimate citizenship recounted by their interviewees – illustrating the gender and sexual inequalities, violence and problems of minoritization that continue to haunt people's intimate lives, and highlighting how much remains to be achieved. They argue that the longing for full intimate citizenship, conceptualized as 'the freedom and ability to construct and live selfhood and a wide range of close relationships safely, securely, and according to personal choice, with respect, recognition and support from state and civil society', is shared by most of the people living outside conventional family forms across the four countries whom they interviewed. Whilst it seems more pressing for women, lesbians, gay men and bisexuals, many of the heterosexual men interviewed also sought these freedoms and rights. This chapter clearly points to the importance of the intimate sphere as a dimension of citizenship and to the need to extend the concept of citizenship to encompass the gendered, embodied, sexual, emotional and relational experiences of intimate life.

From the transformations in personal life that women's movements have, more or less successfully, sought over recent decades, we turn our attention in the following chapter to the sphere of paid employment, and the claims that movements have posed around questions of economic citizenship. In Chapter 4, *Remaking Economic Citizenship in Multicultural Europe*, Nicky Le Feuvre, Rune Ervik, Anna Krajewska and Milka Metso, provide an exploration of this implicitly well recognized, but relatively under-theorized, dimension of citizenship. The authors interrogate the widely held assumption that second wave women's movements have had a radically transformative impact on the gender division of paid work.

The first part of the chapter explores the ways in which economic citizenship claims have been framed by women's movements in five contrasting national contexts – Finland, France, Norway, Poland and the UK. It presents the results of an analysis of a selection of women's movement publications that shows firstly, and surprisingly, that, across all five countries, issues of economic citizenship – including issues of education and training, pay and working conditions, promotion, strike action and trade unionism, domestic labour and the segregation of the labour market – did *not* feature heavily in grass-roots movement publications, in contrast to feminist academic journals, where such matters were of central importance. When grass-roots publications did address questions of paid work, their attention was directed primarily to the experiences of women in non-traditional occupations, rather than on women in 'typically female' sectors of the labour market. Le Feuvre et al. conclude from this research that women's movement publications have regarded paid work as the preferred route to women's 'emancipation', and whilst rarely using the notion of citizenship, let alone economic citizenship, movement claims concerning economic life articulate what might now be called 'an adult citizen worker' model of emancipation. Pointing to the congruence between these claims and the now hegemonic 'adult citizen worker' model in contemporary European economic and social policy, the authors nonetheless are cautious about imputing a causal relationship between movement claims and the current policy regime. They point out that the promotion of part-time work and other flexible employment practices, and the commodification of care – which are central aspects of the adult citizen worker model – were not part of the portfolio of claims articulated in the grass-roots women's movement publications they studied.

The chapter then moves on to a portrayal of the demise of the masculine 'economic citizenship package' as the backdrop to the presentation of the authors' in-depth study of the elderly care sector. They argue that the nature of the labour market that women are entering now has undergone radical change under advanced capitalism, pointing to the increased risk of unemployment, and the prevalence of part-time, temporary and insecure jobs in the most feminized sections of the labour market. The elderly care sector is a particularly suitable case for an analysis of economic citizenship issues in multicultural Europe since similar demographic trends across the continent have led to a significant increase in employment opportunities in this sector, and because migrant and minoritized groups are well represented in the sector. Despite this convergence of conditions across the three countries studied – France, Norway and Poland – the authors found significant differences in the organization of the sector, and hence in the economic citizenship experiences of those employed within it. The degree to which elder care jobs offer adequate wages and are occupied by minoritized workers varies considerably cross-nationally and between different segments of the sector. The chapter ends with a call for full recognition of the care duties of all 'adult citizen workers', to produce the radical shift in power relations that is at the heart of the claims of women's movements.

This focus on the centrality of care in the feminist project of remaking citizenship echoes the work of many feminist citizenship scholars, and is further developed in Chapter 5. *Remaking Social Citizenship in Multicultural Europe*, by Solveig Bergman, Hana Hašková, Kateřina Pulkrábková, Minna Rantalaiho, Celia Valiente and Zuzana Uhde, analyses women's movements' agency in relation to child-care politics and policies. This chapter has a particular interest in the diversity of claims that might be articulated around the same issue, and looks specifically at the differing concerns of majority and minoritized women, in this case, Roma women. Arguing that child care has gradually been recognized as a social right of parents and children, that is, as an issue of social citizenship, the authors discuss how child-care claims have been framed by different actors in women's movements, and across time and place – focusing on the Czech Republic, Finland, Norway and Spain. They highlight three major types of claims around child care: public provision of day-care services, public support for the home-care of the youngest children, and parental leave policies for fathers.

The authors show that whilst parts of the women's movement have regarded institutional child care as a universal social right that can improve women's social status and living conditions, as well as those of children and families, other sections of the movement have employed a maternal frame, claiming that home care of the youngest children should be supported through welfare benefits. The development of social politics around care has been affected by the existence of these opposing arguments, articulated by feminist and traditional women's organizations respectively. The analysis documents the limited cooperation that has existed between minoritized women activists and majority women's organizations on this issue. It argues that Roma women's groups tend to formulate their social citizenship claims on a more materially existential level than majority women's organizations, which reflects their different experiences of discrimination and injustice. The chapter also underlines the significance, amongst transformation-oriented feminist actors across the four countries, of claims addressing the role of men in child care: the argument that to change women's lives requires changes in men's lives as well.

This chapter clearly illustrates the differences that have developed in the organization of child care in Europe, and points to the complex relationships between national, institutional and political contexts, welfare regimes and 'care cultures', and the range of discourses and strategic framings of demands about child care articulated by women's movements. Women's movements' sometimes conflicting goals reflect differing cultural understandings of 'good child care', 'good motherhood', and 'good fatherhood'. Yet, notwithstanding the diversity of positions taken within women's movements around the issue of child care, movements in all four countries have shared a concern with the recognition of care needs and the redistribution of care responsibilities that has a significant impact on the public provision of child care. Despite welfare state retrenchment across much Europe, publicly subsidized, affordable and high-quality day care, as well as good parental leave arrangements, are increasingly recognized as central to state projects of 'social investment', as well as a key element of gender equality politics. Whilst women's movements' demands that state, civil society and citizens (particularly men) should fully recognize and value the care of children is still far from being achieved, the authors conclude that their claims around child care have contributed significantly to the remaking of social citizenship.

In contrast to the concept of social citizenship, which is well established as part of the canonical literature on citizenship, dating from the work of T. H. Marshall (1950), the notion of bodily citizenship, developed in Chapter 6, emerges – like that of intimate citizenship – from the radical agendas of second wave feminism. In *Remaking Bodily Citizenship in Multicultural Europe*, Joyce Outshoorn, Teresa Kulawik, Radka Dudová and Ana Prata point out that the body has been largely absent from scholarly discussions of citizenship, despite the significance of the body within women's movements' demands over recent decades. Their exploration of bodily citizenship starts from the recognition that whilst the right to bodily integrity has been gradually incorporated into the legal frameworks of most democratic states, it is still riddled with ambiguity, and the female body, in particular, remains a highly contested site. The struggle for bodily autonomy and self-determination has been a major concern of women's movements.

The authors examine how women's movements have challenged state governance of, and dominant political discourses about, women's bodies through a detailed analysis of two issues: abortion and prostitution. The legalization of abortion has been one of the top priorities for feminist movements in Europe in recent decades, and has been a key issue in distinguishing feminist movements from wider women's movements. In contrast to abortion, prostitution had not been a major concern for women's movements across most of Europe in recent decades, until trafficking emerged as a political issue in the 2000s. Yet feminists are deeply divided about prostitution, disagreeing particularly about whether it should be understood as a form of sexual violence against women, or as a legitimate form of employment in which workers should accrue rights.

The authors approach the issues of abortion and prostitution through a comparative analysis across four countries: the Czech Republic, the Netherlands, Portugal and Sweden. Tracing the life cycles of the two issues, they identify dominant public discourses and crucial moments of policy change. They then highlight which women's organizations had been active on the issues and how they framed their demands, in order to analyse their impact. The chapter also examines the ways in which debates about migration and racialized difference have been significant in very different ways across the four countries, both within women's movements' framings of the issues, and in wider public debates about abortion and prostitution. A key finding on the issue of abortion is that women's movements in the four countries studied did not employ the language of citizenship in claiming abortion rights; rather, they framed their claims predominantly in terms of bodily autonomy and self-determination. Yet, the chapter clearly shows that feminist movements have made a crucial difference in abortion debates: control over access and availability remained in the hands of medical professionals when there was no feminist movement. With regard to prostitution, the differences between women's movement positions in the four countries are highlighted, as are the role played by feminists in placing human trafficking on the agenda of transnational political bodies, and the increasingly fraught debates between feminists about the relationship between prostitution and trafficking. The overall conclusion of the chapter is that full bodily citizenship for women is still a distant dream: despite abortion law reform, women still lack control over reproduction, and sex workers do not have full civil, social, economic and bodily rights.

In Chapter 7, Monica Threlfall, Lenita Freidenvall, Małgorzata Fuszara and Drude Dahlerup draw us back to one of the oldest preoccupations of women's movements – that of political citizenship – but this time examine it through the lens of new concerns about the unfulfilled promise of full political citizenship. Against the backdrop of relatively stagnant, low levels of representation of women in parliaments in many western European countries, and the sharp drop in women parliamentarians in post-communist countries, discussions reopened in recent years about the quality of women's and men's formal political representation. The effectiveness of quotas and gender parity projects in including members of minoritized groups, such as settled ethnic minority nationals and recent migrants, has attracted a lot of attention. Moreover, the recognition of, and respect accorded to, women political representatives is still a crucial issue in contemporary democracies. In this context, *Remaking Political Citizenship in Multicultural Europe* identifies three separate but related 'deficits' in contemporary political citizenship: the deficit in citizens' satisfaction with their political representation; the ethnic representation deficit; and the agency deficit of women parliamentarians themselves. The authors carried out a three-part study involving discussion groups with ordinary citizens and non-national residents, key informant interviews with leaders of grass-roots ethnic minority organizations, and individual parliamentarians in five countries: Macedonia, Poland, Spain, Sweden and the UK.

The analysis presented in the chapter shows a striking deficit in citizens' subjective satisfaction with their political representation, in established democracies as well as in younger ones. Ordinary citizens expressed feelings of marginality, and even exclusion, in relation to their parliamentarians. Contrary to the popular notion of the engaged, empowered citizen of 'the information society', they spoke about their lack of knowledge, know-how, and control over politics, politicians, and the performance of representatives. Yet for most citizens, symbolic inclusion in the representational order could be effected with relative ease through greater interaction with their representatives. When it comes to the 'ethnic representation deficit', the authors argue that the main citizenship deficit experienced by minority women's organizations is not primarily a lack of agency, since the minority women interviewed were politically active. Instead, women activists identified as their major dissatisfaction the lack of attention by established political parties to their concerns as ethnic minority women and new residents. The third citizenship deficit that prevents women from enjoying full political citizenship was experienced by women parliamentarians as an 'agency deficit', or the unequal opportunity to perform representation. The lack of recognition of and respect for women parliamentarians – struggling to be taken seriously by political parties and male deputies – constitutes a significant failing in political citizenship.

Overall, the chapter makes a case for the 'intersectionalizing of representation' and highlights the ongoing political exclusion experienced by women, particularly minoritized women. The authors argue that without an intersectional perspective the struggle for gender-fair political citizenship risks benefiting only majority women. They conclude with a proposal to broaden and deepen public debate about the political and policy priorities of women and men, suggesting a number of means for the enhancement of the deliberative and dialogical aspects of political citizenship.

Chapter 8, *Remaking Citizenship from the Margins*, takes up and extends the focus on minoritized women's organizations introduced in the previous chapter. madeleine kennedy-macfoy develops the discussion of the political representation of minoritized women into a more general assessment of the extent to which migrant and minoritized women's organizations are able to remake citizenship. The chapter addresses, firstly, the issue of the extent to which migrant and minoritized women's organizations in different national contexts use the notion of citizenship as a framework for their mobilization and claim-making, a question also addressed in the final chapter of the book. Secondly, kennedy-macfoy examines how the organizations perceive their relationship to wider women movements, and thirdly, she discusses the particularities of minoritized women's efforts to mobilize autonomously. The research presented draws on ethnographic field work and interviews carried out in four African/descent women's organizations in the capital cities of three countries: Belgium, England and Norway.

kennedy-macfoy argues that the relevance of the concept of citizenship in the work of these organizations is inextricably linked to the specificities of context: engagement with the concept of citizenship was part of the funder's requirements in Belgium, but not in England or Norway. In England, where a concern to promote citizenship has been a key plank of government policy in recent years, the notion of citizenship was employed by one organization to advance feelings of belonging and awareness of rights. In the Norwegian organization, by contrast, citizenship was understood in terms of a distinction between 'basic rights' and a 'higher' stage of citizenship, with the women in, and represented by, the organization seen as exercising only the former, and therefore not finding the framework of citizenship relevant to their work.

The chapter also suggests that the migrant and minoritized women's organizations studied tend to view themselves as being 'on the margins' of the wider women's movements. The chapter discusses existing research on the relationship between majority and minoritized women's organizations, and it is clear that ignorance or exclusion of the experiences of these minority organizations by these mainstream women's and feminist movements do not differ from the general pattern described in previous research. Yet, kennedy-macfoy insists that marginality should not be seen as the defining characteristic of these minoritized organizations. They should rather be seen as broad political platforms for migrant and minoritized women to engage in the ongoing struggles for women's rights in European contexts, on their own terms. The claims and demands that such organizations make, the author argues, as well as the specific ways in which they choose to position themselves in relation to feminism and (trans)national belonging, indicate the diversity between and within groups of migrant and minoritized women. The chapter's fresh approach to the work carried out by these organizations contributes to understanding the multilayered, differentiated lived citizenship experiences of migrant and minoritized women. This combined reflection on identity-positioning and organizational activism provides empirical evidence that is indispensable for a contemporary feminist politics of citizenship.

Following on from kennedy-macfoy's discussion of organized migrant and minoritized women's mobilizations, and the relevance of the notion of citizenship to their interventions, the final chapter extends the book's consideration of citizenship as a lens for thinking about women's activism, feminist politics and lived experiences of inclusion, belonging and their lack. *'Citizenship Is Not a Word I Use': How Women's Movement Activists Understand Citizenship*, by Line Nyhagen Predelli, Beatrice Halsaa and Cecilie Thun, engages empirically with understandings of citizenship among majority and minoritized women's movement activists. The complex relationship between theory and practice is a central concern for feminism, and the chapter provides insight into the relationship between academic feminism and grass-roots activism. The authors discuss citizenship as a central normative, analytical and descriptive notion in feminist scholarship, and explore how activists frame their demands. The research is based on a mapping of the organizational landscape of women's movements and in-depth interviews with activists from majority and minoritized organizations.

The authors situate their analysis in the historical and socio-political contexts of Norway, Spain and the UK, providing an account of the very different connotations of the term 'citizenship' in these three countries. Their comparative study of the use of citizenship by women's movement activists clearly demonstrates, in line with the previous chapters, the importance of attention to the historical and contemporary contexts within which social movements are embedded. In Norway the term 'citizenship' was unfamiliar to most of the interviewees who rather emphasized the responsibilities of individuals to society. While activists in Spain focused on the rights of the individual, and on freedom from gender-based violence, activists in the UK associated the term with issues of national identity, belonging, and with racist practices by the state, and in society. The authors argue that citizenship is really not a widely used concept among activists, who tend to prefer other frames, such as human rights and gender equality. The second part of the chapter explores the activists' reflections on the possibility of practising full citizenship. Despite the finding that 'citizenship' was not a widely used term, the activists had a lot to say about their own experiences of rights and duties, participation, and belonging, of inclusion and exclusion, providing rich data for the analytical notion of 'lived citizenship'.

Based on their empirical analysis, Nyhagen Predelli, Halsaa and Thun identify a divergence between the feminist scholarly focus on an inclusionary notion of citizenship as *lived practice* – as social relations and participatory practices across all spheres of life – and the ways in which activists understand and use the notion of citizenship. The notion appears to have little relevance in enabling movement activists to mobilize politically. But, the authors argue, this should not imply an abandonment of the concept: it should rather be remade as a normative and empirical concept to serve more appropriately as a bridge between women's movements and formal politics. The clue here is to produce knowledge of lived citizenship that translates to feminist activist communities as well as to institutional politics.

In sum, through our empirical studies and theoretical explorations of the complex relationships between the claims and demands of women's movements and the diverse lived realities of citizenship in contemporary Europe, we come to the conclusion that the collective action of women has, over recent decades, radically changed the world that we now inhabit. Against great odds, yet always also implicated in, and constructed by, the power relations they have sought to contest, women's movements have remade citizenship. Whilst many of the transformations in gendered, sexual and racialized inequalities for which women's movements strive are yet to be realized, this book should, we believe, provide sustenance for further struggle.

Notes

1. FEMCIT – Gendered Citizenship in Multicultural Europe: The Impact of Contemporary Women's Movements – was an Integrated Project, funded by the European Union Framework 6 initiative (2007–11), under the thematic priority 'citizens and governance' (project number: 028746). For more information see Appendix I.
2. A project of the scale and scope of FEMCIT, involving researchers with differing theoretical and political allegiances, is necessarily an exercise in coalition and compromise, and it should be noted that not all the contributors to this book agree with every claim, argument and assertion herein: such is the politics of feminist research collaboration.
3. In this introduction, we are not seeking to provide a comprehensive review of the relevant literatures, but rather to indicate particular work that has been of significance for our research. To identify just a few key texts on women's movements: Griffin (1995), Ferree and Martin (1995); Threlfall (1996); Sudbury (1998); Smith (2000); Ferree and Tripp (2006); McBride and Mazur (2010); Outshoorn and Kantola (2007); Grey and Sawer (2008). For further references to the literatures on women's movements across the 13 countries included in the FEMCIT project, see the FEMCIT Working Papers listed in Appendix III.
4. For example, Hernes (1987); Pateman (1988); Mouffe (1992); Phillips (1993); Walby (1994); Lister, (1997; 2007); Yuval-Davis (1997a; 1999a; 2008); Yuval-Davis and Werbner (1999b); Siim (2000); Lewis (2004a); Abraham et al. (2010); Friedman (2005); Siim and Squires (2008); Erel (2009); Lister et al. (2007); Hobson and Lister (2002).
5. For example, hooks (1982); Moraga, and Anzaldúa (1983); Hill Collins (1991); Mirza (1997); Sudbury (1998); Breines (2006); Roth (2004); Srivastava, (2005); Stoltz (2000).

6. For example, Crenshaw (1991a); Brah (1996); Gilroy (2004); Alcoff (2006); Narayan and Harding (2000); Mohanty (1986; 2003); Frankenberg (1993).
7. Following Gunaratnam, we use the term 'minoritized' to signal 'the active processes of racialization that are at work in designating certain attributes of groups in particular contexts as being in a 'minority" (2003:17).
8. For other research exploring the relationship between women's movements and public and social policy, see, Charles (2000), Banaszak, Beckwith and Rucht (2003), Lombardo, Meier and Verloo (2009), Squires (2007), and the publications of the RNGS (Research Network on Gender, Politics and the State) project McBride and Mazur (2010), Hausmann and Sauer (2007), Lovenduski (2005b); Outshoorn (2004b) and McBride Stetson (2001).
9. These countries are: Belgium, Bulgaria, Czech Republic, Finland, France, FYR Macedonia, Netherlands, Norway, Poland, Portugal, Spain, Sweden and the UK. Appendix II provides background data and profiles of each country across several dimensions of citizenship.
10. We use the notion of 'multiculture' and the 'multicultural' to refer to the empirical reality of the diversity of 'cultures' that co-exist within the nation-states of contemporary Europe. We understand these cultures to be constantly changing, even as they invoke history, tradition and nature, and as intermingling, even as they are seen to be rooted in group identities and practices associated with ethnic, national, racialized, religious and sexual categories and differences. 'Multiculturalism', in contrast, refers to the – increasingly contested (e.g. Vertovec and Wessendorf, 2010) – social policies developed to manage this diversity, and in response to the claims of members of cultural and religious minorities for recognition and rights (Kymlicka, 1995; Glazer, 1997).
11. 'Denizens' are those who have legal and permanent residence status, and normally full social and civil rights, but lack full legal 'citizenship' (Hammar, 1990).
12. For instance, there was an ongoing debate within FEMCIT about the relationship between the concepts of bodily citizenship and intimate citizenship. See Halsaa, Roseneil and Sümer (2011).
13. See Roseneil (2012) for a discussion of the FEMCIT project as an example of feminist case study-based phronetic research.
14. Language is a major challenge in comparative research; core notions do not necessarily have similar connotations across national contexts (see Nyhagen Predelli, Halsaa and Thun, this volume), and crucial research is often available only in a single language. Within FEMCIT, we worked together largely in English, and this has meant that non-English words and concepts have had to be translated into English. However, we have also drawn heavily on non-English language literatures, both in this book and other publications.
15. For example, the work of Bergman et al. within FEMCIT shows that Finland had, until the 1980s, the highest share of mothers in paid work in western Europe, but today is one of the few European countries where mothers' employment rates are declining, and where the 'home care allowance' for child care is very popular and uncritiqued by the women's movement, despite the existence of well-established publicly provided day care (Halsaa, Roseneil and Sümer, 2011:82).
16. See, for example, Jenson (2008) and Le Feuvre et al. (this volume) on how the economic citizenship claims of second wave women's movements for gender equality in the labour market have been incorporated into the increasingly hegemonic 'social investment' model of welfare. See also Strasser (this volume) on how legislation against forced marriage refracts feminist concerns about

women's sexual autonomy and self-determination through a racist and anti-immigration prism. There is also a growing literature that identifies how claims for intimate citizenship, particularly for lesbian and gay rights and equality, are being mobilized in the post-9/11 era as part of a racist and xenophobic politics of 'homonationalism', or sexual nationalism (e.g. Puar, 2007; Kuntsman and Miyake, 2008).

17. See Halsaa (2009) for an extended discussion of the challenge we faced within FEMCIT in attempting to grapple with 'the question of impact'.

18. The idea of convergence of social policy within the EU is contested. See Sümer (2009) for a discussion of this in relation to EU gender policy.

2
Rethinking Citizenship in Multicultural Europe: Critical Encounters with Feminist, Multicultural and Transnational Citizenship

Sabine Strasser

Since the 1960s social movements and the intensification of flows of migration and of global interconnectedness have fundamentally challenged the political and theoretical assumptions of citizenship.[1] Disadvantaged and minoritized groups have made claims for economic, political and social equality that would take into account different experiences and practices. Women, members of racialized and minoritized groups, lesbians and gay men 'still feel excluded from the "common culture", despite possessing common rights of citizenship' (Kymlicka and Norman, 1994:370). Feminists have pressed for the engendering of citizenship, critiquing the universal male concept, and arguing for the recognition of difference (e.g. Lister, 2003 [1997]; Yuval-Davis and Werbner, 1999a; Siim and Squires, 2008; Halsaa, Roseneil and Sümer, 2011). 'Denizens'[2] have demanded rights of belonging and participation without a passport of the country of residence (Hammar, 1990; Soysal, 1994), and 'transnational migrants' have challenged the boundaries of political communities by living in more than one nation-state and acting across borders (Glick Schiller, Basch and Szanton-Blanc, 1992). Furthermore, the relationship between national territories and the sovereignty of the political communities of nation-states – the political container of notionally equal citizens – has been increasingly challenged by liberalized financial markets, deterritorialized legal regulations as well as by cross-border struggles of grassroots movements. The European Union introduced the idea of 'Citizenship of the Union' in the 1992 Treaty of Maastricht, a joint or transnational legal status based on national citizenship of one of the member-states, in order to strengthen and enhance processes of social and political unification (Article 20, EU Treaty). Simultaneously, however, access to the Schengen area and to full membership for third-country nationals has been further restricted by post-9/11 security regulations and measures such as border patrols, language tests and the raising of the minimum age for family reunification.[3] In the course of a new 'integration' debate, gender equality has often become an argument for the restriction of immigration.

Scholars concerned with questions of justice and equality have responded to these challenges by seeking to extend the concept of citizenship, in order to make it more inclusive (such as Bauböck, 1994; Kymlicka, 1995; Yuval-Davis, 1999; Yuval-Davis and Werbner, 1999a; Benhabib et al., 2006). In this chapter I trace feminist, multicultural and transnational reformulations of the notion of citizenship, and I highlight some of the tensions that are inherent in the concept. I reflect on the ways in which the proliferation of feminist, multicultural and transnational theory on citizenship is productive, and perhaps provocative, for a fuller, or more gender-fair, citizenship (Halsaa, Roseneil and Sümer, 2011:72–3).

Since the complexities and contradictions of 'messy' social realities are difficult to grasp, simplifications such as 'cultural essentialism' or 'methodological nationalism'[4] appear in everyday life, in political interventions and in scholarly debates. Coming from an anthropological perspective, I propose a 'critical relativist' approach to dealing with the complexities of contemporary social life. Whereas conventional relativism would suggest studying practices of lived citizenship without subjecting them to evaluation and 'taking sides' (Armbruster, 2008), critical relativism brings together a social anthropological interest in understanding the particularities and complexities of everyday lives without judging by a priori standards (Stocking, 1968:230), and a feminist desire to critically intervene in everyday life in the struggle for gender equality (Young, 1990). I use the example of 'forced marriage' to illustrate how citizenship is lived both locally and transnationally in contemporary multicultural Europe and in so doing, illuminate how critical relativism can enable the sound interpretation of social life, and 'critical' intervention and action for change.

Rethinking a universal concept

The modern concept of citizenship was born of the nation-state (Işın and Turner, 2002:3), and has always referred to a legal status as well as to the rights and obligations of defined groups of people within the bounded territories of a state. People have been expected to participate in elections, to pay their taxes and obey the laws. This way of framing citizenship as legal status, rights and obligations has required an independent judiciary, an elected parliament, a system of public school education, public regulation of labour contracts, and the social benefits of a welfare state (Smith, 2002:107). T. H. Marshall (1963) identified the civil, the social and the political as the elements of universal citizenship. Civil citizenship refers to the rights necessary for individual freedom, such as freedom of speech, thought and faith, or the right to conclude valid contracts. Political citizenship concerns the right to participate and exercise political power, and social citizenship comprises rights such as minimum standards of living and the right to education (Marshall, 1963:78). Citizenship is a status bestowed on those who are full members of a community:[5] 'All who possess the status are equal with respect to the rights and duties with which the status is endowed' (Marshall, 1963:102). Since the time of Marshall's definition, and against the background of accelerating globalization and diasporization, citizenship has become the object of a lively field of study, as it has been increasingly challenged by conflicting equality demands, and as it has shifted from its exclusive focus on nation-states towards a concept of multilevel governance.

Citizenship shaped up as a 'buzzword' in theory in the mid-1990s, when the diversification of populations in western Europe, the post-socialist transformations, the intensification of racism[6] and new armed conflicts in Europe raised questions of justice and membership and the need to revisit the relationship between individuals and states (Kymlicka and Norman, 1994). A number of new terms emerged in order to grasp these issues, such as the problem of 'being accepted and feeling welcome' (Parekh, 2000:342), differentiated (Young, 1990), transnational (Bauböck, 1994; Fox, 2005), multilayered (Yuval-Davis, 1999), nested (Bauböck, 2001), global (Lister, 2003 [1997]) and cosmopolitan (Benhabib et al., 2006; Beck and Sznaider, 2010) citizenship.

Despite the multiplicity of theoretical notions of citizenship and the fact that every country has its own legislation regarding citizenship, there are two main principles organizing access to legal citizenship. *Ius sanguinis* is the principle of blood, which confers recognition as citizen by descent. Rather than the place a person was born, it is the person's ability to document ancestry in the respective country that permits inclusion. All those in the population whose heritage cannot be traced back to the host country are seen as foreigners, and their naturalization is, in principle, not welcome. Even children born in the country are not eligible for citizenship unconditionally and those applying for naturalization usually have to meet a list of integration criteria including minimum income, appropriate housing, language skills or knowledge of the country's culture and history. The alternative principle, *ius solis*, accepts people born in the country as citizens, irrespective of the citizenship of their ancestors. Foreign-born residents can become citizens through naturalization. Naturalization regimes of most European countries today do not follow one of the principles but combine elements of both, such as facilitating access to citizenship for children born in the country and by conferring basic social rights on non-citizens (Soysal, 1994). These principles of membership are shaped by, and embedded in, the liberal tradition of citizenship, which is associated with individual rights, autonomy and equality, the 'communitarian' tradition, which emphasizes social cohesion, and the 'republican' tradition, which is more interested in the obligation of political participation and solidarity (Işın and Turner, 2002:1–4).

Feminist rethinking of citizenship

Feminist theorizations of citizenship have been predominantly concerned with the double-edged nature of the concept, addressing questions of inclusion and exclusion, private and public, emancipation and discipline, as well as of citizenship as enforced 'from above' and struggled for 'from below' (Hernes, 1987; Pateman, 1988; Siim and Squires, 2008). Citizenship was not seen as an aggressively male or exclusionary concept until feminist scholarship revealed how its universalism has been substantially male dominated.

> For some, the historically gendered nature of citizenship, together with its inherently exclusive tendencies at the boundaries of nation-states, render it a concept of little value for contemporary feminism. ... Nevertheless, it is an avenue which has become positively crowded by feminist scholars, in a wide range of countries, intent on re-gendering citizenship from the standpoints of women. (Lister, 2004:325)

Debates about the value of citizenship for feminism have come to occupy centre stage in feminist politics and theory. Important contributions have been developed by feminists participating in debates on justice as a question of equality and difference (such as Young, 1990; Fraser, 1995; Phillips, 1999). Iris Marion Young, for example, commented on justice in the late 1980s, when she suggested focusing on five different 'faces of oppression' (exploitation, marginalization, powerlessness, cultural imperialism and violence), and concluded that different experiences of oppression according to gender, class, age, sexuality, and so on overlap, and need different forms of intervention and resistance. This concept of 'differentiated equality' (1990:39–65) was developed as 'differentiated universalism' by Ruth Lister (2003 [1997]:68–92), in which she explicitly tries to integrate diversity and the ideas of equality and universality. She argues that a creative response to the tension between the universal and the particular should include all social cleavages simultaneously, thereby contributing to the inclusionary and democratic potential of citizenship. Lister rejects the 'false universalism' of the dominant theories of citizenship, and aspires 'to a universalism that stands in creative tension to diversity and difference and that challenges the division and exclusionary inequalities, which can stem from diversity' (2003 [1997]:68).

The contributions of Young and Lister to the citizenship debates expose a feminist concern about whether women's claims to full membership should be conceptualized using a universalistic idea of equality or a gender-differentiated one (Yuval-Davis and Werbner, 1999a; Lister, 2003 [1997]; Halsaa, Roseneil and Sümer, 2011:38–9). Early contributions to this 'equal versus different' debate by feminist scholars on citizenship also focused on the critique of the private/public dichotomy (e.g. Elshtain, 1981; Walby,

1994). The divided realms of the private and the public are associated with women and men respectively, and have given rise to the dominant concept of citizenship that is based on the public male citizen to which women should adapt in order to achieve equal rights. Lister, amongst others, proposes an alternative 'women-friendly' conceptualization of citizenship that transgresses the opposition of private and public, as well as the binaries of dependence and autonomy, and justice and care (Lister, 2003 [1997]).[7] Nira Yuval-Davis and Pnina Werbner call this strategy of transgressing oppositions the 'logic of encompassment' (1999a:10):

> Hence, rather than a model which posits an opposition between two diametrically opposed approaches – 'liberal' individualist and 'republican' communitarian – feminist scholars seek to formulate models that highlight citizenship and civic activism as dialogical and relational, embedded in cultural and associational life.

In the context of infringing dichotomies, attention to agency has become particularly relevant because agency highlights how rights bestowed by citizenship have been practised by women, particularly by minoritized and vulnerable women (Lister, 2003[1997]:323–7).

Feminist contributions to the theoretical reconceptualization of citizenship (Lister et al., 2007; Siim and Squires, 2008; Halsaa, Roseneil and Sümer, 2011) have identified three main elements of citizenship: rights (and responsibilities), belonging and participation. Furthermore, they suggest that a feminist concept of citizenship should identify theoretical tensions and contradictions and strive towards transgressing dichotomies. They have urged the study of 'lived experiences of citizenship' within the respective spatial and historical contexts of national regimes of gender, welfare and migration, and cross-nationally from the intimate to the global constellation, 'from above' and 'from below' (Lister et al., 2007:167–8; Halsaa, Roseneil and Sümer, 2011:68). The following sections will provide a feminist perspective on scholarly debates about lived experience of citizenship in multicultural and transnational contexts.

Rethinking multicultural citizenship

All over Europe, the question of the regulation of diversity and social cohesion is high on the political agenda. In the 1990s, multiculturalist policies were seen as an inevitable and essential response to the ongoing diversification and diasporization of European societies. Yet, just as multiculturalism was identified as a powerful and important approach to social policy and theory (Kymlicka, 1995; Glazer, 1997), a 'new realism' brought the multicultural project to a halt in many European countries (e.g. Vertovec and Wessendorf, 2010). Multiculturalist policies imply increased recognition of, and accommodation of special rights for, minoritized, national and immigrant groups, and the 'new realism' (Prins and Saharso, 2010:76ff) refers to a backlash against multiculturalism as the triumph of a dominant populist discourse. This discourse includes the claim to address problems frankly and to break existing taboos. Furthermore, it emphasizes the need to defend 'ordinary people' (who are assumed to be white, majority populations), and it hails the affirmation of national (Western, liberal and democratic) identity against the 'threat' of Islamization and immigration. In this populist discourse multiculturalism is seen as responsible for segregated 'parallel lives', unemployment and failed social mobility. Assimilationism disguised as 'integration' (Brubaker, 2001) has come to dominate the political debate, promoting the idea of shared values and national language as the vehicles for wealth and social solidarity. Enthusiasm for multiculturalism, and the protection, or granting, of 'special' rights to ethnic and religious minorities, have always been fundamentally questioned by some egalitarian liberals, who have insisted on citizenship as an instrument for equal rights for all individuals, and on the normative standards they must share in order to guarantee autonomy, freedom and equality. The accommodation of 'special rights' and exemptions from specific regulations and obligations for cultural (ethnic, religious or sexual) or ascriptive minorities might, in their opinion, cause social fragmentation and thus threaten equality rather than contribute to it. What actually are those multiculturalist tools of which liberals are so sceptical and what do we gain in terms of a feminist reconsideration of lived citizenship if we reject multiculturalist measures?

Proponents of multiculturalism (Parekh, 2000; Modood, 2005) demand its affirmation at all political levels, in adaptations of school curricula, in protection from discrimination (e.g. equal treatment as well as affirmative directives for discriminated groups) and the promotion of cultural claims (particular holidays, alternative dress codes, public space and buildings for religious practices, funding of cultural and ethnic associations, etc.). Since migrant groups are disadvantaged historically compared with locally established people, special cultural resources are meant to create self-respecting persons and socially, politically and economically autonomous citizens. In this context, and in order to 'help build fairer and more inclusive democratic societies' (Kymlicka, 2010:37), Will Kymlicka suggests a liberal model of multicultural citizenship that is based on human rights and the rejection of hierarchies and exclusion. Yet no European country has adopted all or most of these suggestions and many prefer only a very weak support of cultural differences. 'Speaking and writing about multiculturalism (including academic writing in a philosophical and normative vein) is often based on an imagined (strong) multiculturalism rather than its reality, (Grillo, 2007:993).

One major argument for the rejection of multiculturalism in scholarly debates is the difficulty of avoiding an essentialist notion of 'culture'

(Phillips, 2007; Strasser, 2010). Despite the widely shared scholarly understandings of 'culture' as an historically created and changing system of meanings, which is never settled, never static or free of ambiguities, 'culture' remains the stumbling block of multiculturalist theories. Critics of multiculturalism assume an essentialist, primordial and a-historical concept of 'culture' as underlying (strong) multiculturalist theories (Taylor, 1996), and they ignore efforts at developing anti-essentialist or culture-sensitive theories and approaches (as suggested by, for example, Gilroy, 2004; Modood, 2005; Phillips, 2007).

Considering the limits of the distinction between essentialism and constructivism Seyla Benhabib (1998, 2002) has had doubts about the effectiveness of constructivist views in combating essentialism (Benhabib, 1998). She suggests the alternative differentiation between 'social observers' and 'social agents' (Benhabib, 2002:5). She maintains that outsiders, 'social observers', impose unity and coherence on cultural groups for the sake of understanding and control. 'Social agents', on the other hand, experience the rituals, activities, stories and traditions of cultural groups as shared, but also as contested and contestable. Benhabib thus distinguishes between the changing practices of social agents within a culture, and essentialist reports of external observers.

Some social anthropologists challenge the goal of 'solving the problem of culture', and with it the 'paradox of multicultural vulnerability' (Shachar, 2000)[8] by avoiding 'essentialism' and applying anti-essentialist or constructivist approaches. Through their studies of everyday practices, they have come to see essentialism and constructivism as two sides of one coin, and suggest scrutinizing essentialist and deviant practices and representations simultaneously. Gerd Baumann (1996, 1999) and Ralf Grillo (2003), for example, explicitly suggest that people 'out there' essentialize their own and other people's cultures in processes of segregation as well as in their everyday relations. Baumann (1996, 1999) has emphasized the need to include both essentialist and transformative (in his terms, 'dominant' and 'demotic') aspects of cultural discourses in empirical studies. As Friedman (2002:30) says: 'If people are doing this thing called bounding and closure and essentialism, should this not be recognized as a real social phenomenon rather than shunned as a terrible mistake?' So, whilst the distinction between social agents and observers (Benhabib, 2002) contributes to the aim of studying the diversity and contestation of practices and narratives within social arenas, it does not sufficiently take into account the essentialism that is often an aspect of everyday practices and lived experiences. Looking at cultural practices reveals segregation as well as interrelation, rejection as well as acceptance, essentialism as well as transformation, continuity as well as rupture and exclusion as well as inclusion.

Anne Phillips likewise argues that 'cultural straitjackets' (2007:14) tailored of essentialism actually encumber the aims of multiculturalist politics. Yet, she wonders what to do 'if culture imputes a false stability to experiences that are intrinsically fluid, what exactly is left to be recognised, accommodated, or equalised?' (2007:14). Since she does not find a solution to this problem in anti-essentialism, she suggests political pragmatism:

> [A] multiculturalism that dispenses with the reified notions of culture that feed those stereotypes to which so many feminists have objected, yet retains enough robustness to address inequalities between cultural groups, a multiculturalism in which the language of cultural difference no longer gives hostages to fortune or sustenance to racists, but also no longer paralyses normative judgment. (2007:8)

In addition to the challenge of cultural essentialism, multiculturalism has been accused of strengthening differences instead of dissolving them, and thus of upholding boundaries and divisions instead of promoting economic integration and social cohesion. The 'retreat from multiculturalism' (Joppke, 2003) and the argument for the 'new assimilationism' all over Europe (Brubaker, 2001) intensified rhetorically in the aftermath of 9/11. Muslims were blamed for living 'parallel lives' and rejecting integration. The murder of Theo van Gogh in the Netherlands 2004, the London bombings in 2005, and the 'cartoon affair' in Denmark in 2005 fuelled cultural anxieties. Ruud Koopmans (2010), for instance, argues that there is evidence that multiculturalism has failed to establish social integration and is responsible for spatial segregation, social exclusion, increased criminality and unemployment.

While the debate about terrorism and arguments against multiculturalism have been generally linked with marginalized young men, feminist activists have rather focused the debate on minoritized young women. Debates about wearing the hijab, genital cutting, forced marriage and honour killing intensified publicly after a series of events such as the murder of Fadime Şahindal by her father in Stockholm in 2002 and of Hatun Sürücü by her brother in Berlin in 2005. Whilst politicians and the public at large had, for a long time, turned a blind eye to various forms of violence in the name of culture, tradition or honour, preventative measures and sanctions against gender sexual violence among minoritized groups were established in many European countries during the past decade. Feminists argued strongly for the protection of women and girls from violence and coercion, and many simultaneously critiqued the use of violence against minoritized women as grounds for further restrictions on immigration. Yet Anne Phillips and Sawitri Saharso argue that 'the critique of minority culture and religions is [now] played out largely on the bodies of young women' (2008:292).

In this context, gender relations and the issue of sexual autonomy have gained new momentum in the debate about multiculturalism: what if the groups claiming cultural acknowledgement and group rights do not promote gender equality and sexual autonomy but consider different forms of hierarchy (e.g. age, gender and ethnicity) as intrinsic to their group identity? How can group rights be accommodated without contributing to the disadvantage of women, youth, gay men, lesbians and others within these minorities? Since much of what is perceived as 'culture' also revolves around gender and practices of sexuality, marriage and divorce, different effects on men and women, old and young seem inevitable. This problem is familiar to feminists, who have for a long time been criticizing the consequences of male-dominated cultural regimes for gender relations in their own societies, in receiving and sending countries (e.g. İlkkaracan, 1998, 2000; Narayan, 1997).

The tension between cultural rights, gender equality and sexual autonomy has caused a lively scholarly, as well as a heated political and public, debate over whether women's rights are compatible with ethnic minority rights or whether the politics of multiculturalism is reconcilable with feminism and the claims of sexual minorities (Okin et al., 1999; Shachar, 2000; Saharso, 2003; Spinner-Halev, 2005; Okin, 2005; Strasser and Holzleithner, 2010). Feminists, in theory and political practice, have developed contradictory positions in the face of this challenge. They either criticize liberal democracies for their inactivity and naivety concerning the culturally legitimized violence against women (Okin, 1999; Wikan, 2002; Kelek, 2005; Ateş, 2007), or they warn about the stigmatizing effect of the whole debate with its often homogenizing attacks on ethnic and religious minorities (Narayan, 1997; Razack, 2004; Phillips, 2007; Ongan, 2008). Yet, across this divide they all aim to draw attention to the role women play in the current crises of multiculturalism.

The academic debate about the relationship between gender, sexuality and multiculturalism has provoked new efforts to overcome citizenship's inherent dichotomies, multiculturalism's ambivalent effects, and perceived antagonism between feminism and multiculturalism (Saharso, 2003; Phillips, 2007; Strasser, 2010). Unfortunately, the debate about violence against minoritized women has been played differently in populist discourses. Majority women have been often depicted as liberated equals in gender and sexual relations, whereas minoritized women have been encapsulated in narratives constructing them as victims of their cultures. Public concern about 'violence in the name of tradition' has had a remarkable career (Strasser, 2008; Ongan, 2008), culminating in legal and political interventions in a range of European countries from 2000 onwards. Before I focus on the debate about, and measures against, 'forced marriage', I briefly sketch the transnational dimension of lived citizenship.

Rethinking citizenship from transnational arenas

Contemporary social arenas are simultaneously marked by increasing local diversity and the emergence of new forms of global interconnectedness.

These processes are unsettling membership of nations and give rise to a need for diversified and multiple notions of citizenship. Whereas a concern with cultural essentialism has been pivotal in discussions of multiculturalism, methodological nationalism has been identified as the major obstacle to understanding lived experiences of citizenship across borders. Since the 1990s, the concept of transnationalism has methodologically challenged the national frame of citizenship. A transnational approach to migration has drawn attention to the border-crossing activities that link migrants with their countries of origin and their countries of residence, and underline that migration does not have to be a one-way process. Many migrants maintain multiple relations with their former homeland and insist on belonging 'here' *and* 'there' (Glick Schiller, Basch, and Szanton-Blanc, 1995; Rouse, 1991; Vertovec, 1999; Ong, 1999). Supported by reduced costs of transportation and by accelerated communication, contact is maintained with their regions or countries of 'origin' on a regular basis, and even after years abroad, migrants regard their place of birth as 'home', or at least feel responsible for kin, neighbours, or the environment and economy in their birthplace. There is, for example, a working-class woman in New York who has internet-breakfast with her sister in Istanbul on an almost daily basis. Assyrian Christians living in Sweden, Germany, Switzerland or Austria for three generations still see their region around the Tur Abdin in Turkey as homeland and send their children 'back' to religious institutions to study vanishing languages and the cultural roots of their identity, which is actually shaped in Europe (Armbruster, 2003). For some migrants their preferred marriage arrangement points to the country, region or village of origin in order to confirm social relations, belonging and cultural practices. People participating in transnational politics might feel a sense of belonging and welcome to places 'of origin' even if they have never been 'there' (Appadurai, 2003; Strasser, 2009).

Thus, transnational relations have economic, political, social, intimate and cultural dimensions. Across all dimensions people make use of opportunities in the country of residence to advance their claims by employing their familiarity with their respective town, region or nation-state of 'origin'. For example, the success of migrant minorities' political representatives is often related to the ability to mobilize constituencies originating from the same place (Threlfall et al. this volume). Policy-makers with 'roots' in a different country make use of their local knowledge 'there' to influence politics 'here' and 'there', in order to promote economic and political transformation. Information about how to influence politics across borders and how to mediate between governments plays a vital role in these processes (Østergaard-Nielsen, 2003). Economic interventions aim to take advantage of 'insider information' about local markets in at least two nation-states. Actors in the field sometimes even want to develop their region of origin economically by means of their personal investment. Their engagement is frequently supported by close kin in the area who are often an additional motivation for their activities (Landolt, 2001).

Despite the great potential inherent in transnational activities, transnational formations are not naturally progressive and critical. Transnational migrants do not necessarily reject the nation-states (Al-Ali and Koser, 2002). Indeed some transnational activists go further than simply not acting against nationalism and may share nationalist views prevalent in their countries of origin. Long-distance nationalism (Anderson, 1998) strengthens homogenizing and essentializing dimensions of identity and aims at control, continuity and coherence beyond borders. In this sense it seems obvious that transnational constellations do not necessarily create new possibilities for liberation but may actually contribute to restrictive boundaries. Finally, while transnational practices thus may not always represent creativity and innovation across borders, they may well also be an expression of poverty or exclusory integration regimes.

Having briefly sketched the main issues discussed in the field of transnational studies I will now focus on the question of whether border-crossing experiences are likely to contribute to the construction of a more gender-fair citizenship. The challenge of the notion of 'transnational citizen' is the tension between a concept speaking of a member of a particular well-defined political community (citizen) on the one hand, and referring to a person's connectedness across nation-states (transnational), on the other hand. Does the study of rights and responsibilities, belonging and participation beyond the nation-state (i.e. beyond 'methodological nationalism')[9] require a conceptualization of citizenship beyond its existing vocabularies, or are 'dual citizenship', 'multiple citizenship' or 'multicultural citizenship' sufficient to meet the demands of transnational migrants?

In practice we have to differentiate at least four distinct sets of actors that raise questions about nation-state-based citizenship: first, immigrants challenging assumed cultural monism and ethnic purity and including not only long-distance nationalism but also transnational families and social relations; second, transnational social movements such as feminist, environmentalist, indigenous and human rights networks; third, regional collaboration such as the EU expanding rights across national borders to improve global economic and political influence;[10] finally, global business causing tensions between 'investor rights' and national efforts to protect the social rights of citizens (Fox, 2005:173).

When one tries to define transnational citizenship with any degree of precision the most challenging question is:

'What counts?' After all, not all migrant political participation involves crossing borders, and not all transnational public interest campaigning leads to the construction of citizenship. ... Although transnational action can influence the balance of power between civil society actors and states, this process does not necessarily create transnational citizenship. (Fox, 2005:174)

Fox concludes that much of what is demanded by activists across borders cannot be met by citizenship rights. On the contrary, he suggests that rights, responsibilities and membership in the context of transnational experiences are more precisely described by notions of dual or multiple citizenships, and that the notion of transnational citizenship is dispensable.

However, from a feminist approach that is concerned with 'lived experiences' and 'gender-fair citizenship', Fox's perspective does not sufficiently grasp the effects of transnational practices on rights, belonging and participation. Transnational domestic work (Lutz, 2008 Le Feuvre et al., this volume) or transnational mothering (Erel, 2009) provide examples of families scattered over several countries (Fog-Olwig, 1998, Ong, 1999), and highlight experiences often neglected by national governments and its constituencies. Mothers are involved in 'global chains of care' (Hochschild, 2000) in which their own children are often left behind with siblings or grandparents whilst they care for children or elderly people in richer countries. Nonetheless, such mothers seek opportunities to be involved in their own children's education and engage in 'long-distance care' enabled by new communication, such as skype and cell phones (Zontini, 2007). In some contexts 'commodified motherhood', referring to affection expressed predominantly by expensive presents, has been identified (Parreñas, 2001). Yet, in general the experience of separation from children is painful for parents and the damage for children is often underestimated and still neither studied thoroughly nor politically recognized (Erel, 2009:122).

In Europe, where 'childcare is no longer exclusively regarded as a responsibility of the family but also as a social right of parents and children' (Bergman in Halsaa, Roseneil and Sümer, 2011:21), transnational care systems and the experiences of children and elderly people left behind have become important fields of research but have rarely been considered by women's movements. Similar examples of practices that demand transnational perspectives can be found in the field of politics, reproduction, intimate relations and in women's movements themselves (examples in this volume). Needs and claims with transnational dimensions demand the reconsideration of rights, belonging and participation as dimensions of lived experiences of citizenship. Sasha Roseneil and her team argue

...that at national and transnational levels, there is a profound tension between attempts to recognize the needs of particular groups in relation to intimate citizenship (e.g. to protect the rights of women subject to forced marriages or in danger of 'honour killings') and the mobilization of racist/Islamophobic discourses that construct certain minority groups as particularly patriarchal and/or homophobic. (Roseneil in Halsaa, Roseneil and Sümer, 2011:66)

Following Nira Yuval-Davis and Pnina Werbner (1999a), I consider 'transnational citizenship' to be a highly relevant concept for the study and description of individuals' involvement across borders, and for understanding their claims for rights, belonging recognition and participation.

> Against those who regard citizenship as confined to the nation-state, ... we argue here that, both historically and ideologically, the discourse of one implies the other, so that national and transnational citizenships constitute two coexisting and interrelated modalities of citizenship. (Yuval-Davis and Werbner, 1999a:3)

People living transnational lives are facing the complexity of 'differentiated citizenship'.[11] Complexity (Hannerz, 1992; Eriksen, 2007) stems from the fact that locally as well as transnationally embedded people have to deal with cultural multiplicity in different ways. People who are connected across national borders simultaneously have to engage with different regions, political regimes, economic challenges and religious movements in a multicultural environment that is only slowly including their transnational needs and claims. Transnational marriage is one of the cross-border practices of an increasing number of people.[12] To highlight some threads of the entanglement of transnational and multicultural practices, I will consider the inherent tensions and contradictions of rights, belonging and participation, focusing on the example of 'forced marriage'.

Contemporary citizenship contestations: the case of forced marriage

Forced marriage has been the subject of considerable controversy across Europe during the past decade. While the lack of protection from forced marriage of young women and (presumably less frequently) men has been identified as 'generous betrayal' in the name of culture (Wikan, 2002), interventions by state institutions have been criticized for contributing to restrictive immigration policies (Razack, 2004). Whereas some feminist activists and scholars have argued against harmful traditions and for the equal protection of minoritized women and young people (Kelek, 2005; Ateş, 2007), others have emphasized the danger of focusing on violence in minoritized contexts, and have insisted on the integration of feminism and multiculturalism, and on a culture-sensitive debate (Phillips, 2007). Contributors to the debate generally agree with the definition of the United Nations Expert Paper prepared by Cheryl Thomas, Director of the Women's Human Rights Program, in 2009.

Forced marriage describes a marriage that takes place without the free or valid consent of one or both of the partners and involves either physical or emotional duress. Early marriage is related to forced marriage because minors are deemed incapable of giving informed consent. Forced and early marriages are serious human rights violations. The requirement for the free and informed consent of both parties to a marriage is recognized in numerous legal instruments at international, national and local levels. These instruments, along with all major world religions, condemn forced and early marriages. (Thomas, 2009:2)

If a person is forced into marriage it means severe harm for the victim since everyday life is transformed into a daily experience of bodily, emotional and sexual violence. According to empirical data often based on expert interviews (as criticized by for example Thomas, 2009; Schiller, 2010) forced marriages are likely to occur more frequently among people who are practising arranged marriages since accepted or even requested third parties facilitate the slide from persuasion into coercion (Phillips, 2010:3–4). Although attitudes towards *arranged* marriages amongst minoritized groups within Europe are changing rapidly, and many assume that the practice is declining, this does not mean that *forced* marriages simply disappear. Particularly if adolescents do not silently consent to parental decisions on possible marriage partners, control and violence in the context of marriage might even increase in future (Phillips, 2010).

However, we still do not have detailed knowledge about forced marriage, about how and why particular forms of violence occur in particular social, economic, cultural or religious contexts amongst minoritized groups, about differences within and between groups regarding forced marriages, or about challenges to sexual control and violence. Information on forced marriage is still mainly commissioned by state and city institutions and based on expert knowledge (Schiller, 2010). In contrast, academic research on forced marriage tends to include the voices of representatives of minoritized groups, including women and girls affected by these practices (Samad and Eade, 2002; Latcheva et al., 2006; Bredal and Skjerven, 2007). Simultaneously, we can observe extensive media coverage of cases of forced marriage, with a consequent impact on public opinion, and on relations between minoritized groups and majorities. These stories are often sensational and tend to represent extreme cases. Such representations contribute to the racialization and culturalization of women, constructing women as victims of their culture which is presented as patriarchal, if not as outright violent against women.

The growing awareness of forced marriage has provoked measures at different levels, including the extension of legal punishment, the provision of educational services, the protection of victims (including interventions in non-EU countries), and the call for the cultural transformation of minoritized groups that reject gender equality. Forced marriage was banned by UN conventions and illegal in all European countries even before this new wave of public debate and legal measures. These policy measures thus not only show the growing awareness of the issue, but also represent and perform increasing cultural and political anxiety about the incorporation of migrant minorities. In the course of these contestations, some feminist activists and scholars have contributed, unintentionally or not, to the retreat of multiculturalism in the name of equal citizens and human rights (Wikan, 2002; Kelek, 2005; Ateş, 2007), while others insisted on the reconciliation of gender equality and cultural diversity (Saharso, 2003; Phillips, 2007, 2010).

In the context of public concern about forced marriage the EU revised its directive on family reunification. Although in the EU directive (2003/86/ EG), the ability to secure family reunification is considered important for the integration of minorities, member-states have the option of including a minimum age for reunification in national legislation: 'In order to ensure better integration and to prevent forced marriages Member States may require the sponsor and his/her spouse to be of a minimum age, and at maximum 21 years, before the spouse is able to join him/her' (Directive 2003/86/EC, Article 4(5)).[13]

Despite reasonable doubts whether this optional clause is reconcilable with the European Human Rights Convention (Articles 8 and 12), many member-states – such as Austria (2010), Denmark (2002), the Netherlands (2004) and the United Kingdom (Phillips, 2010) – have introduced a minimum age of between 21 and 24. Denmark, not bound by the directive, introduced 24 years for family reunification of third-country nationals (the EU term for citizens of a non-EU state). Obviously, this measure does not punish actual crimes but pre-emptively 'protects' all members of non-European countries from living with their partners up to a certain age. This measure is meant by its authors to protect young people from being forced into marriage and simultaneously helps nation-states to prevent 'marriages of convenience' and to control immigration in general. The crime of forced marriage is tackled by restricting immigration rights and setting limits to the free choice of a marriage partner. Instead of punishing perpetrators, (young) women and men are prevented from exercising their intimate citizenship rights.

The EU considers it appropriate to control the cohabitation of third-country nationals in the name of combating violence. The EU also considers it lawful to define the age of maturity, not for marriage and sexuality, but for immigration to the EU. This intervention amplifies the distinction between 'free' European citizens encouraged to marry across borders by EU citizenship initiatives (European Commission, 2010a), and 'forced' third-country nationals protected from cohabitation until a certain age to promote freedom of choice.[14] In the course of this 'post-multiculturalist' debate, gender equality has become an argument for new legislation including the restriction of immigration.

Dustin (2006:1) concludes from a comparison between EU member-states, including Norway:

> In many countries, immigration measures are the principal means of discouraging and preventing forced marriages – leading to potential confusion about the motives behind new regulations, a failure to tackle abuses with no overseas dimension, and a lack of credibility among members of minority communities.

In the course of developing policies against forced marriage, culture has become essentialized and misrepresented as a 'threat' to the seemingly more liberal European societies. This cultural essentialism suggests that everyone belonging to a particular group shares the same ideas and practices. If this is not the case, why should all third-country nationals be punished by an EU directive? Third-country citizens are not thought mature enough before the age of 21 to make autonomous decisions. Such actions against forced marriage try to grapple with a perceived, and sometimes real, lack of autonomy and freedom among some minoritized women, and end up restricting the autonomy of young women and men of all third countries. In particular, transnational marriage is collapsed into forced marriage, a move that affects all women and men who explicitly and autonomously wish to marry third-country nationals below the age of 21.

As I have shown elsewhere (Strasser, 2010) many minoritized women might support depicting forced marriage as a crime. Nonetheless they may consider it *not* part of their culture, and consequently might feel discriminated against when being prevented from choosing their marriage partner independent of his (or her) country of residence. Others might probably reject the existence of the practice or not consider their practices or arrangements as harmful (Strasser, 2010).

Detailed studies of the contestation and enactment of issues such as forced marriage focusing on all of those involved – perpetrators, family members supporting control and punishment, critical voices arguing for more freedom and autonomy, community and religious representatives taking sides, and above all those experiencing such practices – are still largely missing. Researchers need to include the various positions and interventions of policy-makers, teachers, social workers, journalists, police officers and activists. Last, but not least, we need information about the complex power relations between participants in violent practices and social observers of the practices (Benhabib, 2002) in order to address the problem effectively. Thus research on issues of violence in minoritized contexts has to be based on the detailed understanding of the complexities, contestations and enactments of the practices in order to avoid premature evaluation and action. I am, therefore, suggesting a critical relativist approach.

'Relativism' as a conventional way of approaching ethnographic fieldwork enables the researcher to examine complex and contradictory issues, such as forced marriage, with many actors at play. In order to allow close readings of the practices, relativism is an epistemic tool for including the points of view of 'insiders' (whether they are essentialist, critical, and/or deviant social agents) as well as 'outsiders' (whether they are constructivist and/or essentialist social observers). Insiders are engaged in reformulating, negotiating, rejecting or affirming and sometimes freezing practices, thoughts, structures, rumours and humours (Navaro-Yashin, 2002:19), whereas outsiders (journalists, social scientists, development workers etc.) try to make sense of – or control – these volatile practices. Some do this by applying constructivism, while others by emphasizing coherence and continuity or universal norms. This form of 'relativism' aims at critically scrutinizing both insiders and outsiders in order to grasp discourses on difference and diversity at various and shifting positions. Relativism facilitates the inclusion of marginalized and publicly muted voices, whereas 'critical relativism' aims at making these voices politically relevant.

Feminist interventions in the field of everyday experiences of rights and responsibilities, belonging and participation in a multicultural society represent a desire for a theoretically informed and critically engaged scholarship. 'Critical relativism' thus aims at developing a 'stand' or 'taking sides' (Armbruster and Lærke, 2008). However, over recent decades 'taking sides had become more complicated, perhaps because what constituted side was no longer so clearly graspable, epistemologically and empirically' (Armbruster, 2008:11). Since any standpoint in a multicultural and transnationally related society is based on complex and shifting grounds, a conventional relativist examination (including many actors and different positions, enactments, reconsiderations and cultural essentialisms, diversities within and across nation-states) appears as an auxiliary of a critical evaluation and claims for action. Enjoining a 'critical' perspective not only includes human rights claims, feminist or queer critiques of culture, but also enables the identification and deconstruction of the interrelation of essentialism and political power in all (hegemonic and subordinated, insider and outsider) contributions.

The diversity of practices of partnership, the existence and emergence of contestations of traditional arrangements, the transformation of sexual behaviour, and enactments of autonomy within minoritized groups are neglected when all third-country nationals are 'punished'. Actually existing individual and collective attitudes towards forced marriage are ignored in the name of 'protecting' minoritized women. The by-product of the Schengen area's struggles to protect women and enhance their citizenship rights independent of their (essentialized) ethnic and religious background (universal rights and human rights) is exemplary of how European countries are (willingly or not) conflating gender equality claims with control of migration, transnational marriages and family reunification.

The assumption that culture is determining, and the diminution of choice around marriage, do not contribute as intended towards increasing the autonomy of young women and vulnerable people within minoritized groups. Indeed, measures such as imposing barriers to family reunification up to a certain age will almost certainly reduce confidence in the institutions of the countries concerned. The debate about forced marriage has not only enabled heightened awareness of violence legitimated through culture and religion, but has also generated discursive violence, and the devaluation and exclusion of migrant and minoritized women 'in the name of gender equality, sexual autonomy and human rights' (Strasser and Holzleithner, 2010).

Conclusions: towards citizenship as lived experience

The concept of citizenship has been extended and diversified in the course of feminist, multicultural and transnational societal transformations, and as the product of activist, political and scholarly debates. In this context, this chapter has identified a universal concept of citizenship, cultural essentialism and methodological nationalism as obstacles to a fuller and more gender-fair notion of citizenship in a multicultural Europe.

Engaging with a universal notion of citizenship, some feminists have rejected the concept. Others have insisted that citizenship is a fruitful framework for the feminist analysis and activism. Feminist theorists, well versed in the critique of universalism and seeking equality without losing sight of differences, have developed a concept of citizenship as 'differentiated universalism' (Lister, 2003[1997]). They thus have provided important tools for understanding and transforming some of the contradictions and tensions inherent in the complexity of citizenship. Transnational relatedness and multicultural experiences have required the adaptation of citizenship to new constellations in a diversifying and globalizing world. These experiences and practices have been particularly significant in feminist considerations of differentiated models of citizenship. Feminists have focused on the study of the complexity of practices and everyday experiences of lived citizenship. The example of violence against women in a transnationally connected multicultural environment shows some of the tensions and difficulties inherent in contemporary discussions of citizenship, gender and migration. Awareness of violence does not prevent sensationalism or the discursive devaluation of minoritized groups, nor do attempts at protection necessarily avoid exclusionary practices. Citizenship then is not just a set of regulations for inclusion, but may simultaneously be an experience of discursive violence and exclusion.

A relativist perspective on the increasingly complex struggle to achieve gender-fair citizenship enables a focus on the tensions, contradictions and enactments of lived citizenship in a multicultural, and transnationally connected, Europe. *Critical* relativism consolidates inclusive, yet multiple, perspectives (universal and particular, insiders and outsiders, participants and observers) in order to contribute to the reconciliation of the tensions inherent in the concept of citizenship (such as those between inclusion and exclusion, liberation and discipline, a focus on citizenship 'from above' and 'from below'). This dual perspective furthermore allows thinking across territorial, cultural and social borders, and facilitates the study of different dimensions of citizenship (political, social, economic, racial/ethnic, bodily and intimate) on a local, national and global scale – as is the shared project of contributors to this book.

Notes

1. First versions of this contribution were presented at the FEMCIT conference at Cumberland Lodge in September 2007 and in Istanbul 2009. I am grateful to Beatrice Halsaa, Sasha Roseneil, Sevil Sümer and to all FEMCIT researchers for comments and suggestions on the draft versions.
2. Hammar calls migrants who are no longer regular foreign citizens but are still not naturalized citizens of the host state, '*denizens*' (1990:13).
3. The Schengen *acquis* has been integrated to the legal framework of the European Union (EU) by the Treaty of Amsterdam of 1997. However, there are still differences between EU countries because some do not want to lift border controls or because they do not yet fulfill the required conditions. On the other hand countries that are not member states of the EU, such as Norway, Iceland and Switzerland, have joined the Schengen area http://europa.eu/legislation_summaries/justice_freedom_security/free_movement_of_persons_asylum_immigration/l33020_en.htm (accessed 10 October 2011).
4. 'Methodological nationalism' is the 'assumption that the nation, the state or the society is the natural social and political form of the modern world' (Wimmer and Glick Schiller, 2002:301). For a critique of methodological nationalism see Wimmer and Glick Schiller (2002).
5. Even after the extension of citizenship to women in many countries at the beginning of the twentieth century and in the age of globalization, cosmopolitan norms and global rights there are still groups of the population who are excluded from citizenship, for example minors, foreigners, prisoners and people with severe mental health issues (Bauböck, 1994:23).
6. This intensification of racism has been discussed in various EU reports on racism and anti-semitism in Europe (Bell, 2002), and contribution to the introduction of the anti-racism directive in the EU 2000 (Council Directive 2000/43/EC, 29 June 2000 implementing the principle of equal treatment between persons irrespective of racial or ethnic origin, http://eur-lex.europa.eu/LexUriServ/LexUriServ.do?uri=CELEX:32000L0043:en:HTML, accessed 10 October 2011).
7. These new debates on citizenship meant to transgress dichotomies, yet unintended established new ones. As argued by Nira Yuval-Davis and Pnina Werbner some feminists support a division between universal egalitarianism seen as masculine and particular discourses of needs and care seen as feminine (1999a:7).
8. The paradox occurs when state policies to accommodate vulnerable minorities and 'to mitigate the power differentials between groups end up reinforcing the power hierarchies within them' (Shachar, 2000:65).
9. Andreas Wimmer and Nina Glick Schiller do not only focus on transnational experiences and practices but also tackle national boundaries and boundedness

of social sciences in their concept of 'methodological nationalism' (Wimmer and Glick Schiller, 2002).

10. For information on EU and legal citizenship see 'The EU Observatory on Citizenship (EUCITAC)', at http://eudo-citizenship.eu.

11. Bauböck (2001) suggests three structures of 'differentiated citizenship': first, a federal multilevel citizenship, which is vertically nested in local, regional, national and transnational contexts, second, a transnational citizenship, horizontally overlapping and finally, a multicultural citizenship differentiating groups within political communities.

12. 'More and more citizens are moving across national borders to EU/EEA countries other than their own, where they study, work, live – and fall in love. An increasing number of couples live in a member state of which they are not nationals. Out of the approximately 122 million marriages in the EU, around 16 million (13%) have such a cross-border dimension.' (European Commission, 2010a:5)

13. Council Directive 2003/86/EC of 22 September 2003 on the right to family reunification. Three member states, namely the UK, Ireland and Denmark are not bound by this directive (see preamble article 17 and 18 of the Directive). Whereas UK and Denmark have risen the age for reunification to 24, Ireland has not adopted any regulation. In six member states (Cyprus, Denmark, Ireland, Lithuania, Germany and the UK) the rules regarding family reunification with nationals are less favourable than those provided for family members of third-country nationals in Directive 2003/86.

14. Only a minority of the member states provide the right to family reunification for unmarried partners. This is the case in Belgium, Denmark, Finland, France, the Netherlands, Sweden and the UK (Groenendijk et al., 2007).

3
Remaking Intimate Citizenship in Multicultural Europe: Experiences Outside the Conventional Family

Sasha Roseneil, Isabel Crowhurst, Tone Hellesund,
Ana Cristina Santos and Mariya Stoilova

Introduction

How can we understand the ways in which, and the extent to which, movements for gender and sexual equality and change have contributed to remaking *intimate citizenship*?[1] The thorny question of the role of women's movements in transforming citizenship in Europe is at the heart of this book, and this chapter extends this focus to encompass lesbian and gay movements, casting its gaze on a dimension of citizenship that owes its very conceptualization to these movements. In this, we are contributing to two theoretically and normatively significant moves within recent scholarship on citizenship: the feminist extension of the concept beyond its classical roots, its republican revolutionary reworkings and its traditional usage in political theory; and the sociological turn which has seen increasing emphasis on practices, meanings and lived experiences of citizenship.[2]

Our feminist point of departure proposes that if citizenship is about 'full membership of community', as T. H. Marshall (1950) famously asserted, then it needs to encompass not only the spheres he delineated as civil, political and social, but also the realm of intimacy and personal life (Plummer, 1995; Plummer, 2003; Lewis, 2004a, b) because this is a core arena for the exercise of agency and the three 'key elements of citizenship – "rights and responsibilities, belonging and participation"' (Lister et al., 2007). The study of citizenship should include attention to the laws, policies and cultures that construct and regulate experiences of intimate life – experiences of, inter alia, inclusion and exclusion, recognition and misrecognition, freedom and oppression, autonomy and dependence, choice and constraint, and of the tensions and spaces between these binaries. The research on which this chapter draws addressed both intimate citizenship law and policy, *and* cultures, practices and experiences of intimate citizenship, seeking to tease out the influences of women's and lesbian and gay movements on each, and to trace the relationships between the legal, policy and cultural practice dimensions of intimate citizenship.[3] Our more limited focus in this chapter is on exploring how these movements might have impacted upon everyday experiences and subjective understandings of intimate citizenship.

Intimate citizenship and intimate life: movements and socio-cultural change

Although the concept of *intimate citizenship* has not been used by women's movements, it emerges from the radical rethinking of personal life set in train by the second wave feminist claim that 'the personal is political' (Hanisch, 1969). It is a feminist concept in its explicit connection of intimate life and citizenship, in its assertion that 'public' and 'private' are always mutually entangled, and that there is no clear, real or ultimate distinction to be drawn between them. With a broader referent than the notion of sexual citizenship (Evans, 1993; Bell and Binnie, 2000; Richardson, 2000), or bodily citizenship (Outshoorn et al., this volume), intimate citizenship is concerned with the processes, practices and discourses that regulate and shape the exercise of agency in intimate life: both the laws and policies enacted by states and polities, and the social relations between individuals and groups within civil society.

Our use of the term draws on the work of Ken Plummer (1995, 2003) who situates the emergence of intimate citizenship as a terrain of struggle within late modernity. Plummer regards feminism and lesbian and gay liberation movements as the progenitors of the new 'life politics' concerning the decisions people have to make about 'the *control (or not)* over one's body, feelings, relationships; *access (or not) to* representations, relationships, public spaces, etc.; and *socially grounded choices (or not)* about identities, gender experiences, erotic experiences' (1995:151, emphases in original). The seemingly oxymoronic notion of intimate citizenship implicitly refers to the fact that, in the wake of movements for gender and sexual equality and change, 'our intimacies are now thoroughly contested' (Plummer, 2003:13). This means both that the realm of personal life and close relationships is an arena of politicized struggle to change law, policy, and culture, and that, as individuals, we face a 'growing array of 'choices' in our personal life…concerning families, gender, bodies, identities and sexualities' (2003:4). Plummer (1995) emphasizes the centrality of story-telling in the construction of intimate citizenship – the 'family' stories, emotional stories, bodily stories, gender stories, erotic stories and identity stories that mediate between personal experience and the collective realm, and he explores the contestations and disputes that characterize what Lauren Berlant (1997) calls the contemporary 'intimate public sphere'. As such, the concept of intimate citizenship offers a new way of thinking about citizenship that recognizes the importance of political, social and cultural transformations of recent decades, and grants a central importance to women's movements and lesbian and gay movements.[4]

In a similar vein, Plummer is one of a number of sociologists (Giddens, 1992; Beck and Beck-Gernsheim, 1995; Castells, 1997; Weeks, 2007) who have asserted that post-1960s women's and lesbian and gay movements have been key drivers in the profound changes that have taken place in the sphere of intimacy over recent decades. They regard processes of individualization, de-traditionalization and increased self-reflexivity, fundamentally linked to feminist and sexual liberationist political projects, as opening up new possibilities and expectations in personal relationships, and radically transforming gender relations and family life. However, these theorists have not carried out empirical analyses that put their claims to the test or that investigate the processes of influence by which this might have happened. Moreover, the historical agency granted to social movements in transforming intimate citizenship and intimate life more broadly has been asserted in relation to north-western Europe and North America, and possible differences within Europe (or beyond) have not been explored. Notably, scholars of both intimate life and social movements have not explicitly addressed the relationship between the two: empirical research on intimacy rarely considers the meso-level realm of collective action, and work on social movements has not, as yet, paid significant attention to personal life.

Researching intimate citizenship in contemporary Europe

The context of our research is, then, the transformation of intimate life that has taken place over the past 40 years. Across European populations more and more people are spending longer periods of their lives outside the heterosexual, co-resident nuclear family unit that became the dominant model during the twentieth century (Roseneil and Budgeon, 2004). The change in the pace of migrations in Europe, which is producing increasing cultural diversity, has also challenged the hegemony of the modern western European nuclear family, as different models of intimate and family life prevail in different ethnic groups (Bryceson and Vuorela, 2002; Mason, 2004; Smart and Shipman, 2004; Grillo, 2008). Recent decades have also seen more and more people living openly in same-sex relationships in many European countries (Roseneil, 2000; Mercer et al., 2004). These changes in the organization of intimate life are dependent upon the successes of first wave feminist demands for political citizenship and access to education and employment. More recently, they are fundamentally entangled, in complex ways, with the emergence and development of welfare states, women's increased labour force participation, mass entry into higher education, and the concomitant increased possibility of economic independence (see Le Feuvre and Roseneil,

2011). As such, transformations in intimate life are uneven across Europe (Therborn, 2004; Cooke and Baxter, 2010).

We carried out our research on four countries, chosen according to a 'most different' comparative methodology to give a range of welfare regimes and both long-standing and newer democracies with different histories of civil society/state relations: Bulgaria – a 'post-Communist' state; Norway – a 'social democratic' Nordic 'woman-friendly' (Hernes, 1987) welfare state; Portugal – a 'southern European', Catholic, post-dictatorship state; and the UK – a north-western European '(neo-)liberal'/ 'social investment' welfare state.[5] In each country we addressed three spheres of intimate citizenship: civil society action, state activity, and everyday life. We carried out a historical study of the claims and demands of movements for gender and sexual equality and change in relation to intimate life and intimate citizenship (see Roseneil et al., 2009; 2011), a critical analysis of (national and EU) law and policy concerning intimate life (see Roseneil et al., 2008), and a socio-biographical study of everyday experiences of intimate citizenship. In the latter, we focused on people living outside conventional nuclear families and couples – people who might be seen to be at the forefront of the processes of individualization and de-traditionalization in intimate life that have been linked to the impact of women's and lesbian and gay movements.

We interviewed 67 people (41 women and 26 men) aged between their late twenties and their mid-fifties, who were one or more of the following: un-partnered; in a non-cohabiting (living-apart-together, LAT) relationship; lesbian, gay, bisexual/in a same-sex relationship; living in shared housing.[6] In each country we interviewed both members of the national majority population (26 in total) and of two different minoritized/racialized groups (41 in total).[7] We deliberately avoided interviewing activists, wanting to talk to 'ordinary' women and men living unconventional intimate lives, to explore the ways in which their unconventionality might be related to the interventions and impacts of women's and lesbian and gay movements.

Concerned to explore the relationship between biographical experience and wider socio-cultural processes and context, we used the biographical-narrative interpretive method (Wengraf, 2007) to gather and analyse life histories and accounts of particular incidents and events in the personal lives of our interviewees. The first part of the interview involved posing a single question which was designed to elicit uninterrupted, self-organized narratives from our interviewees: 'Can you tell me the story of your life and personal relationships, all the events and experiences that have been important to you...?' After the interviewee had exhausted what they had to say in response to this question, we followed this by asking for more detail about the intimate life events and experiences they had recounted. The method meant that interviewees decided for themselves what to speak about, and we only asked for more detail about events and experiences that they themselves first discussed. We did not, therefore, explicitly elicit information about attitudes and orientations towards the issues focused on by movements for gender and sexual equality and change, but were able to see how these issues arose *in vivo* in the course of the interviewees' narratives. We carried out a 'twin track' group process of data analysis, with workshops focusing, case by case, on each individual's 'lived life' and then on their 'told story'. After writing up individual case studies, we worked inductively across the set of case studies looking for patterns and themes in order to analyse narratives of intimate citizenship and the overall impact of the movements on experiences of intimate citizenship.

Struggles to remake intimate citizenship

In order to understand the role that social movements might have had in transforming lived experiences and subjective understandings of everyday intimate citizenship, we first have to know something about the struggles of social movements in this area. We can only outline the findings of this aspect of our research here, inevitably sacrificing detail and some nuance in the process.[8]

We identified four main areas of intimate citizenship claim-making and intervention by women's and lesbian and gay movements, around issues of: partnership, reproductive rights and parenting, sexual and gender identities and practices, and gender and sexual violence. Many claims highlighted the traditionally gendered and heteronormative character of states and political parties, demanding changes in law, policy and welfare provision in favour of women and those living outside normative heterosexuality. But culture and civil society were equally, and in some cases more, important terrains of struggle as movements sought to transform cultural understandings about intimate relationships and sexuality. This has involved the efforts of women, lesbians and gay men to remake their own deeply engrained patterns of thought and behaviour, their intimate selves and subjectivities, and has also challenged men and heterosexuals – individually and as social groups. In their more liberal, rights-orientated modes, movements have focused on demanding equality, justice and self-determination in intimate life for women, lesbians, gay men and trans-people, and for the recognition of sexual difference. At their most expansive and radical, they have sought to combat the systematic privileging of male and/or heterosexual interests and needs in both everyday intimate life and in the laws and policies that regulate intimate life, arguing that ways of living gender and sexuality in intimate life need to be fundamentally remade.

So, for instance, radical, liberationist, and queer elements within women's and lesbian and gay movements (particularly in the UK) have challenged the hegemony of marriage, the nuclear family and monogamy as institutions which serve to control the expression and exploration of love and sexuality, whilst others have demanded access to the institution of marriage for same-sex partners. Women's movements have claimed the most basic liberal right of bodily integrity, and that women should be able to choose when and how to have children, and not to have to deal with child care alone. They have argued that women should have access to sexual pleasure, that sex should not just be on men's terms, and they have struggled to liberate women from sexual shame, to enable the freer exploration of sexual desire, with men, and, in parts of the movements, at least, with women. Women's movements have politicized the interpersonal power relations and unequal negotiations that take place between intimate partners. They have drawn attention to the pervasiveness of gender and sexual violence, to the ways it shapes, constrains, and sometimes destroys and ends the lives of women and children, and they have tried to reduce its prevalence and ameliorate its impacts. In so doing, the needs and experiences of women and sexual minorities as intimate subjects that hitherto had been understood as individual and private have been asserted as central to human well-being, to social justice and 'full membership of community' (Marshall, 1950): in other words, to citizenship.

However, there are significant differences between the four countries we studied. Developing out of different historical and political contexts, facing distinct political opportunity structures and gender and welfare regimes, movements constructed agendas around intimate citizenship with differing emphases, and subject to different internal debates and conflicts. In addition the salience of intimate citizenship claims has waxed and waned over the years, and some of the issues have been keenly contested within national movements, and within and between movements. In Norway and the UK, on the one hand, there were significant 'first wave' feminist demands, in the early years of the twentieth century, around intimate citizenship issues (e.g. around divorce and marriage laws, child custody, male violence, prostitution, contraception, abortion, sex education and the social conditions faced by single women), but little comparable mobilization in Bulgaria and Portugal. And in Norway and the UK, grassroots women's liberation movements made vigorous and wide-ranging demands in each of the four areas we have identified from the early 1970s onwards. In contrast to the more open civil societies of Norway and the UK, the right and left wing authoritarian regimes in Portugal and Bulgaria meant that there was little social movement activism (Sousa Santos, 1992; Estanque, 1999; Viegas, 2004; Daskalova, 1999; Brunnbauer, 2008), and a relatively small urban middle class of the type that was the backbone of the new social movements in the 1970s and 1980s in western Europe (Kriesi, 1989; Rodrigues, 1995). In Portugal, the women's movement came later, and has been weaker, than in Norway and the UK, focusing particularly on issues of reproductive rights, rather than the broad sweep of intimate citizenship issues (Roseneil et al., 2011). In Bulgaria, there was little autonomous feminism in the 1970s and 1980s, and since the fall of communism there has been the growth of 'NGO-activism', much of which has been instigated by transnational funding bodies and pressure groups, and which has had a focus limited largely to gender and sexual violence (Roseneil et al., 2011).

With regard to lesbian and gay movements, in both Norway and the UK active campaigning for homosexual (UK)/homophile (Norway) rights began in the 1950s, with the emergence of a more radical gay liberationist movement in the early 1970s in the context of the New Left and the development of feminism. In both countries lesbian and gay sub-cultures developed during the 1970s, although lively urban 'gay scenes' have been much stronger in the UK than in Norway. The most significant difference between the two countries during the 1980s and 1990s was that the lesbian and gay movement, like the women's movement, was much closer to the state and political power in Norway than in the UK, where the Thatcher government engaged in openly homophobic politics in the 1980s (Weeks, 2007). In Portugal lesbian and gay politics emerged in the early 1990s, and was highly effective in securing publicity, engagement with the political parties, and legal change (Santos, 2008). In Bulgaria there has been a weaker and NGO orientated lesbian and gay 'movement', which has achieved much less visibility and as yet little success, but which has been supported and reinforced by Bulgaria's accession to the European Union (Roseneil and Stoilova, 2011).

Given these differing histories, it might not be seen as surprising that it was in the countries with the longer and stronger histories of social movement activism around intimate life – Norway and the UK – that we found clearer evidence of the impact of the movements on the narratives and lives of our interviewees, with Norway, the country with the closest relationship between movements and the state, evidencing the greatest impact. Social movement activism came later to Portugal, after the fall of the dictatorship, but has flourished in recent years, and there is considerable evidence of the difference that movements have made. In Bulgaria, where women's and LGBT movements lack a grassroots base, there is considerably less evidence of impact on intimate lives and narratives.

Impacts of the movements on experiences of intimate citizenship

What difference have women's and LGBT movements, and the legal and policy changes that have taken place in the wake of these movements, made in the lives of people living outside conventional couples and families?

We analysed the life stories offered to us by our interviewees in terms of how women's and LGBT movements might have impacted upon their experiences of intimate citizenship. We sought to track the role played by transformations in intimate citizenship law and policy that had been the subject of movement claims and demands, and we read our interviews for the expression of discourses and ideas about feminism, gender and sexual equality, lesbian and gay rights and sexual liberation. We tried to understand the ways in which the claims and demands of the movements, and the institutionalization of these claims and demands, might have been part of the framing and structuring of our interviewees' intimate lives and their self-interpretations and understandings. We also looked more broadly at the ways in which other transformations related to feminist claims for economic and social citizenship, such as the possibility for women to earn an independent income, or to receive state benefits in their own right, have impacted upon our interviewees' lives. This was a complex and challenging task that involved reference back and forth to our body of knowledge about the nationally specific claims and demands of the movements (Roseneil et al., 2009), and about the ways in which these demands had, or had not, been incorporated into law and policy (Roseneil et al., 2008). Moreover, we were acutely aware that there had always been multiple factors at work in bringing about legal and policy change, and in the construction and narration of our interviewees' lives; we do not wish to suggest that *only* women's and lesbian gay movements are to be understood as determining.

That said, when people mentioned making use of state-provided child care (in countries where this had been a feminist demand), drawing state benefits as lone mothers (where this had been a feminist demand), having (safe, legal) abortions, sharing custody after divorce, entering a state-recognized same-sex partnership, or staying in a women's refuge to escape domestic violence, it was clear that their experiences had been impacted by the successful realization of some of the demands of women's and lesbian and gay movements. When people talked explicitly and critically about their encounters with gender inequality and gendered roles, patriarchal attitudes or relations, discrimination on the grounds of gender or sexuality, the cultural impact of the movements was clear: the very possibility of speaking about these issues was directly related to these movements. When their stories revealed an expectation of, or search for, gender equality in intimate life, for a democratic form of intimacy, and when they suggested a sense of ease with lesbian, gay or bisexual identities, an assumption that living outside heterosexuality was legitimate and should be fully socially acceptable, that having and raising children in a same-sex partnership was possible, it was also clear to us that the movements had made a difference: such lives would not have been possible without these movements.

On the basis of this analysis, we grouped the interviewees into three clusters (see Table 3.1). The largest was the 43 interviewees in whose accounts we saw *clear, direct* evidence of the *impact* of legal/ policy changes, and/or cultural transformations – objective and/ or subjective impacts – that we understand as related to the movements. The second cluster was 11 interviewees where there were *traces of impact* – or what could be seen as *movement reverberations* – that were less definite and clear than the impacts we registered amongst the first group, and that were often indirectly exercised through the lives of others, particularly partners whose lives were more clearly affected by the movements. The third cluster was the 13 interviewees for whom we discerned *no impact* of women's and lesbian and gay movements. Below are some brief examples of these three clusters:[9]

Brief Examples of the Impact of Women's and LGBT Movements on Experiences of Intimate Citizenship

Clear impact

Ashen, a heterosexual Turkish woman in her late thirties, living in the UK, and now in a non-cohabiting relationship, had stayed in an abusive marriage because she was afraid that her parents would find out from her husband that she had not been a virgin before marriage. She came to understand her inaction as the result of a gendered and unequal culture that shames women for having sexual desires. She feels she was treated as a 'sexual object' and as 'a hole' by her husband. She benefited from changes in policies around domestic violence which had been the result of feminist campaigning. When she first escaped to a women's refuge, the police considered domestic violence a private matter in which they would not intervene. Some years later, however, she was able to obtain a court injunction against her husband, protecting her from further violence.

Mariana, a majority Bulgarian lesbian in her late twenties, describes herself as somebody who objects to the patriarchal model of family relations, and explains that she had left her boyfriend because he was limiting her freedom and suppressing her individuality. She is damning about a system that fails to recognize her female partner, whom she refers to as 'my wife', and the family they want to create.

Shirin, a divorced Norwegian Pakistani woman in her late thirites, now leads a financially independent life, has a full-time job and owns her own flat. This is possible because after her husband left her, she was supported by state-provided child care and benefits for lone mothers. She is highly critical of the norm of obedience to the family, and of the 'shame culture' that affects Pakistani women whose arranged marriages fail and who are then stigmatized by their community. She seeks a different kind of relationship in the future.

Vera, a heterosexual majority Portuguese woman in her late thirties in a non-cohabiting relationship, speaks about the importance of autonomy as a woman, about the value of friendship, and the influence of the strong women in her family. She has chosen not to have children and is critical of the pressure to cohabit and reproduce.

Traces of impact

Bobby, a heterosexual majority Bulgarian in his late thirties in a non-cohabiting relationship, has rather traditional ideas about gender and the domestic division of labour, but has had to grapple with the desires of his partners for greater equality. His ex-partner, with whom he has a child, was critical of his lack of involvement with child care, and since they split up she has emigrated with their son. His current partner is reluctant to move in with him and take up the domestic responsibilities that he seems to regard as naturally hers.

Luisa, a single heterosexual Portuguese Roma woman in her late forties, describes having wanted a love marriage, which when she was young was not possible for a Roma woman. Whilst she regrets that marriage has 'passed her by', she was able to persuade her mother to allow her to learn to drive so that she could earn a living, and she expresses pleasure with her 'full life', her ability to work and relief at not having 'a Gypsy man giving me orders, having to obey his rules, maybe even being beaten on top of that'.

Paul, a single heterosexual Pakistani man in his early forties living in London, has rejected the brides proposed to him by his family because they have not been fair-skinned enough or have been from a lower caste. He feels that he learnt a lot about sex from his 'equal relationship' with a 'Western liberated woman', in which 'there was no point of domination'. He regrets the loss of that relationship, and how he remains single. He idealizes the exciting 'Western woman' and rejects Pakistani women for being backward and lacking 'real beauty'.

No impact

Adrian, a divorced heterosexual Bulgarian Roma man in his late forties, has a traditional, patriarchal understanding of the roles, responsibilities and power relations between men and women in the family. He believes that he had the right as a husband, and even as an ex-husband, to demand and enforce, with violence if necessary, the fulfilment of his expectations of his wife.

Frank, a single heterosexual majority British man in his late thirties, seems rather uninterested in matters of intimacy and sexuality, recounting having had sexual encounters with six women in his life so far, and two relationships of a couple of years which drifted apart because of his 'apathy'. In the context of his lack of relational attachments, he seems unaffected by women's and lesbian and gay movements.

Rute, a single Portuguese Roma woman in her early thirties, has never been able to pursue any sexual/love relationships, having always been busy with familial care responsibilities, first for her sick and disabled father, then for her sisters' children. She accepts the gendered expectations and demands on her as the youngest daughter with no discernable critique or resentment.

Table 3.1   The impact of women's and LGBT movements on experiences of intimate citizenship

	Clear impact		Traces of impact		No impact		
	Women	Men	Women	Men	Women	Men	Total
Bulgaria	2	–	5	2	1	6	16
Norway	13	4	–	–	–	–	17
Portugal	8	2	2	1	1	2	16
UK	9	5	–	1	–	3	18
Total	32	11	7	4	2	11	67

Whilst we certainly cannot generalize to the whole population of people living outside conventional couples and families on the basis of our qualitative study, the simple numerical patterns in our sample are of analytic interest for what they *might* suggest about the varying impacts of movements across national contexts, between women and men, and between heterosexuals and non-heterosexuals (see Table 3.1).

In terms of differences between the four countries, we found the greatest impact amongst the Norwegian interviewees, where all the interviewees were considered to have been clearly impacted by the movements. Norway is followed by the UK, where 14 of 18 interviewees were considered to have been clearly impacted, 1 showed traces of impact and 3 no impact. Of the Portuguese interviewees, we analysed 10 as having been clearly impacted, 3 as showing traces of impact and 3 no impact. Amongst the Bulgarian sample, we only identified 2 interviewees who had been clearly impacted by the movements, 7 who were not impacted at all, and 7 for whom there were traces of impact. These findings resonate with our analysis of the strength of the movements in the four countries, their scope, and the extent to which movement claims and demands have been taken up by state institutions and political parties.

Looking at differences between women and men, we found only 2 of the 41 women not to have been impacted by the movements, in contrast to 11 of the 26 men; 32 of the 41 women were considered to have been clearly impacted, compared with 11 of the 26 men. However, amongst the Norwegian interviewees, the lives of both women and men had been impacted by the movements. In the UK, all the women interviewees evidenced movement impacts. In Portugal, where we had a smaller sample of men, 8 of 11 women showed clear impact, against 2 of the 5 men. Bulgaria showed the greatest gender differences, with 6 of 8 men showing no impact, against 1 of 8 women, and only 2 men showing traces of impact, against 5 women.

With regard to sexuality, 16 of the 20 lesbians, gay men and bisexuals we interviewed were clearly impacted by the movements, and we categorized two as showing traces of impact, and two as not impacted, both of whom were Bulgarian, where the lesbian and gay movements has been weakest. The large proportion of our non-heterosexual sample whose lives had been impacted by the movements suggests that the very possibility of adopting an openly lesbian/gay/bisexual identity, and being able to speak of such a life in positive terms, is directly related to the lesbian and gay movement.

Narratives of intimate citizenship

How did our interviewees talk about their intimate lives and see themselves as intimate actors? How did they narrate themselves as intimate citizens?

Asking these questions of the biographical narratives given to us by our 'non-conventional' interviewees was the second way in which we tried to understand how women's and lesbian and gay movements have made a difference to intimate citizenship. Reading across the whole set of case studies, we inductively identified the different narratives of intimate citizenship in the interviews, teasing out our interviewees' subjective constructions and representations of their experiences in terms of their overall tone and focus. Having wondered if there might be narratives that could be understood clearly with reference to the discourses and claims of women's and lesbian and gay movements – as feminist, gay liberationist, or queer, for example – we found that there was no straightforward mapping of movement discourses onto the complex life narratives of our interviewees; even the 7 self-identified feminists amongst our interviewees did not offer us narratives of their 'life and personal relationships' that would best be summarized in their totality simply as 'feminist'. Instead, we found five main narratives of intimate citizenship amongst our interviewees: narratives of self-realization and authenticity; narratives of struggle; narratives of un-fulfilment or failure; conventional narratives; and narratives of oppression. The stories of many interviewees featured more than one of these narratives – for instance, narratives of struggle often featured as secondary narratives, alongside narratives of self-realization and authenticity, or narratives of un-fulfilment. And attempting to summarize a long, complex, multifaceted story of 'life and personal relationships' in terms of a single dominant narrative inevitably does an injustice to the particularity of the story-teller's subjectivity and meaning-making process. For our purposes here we have categorized each interview in terms of its dominant narrative of intimate citizenship, in order to look at the patterns across the sample as a whole.

Narratives of self-realization and authenticity

Nearly half our interviewees (31 of 67) offered us narratives that we understand primarily as ones of self-realization and authenticity, in which the dominant theme in relation to intimate citizenship was the process of 'becoming oneself' in terms of identity and/or relationships with others. In most of these narratives this was seen as a 'work in progress', a process in which they were actively engaged and to which they were more or less explicitly committed. A number of interviewees spoke of self-realization and fulfilment as successfully achieved, expressing considerable satisfaction with their intimate lives and citizenship experience. These were agentic narratives, in which the creation of the self and the building of intimate relationships were reflexive projects, subject to thought and ongoing attention. They were not without the pain of loss and failure, or struggles with oppression and marginalization, but in these narratives these negatives were material with which to work, in order to create a better, more fulfilled future.

Narratives of self-realization were more prevalent amongst our women interviewees – 25 of 41 – than amongst men – 6 of 26, and it is notable that only one heterosexual man offered us a narrative of self-realization: they were overwhelmingly the stories of women and gay men. It is also interesting to note variation between countries: they were the predominant narrative amongst the relatively economically and socially secure Norwegian interviewees, with slightly fewer than half the UK and Portuguese interviewees offering such narratives; they were least common amongst the more precariously positioned Bulgarian interviewees. And whilst narratives of self-realization were not in themselves necessarily explicitly aligned with the claims and demands of women's and lesbian and gay movements, the overwhelming majority of those who offered narratives of self-realization were also categorized as showing clear impact of women's and/or LGBT movements in their lives – 28 of the 31, with 3 showing traces of impact, and none showing no impact.

Hanna's story is a strong example of the narratives of self-realization and authenticity amongst our interviewees. Born in Oslo in the mid-1970s, a majority Norwegian, educated to Masters level, and identifying as bisexual, Hanna was interviewed as someone living in shared housing.

Hanna's life had been far from conventional. She grew up in a culturally alternative milieu, and became active in left wing politics in her late teens. After high school she shared an apartment with a lesbian friend, Lisa, and then she moved abroad to study, during which time she had a four-year relationship with a woman. After graduating, she travelled to Asia and had a four-year relationship with a man. At the time of the interview she had returned to Norway and was living with Lisa – her (platonic) 'big love' – Lisa's ex-partner, and two cats, in her own 'family of friends'. Her account of her life was rich in descriptions of her travels between continents, of living, studying and working during her twenties in many different countries, of dramatic events, and of important intimate and sexual relationships with men and women, as lovers and friends. Yet the thread that ran through the intricate detail of her story, of her movement between places and her intimate travels, as one relationship ended and another began, was an overarching narrative of a personal, self-reflective, introspective journey, of a quest for self.

One major theme in this narrative was her relationship with her parents, for she had spent much time and energy contemplating her relationship with her father, whom she saw as having shaped her in a negative way. Hanna emphasized that she loved both her parents, and that she now had a good relationship with both of them. She described them as 'radical, intellectual', and remembered exciting family back-packing holidays when 'we had a really good time. Then they were all in a good mood.' Yet more formative was the rest of the year, 'everyday life':

Mum was always exhausted...I just didn't want to have it like that. Didn't want to live in a loveless – they did love each other, but, I felt that mum was not appreciated. I was always on my mum's side. Poor dad [laughs]. Uhm, uhm...but it was – I didn't want to be like them, and I realized that very early: I *do not* want to have it like that.

Her father was very focused on his work, and when he was at home he was often bad tempered. Hanna was interested in society around her, but when she discussed social issues with her father she felt that he ridiculed her. She later came to understand that he wanted to develop her intellect, but at the time she experienced him as bullying. Emphasizing the pressure she felt she was under, she recounted how, at the age of 15 she almost died in an accident, and how she felt that she would be happy to die, to let go, to avoid all the expectations on her, and the pressure to 'become something': 'It wasn't like enough to just be present and to be me.' She talked about coming to realize much later on that she had probably spent so much time travelling and living abroad in order to 'get away from all those expectations.'

Moving to Asia with her boyfriend, Emilio, living in a beautiful spot in the jungle by the beach, Hanna 'felt free because – it was out in nature, it was a different place, it was an exciting culture', but she ended her relationship with her boyfriend because it went sour. 'The relationship between him and me, it suddenly was totally similar to my mum and dad…. He was grumpy and moody [laughs], and I was nice and kind [laughs]…. He was very much like my dad, just grumpier.' Moreover, their relationship was highly gendered, Emilio did not treat her well, and she started to worry about being alone with him in the jungle. She began to think about sexual orientation, and about whether 'lesbianism might be more her.' She had kept her former relationship with a woman secret, although she realized her feelings for her girlfriend had been stronger than for Emilio. She wondered how much she was with a man because of convention, because 'being with men is what you do', and because it is easier to be with a man. But after these reflections she decided, 'no, I'm just bisexual'.

Back in Norway after more travelling, Hanna was stressed and tense, and she started seeing an alternative therapist. The first time she went, she had a strong response:

Memories and feelings, and things like that, things you haven't been able to express. It is stuck in muscle tension, in your breathing, everything. It was a revelation for me…I feel that after I came back to Norway, I haven't been out travelling, but have gone inwards…. It has been a journey, inwards, like starting to understand myself more and more. So I want to become a therapist now [laughs]. It is the first time I am studying something that…I do not feel is like a *good girl* thing.

At the time she was interviewed, Hanna was training as an alternative therapist, whilst working as an office assistant. For the first time in her life she felt she was doing what she really wanted, and was no longer worried about being successful in a conventional way. Reflecting on her life, she spoke of how she had realized that she had been caught up in parental and social expectations of what a 'good girl' should be, in terms of education, career and sexuality. She had now reached a point in her life journey when she had stopped drifting, had created a 'safety point' in her shared home, and was, finally, moving in the right direction towards what she felt would be a happy outcome. At the time of the interview she was in a new relationship with a man. Her story was one of a tortuous coming to terms with who she was and what she wanted from life.

Hanna's story can be seen as a quintessentially late modern narrative, highly reflexive in its discussion of intimate life and self-hood (Giddens, 1992), concerned with the quest for authenticity, and mobilizing, at times, a therapeutic, psychological language (Zaretsky, 2005; Furedi, 2004) to make sense of her experiences. It is a story with a teleology, the goal of which is self-realization. Hanna speaks about grappling with the normative expectations about the contemporary Norwegian 'good girl' – heterosexual, successfully coupled, successful academically and in work. Seeing these expectations as impressed upon her by her parents, Hanna understand them as having impacted upon the secrecy that surrounded her first significant love relationship – with a woman – and on the time she stayed in an unsatisfactory relationship with a man. Like many of the narratives of self-realization and authenticity that we were told, there is, then, a powerful undercurrent of feminism running through Hanna's story, as much of what Hanna seeks for herself, as woman living outside the conventional couple and family, has become thinkable and desirable in the wake of the post-1960s women's movements.

Narratives of struggle

The second most common intimate citizenship story amongst our interviewees was the narrative of struggle. For 13 interviewees their dominant story was of struggle, resistance, and/or challenge to relations of oppression, restriction or dependence in intimate life and with social norms about how they should be leading their intimate lives.[10] Interviewees talked about their struggles to resist the pressure to marry and have children and/or to marry within their faith, to leave marriages and intimate relationships that they found oppressive, abusive or violent, to separate from parental control, for sexual autonomy as women and as non-heterosexuals, and to survive (emotionally, financially, socially) without a man, as single women and lone mothers:[11] here we see, again, then, many threads of feminist and lesbian and gay movements' struggles. Some of this group also talked explicitly about facing racism, ethnic prejudice and discrimination, and about their struggles to develop or maintain a sense of themselves as valuable and worthy human beings in this context. Like the narratives of self-realization and authenticity, narratives of struggle were agentic narratives, but in the latter the emphasis was more on the process and difficulty of the struggle, of the power of the forces ranged against the narrator, rather than on that which was longed for.

The struggles narrated were experienced in three different ways, sometimes simultaneously. They were, first and foremost, experienced as interpersonal struggles, particularly in relation to the expectations and demands of parents and other family members, and sometimes as struggles with oppressive partners or ex-partners. Secondly, they were experienced as internal/psychic and emotional struggles with self, with many interviewees describing considerable psychological turmoil, and sometimes struggles with long-term mental ill health, depression and even attempts at suicide. And thirdly, they were experienced by some as political struggles in relation to established gender relations and intimate normativities, in which interviewees named their struggle as one against 'the patriarchal model', against a 'patriarchal father', against their oppression as women and as lesbians and gay men.

These narratives were similarly prevalent amongst Bulgarian (2), Portuguese (2) and Norwegian (3) interviewees, but 6 UK interviewees offered us such stories, suggesting, perhaps, an unexplained more consciously agentic dissatisfaction amongst our London interviewees. It is interesting to note that all but one of the 13 interviewees who offered a dominant narrative of struggle were from racialized/minoritized groups (10 of the 13) and/or were lesbians or gay men (4 of the 13); there was one heterosexual majority ethnic woman amongst this group. Of the 13, 10 were also categorized as showing clear evidence of movement impact, 2 traces of impact, and one, no impact.[12]

Ismail was born in the early 1970s in London, a second generation British Pakistani. His parents were both professionals, although his mother did not work after her marriage. Ismail attended a leading fee-paying school, where he excelled, and he went on to study law, and to become a successful lawyer. His parents were not, he said, strict Muslims, but brought him up with 'Muslim values', and from the age of 14 his friends were primarily Muslim boys from his local community rather than the white boys at his school. At law school he socialized mostly with people of an Asian background, and became very religious and active in the student Islamic Society. During this time he had his first relationship, with a Hindu fellow student, and he found their relationship being frowned upon by both Muslims and Hindus. After he began working, he became less religious, and stopped following Islamic teachings, by drinking alcohol for instance. He also began a relationship with Karen, a white British woman from a working class background. They were together for four years, and he never told his parents about the relationship. This caused friction in the relationship, which deteriorated as it became clear to both of them that he was not going to tell his family about it, and eventually he ended the relationship: 'I think I had a difficulty in accepting the fact that we might have a future, I think, because of our different backgrounds.' Ismail started seeing other women, and in his early thirties began a new relationship with Eleanor, a white middle class woman. A year later they bought a house together. He met her family, and they all got on well, and eventually he decided to tell his mother and sister about the relationship. A year later, however, the relationship ended, and he embarked on what he described as a 'bachelor's life'. During this time his mother tried to pressurize him into having an arranged marriage, but he has continued to resist.

Ismail's intimate life story was one that emphasized the emotional and interpersonal struggles he faced navigating between parental expectations and his own desires and choices, and between British and Pakistani cultures – what he called the 'double life phenomenon' that he regarded as common amongst British Pakistani. His story of his childhood and teenage years spoke about his sense of duty, and how he followed the 'rules' and 'values' he had been taught 'about certain things about kind of morality and family and things like that, so, you know, you, I mean you are not meant to have sex before you're married, you know, you're not meant to have girlfriends and things before you get married...'.

He described everything as being against him from the start in his first relationship with his Hindu girlfriend, and the conflict between his 'culture', represented by his family, and the way he was actually living his intimate life continued to the present day. After leaving university he 'went a bit crazy for a year', doing 'all the things that people did when they were 14 or 15', which he felt, in retrospect, 'a bit traumatized by'. His two major cohabiting relationships, with white women, were characterized by his struggle to 'come clean with my family'. When he finally told his mother about Eleanor, 'she wasn't very happy, really, she wasn't very happy'. He explained that it was difficult to introduce Eleanor without having plans to marry her straight away, and when his mother found evidence that Eleanor was staying over at his house, she was 'horrified': 'she was actually mortified. And, I mean, I think she actually cried, which made me feel very [laughs] but she kind of, I think she gradually accepted it, but every time that she would come she would always try to convince me out of it, wonder when I would come to my senses.' He realized that his mother would always be disappointed with his choice, and although he attempted to brush this knowledge aside, it affected his life too deeply:

> My mum was dead set against the idea [of me having a non-Pakistani girlfriend]. I mean, the biggest thing to deal with was her disappointment. I mean, she wasn't angry, and she wasn't upset, it was just intense disappointment.

Threatened by Eleanor with the ending of the relationship, he eventually told his father too, 'And my dad, bless him, he was so good, he was like, "Oh I don't really care that much". So it was a big who-ha over nothing really.' But the situation, and his internal conflict about the anticipated negative reactions of his parents, had ultimately put too much of a strain on the relationship: 'All that kind of puts cracks in the relationship that even though you kind of do it, it's almost you know, it's almost broken by the time you get there.' Ismail found himself pressuring Eleanor to get married, but she resisted this, and ultimately left him.

Ismail saw many of his intimate life experiences as typical of those 'making a new identity, which is that of British Asians, which is completely different from Pakistani and different from British, in a way'. It meant living a 'double identity', and struggling to reconcile his British lifestyle with the values and ways of life deriving from his Pakistani cultural background. In trying to explain this to the non-Pakistani interviewer, he moved between using the collective 'us/ we' to speak about 'us Pakistani/ Muslims' and the singular 'I', when talking about his Britishness, thereby emphasizing the ways in which his Britishness constituted him as distinct from, and alone, in relation to his community of origin.

Compared with many of our interviewees, in the light of changing practices of intimacy across Europe, Ismail's story of love, sex and cohabitation outside marriage does not seem particularly unconventional, and as a heterosexual man, he does not speak of struggling with oppressions of gender and heteronormativity. However, the emotional turmoil and familial tensions he narrates concerning his unconventionality in relation to his cultural background was potent, and was echoed and amplified in the stories of many other interviewees. His story does not speak explicitly of the impact of women's movements or lesbian and gay movements, although he does articulate a post-feminist consciousness of the gendered power relations in his family; rather his case points to the important intercultural dimensions of the remaking of intimate citizenship in contemporary Europe.[13]

Narratives of un-fulfilment or failure

Eleven interviewees offered narratives in which the dominant theme in relation to intimate life was one of un-fulfilment or failure, of not having what they had desired or hoped for, or what they feel is expected of them in their intimate lives – generally a partner/spouse and a loving stable relationship, and in one case, children. Whilst some of these narratives were tempered by a recognition that this un-fulfilment or failure might pass and prove to be temporary, as divorced interviewees hoped to repartner, others looked back over their life histories with considerable regret and disappointment about relationships that had ended and about relationships that had proved impossible because they crossed ethnic boundaries, without much hope that things would change in the future. Compared with the narratives of self-fulfilment/authenticity and the narratives of struggle, narratives of un-fulfilment/failure are much less agentic, focusing less on the action of the narrator and more on that which has been lost or never achieved.

These narratives of un-fulfilment/failure were fairly evenly spread across the four countries – with 3 in Bulgaria, Portugal and the UK, and 2 in Norway. However, they were considerably more common amongst men than women: 8 of 26 men offered such stories, compared with only 3 of 41 women – suggesting perhaps that men are more inclined to feel themselves to be losers in the contemporary intimate sphere. Two of those offering narratives of un-fulfilment/failure were (Bulgarian) gay men; the rest were heterosexual. Of those who offered narratives of un-fulfilment/failure, 5 were categorized as showing no evidence of the impacts of women's and lesbian and gay movements, 4 showed clear evidence of impact, and 2 showed traces of movement impact.

Vasil was born in the early 1970s in Sofia, the second child of a Muslim Roma family. In the mid-1980s, like all Bulgarian Muslims, he was forced to change his Arabic name to a Bulgarian name, and not long afterwards his family joined the Evangelical church, where he met a girl, Lina, with whom he became friends. At the age of 12 he fell in love with a boy at school, and a year later he was raped by an older man, who continued to harass him for some time. As his teenage years went on, Vasil started to make gay friends and to explore his sexuality at gay clubs and private parties. Meanwhile, aged 15, he and Lina decided to get married, and 'ran away' together to have sex, after which they were considered married according to Roma custom. After failing to get pregnant, they found out that Lina had health problems and would not be able to have children, and around this time Vasil developed a degenerative condition, which would gradually cause him to become quite seriously disabled. Lina and Vasil began to argue, and they broke up when Vasil was 19.

Following the end of his marriage, Vasil began a relationship with Boris, and his increasing association with gay friends made his father very angry. After a row with his father, Vasil moved with Boris to another city, where they lived together for a year and a half, but the relationship broke down, and Vasil moved back to Sofia. Around this time, in his early twenties, he met Stanislav, with whom he began a relationship. It was Stanislav who realized that rather than being offered a job as a cleaner in a sauna in Spain, Vasil was on the verge of being trafficked as a prostitute; Stanislav's intervention meant that Vasil stayed in Sofia, and they began living together. Some time later Vasil discovered that Stanislav was married and had two children. Vasil was very upset and asked Stanislav to leave, but the relationship did not end at this point; they stayed together seven years in total. By his late twenties, Vasil was having more serious health problems, and spent more and more time in hospital. He had several unsuccessful operations, one of which left him seriously incapacitated, and at one time he was in a coma for six weeks. Gradually his health improved a little, he found work as a taxi driver, and began an online romantic relationship with a man. Six months into the relationship, they were arranging to meet in person for the first time, and Vasil told the man he was Roma. He did not hear from the man again. At the time of the interview Vasil was single and living with his parents.

Vasil's life had been characterized by the experience of multiple, and multiplying, forms of marginalization and intimate violence – the racist violation of being made to change his name as a child, the sexual violation of being raped as a teenager, rejection by his father because of his sexuality and by the gay community (gay clubs, and a boyfriend) because he was Roma, whilst facing an increasing level of disability. His story was detailed, complex, and at times difficult to follow, but he was eager to speak about his life, and to try to explain how he felt. Whilst he sought, at times, to put a positive spin on his life experiences, the dominant narrative regarding his intimate life was one of un-fulfilment; his romantic relationships were a great source of disappointment for him, and he held great sadness about how things had turned out. His 'first and last love', for Stanislav, had been 'love at first sight', passionate, close and mutual; Stanislav had meant 'simply everything' to Vasil, offering him stability, comfort, support and belonging.

Everything that I wanted, I had it with him, all that he wanted, as far as I could, I was giving him. We worked together, we bathed together, lived together. We did everything together. We simply did not part, we did not part in any way.

His story of the end of their relationship was confusing to follow, but there was a strong fatalism about the narrative:

I told him that I might die from the pain, but simply we can't be together anymore because he does not belong to me. Because I am not the right thing in life. I'm not a woman, with whom he can live and have a family. I'm a man like him, and I can't give him what a woman can.

Their break-up caused him great distress, and with the loss of the relationship, Vasil 'saw that I can't be with a man for life'.

After him I have been alone for a while. I don't let anyone close to me. I don't even look people in the eyes, because I'm scared. I felt fear, horror, because I have felt the pain I feel.…I was very traumatized. I started thinking in a completely different way…. At some point I hated myself. I couldn't fit into my skin because I love somebody and I want to be with him.

He believed very firmly that 'when two men truly love each other, they love each other more than a man and woman do…this is the tenderest and most sincere love', but it 'is normal to be a man and a woman', and as a man he is not able to give another man 'what a woman can' – a family. 'I can't share my life with a man for life because this is not normal. Well, it can be normal for me, but it is not normal for people; they don't look at this as a normal thing, at least here in Bulgaria.'
As his story moved closer to the present day, he talked a lot about his disability, his desperation when he was confined to a wheelchair, about the reactions of others to his disability, and how he has had to come to terms with his deteriorating body. The combination of his disability and his sense of the impossibility of same-sex relationships mean that he holds out little hope for a future relationship with a man. He seems to have given up on what he prefers, and suggests that maybe he should be with a woman, to avoid a lonely old age.

Vasil's narrative of un-fulfilment as an intimate citizen was one of those that seemed most unaffected by women's and lesbian and gay movements; his defeated, depressed story of a failed, seemingly impossible relationship with his male lover highlights how much remains to be achieved in changing the cultural conditions of intimate life for those suffering multiple forms of marginalization, in a context where lesbian and gay movements have had little cultural or political impact. Other interviewees whose narratives we categorized as ones of un-fulfilment and failure, who were facing less severe marginalization, and were without a deteriorating physical impairment –

particularly the two divorced majority heterosexual men – were less defeated than Vasil, holding on to a greater degree of hope for a turn-around in their intimate fortunes; they had *failed*, but they might yet not see themselves as *failures*.

Conventional narratives

Eight of our 'non-conventional' interviewees offered us what we understand as conventional, or normative, narratives – narratives that do not problematize the interviewee's experiences of intimate citizenship and that imply, or sometimes explicitly state, that they have largely followed expected paths and conventional norms. Where there have been breaches of conventional norms, such as divorce or adultery, this is seen as morally wrong, and attempts have been made to move back towards a more normative form of intimate life. The conventions that are being followed vary, between place and ethnic group, but these stories share an uncritical, unreflexive attitude towards established gender relations and traditional family structures and relations, despite the fact that objectively each of the narrators was living outside the normative European family form. These narratives were notably much shorter than the others: the mean length of the answer to the first question of the interview was 29 minutes, compared with 65 minutes for the sample as a whole. [14] These were the narratives of those who did not have much to say about their intimate lives, who felt their own experiences to be relatively unremarkable, and who tended to speak in generalizations rather than offering rich narratives of significant incidents in their lives.

Perhaps unsurprisingly, all but one of the conventional narratives were offered by men, and all but one were heterosexual. Four were Bulgarian, 3 Portuguese and 1 from the UK. Only 1 of the conventional narrators was identified as having been impacted by the movements for gender and sexuality equality and change 5 showed no trace of impact and 2 showed traces of impact.

Albay was born in the late 1950s to a Bulgarian Turkish family in rural Bulgaria. Whilst at high school he took part in a number of talent competitions, and at one of these he met an actress with whom he had his first sexual encounter at the age of 18. After two years of compulsory military service, he was allocated a job in a factory, and whilst working there he started dating Anna, a majority ethnic Bulgarian. During his early twenties he was seeing both Anna and other women, and after three years he and Anna split up, and shortly afterwards Anna married another man, a majority Bulgarian. A few months after the wedding Albay and Anna resumed their relationship, which continued for another nine years. Four years after Anna's wedding, Albay began a friendship with Silvia, who was also from a Turkish background. He continued to see other women, including Anna, whilst seeing Silvia. However, Albay's emigration with his family, as part of the 'Big Excursion', when over 300,000 Bulgarian Turks fled the country after the forceful changing of Muslim names, meant that his relationship with Anna ended, whilst his relationship with Silvia was strengthened, as she and her family also moved to Turkey. Nearly a year after their migration, Albay and Silvia returned to Bulgaria together, she moved in with him and they married, eventually having a son. During the years that followed Albay was forced to find work abroad, and he sought to improve his position by studying part time at university. Eventually he secured a prestigious job in Sofia, and he moved to the capital to work, leaving his wife and son behind. His career flourished, and at the time of the interview he had been living apart from his wife for seven years, during which he had had several short-term relationships with other women.

Albay's story of his educational and working life was detailed, as he described his journey from factory worker to accomplished professional, and his emotional account of the humiliations of the period of anti-Turkish oppression through which he lived was similarly rich. However, apart from dwelling at some length on his 'first love', Anna, which was a 'forbidden love', impossible because of their different ethnic backgrounds, he spoke only briefly about his marriage and his various 'promiscuous' relationships. He described meeting his wife, their long friendship before marriage and their wedding in a rather laconic and distanced way, particularly in comparison with how he talked about his feelings for Anna, and about the 'very nasty' experience of his forced migration. He married in the context of this period, which his family and Silvia's family had shared, thinking 'Let me be like other people: the years are passing by', and because his relatives were 'mocking' him for not being married. The greatest joy in his life was the birth of his son: men feel 'instinctively happy' he said, when they have a boy, but he spoke very little about his son or his wife as individuals. He presented himself as a man of family values, believing in the will of the Creator, and demonstrating a certain resignation. Alongside this, though, there was a sense of himself as something of a Casanova, passionate, sexual, sensitive and romantic – who wanted the interviewer to know about his 'delicate relationships with ladies', and that he could resist 'any benefit that life on earth offers, any benefits in the sense of wealth, money, ummh, and others, but I am not sure I can resist a beautiful woman'. Rather undercutting the picture he seemed to be wishing to paint of a romantic seducer, and revealing his rather misogynist attitudes, he assured the interviewer 'of course, I wouldn't go out with a crocodile'. He justified having had 'quite a lot of relationships', as impulsive actions, driven by the 'calls of nature', and spoke about the aftermath of regret and self-blame, because now he was married.

Albay is aware that his intimate life had not, at times, followed normative injunctions to the letter – he had had a 'forbidden' cross-ethnic relationship, he had been 'promiscuous', he has a wild streak. Ultimately, however, he sees himself as an ordinary man, who accepted the impossibility of the relationship with Anna, and settled down with the Turkish woman whose parents he respects. Accounting for himself in conventional ways, as a good family man, he presents himself as subject to normal, natural male desires, which he tries, not always successfully, to control, for the sake of his marriage, to which he remains committed despite living away from his wife.

Albay's narrative speaks of the traditional gender identifications and attachment to ideals of family that were characteristic of those who told conventional narratives, and underlines how far the ripples of women's and lesbian and gay movements were from reaching everyone we interviewed. His self-understanding and representation as a 'normal' man, subject to biological urges that need to be curtailed for the sake of family life, articulates a subject-position that resonates strongly with patriarchal tradition, but that was far from dominant amongst our 'non-conventional' interviewees.

Narratives of oppression

The smallest group amongst our interviewees were the four who offered us narratives which we understand as primarily narratives of oppression in relation to intimate citizenship. In these narratives, interviewees recounted experiences of grave restriction and patriarchal control of their intimate lives, and/or of violation of their autonomy and personhood, with little or no discussion of resistance to, or critique of, their intimate life conditions and experiences. In contrast to the conventional narratives which were largely offered by men, the narrative of oppression were women's stories – all were Roma women (3 Bulgarian and 1 Portuguese). In terms of the impact of social movements on those who offered stories of oppression, 2 showed no impact (including Alexandra below) and 2 showed the mildest traces of impact, in the desires they expressed, for themselves and/or their daughters, to improve their education and to find employment.

Alexandra is a Roma woman who was born in Lisbon in the late 1960s. At the age of 16, following her uncle's orders, she 'ran away' with one of her cousins, and was thereby married according to Roma custom, moving with her young husband into a shack at the back of her parents' house. A year after marrying, Alexandra became pregnant with their first child, but she had already become used to spending nights alone because her husband was seeing other women. Just before she was due to give birth, she found the address of an alleged mistress, and her mother and grandmother beat this woman up. The woman told them she was his drug dealer, not his lover. Not long afterwards Alexandra got pregnant again, and after this her husband stopped seeing other women but became seriously addicted to heroin. Alexandra's father and grandmother knew about this, but Alexandra was slower to find out. During this period, Alexandra had hardly any money to eat, because her husband was taking all the money he could find to spend on drugs, and he would sometimes disappear for weeks on end, stealing the only beautiful things she had possessed, her 'bottom drawer' of nightgowns and bed spreads, furniture and crockery. Alexandra relied on her parents for food and clothing for herself and her children, as her own possessions disappeared.

Five years after being married Alexandra began to have epileptic seizures, one of which temporarily paralysed her from the waist down. Whilst she was paralysed she got pregnant with her third child, and she continued having seizures throughout the pregnancy. Eventually, her father intervened, seeing how sick both Alexandra and her husband were. First he instructed her husband to live and sleep separately from his daughter, and when that failed, he 'decided that I shouldn't be there, with him...He stopped being clean, cleaning himself, and so my father said, "No, this can't go on. You have your children to raise and I am also a widower. I've no longer got your mother, so this ends here. Come on. Grab your things, whatever is yours, your children, and you'll come to my house." So that was it. I got separated.'

Alexandra moved out, but continued to give her husband money for food via her children. In the wake of the separation, and a period in which she had cared for her dying mother, as well as her three children, Alexandra started to experience mental health problems, which led to her referral to a psychiatrist who prescribed her medication. Around this time she found out that her former husband had contracted AIDS, from which he later died. Alexandra tends his grave, and at the time of the interview was living with her children, daughters-in-law and grandchildren in her father's home. She draws benefits, and occasionally sells clothes door-to-door.

Alexandra began the interview by stating that there was not much to be said about her life, and went on to narrate a life with little room for autonomous, informed, and self-determined agency. Most of her story is about the bad things that have happened to her, and that have been beyond her control. Her narrative revolves around the actions of three male relatives, her husband, father and uncle. Her (dead) husband is described as the cause of all her sorrow and suffering, including stress, illness, hunger, poverty and betrayal. Her (living) father is described as the source of support and knowledge, who has helped her and her children financially, and who 'cured' her illness. It was her uncle who organized her marriage. She emphasized how her marriage had not been her idea, and how she was still really a child when it took place:

I never thought about getting married. I never thought about it. I was too young, and I'll tell you this, umm, I was a Mary-man [a tomboy]. [laughs]. I was a Mary-man. My life was about throwing the whipping top. I wasn't thinking about anything. Being 16 I had a very childish brain.

She went on;

'I never had, umh, I never intended to, umm, get married. I didn't. At that time, I didn't. All I wanted was to play and so on. So, I had an uncle, who must have spoken to my husband or with my granny, because he decided he would like me to get married to my husband. And so my uncle grabbed me. They must have agreed, or, I don't know. My uncle grabbed me and he grabbed my husband and he put us, umm, we ran away from home. He grabbed me and my husband and put us inside a taxi, and we ran away to a relative's house....I was never asked.'

Alexandra's story is one of almost unremitting patriarchal oppression, of a woman who cannot read or write, whose life-changing decisions were made by others, invariably male, and who additionally has suffered from physical and psychological illness, at times severely life-limiting. The only decision that she speaks of having made in relation to her intimate life is not to repartner:

'From a young age, younger than I am now, because of the life I had with my husband, it made me decide that I didn't want any other man. Never again. And I don't. And I stayed like this. I will raise my children....Men to me are dead. He died already, and I no longer want any other.

And I remained like this. I never wanted men anymore.' However, this 'choice' is in the context of a life that had been overwhelmingly shaped by her marriage, and she does not speak of herself autonomously without reference to the impact of her marriage.

Alexandra's story was very similar to the other narratives of oppression in lacking in a sense of agency. Whilst she was just able to formulate criticism of her uncle for making her marry too young, and for not consulting her about the marriage, her narrative, like the others in this group, did not express outrage or anger about the conditions of her life. These were stories in which the interviewees often seemed overwhelmed by their experiences, and to have little personal capacity to effect change in their lives. They were narratives of highly constrained intimate citizenship. However, it must be noted that there were relatively few such stories amongst our interviewees; it might be imagined that 40 years ago there might have been many more.

Failures of full intimate citizenship

Finally, in seeking to understand the impacts of women's and lesbian and gay movements on experiences of intimate citizenship, we must draw attention to the extent of the failures of full intimate citizenship that were recounted by our interviewees: failures of the possibility of fully experiencing and enacting 'rights and responsibilities', 'belonging' and 'participation'. Across the sample, almost all of our 'non-conventional' interviewees spoke of at least one incident or experience in their intimate life that social movements have challenged as oppressive, discriminatory and marginalizing; this included almost all of those whose experiences of intimate citizenship show clear impact of women's and lesbian and gay movements, and those whose overarching narratives of intimate citizenship emphasized self-realization/ authenticity. Amongst the few who did not speak of such experiences, we heard a little about 'the other side' of oppression in intimate life, the failure of the intimate citizen's responsibility to treat intimate others with respect, and to recognize their bodily integrity.

With regard to *partnership*, a number of interviewees spoke about encountering a lack of respect and recognition of their partner/lover – from their own families, communities and/or the wider social world, and from legal and state institutions – because s/he was the same-sex, of a different ethnicity, transgender or the 'wrong age'. Some interviewees faced limitations on their freedom of choice in their intimate relationships, particularly in mixed ethnicity relationships. Others discussed violations of self-determination and personhood, being 'stolen', forced, coerced or bribed into marriages and sexual relationships, or, less extremely, experiencing considerable moral and social pressure to be married or just partnered. For some, choosing to leave a marriage, or being left by their spouse, resulted in shame and humiliation, a sense of personal failure, social marginalization by family and community, and/or economic hardship. In terms of *reproduction and parenting*, interviewees talked variously about the negative impact of social and parental pressure to have children, about the difficulty of having children as a lesbian, about losing, or fearing the loss of, custody of their children, as well as about the unequal gendered burden of caring for children. When it came to *sexual practices and identities*, some women talked about the shame they had been made to feel about having and acting on their sexual desires. Lesbians, gay men and bisexuals described their struggles to come to terms with their same-sex desires, to deal with the social disapprobation they encountered, and some with finding private space to pursue their intimate relationships. In terms of *gender identities*, many women talked about how their personal development, social and educational opportunities and sense of self had been restricted as girls and young women, by patriarchal fathers, controlling mothers and communities that did not value women as autonomous human beings. Many interviewees, including a small number of men, also talked about *gendered and sexualized violence* disrupting their bodily integrity – about violent, abusive and domineering partners, about rape and sexual assault, about sexual harassment at work, and we heard about experiences of violence, abuse and neglect by parents and in state institutions, as children, much of which had long-term psychological impacts on the narrators. In all of this, there was evidence of the failure of law and policy to protect people from intimate forms of violence. From the other side, a small number of men revealed the violence they had meted out to wives and partners.

For some, such experiences were discrete incidents that could be recounted as located firmly in the past; but for many, the experiences ranged across the years, and sometimes decades, from childhood onwards, with long-term consequences for interviewees' sense of self and future relationships. The unhappy psychic states and mental health problems – depression, detachment, alienation, loneliness and suicidality – that many interviewees spoke about, sometimes elliptically, sometimes explicitly, might well be related to the experiences of intimate violation and impingement recounted as part of their life stories. Interviewees varied in the extent to which they railed against these experiences. For many they were the source of explicit critique and anger, whilst others described them as part of their life stories, often with considerable emotion, but without an obvious sense of having experienced a social or interpersonal injustice.

The failures of full intimate citizenship described by our interviewees can be understood at different levels: some were failures of respectful, equal relating between two or more people bound together intimately, others were failures of civil society communities, and/or the state to offer recognition, support or sensitive, appropriate protective intervention. Many of these failures offer evidence of the ongoing problems of gender inequalities in intimate relations, which at times might be understood as patriarchal power and women's oppression. Others point to varying problems of minoritization, which produce inattention to the intimate needs and suffering of members of some social and ethnic groups, or which problematize the intimate lives of particular groups.

Remaking intimate citizenship?

In this chapter, we have sought to understand the difference that women's movements and lesbian and gay movements have made to intimate citizenship by studying the lives and stories of a relatively small number of people, in four European capital cities, who are, in various ways, living outside the conventional Western couple and family form. The people we interviewed were not a representative sample, but the sample was strategically designed so that we might be able to comment on ongoing processes of transformation in intimate life, as experienced by members of both majority and minoritized/racialized groups in the four countries.

Drawing together the analysis we have presented, we suggest that there is evidence that women's and lesbian and gay movements have made a radical difference to the possibilities of intimate citizenship for people living outside conventional families. We identified multifarious ways in which the conditions of intimate life and the intimate subjectivities of our interviewees had been affected by these movements. Feminist and sexual/gay liberationist/queer discourses were only occasionally explicitly articulated by our interviewees. However, the narratives of self-realization and authenticity, and the narratives of struggle that were the dominant narratives of two thirds of our interviewees, and the majority of the women, expressed desires for fuller experiences of intimate citizenship, and to transcend restrictions, oppressions and impingements in intimate life. The longing for 'the freedom and ability to construct and live selfhood and a wide range of close relationships ... safely, securely, and according to personal choice, with respect, recognition and support from state and civil society' (Roseneil, 2010b:81–2) – for full intimate citizenship – is shared by most of the people living outside conventional family forms across the four countries we studied. Whilst it seems more pressing for women, lesbians, gay men and bisexuals, many of the heterosexual men we interviewed also sought these freedoms and rights.

We also found that almost all of our 'non-conventional' interviewees had experienced violations of their intimate citizenship, ranging in severity and duration, that underline how far from realized are the far-reaching ideals of feminist, lesbian and gay activists and visionaries. Our research suggests that the struggle for fuller intimate citizenship is being pursued in the everyday actions and relational practices of individuals, as well as by women's and lesbian and gay movements, but there remain significant inequalities in access to the cultural and personal resources that enable people to mobilize and flourish as intimate citizens. Whilst the longing for fuller intimate citizenship crosses nation and ethnic group, for some, the impact of multiple forms of marginalization over a lifetime is to produce resignation, a sense of hopelessness, desperation and a lack of personal agency in intimate life.

Our research is suggestive of notable differences between the four countries we studied. Norway, the country where women's and lesbian and gay movements have been most effective in securing integration into state institutions and policy, appears to show the strongest evidence of impact on people's lives, followed by the UK, Portugal and then Bulgaria, in ways which might be seen to reflect the historical development, strength and cultural reach of the movements in each country. However, future research might consider how other factors, such as absolute levels of national wealth and gross domestic product and relative levels of economic and social inequality within countries, mediated by welfare states and redistributive social and economic policies, might also impact upon the stories people tell about their intimate lives, their intimate subjectivities, and the intimate futures they are able to imagine and seek. Moreover, the rich, complex biographical narratives offered to us by our interviewees – in which they discussed their intimate lives in the context of their experiences of education and personal development, early family life (from loving and supportive to violent and alienating), employment and unemployment, health and illness, and positive and negative encounters with state institutions, communities and social groups – underline the complexity of understanding the influences on any individual's experience of intimate citizenship. Disentangling the impacts of movements for gender and sexual equality and change on intimate citizenship from those of other social forces and cultural processes, such as the emergence of 'intimate public spheres' (Berlant, 1997) and the diffusion of 'therapeutic culture' (Furedi, 2004), is an inherently fraught, and maybe impossible, task, given that the very ability to speak about intimate life, its troubles and vicissitudes, its joys and pleasures, has been conditioned both by those very movements, and by their imbrication with these other trends.

Notwithstanding the problems associated with the project of seeking to understand the role of social movements in remaking intimate citizenship, the research that we have carried out points clearly to the salience of the intimate sphere as a dimension of citizenship. And in extending the concept of citizenship to encompass the gendered, embodied, sexual, emotional and above all relational experiences of intimate life, the rational, autonomous citizen of liberal and republican heritage is reimagined as a more fully human, complex, connected being.

Notes

1. We use the phrase 'movements for gender and sexual equality and change' to encompass women's movements, feminist movements, and lesbian, gay, bisexual and transgender movements, both in their autonomous formations and as elements within other movements, political parties and non-governmental

organizations. For brevity, we also refer to these movements as women's and lesbian and gay movements.

2. On the feminist reconceptualization of citizenship, see Hernes (1987); Lister (1989; 1997); Siim (2000). An early example of the sociological turn in citizenship studies was Werbner and Yuval-Davis's (1999:4) definition of citizenship as 'a more total relationship, inflected by identity, social positioning, cultural assumptions, institutional practices and a sense of belonging'. See also Strasser (this volume).

3. See Halsaa, Roseneil and Sümer (2011:55–67) for an overview of the findings of the research, which was part of the EU FP6 FEMCIT project.

4. It should also be recognized that whilst the concept of intimate citizenship has only become imaginable in the wake of the post-1960s movements for gender and sexual equality and change, intimate citizenship itself has a much longer history; citizenship should be understood to have always incorporated an intimate dimension, to have always assumed and promoted, as part of the 'fraternal social contract' (Pateman, 1989), particular forms of (largely heterosexual) intimate relationship and family form, and to have rested on familial practices of reproduction and national birthright (Stevens, 1999). Citizenship cannot be understood without attention to the legal and normative regulation of practices of intimacy.

5. Due to resource limitations, it was not possible to include a fifth 'conservative/ corporatist' welfare regime.

6. We interviewed 16 people in Sofia, 16 in Lisbon, 17 in Oslo and 18 in London; 40 people were unpartnered, 20 were lesbian/ gay/ bisexual, 21 were in a non-cohabiting relationship and 21 were living in shared housing.

7. The minoritized interviewees were Roma and Turkish in Bulgaria, Cape Verdean and Roma in Portugal, Sami and Pakistani in Norway and Pakistani and Turkish in the UK. We selected the minoritized/racialized groups for each country with reference to the relative size and salience of the groups to recent debates about intimate citizenship, with reference to the colonial histories of Portugal and the UK, to include important national minority groups in Bulgaria and Norway, and to include groups that exist across two or more of the countries.

8. See also Roseneil et al. (2009, 2011).

9. All cases have been anonymized.

10. It should be noted that struggle was a subsidiary theme in many more interviewees' narratives.

11. There was also one heterosexual man whose struggle was against his wife's accusations of domestic violence, and for increased access to his children.

12. This was a Turkish-speaking heterosexual man whose intimate struggles concerned the familial pressure he faced to get married, and the cultural differences he encountered in relationships with women from different backgrounds.

13. By 'post-feminist' consciousness we mean reliant upon the insights of feminism.

14. The interviews were between 17 minutes and 5 hours 22 minutes in length, with the mean length being 2 hours 6 minutes.

4
Remaking Economic Citizenship in Multicultural Europe: Women's Movement Claims and the 'Commodification of Elderly Care'

Nicky Le Feuvre, Rune Ervik, Anna Krajewska and Milka Metso

Introduction

It is widely assumed that one of the most visible legacies of the second wave women's movement has been a radical transformation of expectations regarding the gender division of employment and, to a lesser extent, unpaid care activities. However, some recent feminist research has stressed the unintended consequences of the claims made in the final decades of the twentieth century for women's 'emancipation through employment' under what has sometimes been called the 'paid work paradigm' for gender equality (Méda and Périvier, 2007; Lewis 2003, 2007). In European policy terms, there are now quite clear signs of a shift from measures predicated on women's widespread exclusion from the labour market to policies explicitly aimed at encouraging their continuous employment over the life-course (Jenson, 2008, 2009). However, this shift has been received with ambivalence in feminist circles, notably due to its potentially divisive effects on women as a social group and to its ineffectiveness in transforming the gender division of (paid and unpaid) care activities more generally. Despite the partial shift 'from private to public reproduction'[1] (Hernes, 1987), the main burden of care activities continues to fall principally on women's shoulders (Bambra, 2007), but not necessarily equally on women of different social and racial origins, and not necessarily to the same extent in all national contexts.

On the basis of empirical research carried out under the FEMCIT project,[2] this chapter aims to investigate the citizenship issues raised by the 'commodification of care' processes currently observed in a number of European countries (Lyon and Glucksmann, 2008). After defining the notion of 'economic citizenship' and outlining the methodology used in our research, the first section of the chapter presents the terms in which 'economic citizenship' claims have been framed by women's movements in five contrasting national contexts (Finland, France, Norway, Poland and the UK). We show how, since the early 1970s, the 'adult citizen worker' model (Fraser, 1994; Orloff, 1993) has emerged as an implicit point of reference in the selection of grass-roots publications from all the countries studied here, despite their very different positions in gender and welfare state typologies (Esping-Andersen, 1990; Lewis, 1992, 1997). Secondly, we assess the shifting context in which these women's movement claims have been (at least partially) translated into policy orientations and social practices. We take the elder care sector as a focal point of comparison. Analysing the degree to which elder care jobs provide the conditions for full economic citizenship in three national contexts (France, Norway and Poland)[3] enables us to illustrate the potential hiatus between the claims for women's emancipation through employment and the concrete economic citizenship experiences of a particular group of (largely female) workers in specific societal contexts. In conclusion, we will argue that the externalization of the elder care work previously carried out unpaid by successive generations of women in the home does *not necessarily* lead to the increase in inequalities between different groups of women, and does *not necessarily* imply the emancipation of white, majority, middle-class women at the expense of their poor, migrant or minoritized counterparts. The precise characteristics of elder care jobs vary considerably from one national context to another, as does the degree to which minoritized women are normatively assigned to them (Simonazzi, 2008). We argue that there is nothing inherent about elder care work that makes it impossible to envisage as a route to full and fair economic citizenship. It is the conditions under which elder care is materially organized and symbolically framed that determine the economic citizenship experiences of elder care workers and we argue that this opens up opportunities for renewed feminist claims-making in a multicultural European context.

Defining economic citizenship

The notion of 'economic citizenship' is not widely used in the existing literature on women's work and employment,[4] since access to economic resources has usually been subsumed under the notion of 'social citizenship', as defined by T. H. Marshall. According to Marshall: 'the right to follow the occupation of one's choice in the place of one's choice' (1950:10) is a basic civil right. However, a great deal of feminist research has highlighted the fact that, contrary to the vast majority of their male counterparts, most women have historically gained access to a range of social rights and benefits through marriage and/or motherhood rather than employment (Fraser, 2000; Hobson, 2000). It thus seems necessary to distinguish more clearly between 'social citizenship' issues, which refer to various social benefits (including maternity leave, child-care facilities and parental leave, cf. Bergman et al., this volume) and women's direct access to the rights, resources, recognition (Lister, 1997) more directly associated with their own participation in paid labour.

Along with Barbara Hobson (2000), Alice Kessler-Harris is one of the rare feminist scholars to have developed the notion of 'economic citizenship' (Kessler-Harris, 1996, 2003). According to her, this notion encompasses 'the right to work at the occupation of one's choice (where work includes child-rearing and household maintenance); to earn wages adequate to the support of self and family; to a non-discriminatory job market; to the education and training that facilitate access to it; to the social benefits necessary to support labour force participation; and to the social environment required for effective choice, including adequate housing, safe streets, accessible public transport, and universal health care' (Kessler-Harris, 2003:163). She claims that, from a gender perspective, Marshall's definition of social citizenship remains unsatisfactory, since it fails to encompass what she calls the 'three-way tug' between care-giving, family life and wage labour, thus '[posing] severe challenges to achieving gender equity and full citizenship' (Kessler-Harris, 2003:158).

In short, Kessler-Harris argues that the perceived tensions between paid work and unpaid care work that infuse many policy measures (including equal opportunity policies to promote 'work–life balance') are largely due to the legacy of the (historically and geographically situated) 'normative assumption that women would spend most of their lives in household production and maintenance and in biological and social reproduction' (2003: 161). This stunted 'gendered imagination' (Kessler-Harris, 2001) has led to a historical difference in the provision of civil and social rights according to an individual's sex and marital status: 'policy makers and advocates of women chose to protect the social rights of women through families, rather than insisting on civil rights to work...By assigning some social benefits through wage work, and others through state indulgence, a divided labour force limited possibilities for either sex to create balanced lives, inhibiting political participation for women and family participation for men...The result is a deeply class- and racially divided system, for it leaves those without work (often women, African Americans, recent immigrants, and the poorly educated) with a problematic form of social citizenship and a questionable 'right to work' that smacks more of obligation than of benefit.' (Kessler-Harris, 2003:163–4).

Although Kessler-Harris has been criticized for her excessive focus on the North American case, and for her perceived advocacy of the widespread 'commodification of care' (Lewis, 2002, 2003), her line of reasoning is, in fact, more subtle. She shows quite clearly that those jobs primarily labelled as 'women's work' generally fail to met the criteria for full economic citizenship, precisely because many categories of women continue to benefit from three distinct sources of social protection; one that is related to their own direct labour market participation (putting them on a par with most men) and two which are not: those benefits offered to them as the spouse of an employed male partner (widow's pensions, for example) and those offered to them by the state, on the basis of their domestic caring and household maintenance roles (paid carers' leave, single mothers' allowances, for example). According to Kessler-Harris, one of the results of these potentially multiple sources of social protection has been to reduce the effectiveness women's claims for rights, economic redistribution and social recognition (i.e. citizenship) directly through their own employment experiences.

Kessler-Harris' definition of economic citizenship is largely echoed in the more recent work on 'defamilialization'. According to Bambra, for example, 'defamilialization refers to the extent to which the welfare state enables women to survive as independent workers and decreases the importance of the family in women's lives. Defamilialization is therefore concerned with women's freedom from the family, rather than the freedom of the family' (Bambra, 2007:331). These conceptualizations allow us to consider not only the characteristics of women's jobs (levels of pay, working time patterns, health and safety issues, qualifications and training, promotion prospects, etc.), but also the ways in which these particular jobs affect women's ability to work and simultaneously carry out the care tasks that are necessary to maintain a satisfactory relationship with their 'intimate others' (cf. Roseneil et al., this volume).

Methodology

In order to understand the challenges placed on women's economic citizenship in a multicultural Europe, a variety of research methods were mobilized. First, we carried out a mapping analysis of a selection of women's movement grass-root publications and Women's Studies journals from the early 1970s to the present day. Our aim was to identify the claims framed in relation to women's work and employment, and their evolution over time, in five national contexts (Finland, France, Norway, Poland and the UK). We also mapped the degree to which these publications addressed the intersection of gender and race/ethnicity in relation to women's economic citizenship rights and practices (Metso et al., 2009). In addition, we carried out a secondary analysis of the statistical data and academic literature available at national or European level, in order to identify the effects of the intersection of gender, class, nationality and/or ethnicity on the labour market position and experiences of men and women in three of these national contexts (France, Norway and Poland) (Le Feuvre et al., 2009). We then analysed the policy orientations, policy apparatus and measures adopted to promote gender equality and/or racial and ethnic diversity in each national context, with an aim to identifying the coherence, congruence or conflict between these two sets of policy initiatives (Gullikstad, 2009; Krajewska and Orłowska, 2009; Metso and Le Feuvre, 2009). Finally, in order to gauge the actual influence of gender equality and diversity policies on daily practices of economic citizenship, we carried out an empirical study of the elder care sector, including expert interviews with employers and trade union representatives and a series of 75 biographical life-history interviews with male and female, majority and 'minoritized' elder care workers in a range of employment niches. The main aim of these interviews was to analyse the complex effects of the intersection of gender, age, class, nationality and/or ethnic origin on the access of elder care workers to full economic citizenship in a rapidly expanding and increasingly segmented elder care labour market.

The publications mapping exercise enabled us to identify the ways in which potentially consensual, competing or conflicting claims with regard to women's access to economic citizenship rights and responsibilities, either through paid work, unpaid work and/or welfare transfers, have been framed by the contemporary women's movements in different national and historical contexts. We selected texts both from the 1970s and from the more recent period in the five countries, which were chosen for their contrasting positions in a number of welfare state typologies.[5] For each of the publications selected (see Figure 4.1), we produced a quantitative overview of the relative importance of issues pertaining to women's economic citizenship, in relation to other dimensions of gender relations, including those covered by the FEMCIT project.

Our aim was not to achieve a fully representative sample, but rather to concentrate on a selection of publications that provided a picture of the nature of the issues discussed in relation to economic citizenship issues within the autonomous women's movement and within academic feminism over the past 40 years.[6] We wanted to determine to what extent issues relating to women's economic citizenship in general and to the employment rights of women from different ethnic backgrounds in particular had featured in the written production of the movement and in academic feminist research. We were particularly interested in establishing the extent to which the field of economic citizenship had been seen as a primary locus for the intersection of gender, race and ethnicity and in the variations of the framing of this 'intersectionality' (Crenshaw, 1991b; Dorlin, 2008) in different national contexts and across time.

It should be stressed here that we were not interested in looking back on these publications with the idea that they could, or indeed should, have been more sensitive to any particular issue at any particular time. We are all too aware that the women's movement is historically situated and that issues that have become important within academic feminism in recent years may not have been seen as vital or challenging in other historical contexts (Lykke, 2004; Picq, 1993). We were simply concerned with the idea that the women's movement has, over time, developed potentially conflicting or contradictory claims concerning women's economic citizenship: should women be given equal access to the labour market on the same terms as men, or should their contribution to the economic well-being of the nation through their care activities in the domestic sphere be recognized as having an economic value and, therefore, be paid in some form? (cf. Bergman et al., this volume).

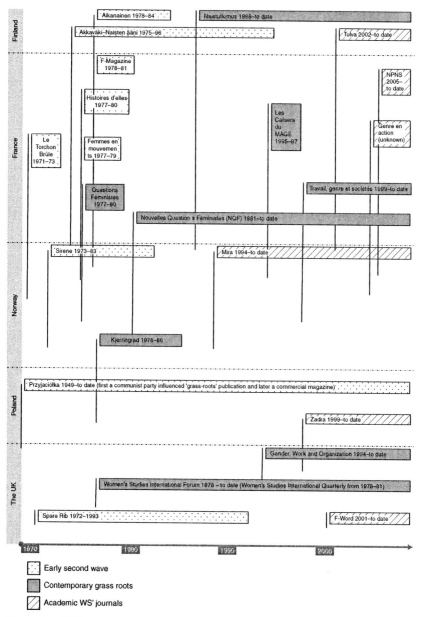

Figure 4.1 Publications selected for analysis, type of publication and duration

In order to have some idea about the influence that this vast social movement has had on policy debates and changes in contemporary European societies, it is obviously important to take a closer look at precisely which claims were being made, by whom, where and for which categories of women. We worked with the idea that there had probably been changes over time and tensions within the movement as to the precise models of 'women's emancipation' (or 'gender equality') that were being promoted in different national contexts, at different periods of time (Metso et al., 2009).

Although we will not be developing this point further here, it should be noted in passing that the mapping exercise also revealed some interesting information about the characteristics of the women's movements in the different national contexts (Offen, 2000). The 'life lines' of the publications selected show that the national context clearly influenced the ability of the women's movement to disseminate ideas and debates to a wider readership. In some countries, the limited duration of many publications would seem to suggest a lack of access to the economic resources required to produce journals or magazines, whilst this is less the case in other countries. The fact that a given national women's movement produced a single or several publications between given dates would also seem to point to variations in the ways in which divisions within the movement translated into their publication practices. In some countries, such divisions were clearly expressed through the channels of separate (competing) publications, whilst in other countries a single publication was used to express a diversity of opinions and claims.

The 'adult citizen worker' model in women's movement publications

The first result of this mapping exercise enabled us to observe that the notion of 'economic citizenship' was not mobilized as such in any of the publications studied. Although women's rights to health care and social security benefits were occasionally framed in 'citizenship' terms (at least outside the Nordic context, cf. kennedy-macfoy, this volume), their access to the labour market and to economic resources were associated with notions of 'equality' or 'emancipation', rather than citizenship. In the absence of specific and explicit references to the notion of 'citizenship' in the publications studied, we adopted a relatively broad definition of those claims that could legitimately be seen to cover such issues. We used the general definition of citizenship proposed by Lister (1997, 2004) to include issues relating to economic resources and redistribution issues, to women's labour market and employment rights, to recognition for paid or unpaid work, as well as issues relating to women's experiences of employment. Given the contrasting nature of our case study countries, we expected to find some differences in the way that these issues had been framed in the different national contexts. Our results suggest that national differences are relatively limited, and, in fact, the similarities in the themes evoked and the claims made with regard to women's economic citizenship are striking.

Firstly, even when a very broad definition of 'economic citizenship' was adopted (including issues of education and training, pay and working conditions, promotion, strike action and trade unionism, domestic labour and the vertical and horizontal segregation of the labour market, etc.), the question of women's work did not prove to be a major topic of discussion within the selected grass-roots women's movement publications in any of the national contexts studied here. The proportion of articles referring to women's work proved to be relatively similar from one country to another, from one historical period to another. On average, *less than one in ten* of the articles published relate to economic citizenship issues in any way. This is the case for the publications of the 'radical', autonomous, self-funded women's movement magazines from the 1970s in Finland, France, Norway and the UK, but also for the 'semi-official' publication of the women's section of the communist party in Poland under the Soviet regime (Metso et al., 2009). The period covered by these publications saw a radical transformation of women's access to education and the labour market and, albeit according to slightly different time-scales, the decline of the normative 'male breadwinner/female home carer' model (Crompton, 1999) in those countries where it had been present. However, the publications from the grass-roots women's movement tend to pay more attention to the other major changes taking place in women's lives, particularly those relating to the experience of being part of an autonomous women's movement (or, in the Polish case, of not needing to be part of this movement, thanks to the 'emancipation' purportedly already offered by the Soviet political system).

We can only tentatively suggest that these results reflect an internal 'division of labour' within the contemporary women's movement, with some of the claims relating directly to economic citizenship issues being formulated and disseminated through alternative channels, such as women's sections within trade unions and political parties, but also through the university and research institutions that were actively involved in the emerging academic field of Women's Studies (Griffin, 2004). Indeed, in most of the countries studied here, with the partial exception of Poland, there is a clear difference between the relatively limited attention paid to economic citizenship issues within the grass-roots publications of the women's movement and the central importance given to women's work and employment in academic Women's Studies journals.[7]

The thematic content of the articles related to women's economic citizenship in the grass-roots women's movement publications was also surprisingly similar from one national context to another. In each country, there were only very limited signs of a will to chart the experiences of women working in highly feminized occupations. In most of the publications, there are at least twice as many articles on women in non-traditional occupations than on women in the 'typically female' sections of the labour market (and most of the later referred to their involvement in industrial actions, rather than to their employment experiences as such). Thus, there seems to be a shared concern with contesting existing stereotypes. One of the unintended consequences of this focus is to leave the employment experiences of the large majority of women workers largely uncharted. Although these articles invariably cite the numerous obstacles women have had to overcome in order gain access to the existing 'male bastions', they are generally optimistic as to the possibilities that women could and should have to make career choices in a future gender desegregated labour market. As we know, this optimism has proven to be somewhat unfounded to date, since the horizontal gender segregation of the labour market has increased rather than decreased in almost all EU member states over the past 30 years (Franco, 2007). The relative importance that women's movement publications give to women in non-traditional occupations can be seen as an indication of the 'gender equality model' that has been implicitly present throughout the period covered here. None of the articles studied here envisages the remuneration of domestic care work as a solution to women's economic dependency on men, although we know from other sources (Fauré, 1997; Fougeyrollas, 2005) that some women's groups in each of these countries (and elsewhere) did make claims for 'wages for housework'. We can only hypothesize that such claims occupied a minority or marginalized position within each of the national women's movements studied here and never mustered enough support to be expressed through their main publication channels. On the other hand, the claim that men should increase their participation in unpaid domestic work and child care was occasionally expressed. This suggests that those women's groups who had access to the resources required to publish magazines and journals were clearly inspired by a universal *equal rights* philosophy and were less oriented towards the struggle for the *equal value* of the complementary role of women as carers and men as breadwinners (cf. Bergman et al., this volume).

In the five countries studied, women's paid work is undoubtedly seen as the preferred route to their 'emancipation', but the number of articles published about the precise mechanisms through which this radical transformation of women's economic citizenship experiences should be promoted was far smaller than we initially expected. Furthermore, it is difficult to identify any clear policy recommendations within the articles studied, raising some doubt as to the extent to which subsequent 'equal opportunity' policy measures were directly inspired by the claims formulated within the autonomous women's movement organizations of the second half of the twentieth century (Mazur, 2002; McBride Stetson, 1997). However, given the exploratory nature of our research, the reliability of these results obviously needs to be confirmed by more systematic studies in the future.

When women's movement claims meet ethnic diversity

Our analysis of references to the experiences of migrant women or those from minority ethnic groups also brought some rather surprising results.

Once again, the similarities between the five countries were more striking than their differences. In all of the publications studied, there are frequent signs of interest in the situation of women from other cultural backgrounds. Indeed, the number of articles published in grass-roots magazines on issues related to cultural differences is generally greater than the number of texts relating to women's work and employment.

Nevertheless, it is also true that ethnicity is generally conceived in terms of geographical distance and 'otherness' (Özbilgin and Woodward, 2004). The experience of women from 'other cultures' provides a backdrop against which the current state of gender relations in the home country can be measured. Many of the texts published in the 1970s western European magazines reflect a historically tainted positive vision of women's experiences in countries such as the Soviet Union and The People's Republic of China, largely defending the idea that the demise of capitalism would hold the key to women's emancipation in the West. In other cases, the experience of women in other cultural contexts serves to illustrate the advances made by the autonomous women's movements in the West and acts as a reminder for the need to develop a 'global network of sisterhood' across national boundaries. In this case, it is the similarities between women, rather than their diversity that clearly occupy the thoughts of the authors (Metso et al., 2009). In these texts, there is a marked absence of recognition of any (real or potential) 'conflict of interests' between women, either in terms of class, age, sexuality or race. With the notable exception of the UK, where tensions around questions of racial difference and racism were present in the grass-root and academic women's movement publications from a relatively early date, the differences in women's experiences are generally expressed in the binary terms of here/there and the existence of diverse ethnic groups within a single national context is rarely envisaged, at least until the early 2000s. This conception of the multicultural experiences of gender is largely explained by the generally homogeneous ethnic composition of the women's movements themselves (see Nyhagen Predelli et al., this volume) and by the socially constructed invisibility of women from ethnic minority groups within those societies where some degree of (post-colonial) immigration was already in evidence by the late 1970s (see kennedy-macfoy, this volume).

On this point, there are clear similarities between the early grass-roots women's movement magazines and the academic feminist journals. Most of the academic journals do include articles on cultural differences between women, although rarely in relation to economic citizenship. However, these articles also tend to posit that such differences exist 'elsewhere', outside the home country, rather than within it. The Polish case is interesting here, since the women's publications do refer to some extent to the effects of migration on gender relations, but the case of Polish women migrating out of the country, rather than the experiences of migrants to Poland, is at the heart of the issues addressed (Metso et al., 2009).

Overall, there are very few crosscutting references to the two themes of economic citizenship and ethnic diversity. In all five countries, cultural differences are overwhelmingly seen from an international perspective rather than an issue to be addressed within the national (or European) context. This continues to be the case in Poland today, whereas the generalist academic publications and the specialized NGOs in the other countries studied here have begun to address the intersection of gender and ethnicity, particularly in relation to migration and the so-called care drain (Ehrenreich and Hochschild, 2002). We will return to this point later. Nevertheless, it remains the case that the contemporary grass-roots publications that focus on ethnicity and multiculturalism rarely address these questions from an economic citizenship perspective. On the other hand, the academic journals that are specialized in questions of work and employment are less likely to address issues of ethnicity and cultural difference within their home society than are the more generalist Women's Studies academic journals and the grass-roots organizations of women from migrant/minority backgrounds.

At this stage, we can only hypothesize that the 'otherness' conception of ethnic diversity that we have identified in the women's movement publications has played a role in the framing of equal opportunity, migration and anti-discrimination policies as distinct areas of public decision-making, leading to difficulties in translating the more recent feminist theoretical interest in 'intersectionality' into a consolidated policy framework in any of the countries studied here (Gullikstad, 2009; Krajewska and Orłowska, 2009; Metso and Le Feuvre, 2009).

The mapping of women's movement publications over the past 40 years has enabled us to establish that the main claims being made in different national contexts clearly reflect an 'adult citizen worker' (Fraser, 1994; Orloff, 1993) model of emancipation. Somewhat surprisingly, ensuring women's access to male dominated sectors of the labour market appears to have attracted more attention than the elaboration of alternative models for the organization and gender redistribution of care activities. When care work was mentioned, we found few references to the 'commodification of care' as a feminist ideal. Rather, women's increased labour market participation was envisaged as being offset by an equivalent shift of men's time from the labour market to the home. We can note in passing that, in all but a few cases (e.g. Orloff, 2002), this model for a more egalitarian society remains strongly imbued with heteronormative undertones (Roseneil and Budgeon, 2004) and fails to reflect the progressive increase in more varied forms of life-style options, including single living (cf. Roseneil et al., this volume).

It is often suggested that the claims made by the women's movement have had a significant impact on policy orientations and legislative measures introduced during the second half of the twentieth century (Orloff and Palier, 2009), particularly those in favour of women's increased labour market participation. Our results suggest caution here. First, in the Eastern block countries, women's continuous labour market participation was intermittently framed as the norm prior to 1989 (Einhorn, 1993; Heinen and Portet, 2004; Pollart, 2003), even in the absence of an active, autonomous women's movement. Secondly, as Maria Stratigaki has convincingly argued, the so-called 'translation' of women's movement claims into political policies at the European level has almost systematically eluded the question of a redistribution of unpaid care activities between the sexes (Stratigaki, 2004, 2005). In reality, policies have focused on the promotion of two alternatives that were barely mentioned in the women's movement publications we have analysed: the development of part-time and other 'flexible' employment practices for women and the 'commodification' and partial externalization of (women's) domestic care activities. These policy orientations are intended to meet the dual objective of job creation (at a time of rising structural unemployment and the delocalization of many manufacturing jobs) and the labour market 'activation' of those groups who have remained furthest from the new adult citizen worker model of social integration. This very partial translation (or treason) of women's movement claims (Jenson, 2009) obviously needs to be examined against the backdrop of wider economic and policy debates. Two points appear to be particularly important here: first, the transformation of the regulation of the labour market under 'advanced capitalism' (Giddens, 1992); secondly, the relationship between labour market participation and access to citizenship rights and benefits under the conditions of 'second modernity' (Beck, 2000).

A closer analysis of the economic citizenship issues facing workers in elder care jobs in three contrasting national contexts will enable us to explore some of the consequences of the widespread promotion of an adult citizen worker model of gender equality in more detail and to consider the possibilities for 'remaking' economic citizenship in the light of these findings.

The contrasting 'translation' of claims for full economic citizenship into elder care policies

Establishing the 'impact' of women's movement claims on subsequent policy measures relating to economic citizenship issues is a difficult task. The very nature of the labour market that women are now entering in large numbers (particularly through the so-called caring occupations) bears very little resemblance to the labour market from which they were more or less actively excluded. As Taylor-Gooby (2008) has stressed, the 'social contract' of the mid-twentieth century, generally referred to as the 'Fordist period', has undergone radical change, under pressure from a number of sources, including the delocalization of many of the manufacturing and tertiary activities that enabled men to assume their 'breadwinner' roles. As we know, this 'social contract' was premised on particular 'sexual contracts' (Pateman, 1988), 'gender contracts' (Lewis, 1997, 1998), 'gender arrangements' (Pfau-Effinger and Geissler, 2005) or 'gender regimes' (Sümer, 2009; Walby, 2004).

Under these macro-social arrangements, men were expected to invest in the labour market continuously throughout their adult lives, to work relatively long hours on jobs, many of which, through automation and mechanization, offered little intrinsic satisfaction, but which provided them with a host of material and symbolic benefits (Guillaumin, 1992). First, there was the possibility of earning a family wage that was high enough for them to assume the cost of a full- or part-time home-maker wife and, therefore, to adopt strategies for maximizing their income (e.g. over-time, shift work, geographical mobility, etc.), without having to face the difficulties of reconciling work and family life. Second, there was the possibility of covering the cost of raising children long enough to achieve intergenerational upward social mobility. Third, there were opportunities for self-expression and self-realization, either through their work or through various forms of leisure and 'conspicuous consumption' practices. Finally, there was assurance of protection against the inherent risks of their salaried status, through a comprehensive system of welfare benefits that covered the risks of accident, ill-health, unemployment and retirement.

This, then, was the relatively well-documented Western (masculine*) economic citizenship package* to which the second wave women's movement claimed women should also have access in their own right. It is, however, important to remember that this normative model has not had the same impact on the gender division of labour in all national contexts and that its influence has also varied over time (Daly and Rake, 2003; Lewis, 1997; Makkai, 1997; Pfau-Effinger and Geissler, 2005; Sümer, 2009). Although the 'separate spheres' ideology was never officially acknowledged and normalized under the Soviet regime in Eastern Europe, the failure to collectivize care activities and the low levels of men's participation in family life led to a situation where women were still expected to meet most of the care needs of their family members, despite their parallel commitment to paid work. This was achieved at the cost of a particularly heavy 'double burden' for most women (Pollart, 2003) and through the adoption of extended maternity leaves and the informal flexibilization of working time arrangements (Portet, 2004): both widespread practices that were to become increasingly problematic with the transition to a market economy. Likewise, at the turn of the twenty-first century, with the progressive 'demise', to varying degrees, of the 'male breadwinner' (Crompton, 2006; Crompton, Lewis and Lyonette, 2007) or 'family wage' (Fraser, 2000) model of gender relations, the old Western democracies were faced with major new challenges for social integration and cohesion.

The demise of the masculine 'economic citizenship package'

It could probably be argued that the first signs of strain on this masculine *economic citizenship package* appeared with feminist claims for self-determination in the sphere of bodily and intimate life (cf. Outshoorn et al. and Roseneil et al. this volume). The delicate 'balance' of paid and unpaid work that stood as the lynchpin to this particular form of social organization obviously rested to a large degree on the stability of couples and on child-bearing, heterosexual marriage as the adult life-style norm (Cooke and Baxter, 2010). Men's motivation and ability to work long hours required the permanent presence of an unpaid stay-at-home wife; whereas women's ability to provide a host of unpaid care services rested on the assurance of the permanent presence of a 'breadwinning' husband in full-time, continuous employment. If the progressive liberalization of divorce laws and the liberation of women from unplanned pregnancies produced the first cracks in this historically located model of social organization (Tahon, 2004), these fissures were later to be opened even further by the combined effects of long periods of economic down-turn, the delocalization of many industrial activities, the reduced supply of cheap (often post-colonial) migrant labour and concerns about the spiralling of public spending on welfare provisions (Esping-Andersen, 1996). In many European countries, these changes combined to make policy-makers sensitive to the untapped economic resources that lay within the female adult population. It could, thus, be argued that, under considerable tension and with significant time lags between countries, the premises of what some authors have termed the 'social investment' model of welfare provision (Dobrowolsky and Jenson, 2004; Lewis, 2007) appeared at a time when the second wave women's movement was voicing its claims in favour of the adult citizen worker model and that each of these discourses curiously echoed each other throughout the last decades of the twentieth century.

According to Jane Jenson (2008), the 'social investment' model of welfare has since become dominant in most developed (and some developing) countries. The social investment philosophy that now infuses supra-national decision-making bodies (the EU, the IMF, the World Bank, etc.) provides a radical shift in thinking about women's economic citizenship. As Jenson notes, the 'social investment' model of welfare appears to have taken at least some of the claims made by the second wave women's movement (and academic feminism) on board. Firstly, it recognizes that gender equality is a legitimate claim and that women's access to autonomous economic resources contributes to this objective. Secondly, it suggests that women's exclusion from the labour market can be, at least partly, explained by the weight of their unpaid caring duties in the home. Thirdly, it stresses that, notably due to widespread demographic trends, all developed nations can expect a huge increase in the demand for care services (particularly elder care services) in the future. Finally, it claims that women should now be actively encouraged to enter the labour market and to carry out paid work throughout the full duration of their adult lives (irrespective of child-care or other family responsibilities). This social investment philosophy further claims that women's economic autonomy will (1) protect their children from the risks of poverty; (2) protect the women themselves from similar risks, particularly in later life and (3) reduce the demands on welfare benefits created by the economic dependency of large numbers of women on husbands or partners who are no longer in a position to command a 'family wage' throughout their entire adult life – at least not necessarily in a position to share their resources with the same wife or partner throughout their lifetime (Jenson, 2008).

To a certain extent, one could argue that – in a curious twist of events – Western democracies have aligned themselves to the normative models of women's economic citizenship that were prevalent in many of the Eastern block countries prior to 1989, precisely at a time when the transition to capitalism in many of the ex-USSR member states has resulted in a weakening of women's position in the labour market and the emergence of new tensions around normative gender roles in relation to work and caring (Heinen and Portet, 2004; Roth, 2004).

The shift in political thinking in relation to women's economic autonomy raises several questions and presents a challenge for feminist research and activism (Fraser, 2000). Firstly, the conditions under which women are now actively encouraged to become 'adult citizen workers' in their own right need to be considered. As we have seen, several evolutions during 'second modernity' (Beck, 2000) have led to the widespread deregulation of the labour market, producing a risk of precariousness and flexibility for many adults of both sexes, but with considerable variation between societal contexts and social protection regimes. The stable employment relations of the Fordist period enabled most (but not all) Western European men to combine full-time continuous employment with the exercise of their full citizenship rights in the political sphere and the benefit of social protection against the risks associated with their salaried status (Castel, 2003). Not only have rising unemployment rates and the dismantling of public services and welfare provisions made workers more vulnerable to market forces in some national contexts, the regulation of the market now largely escapes the sphere of influence of nation-states, reducing the ability of 'adult worker citizens' to mobilize national political systems to protect their interests (Beck, 2000).

In addition, the 'time bind' (Hochschild, 1997) placed on workers at all levels of the occupational hierarchy has intensified, notably because of the increasing deregulation and de-synchronization of working life in general (Nicole-Drancourt, 2009). The individualization of employment and career paths also means that workers must ensure that their 'employability' is maintained throughout their working life, undertaking retraining and refresher courses at regular periods of time, often at their own expense.

The pressures of global capitalism have not only increased the risk of unemployment, they have also led to the creation of a whole series of part-time, temporary or insecure jobs that do not meet the 'living wage' criteria

and that are not accompanied by the host of citizenship rights and responsibilities that were associated with the masculine 'economic citizenship package' of the mid-twentieth century (Fraser, 2000). Of course, these changes
have not been evenly spread over the labour market or the occupational
hierarchy. They have been easier to impose in those sectors where labour
organizations are weakest and where the tradition of the 'family wage' is
least well rooted, thus hitting the most feminized sections of the labour
market first and hardest (Fraser, 2000).

The economic citizenship issues facing elder care workers in a multicultural Europe

The elderly care sector was selected as our main research object for a number
of reasons. First, similar demographic trends are affecting all European countries. They suggest that the dual phenomena of women's increasing economic
activity rates over the life-course (reducing their 'availability' for unpaid domestic caring activities for their elderly relatives, friends or neighbours) and
the ageing of the population will result in a significant increase in employment opportunities in the elder care sector within the next decade (OECD,
2006). This enables us to analyse the different gender and ethnic configurations of employment patterns in a relatively favourable labour market context, since fears of labour shortages in this sector are expressed in all the
countries studied here. Secondly, the results of our secondary data analysis
show a marked tendency for migrant and 'minoritized' groups to be over-
represented in employment in the 'personal services' sector (Le Feuvre et al.,
2009). Thirdly, the mapping of women's movement and women's studies
publications indicated the recent emergence of a corpus of activist and academic writing on the intersection of class, gender and race with particular
reference to women's employment in care activities (Metso et al., 2009).
Fourthly, preliminary background research has shown that the elderly-care
sector is characterized by a huge variety of employment practices, ranging
from 'standard' work contracts in public-sector and private-for-profit elderly
care institutions to undeclared direct employment by care recipients. This
wide range of employment and working conditions makes the sector particularly interesting to examine from an economic citizenship perspective.
We hypothesized that elderly care work may take very different forms in
different national contexts, depending on gendered expectations about the
availability of women (as daughters, wives, mothers, neighbours, volunteers,
etc.) to provide unpaid support for the dependent elderly, the public policies
adopted to 'formalize' or 'professionalize' work in the elderly care sector and
the national and local 'employment regimes' available to women from different ethnic backgrounds (Simonazzi, 2008; Ungerson, 2003).

In all of the countries studied here, migrant and 'minoritized' social
groups face a series of obstacles in gaining access to economic citizenship

rights on the same basis as majority groups (Le Feuvre et al., 2009). Female migrants not only face similar problems to those of their male counterparts, notably in terms of language skills and recognition of their existing qualifications, they also have to face the objective and subjective tensions created by the potential hiatus between the normative gender expectations of their home culture and those of their host country. These tensions are exacerbated by the discrimination that migrants and minoritized groups face in employment and which leads to their limited access only to the least desirable segments of the labour market (Meurs and Pailhé, 2010; Safi, 2008; Silberman and Fournier, 2008). A dual process seems to be operating here. On the one hand, having a job has become a condition for migrants' access to citizenship – a process sometimes referred to as 'earned citizenship' (van Houdt, Suvarierol and Schinkel, 2011). On the other hand, more women are migrating independently, rather than through various forms of 'family resettlement' (European Commission, 2010a). These recent evolutions have doubtless contributed to the emergence of new forms of labour market inequalities between different categories of women. In those national contexts where policy-makers assert that they have been 'enlightened' by the second wave women's movement, women's claims to citizenship must clearly be framed in relation to their ability to adapt to the model of the adult citizen worker and this poses considerable problems for the carrying out of unpaid care duties (Fraser, 2000; Lewis and Giullari, 2005; Lewis, 2007).

As we have already mentioned, the increased availability of externalized care services also has an effect on the conditions under which women compete with men for access to the most desirable positions in the employment hierarchy. Some contemporary feminist research suggests that certain groups of women (majority, middle class, well-qualified) are exploiting the precarious positions of their less privileged counterparts in order to improve their own competitive chances in the labour market. This is said to lead to a gradual polarization of the experiences of women in relation to employment and care activities (Glenn, 2000; Ehrenreich and Hochschild, 2002). According to this scenario, well-qualified women (usually from majority groups) are being encouraged to adopt the unlimited availability for full-time, continuous paid work that was characteristic of the masculine 'economic citizenship package' of the mid-twentieth century (Fraser, 2000). In order to do this, they are being encouraged to 'out-source' part of what are still largely seen as 'their' unpaid domestic care duties. In return, less well-qualified women (and some men), particularly those from migrant or minoritized groups, are being forced to take up jobs in the care services sector, although these may provide a limited range of economic citizenship rights (often excluding a living wage and access to a full range of social protection benefits). Thus, on the one hand, certain categories of women succeed in gaining access to the labour market on 'men's terms' (i.e. in accordance with the dominant 'scripts' of the standard male career, see Fraser, 2000; Le Feuvre and Lapeyre, 2005;

Lyon and Woodward, 2004). On the other hand, other groups of women are loosing all the ('typically female') alternative routes to social integration and are being forced to take up employment in jobs where the actual content of their work largely mirrors the tasks they are still expected to continue to perform, unpaid, in the home. According to this scenario, although many of the claims made by the second wave women's movement have effectively been met by the (at least partial) demise of the 'male breadwinner/female carer' (Crompton, Lewis and Lyonette, 2007) or 'family wage' (Fraser, 2000) model of gender relations, this relative success story has a darker side. This is reflected in the deepening of class and racial inequalities between women that were largely ignored or underestimated in the early years of the second wave women's movement.

Our research suggests that this account of the growing, global inequalities between different categories of women is over simplistic. Firstly, the degree to which unpaid domestic and care activities continue to be seen as the sole responsibility of women varies considerably across countries. According to the European Time Use Surveys, men currently do about 40 per cent of the housework in Norway and Sweden, whereas they do less than 35 per cent in Poland and France and less that 25 per cent in Italy and Spain (Aliaga, 2006). Secondly, in line with the hypothesis elaborated by the Italian economist Simonazzi, the degree to which (elder) care jobs are 'flexibilized' and the degree to which they are allocated to 'minoritized' workers also varies significantly across national contexts (Lyon, 2010; Saraceno and Keck, 2010; Simonazzi, 2008). As Simonazzi has suggested, the fact that elderly care is seen (or not) as a particularly suitable employment area for migrant and 'minoritized' workers (generally women) depends to a large extent on whether care jobs are regulated and aligned to the 'standard employment contract' or are left unregulated and framed as a field of 'grey' or undeclared work. The regulation of elder care work varies significantly, both between the three countries and between the different care work niches in each country.[8] By carrying out a comparative analysis of the economic citizenship experiences of women from 'minoritized' and majority ethnic groups working in elder care in three contrasting national contexts, we are in a position to provide some insight into what the remaking of economic citizenship for elder care workers could imply from a 'gender fair' and multicultural perspective (Fraser, 2000).

Thus, our research in Norway showed that almost all elder care jobs fall into the declared, formal labour market (Ervik, 2010). Nevertheless, the recent introduction of New Public Management criteria for the provision of elder care services through market tender has increased the rationalization of services and has decreased the possibility previously offered to new migrants to work in tandem with more experienced (usually majority) colleagues. Migrants have fewer opportunities to enter the labour market directly through elder care jobs (Ervik, 2010). However, the immigration policies adopted in Norway place great importance on access to training and qualifications (Gullikstad, 2009). This also holds to a certain extent for the elder care sector, which does enable female workers to ensure their own economic survival, without the support of a 'male breadwinner' or dependency on social transfers. Thus, largely due to the weight of the adult citizen worker model in the Norwegian value system (Forgeau, 2007), although many elder care jobs are part-time, they are highly regulated and protected and they, thus, enable workers to achieve high levels of financial autonomy (Ervik, 2010; Widding Isaksen, 2010). Indeed, in our interview sample of Norwegian elder care workers, we found a wide range of intimate living arrangements, suggesting that the presence of a 'main (male) breadwinner' is not a condition for working in elder care in this country. In this case, the elder care sector can be said to provide many of the conditions for 'full economic citizenship'. Although the progressive 'rationalization' of elder care services through external tendering has made it more important for migrant workers to speak Norwegian fluently, once they have improved their language skills, they would seem to obtain similar jobs to their majority counterparts and to benefit from the same opportunities for training and promotion.

In Poland, on the other hand, the elder care labour market is clearly divided along ethnic lines. Institutionalized care services are almost exclusively provided by Polish female workers who rarely earn enough to satisfy their basic economic needs and who, therefore, need to be married to a male breadwinner in order to survive (Krajewska, 2010). However, formal jobs in elder care institutions are also associated with high levels of symbolic recognition, in a country where the moral obligation to care for elderly and dependant family members within the household remains very pervasive. In contrast, (often undeclared) migrants from countries beyond Poland's eastern borders (Ukraine and Byelorussia) provide almost all the rapidly expanding home-based elder care services. In this sector, there are almost no formal contracts, working conditions are highly precarious, but wages are generally higher than in the institutionalized care homes. Thus, those migrant women who move or commute to Poland in order to work in elder care generally assume a 'main breadwinner' role for their families in their home country, often protecting them from extreme poverty (Krajewska, 2010). Although they are no longer physically present to deliver family-based care to their loved ones (Ehrenreich and Hochschild, 2002), they continue to provide care services intermittently and at a distance, and also benefit more from higher levels of economic autonomy and self-determination than their Polish counterparts. Unlike in Norway, there are few opportunities for training and qualification within the elder care sector. Polish care workers are expected to mobilize the competencies acquired in the course of their gender socialization in order to identify and satisfy the needs of the care recipients. The migrant women who occupy these jobs may not achieve full economic citizenship within the Polish context, but they nevertheless come closer to 'defamilialization' than their majority counterparts in the formal elder care sector.

The French case provides yet another 'configuration of care' (Lyon and Glucksmann, 2008). Here, a succession of policy measures aimed at promoting home-based formal and declared care services to the dependant elderly have been introduced since the 1980s (Dussuet, 2005; Le Feuvre and Martin, 2001). These policies have led to a fragmentation of the elder care labour market. The total number of formal elder care jobs has increased spectacularly over the past 20 years, but growth has been fastest in those sectors that are furthest from the 'standard employment contract' (Jany-Catrice, 2010). Home-based elder care jobs are overwhelmingly part-time and poorly paid and only a very small minority of workers are in a position to live independently on the income derived from them. Direct employment of elder care workers by the care recipients (or their families) reduces the opportunities for care workers to access training programmes and qualifications and also provides little protection against discrimination on the grounds of ethnic or cultural origin (Le Feuvre, Metso and Chaker, 2010). However, the recent policy drive to 'professionalize' home-based elder care services has undeniably increased the opportunities for many poorly qualified women to access the formal labour market and, occasionally, to progress onto better-paid jobs (such as nursing assistants) through experience-based training schemes. Although migrant and 'minoritized' women generally benefit from a symbolic recognition of their outstanding caring capacities, this recognition rarely enables them to access those sectors of the elder care labour market that provide the fullest forms of economic citizenship. However, the degree to which 'minoritized' women are relegated to the least regulated sectors of the elderly care sector largely depends on the opportunities for employment offered to majority women in the local labour market. In those areas (mostly rural) where job opportunities for unqualified women are scarce and where demand for home-based elder care services is growing rapidly, those jobs in elder care institutions and with registered home-care service providers that come closest to the 'standard employment contract' tend to be reserved for majority women. In those areas (mostly urban) where the registered care service providers find it difficult to satisfy the demand for care services (due to more attractive, better-paid employment opportunities for poorly qualified women in other sectors), there are some signs of a progressive 'racialization' of the elderly care workforce. In this case, regional disparities serve to modify the conditions under which majority and 'minoritized' elder care workers achieve (or not) the conditions of full economic citizenship.

Conclusion

In line with the reflections developed by Fraser (2000), Hobson (2000), Kessler-Harris (2003) and Bambra (2007), we have been able to demonstrate in this chapter that 'economic citizenship' covers many more issues than the simple 'right to follow the occupation of one's choice in the place of one's choice' (Marshall, 1950). Many of the financial disincentives and normative barriers to women's labour market participation have now been lifted, to the point that their 'right to work' has been transformed into a moral and material 'obligation to work', in accordance with a largely de-gendered adult citizen worker model (Fraser, 2000). Many elder care workers are nevertheless far from achieving full economic citizenship. However, the diversity of their experiences tends to suggest that this has little to do with the nature of elder care work as such, and more to do with the employment, migration and care regimes under which they access particular segments of the elder care labour market.

Firstly, the jobs they perform may (as in Norway) offer 'wages adequate to the support of self and family' (Kessler-Harris, 2003), but this is not always the case. As the Polish case study illustrates clearly, the ability to earn a 'living wage' through elder care jobs is not necessarily associated with the most stable, formalized and highly regulated segments of the elder care labour market. In some national contexts, a highly flexibilized and unregulated labour market niche may provide women elder care workers with more opportunities for self-determination, particularly in intimate living relationships (cf. Roseneil et al., this volume), than the more 'standard' elder care jobs.

Secondly, the degree to which elder care workers are required to adopt a 'double burden' of paid employment and domestic activities also varies considerably, between countries and between different segments of the elder care sector within a given national context. In those countries where there is widespread provision of low-cost public child-care services and/or an ideological commitment to gender equality in the domestic division of labour, elder care workers may have no more difficulty in achieving some form of 'work–life balance' than workers in other sectors of the labour market. However, the unsocial and irregular hours associated with some forms of elder care work may become particularly problematic in those contexts where the 'defamilialization' of care activities is least advanced.

Thirdly, the degree to which elder care jobs are reserved for 'minoritized' workers, freeing their majority counterparts to access the upper reaches of the socio-economic hierarchy also varies considerably. In some countries, the elder care labour market may indeed be highly discriminatory, with 'minoritized' women being concentrated in those jobs furthest from the 'standard' employment contract (excluding their access to health and security or pension rights, for example). Usually, however, the racial or ethnic division of the elder care sector is far more complex. On some dimensions of economic citizenship (e.g. the ability to earn a 'living wage'), the experiences of 'minoritized' care workers may be relatively better than those of their majority counterparts, whilst the reverse may be true on other dimensions (e.g. the ability to combine paid work with a satisfactory level of work–life balance or with self-determination in intimate life, cf. Roseneil et al., this volume).

Finally, our comparative research shows that elder care jobs are *not necessarily* predicated on the idea that those who occupy them are already in a position to access a range of social benefits (health insurance, pension rights, etc.) through marriage or state transfers, rather than employment. Although this is clearly the case in institutionalized and home-based care services in Poland, it is not true in Norway or in the majority of institutionalized care services in France. The ability of care workers to join trade unions and to collectively defend their employment-related interests depends to a large extent on the degree of regulation of the sector, but also, as suggested by Kessler-Harris, on the extent to which elder care workers consider themselves to be 'adult citizen workers' in their own right. Undeniably, in some national contexts, women's newly acquired 'right to work' has not been accompanied by a significant shift in their 'obligation to marry' and, therefore, in the pressures on them to provide unpaid care services to adult men, children and other dependant family members (Kessler-Harris, 2003). However, without more systematic empirical research, it would seem hasty to suggest that this is any more so the case in professional activities that explicitly mobilize women's normatively defined 'capacity to care' than in many other sectors of the labour market.

Despite the persistence of gender discrimination and the resistance of 'inequality regimes' (Acker, 2009), many of the most highly qualified (and generally majority) women in Europe can now achieve professional goals that were largely beyond the reach of their mothers and grandmothers. As such, their citizenship experiences reflect the claims for 'emancipation through employment' that are central to the women's movement publications we have studied here. In some national contexts, these changes are due to a fundamental shift in the gendered division of unpaid domestic labour (Gershuny and Sullivan, 2003), but they can also be seen as the result of the ability of an increasing number of women to externalize part of 'their' responsibilities for the care of the most vulnerable members of society (children, the sick, the dependant elderly, etc.), with the support of (female) paid care workers.

In some (but not all) national contexts, elder care workers face what could be termed a 'care work paradox'. The competencies developed in the course of their unpaid domestic care duties may provide them with new opportunities to access the labour market and to remain in employment throughout their adult lives (one dimension of 'economic citizenship' as we have defined it here). However, in some (but not all) national contexts, the employment and working conditions associated with elder care jobs fail to provide workers with enough pay to achieve financial autonomy, self-determination in intimate life, or any form of 'work–life balance' (other important dimensions of economic citizenship as we see it). Thus, the fact that the vast majority of European women are no longer (as was generally the case during the immediate post-war period) excluded from the labour market and confined to a life of domestic dependency on a male breadwinner or on the state could be seen as a victory for the claims-making initiated by the contemporary women's movement. However, due to structural changes in the regulation of European labour markets since the 1970s, women are now increasingly expected to work continuously throughout their adult lives, despite the fact that many of them are being ushered into jobs that fail to provide the rights, resources and recognition that were part and parcel of the historically situated masculine 'economic citizenship package' we have described earlier in this chapter.

Therefore, unless the care duties that any adult citizen worker must provide to friends and family (Lewis, 2007) are fully recognized, policy initiatives aimed solely at increasing women's economic activity rates will fail to produce the radical shift in power relations that was at the heart of the claims made by the contemporary women's movement. Indeed, the conflicting interests between different categories of women may well be exacerbated by the illusion that 'defamilialization' and the 'commodification of care' can transform all women into equal 'adult citizen workers' (Fraser, 2000). However, rather than seeing the deepening of class and ethnic divisions between women as an inevitable consequence of the claims made by the largely white middle-class women who made up the European women's movements in the 1970s, it would seem more productive to mobilize collectively to improve the very partial 'economic citizenship package' that is associated with care work in many national contexts. As we hope to have shown here, there is nothing inherent to (elder) care work that makes it incompatible with full economic citizenship rights and practices, or that relegates it to a modernized form of 'subservient domesticity' (Fraisse, 2009).

Notes

1. More recently, this process has also been described with the notions of 'externalization', 'defamilialization' and 'commodification', which are sometimes used interchangeably, but which actually each refer to particular aspects of the changes that have taken place in the organization of care activities. These may involve a reduction in the normative expectations placed on 'families' (usually meaning female relatives) to provide care for dependant family members ('defamilialization'), an increase in the role played by non-family members in the provision of care ('externalization') or an increase in the provision of such services through market-based (rather than voluntary sector or social service based) service providers ('commodification'). We propose to maintain this distinction throughout the present chapter.

2. This chapter is based on research carried out by the authors under work-package 3 of the EU 6th framework FEMCIT project. Anne-Jorunn Berg, Saloua Chaker, Berit Gullikstad, Beata Laciak, Elisabet Ljunggren, Dorota Orłowska and Tone Gunn Stene Kristiansen were also involved in some of the research carried out under work package 3 and the authors of this chapter wish to acknowledge their contributions. See: http://www.femcit.org

3. Due to time and resource limitations, we were unable to carry out comparable empirical fieldwork in two of the countries selected for the publications mapping exercise, Finland and the UK.

4. The term is increasingly used to refer to the partial citizenship rights bestowed on foreign investors in a number of global tax havens, particularly in the Caribbean islands.

5. The countries selected included: 2 Nordic regimes (Finland and Norway), 1 corporatist regime (France), 1 liberal regime (the UK) and 1 Soviet regime (Poland). See Gøsta Esping-Andersen (1990) *The Three Worlds of Welfare Capitalism* (Cambridge: Polity Press).

6. Thus, we deliberately decided exclude those magazines/journals that were published by organizations traditionally involved in discussions around labour market issues, such as trade unions or political parties. Although we recognize that feminists have been active in putting the 'woman question' on the agenda of many of these organizations since the 1970s, we were particularly interested in gauging the extent to which economic citizenship issues were discussed *within* the autonomous women's movement and women's studies publications themselves.

7. The differences in the issues covered in grass-roots and academic publications is a rather surprising, particularly given the widespread tendency for Women's Studies activists to present themselves as the 'academic arm' of the women's movement. See Judith Ezekiel, *Feminism in the Heartland* (Dayton: Ohio State University Press, 2002), 339.

8. Some indication of the overall degree of labour market regulation in different national contexts can be gleaned from the Appendix II to the present volume.

5
Remaking Social Citizenship in Multicultural Europe: Women's Movements' Agency in Child-Care Politics and Policies

Solveig Bergman, Hana Hašková, Kateřina Pulkrábková,
Minna Rantalaiho, Celia Valiente and Zuzana Uhde

Introduction: child care as an aspect of social citizenship

During the latter half of the twentieth century, women's movements across Europe succeeded in placing child care on the political agenda. They have challenged the unequal distribution of care between women and men and between the private and public spheres, as well as the general lack of recognition of care in society (e.g. Bergqvist, Kuusipalo and Styrkarsdóttir, 1999; Bertone, 2003; Bleijenbergh and Roggeband, 2007). As a consequence, in many European countries child care has gradually come to be seen no longer as exclusively the responsibility of the family but as a public issue and a social right of parents and children: that is, as an issue of *social citizenship* (see for example Lister et al., 2007).

The concept of social citizenship arose in the aftermath of the Second World War, out of the question of whether low income, unemployment and lack of access to social security and health care diminish citizenship status. T. H. Marshall (1950) expanded the liberal concept of citizenship beyond civil and political rights to include social rights. Marshall's notion of social citizenship included social and health services, education as well as social benefits and social insurance, and had the aim of reducing social inequalities. The idea of social citizenship is of substantial significance for women because it stresses not only the rights and obligations of citizens but also the opportunities and conditions that can either undermine or enhance full citizenship.

Since the 1990s, feminist scholars have criticized citizenship thinking for ignoring the gendered nature of social citizenship, for failing to acknowledge the value of unpaid domestic labour and for being based on assumptions of traditional male-dominated social and family structures. In particular, feminists have emphasized that mainstream citizenship theories failed to embrace *care* as a social right (e.g. Orloff, 1993; Anttonen and Sipilä, 1996; Lewis, 1997). Care was seen primarily as a family task, grounded in the liberal separation of the private family and the public sphere. As a consequence, care as an activity and a concept was under-researched and under-theorized. Feminists have also critiqued the connection between citizenship and paid employment, and the liberal notion of the independent working individual on which this rests, which are prevalent in mainstream theorizing and which result in limited citizenship status for those outside paid work. Instead, they have argued that the inclusion of care within a rights discourse that serves as a framework for the universal concept of citizenship is crucial in moving towards a more gender-fair citizenship (see also Hobson, 2000; Leira and Saraceno, 2002; Lister, 2003; Lister et al., 2007). In this vein, Selma Sevenhuijsen emphasizes that care is an issue that affects everybody and should thus be approached as a moral orientation and process. She argues for a society in which 'caring citizenship' and an 'ethic of care' are considered important and civil society-based voices and claims-making around care issues are acknowledged as legitimate and relevant (Sevenhuijsen, 1998, 2003). Whilst women's movement activists in Europe have seldom used the concept of citizenship in their claims-making around care, in recent decades child care has been a central concern. Our research suggests that movements have effectively sought to reconceptualize and remake social citizenship through their emphasis on the relevance of care in general, and child care in particular. The importance of this is underlined by the work of feminist scholars who have emphasized that few policies influence gender relations within the family and in the labour market as much as child care and parental leave policies (Sainsbury, 1994; Lewis, 1997; Ellingsæter and Leira, 2006).

The attention that large parts of women's movements have devoted to women's right to continuous employment over the life-course has been echoed in public policies across Europe, culminating in the European Union objectives of increasing women's labour market participation and extending early childhood education and care (Esping-Andersen et al., 2002; Jenson, 2008, 2009). However, the labour market to which women's movement activists of the 1970s claimed that women should have access bears little resemblance to the one they have effectively entered since that date (see Le Feuvre et al., this volume; see also Halsaa, Roseneil and Sümer, 2011). Feminist claims for women's full citizenship rights and gender equality have been partly 'lost in translation' (Jenson, 2009), that is, sidelined by labour market activation and 'social investment' perspectives, under the combined influence of globalization, neoliberal political economy and demographic changes.

Women's movements' claims-making around child care is affected by the institutional terrain in different countries. Cross-national studies show how different welfare state models and political contexts influence the claims-making of the movements and the impact they have in their national contexts (e.g. Bertone, 2003; Bergman, 2004; Bleijenbergh and Roggeband, 2007). In critical response to mainstream typologies of welfare states (particularly Esping-Andersen, 1990), feminist scholars have developed gendered typologies of national welfare models (e.g. Lewis, 1993; Sainsbury, 1999; Leitner, 2003). They have also introduced concepts such as gender regimes (Walby, 2004; see also Sümer, 2009) and care regimes and cultures (Kremer, 2007; Pfau-Effinger, 1998, 2004). Mainstream welfare models have been criticized for insufficient attention to gender relations and care provided by the family, the state and the market (e.g. Orloff, 1996; Lewis, 1997). In later 'mainstream' literature, Esping-Andersen partly recognizes the feminist critique and attempts to integrate it into his model, arguing that gender equality is a major challenge for future welfare state reforms (Esping-Andersen et al., 2002).

In today's globalized world, care work is shaped by the intersection of what we are calling 'child-care regimes' and 'migration regimes' (Williams and Gavanas, 2008). In addition to the redistribution of care between families and the public sector, there has been a transnational redistribution of care work (see Le Feuvre et al., this volume). Fiona Williams and Anna Gavanas (2008) emphasize that female migration is central to institutional policies and practices with respect to child care in many states. Child-care regimes differ in their reliance on migrant labour, and more widely, in terms of the extent and nature of child-care provision, the organization of parental leave schemes and home-care allowances for child care. In addition, there are different 'care cultures' in different societies, depending on the dominant attitudes, norms and discourses about the nature of appropriate or 'good' child care. Yet, there are also differences in care cultures within societies, relating to ethnicity, class and generation (Williams and Gavanas, 2008; see also Isaksen, 2010).

Difference and diversity – challenges for social citizenship

Feminist scholarship and women's movements have been criticized for being implicitly derived from the situation of majority middle-class women whose experiences were taken to be universal. Minoritized women's groups have criticized the neglect of their needs and problems and the marginalization of the values and cultural patterns of diverse social and cultural groups. As a result, in the context of the emergence of a 'politics of difference', which recognizes multiple memberships of every individual and differentiation within groups (Young, 1990), social categories, such as class, 'race' or ethnicity, sexuality, country of origin, and religion, are now regarded as structuring social citizenship (or denizenship).[1] Although the feminist critique still mainly focuses on the gendered nature of citizenship, it is also informed by the significance of the diversity of women's claims to social citizenship according to their multiple social and cultural positionings. Ruth Lister proposes the principle of 'differentiated universalism', which responds to both these issues. First, there is the criticism of the false universalism of citizenship, which primarily values the independent working individual and disadvantages women through the gendered division of labour. Second, there is the criticism of a universalizing notion of women, which neglects the significance of other social divisions and inequalities. According to Lister, differentiated universalism overcomes the equality versus difference dilemma, embracing both equality and diversity (Lister, 2003:91; see Strasser and Nyhagen Predelli, Halsaa and Thun, this volume).

Nevertheless, the obvious limitations of the concept of social citizenship arise with the claims of migrants and minorities. The legal definition of citizenship is based on the distinction between members and non-members of a state or political community, who are not entitled to the same rights. As Evelyn Nakano Glenn points out, 'equality among citizens rested on the inequality of others living within the boundaries of the community who were defined as non-citizens' (Glenn, 2000:2). The concept of citizenship has the capacity to include individuals of different groups within the community as equal members. However, if the entitlement to rights is tied to the status of being a citizen of a given state, the discriminatory division between members and non-members remains and thus it seems that the concept of citizenship does not go far enough. This critique of the concept of citizenship had an impact on the increase of the interest in, for example, cosmopolitan and global citizenship that take into account that many individuals are related to more than one nation-state (e.g. Benhabib, 2002; Strasser, this volume).

Aims, methods and material

This chapter highlights women's movements' agency in the remaking of social citizenship in relation to child-care discourses and policies. It explores the frames used by women's movements to articulate and justify their child-care claims. On an *empirical level*, we discuss how contemporary women's movements in different parts of Europe have helped to shape and construct discourses, practices and policies related to one important social citizenship issue: child care. We pose two research questions:

1. What claims have been articulated by women's movements in relation to child care?
2. How have child-care claims been framed by different actors in women's movements and across time and place?

On a *theoretical level*, we contribute to the reconceptualization of social citizenship by accommodating the care of children in this tradition of thought.

The concept of *frame* refers to collective interpretation processes and strategic attempts to identify and explain social problems, to propose solutions and to mobilize people for collective action (Benford and Snow, 2000). Conflicting views about specific social and political issues – for example, child care – are expressed through various frames. We find an analysis of frames a useful method for exploring women's movements' discourses and claims-making. Here our point of reference is Carol Bacchi's definition of discourse as 'the language, concepts and categories employed to frame an issue' (1999:2).

In our research, we selected three major types of women's movement claims around child care: public provision of *day-care services*, public support of *home care* of young children, and *fathers' role* in parental leave policies.[2] We discuss how these claims are framed by different actors and whose needs or interests are voiced in the claims – women's needs, children's needs, or those of men, families, the employed population, minorities.[3] We also consider whether claims made on behalf of women refer to the universal category of 'women', or whether specific groups of women are addressed. Furthermore, we seek to identify voices and claims of both majority and minoritized women's organizations and to examine the extent to which the claims-making of the majority organizations take into consideration the experience of minorities. The issue of care-claiming by minoritized groups cuts across all three areas but is also addressed separately.

The analytical framework adopted in our research treats social citizenship as a *claims-making* process, that is, we do not only understand citizenship as *rights* and *obligations* but also as an active *practice*. We are interested in the impact of claims-makers, that is women's movements, on the contents of social citizenship in the context of the particular national care regimes and gender regimes.[4] We approach child-care politics as a field of *gender mobilization*, with a focus on the role of women's movements in mobilizing political demands and directing them towards the public and political domains (cf. Bertone, 2003; Bergman, 2004). Thus our emphasis is on civil society actors or claims-making 'from below' (Williams, 2009).

While the state has been an important site for women's collective strategies, negotiations and coalition-building in child-care policies in many European countries, institutions in civil society have had a more significant role in others. In this context, it is important to note that women's movements are made up of a large variety of groups and associations with multiple aims, thematic issues and strategies. Not all movements or all activists have an identical approach to given child-care and parental policies. The relationship of the movements to child care and social reproduction has often been a complex and tense issue.

We researched women's movements' claims-making around child care in four European countries that are examples of different welfare state models, political contexts and historical trajectories, and that represent different care regimes in Europe (cf. Lister et al., 2007, 114–16). We examined how such differences affect the movements' discourses and claims-making and their framing of the issues. We selected the Czech Republic as an example of the post-communist Central European countries and Spain as an example of a

Southern European country that experienced a right-wing authoritarian regime until the mid-1970s. Women's organizing in these two countries has been influenced by the authoritarian political regimes that obstructed and delayed the formation of autonomous women's movements. In contrast, in the Nordic countries women's movements – not least in the form of 'state feminism' (Hernes, 1987) – have had a strong and influential position. Two Nordic countries, Norway and Finland, are included in our study because of the different character of their welfare state development and of the political landscape shaping women's collective agency in these two countries. Today, in the Czech Republic, we can speak of women's organizing and NGO coalitions rather than of an autonomous movement (Hašková, 2005; see also Outshoorn et al., this volume). In Spain and the Nordic countries, we can speak about a tendency to institutionalization and professionalization of women's movements, which in Nordic countries involves considerable engagement by the movement in party politics (Valiente, 2009; Korsvik, Rantalaiho and Bergman, 2009).

This chapter draws on research carried out in FEMCIT, an EU funded research project,[5] in which we examined women's movements' role in child-care politics and policies through a broad approach covering both traditional and feminist women's groups and organizations, and various forms of party feminism. Both majority and minoritized women's organizations as well as women activists in Roma and migrant-focused organizations were included. We carried out a secondary analysis of research literature and a primary analysis of documents (policy and movement texts and organizations' archival material) as well as of interviews with key informants (activists, politicians, policy-makers). Instead of carrying out systematic comparisons of the claims-making in respect of child care in the four countries, we used our case studies to illustrate and contrast different claims and frames used by women's movements in the four countries.

Day-care services and home-care allowances: a long-term struggle

Historically, in Western societies, the overwhelming majority of pre-school children have been cared for at home, mainly by their mothers, on an unpaid basis. Since the 1960s, the development of the welfare state and married women's increasing labour market participation resulted in a new model for organizing care for the youngest children in the form of publicly supported day-care services in both Western countries and state socialist countries (Walby 2009:112–3). However, the extent to which public support should be given to day-care services versus home-based care remained a contested issue, including within women's movements. Claims-making around child care has been strongly affected by the opposing arguments and frames of feminist organizations and traditional women's organizations. Whereas the former have demanded publicly funded, affordable and quality day-care services[6] and shared parenting, the latter have preferred recognition and remuneration of care in the home, predominantly performed by mothers (Lister et al., 2007). In other words, demands for 'defamilialization' of the care for young children (i.e. nursery-based care) are raised parallel with claims for 'refamilialization' (i.e. long care leaves, caring fatherhood) (cf. Esping-Andersen, 1990; Leira, 2006).

Feminist claims-making and framing of day care

Although demands for improved day-care services have been central to feminists' care claims across Europe, the strength, timing and impact of such claims have varied, reflecting different structural and cultural conditions. The women's movements in the four countries we have studied have used different but interrelated arguments and frames to articulate day-care claims, the major ones being the *gender equality frame* and the *employment-centred frame*. The gender equality frame defines child care as a cornerstone for women's economic autonomy, emancipation and well-being, while the employment-centred frame ties mothers' paid work to an instrumental way of developing human capital and supporting economic growth and competitiveness. Our research shows that women's movements have also used other ways of framing their claims on day care. They have often joined forces with other social actors employing arguments based on pedagogic ideas related to *socialization* of children, the need to *integrate care and education* and the *right of all children to quality day care* in order to reduce socio-economic and cultural inequalities.

In Norway and Finland, both party-political and grassroots feminist organizations were already demanding day-care services in the 1960s and 1970s, employing mainly the gender equality frame but also strategically using other ways of framing their claims. Grassroots organizing and extra-parliamentary activities were more significant in Norway. The strategic alliance of Finnish feminist activists with left-wing parties and their integration into formal politics, as well as the greater economic need in families for women's paid work, led to legislation obliging municipalities to provide day-care services much earlier in Finland than in Norway (Korsvik, 2011; Bergman and Rantalaiho, 2011).[7]

In the Nordic countries, day care has become a core element of the welfare state and is regarded as the realization and embodiment of the potentially 'women-friendly' nature of the state (cf. Hernes, 1987), which has taken the dual-earner/dual-carer family as the primary model for policy-making. In Finland and Norway, municipalities are today obliged to provide day-care services after the parental leave period to all resident families with a pre-school child. In other words, publicly subsidized day care has developed into a *universal social right* and is framed as an *integral part of social citizenship* (cf. Ellingsæter and Leira, 2006; Lister et al., 2007).

Whilst women's movements had been demanding institutional child care in most other democratic countries in Europe since the 1970s, the authoritarian regimes in Spain (before 1975) and Czechoslovakia (before 1989) effectively blocked women's mobilization and claims-making. In Spain, Franco's right-wing authoritarian regime defined motherhood as women's primary duty and hindered women's employment. After the fall of the Franco regime in 1975 feminist groups started to mushroom in Spain. However, child care was an issue of only moderate priority for the Spanish women's movement: other issues (e.g. employment, bodily and sexual rights) were considered more important. Because all post-authoritarian Spanish governments feared promoting legislation that would resemble the Francoist ideology that defined women solely as mothers, and as Spanish feminist groups formed close connections to left-wing parties that became powerful after 1975, day-care services were developed – although predominantly for children over the age of three. The fact that day-care services were thereafter regarded as part of education policy contributed an extension of these services, because investment in education was seen as necessary for Spain to catch up with the other EU countries economically. Yet, day-care services for younger children are scarce and a pool of grandmothers and migrant domestic workers take care of many children in this age group (Valiente, 2002, 2009, 2011).[8]

Another dimension of the employment-centred frame is revealed by the Czech example. The communist governments in Czechoslovakia developed day-care services in order to capitalize on women's labour force participation while defining women's employment as part of the route towards their emancipation. After 1989, the turn to a market-driven economy in the Czech Republic, and accompanying ideological changes, resulted in a significant downscaling of day-care services, particularly for children under the age of three.[9] Since the Czech Republic is a country with low fertility, whilst the highest fertility rates can be found in countries with the highest percentage of children under the age of three in day care (Hašková, 2009; Oláh, 2011), Czech feminists have utilized the argument that day care contributes to the demographic and thus economic sustainability of society. In fact, this argument combines both the gender equality and the employment-centred frames because the explanation of the positive correlation between fertility and day-care usage lies in the range of work–life balance options and the extent of gender equality that exist in a society.

Both the gender equality and employment-centred frames have been largely used in EU policy documents on day care in the past decade, such as the Barcelona Agreement's recommended targets for the provision of day care for a third of children younger than three years of age and 90 per cent of pre-school children above the age of three in all EU countries by 2010 (European Council, 2002; cf. Jenson, 2008, 2009).[10]

From 'mothers' wages' to home-care allowances

In the 1990s and 2000s, public support for home care for the youngest children was on the political agenda in three of the countries in our study:

Finland, Norway and the Czech Republic. Nonetheless, discussions started at different points in time in these countries and were more common in Finland and Norway than in the Czech Republic. In contrast, public discourses on the topic were virtually non-existent in Spain.

Demands for mothers' or housewives' wages, that is, remuneration of married women's unpaid care and domestic work, had been raised in the 1970s and 1980s in some Western European countries (e.g. Italy, the UK, Germany). Campaigns for 'wages for housework' paid by the state were advanced by some socialist feminist groups with the aim of raising the class awareness of working-class housewives (cf. Della Costa and James, 1973; Malos, 1980). However, such claims-making was harshly criticized by several other feminist groups and organizations and was not common in the feminist movement in the countries in our study. Instead, in both Finland and Norway gender-conservative women's organizations started to demand allowances for stay-at-home mothers in the 1970s. Later, such demands were reframed as 'home-care allowances' or 'cash-for-care payments', that is flat-rate benefits paid after the statutory maternity or parental leave period to support home-based care, in most cases until the child's third birthday. In both countries, the women's movement was divided. The supporters of day-care services were mainly left-wing women's organizations and feminist movements, and the opponents of such policies, who instead pleaded for home-care allowances, were mainly housewives' organizations, and Christian and centrist-agrarian women's organizations (Rantalaiho, 2010; Korsvik, 2011; Bergman and Rantalaiho, 2011).

Similar demands emerged in some state socialist countries (e.g. Heinen, 2011; Szikra, 2010). In Czechoslovakia, when the need for labour force participation decreased in the 1960s as a consequence of an economic slowdown (Myant, 1989), the critique of women's double burden, low fertility and overcrowded nurseries, often with long opening hours, became pronounced (Hašková and Klenner, 2011). As a consequence, day-care services for the youngest children came to be framed as detrimental to children's well-being and the introduction of a home-care allowance was supported, even by the semi-state women's organization (Čákiová, 2005). A 'maternity allowance' was introduced in Czechoslovakia in the early 1970s for mothers of the youngest children. After 1989, the allowance was increased to cover a period of up to four years while support for day-care services was reduced on the grounds that it imposed 'unnatural collectivism' on young children and burdened mothers with 'over-employment' (cf. Czech EU presidency, 2009). Today, home care has strong support in the Czech Republic and feminist counter-arguments have remained weak.

The relative absence of public discussion of home care in Spain is a legacy of the political past. The official doctrine of the Franco dictatorship defined motherhood as women's main duty and affirmed that the role of mothering was incompatible with that of waged worker. In the late 1960s, the women's branch of the Francoist party elaborated a proposal on housewives' salaries. Opposition to this suggestion was advanced by the Seminary for the Sociological Study of Women (Álvarez et al., 1968), amongst others. The proposal was never adopted. After Spain's transition to democracy, home-care allowances were never established at a national level.[11] The issue became associated with the authoritarian regime, which effectively prevented future discussions and policies. After decades of being bombarded with the idea of mothering and caring as the most important task in women's lives, the last thing Spanish feminists wanted after 1975 was mothers to be paid by the state to take care of their children at home (Valiente, 2009).

A home-care allowance was introduced as a statutory right in Finland in 1990 and a cash-for-care benefit in Norway in 1999. Since part-time employment is comparatively uncommon in Finland, many mothers choose the allowance instead of full-time employment. In Norway, the lack of day-care places prevailing until recently forced many women to look for other child-care alternatives. Consequently, home-based care gained in popularity in both countries. In Finland, broad consensus, including within the women's movement, has been reached by giving families a choice between nurseries and home-care allowances, resulting in the widespread popularity of home care of children under three. The conflict was much more intense in Norway and has divided both the women's movement and political circles. The popularity of home care has decreased in pace with the development of day-care services and the low unemployment rates. Despite the option of a home-care allowance, both the percentage of children in day care and the employment rate of mothers have continued to grow. Today, nursery care – including for one to two-year-old children – is clearly the preferred option amongst parents, state authorities and the women's movement in Norway (Ellingsæter and Gulbrandsen, 2007; Bergman and Rantalaiho, 2011). In September 2011, the left-centre government in Norway tabled a revision of the cash-for-care scheme that would limit access to the benefit to families with children under two years of age. Simultaneously, however, the level of the allowance was raised. The government's expressed rationale for the amendment is the need to increase gender equality and to advance the integration of migrant families in society (BLD, 2011).

Thus, home-care allowances have considerably less political support and popularity in Norway than in Finland and particularly in the Czech Republic. Today, less than a quarter of two-year-old children in the Czech Republic and a half of two-year-old children in Finland attend day care, compared to almost 86 per cent in this age group in Norway (*Nordic Statistical Yearbook*, 2010, 66; Kuchařová and Svobodová, 2006). The popularity of home-care leave in Finland can explain why criticism of the scheme by the women's movement – that was still quite harsh during the 1980s – has weakened. This draws attention to the differences in gender politics *within* the Nordic regimes.

Other frames used by women's movements

The advocates of home-care allowances are mostly to be found on the conservative side of the political spectrum. Within women's movements, they tend to be women's groups that do not consider themselves 'feminist' while opponents of the benefits often call themselves 'feminists' and are mostly on the left-wing or social-liberal side of the political spectrum. Our research shows that proponents of home-care allowances use arguments based on *freedom of choice*, the *recognition and valorization of home-based care* and *children's well-being*. Support for home care is said to allow families to decide what the best type of care is for their children, rather than forcing parents to engage in paid work and putting children in day care. It is argued that families should be able to choose among several alternatives in an environment free from outside interference. Our research findings indicate that in parts of women's movements home-based care is valued for children's well-being, and mothering (parenting) is seen as a socially meaningful activity that should be rewarded financially by the state, and should be recognized. Alongside this, the organization of a work-centred society, where only work performed in the labour market is valued, is criticized. Full-time day care of the youngest children is represented as being detrimental to children's harmonious upbringing, for example by impeding the development of individuality.[12]

In contrast, advocates of day care argue that *children's well-being* and *socialization* is better promoted in high-quality nurseries, where emphasis is put on the pedagogic skills of the staff. Thus, both opponents and proponents use children's well-being as an argument to support their preferred policy option. Similarly, at times champions and detractors of home-care allowances use the argument of *redistribution* to support their own perspective. Critics argue that home-care allowances divert resources from public day-care facilities that are supposed to be accessible to all families. According to them, nurseries can help to reduce socio-economic and cultural inequalities between families and in society. The defenders argue that considerable resources would be saved if societies were to rely more on home-based care because of the high cost of day-care services. Also, they argue that parents who do not use publicly subsidized day care should be compensated economically for not using such costly services.

The neoliberal emphasis on 'freedom of choice' is reflected in the extension of the right to care allowances to employed parents who prefer market-based care arrangements. The tendency towards *supporting private child-care services* intersects both with the freedom of choice-frame and the frame of children's well-being since private care arrangements are often defined as being superior to the public ones and better suited to accommodating different needs of families. They are presumed to help parents to effectively solve the challenges raised by the combination of paid work and family. However, if public resources are redistributed to favour market-based care solutions rather than public day care, we can hardly speak about redistribution that aims at benefiting the most marginalized families.

Moreover, feminist critics of home-care allowances argue that since the overwhelming majority of recipients of such allowances are women, the *traditional gender-based division of labour* in the home, the labour market and society at large is reinforced. Day-care services are more attractive to educated middle-class women since they support women's economic self-sufficiency and career development, while home-care allowances look more attractive to low-income women, especially those in precarious jobs. Thus, it is argued, home-care allowances easily become a 'trap' for women and prevent gender equality. 'Choice' is never free of cultural and structural conditions, which is not only gendered but also structured along the axes of class, ethnicity/'race' and legal citizenship. The economic independence of working-class and migrant women is jeopardized since they are, for structural reasons (such as high unemployment and participation in low paid precarious jobs), particularly attracted to the option of staying at home. However, also many middle-class women prefer to stay at home, for example, due to a 'male' work culture that makes reconciliation of family and career difficult (e.g. Williams, 2000; Lewis, 2002). As Birgit Pfau-Effinger (1998, 2004) points out, family policies, as well as preferences and choices regarding child care, are structured by the prevailing gender norms in society. Similarly, Monique Kremer (2007) emphasizes the importance of the normative framing of child care that is reproduced in the strategies chosen by parents but is also firmly established in institutional structures. If 'alternative ideals of child care' have not been promoted by influential collective actors, such as the women's movement, full-time mothering remains the dominant norm in a society.

Public discourses around child-care policies contain few references to minoritized women or families. Yet in Norway, where employment is seen as the main route for both majority and minoritized women's inclusion in society, recent debates in the media and in the political arena have focused on the negative impact of home-care allowances particularly for migrant women and children. Many women's organizations and political parties, as well as the MiRA Resource Centre for Black, Immigrant and Refugee Women, argue that cash benefits for home-care of children are detrimental to integration (Korsvik, 2011). Institutional day care is also presented as particularly stimulating for migrant children's social development and for learning the Norwegian language, as well as for helping to reduce socio-economic and cultural inequalities between the majority and minoritized populations. Thus, day-care services are defined not only as a *social right of children and parents* but also as a means to *social inclusion* and *integration*. In Finland, the migrant population is smaller than in Norway, and such arguments have not been frequent in public debates or policy-making. Moreover, since home care of the youngest children is politically and culturally institutionalized and broadly accepted in Finland, the sort of criticism heard in Norway is unlikely in the near future.

In the Czech Republic, migrant women's organizations have not specifically included payments for home care in their care claims-making. But such payments are part of their broader deliberation about migrants' access to social benefits. Roma women's organizations support benefits for home care as a way to promote their preferred form of child care. Both in the Czech Republic and in Spain the access of migrant and minoritized children to day care is heavily restricted on a discriminatory and structural basis since a there is no statutory right to affordable day care for the youngest children in these countries and discriminatory attitudes and practices by nursery managers particularly affect migrant and minoritized children.[13] Neither the Czech nor the Spanish feminist movements have raised this issue despite discrimination against Roma in access to pre-schools in the Czech Republic, and despite migrant women performing care tasks in many well-off families in Spain while their own children's access to care services is restricted due to the lack of nursery places and the high cost of day-care services. The dominance of middle-class women's voices among feminists in a society where domestic services are generally accepted as a legitimate form of care provision partly explains the low attention afforded by Spanish feminists to day care in relation to migrants (cf. Kvist and Peterson, 2010).[14]

Men's role in child care

During the past 15 years, the issue of men's role in child care has entered European policy agendas. In 1996, after over a decade of active lobbying from different positions (Fusulier, 2009), the EU member states agreed on a parental leave directive (Council Directive 1996/34/EC), according to which both men and women workers should have an individual, non-transferable right to at least three months' parental leave. The discourse of reconciling work and family responsibilities through leave arrangements played a strong role in the framing of the directive, which was politically justified as a necessary means of advancing gender equality. Yet, the directive was very 'soft', leaving it up to member states to decide whether the non-transferability was implemented or not. In March 2010 the Council of the European Union extended the length of individual leave from three to four months. It further agreed that at least one of the four months 'shall be provided on a non-transferable basis' (Council Directive 2010/18/EU). This directive will be in force from 2012.

The way in which parental leave schemes recognize men's care potential, as well as the extent to which they encourage men to take care leave, varies considerably in Europe (Moss, 2010). Among women's movement activists too, the focus on men's role in child care has differed. Though we can find noteworthy resemblance between the countries we have studied it is clear that in the two Nordic countries women's movements have been more deliberate in the articulation of men's role in child care as a matter of women's social citizenship, compared with the Czech Republic or Spain.

Men's role in child care has become more articulated over time. Yet, the idea of reserving some leave for fathers was introduced by women's movement activists as early as the 1960s, in relation to the time around the birth of the child (Lammi-Taskula and Takala, 2009). The father was primarily seen as 'a helping hand' in order to give the mother time to rest and care for the baby. In such a frame, the sharing of child care is not linked to any fundamental change in the gendered practice of child care – the 'need' is located in the family and not articulated as a matter of gender equality. Paternity leave has typically been legitimated by such a frame.

In the 1970s, women's movements in Norway and Finland put forth the idea that changing women's position in the public sphere requires changing men's role in the private sphere (Korsvik., Rantalaiho and Bergman, 2009). This way of thinking has become a key element in the rationale of using child-care policy actively in order to achieve gender equality, and explains, partly at least, why a clearly more deliberate emphasis on men's role in child care has emerged in the two Nordic countries compared with the Czech Republic or Spain. In the Czech Republic, a limited number of men (e.g. widowers and husbands of women who are imprisoned) obtained the right to some maternity leave in 1985, yet, until the late 1990s, the focus of child-care policy has been on facilitating long care leave without questioning the gender-bias in care cemented by such a leave system (Kocourková, 2009; cf. also Maříková, 2008). In Spain, paid paternity leave (15 days) was introduced only in 2007. Gender sharing of parental leave and child-care has until now not been highly prioritized in Spain and parental leave policies have not been strongly tied to a discourse of gender equality or 'active fatherhood' (Wall and Escobedo, 2009).

In the Nordic countries, parental leave policies are generally understood to advance first and foremost the position of women, but since the late 1980s the focus has been increasingly on men's role in child care. The father's quota (an arrangement which reserves one part of the parental leave for the father's use only) that Norway introduced in 1993, was meant to have a positive effect on women's labour market position but also articulates the idea of men's care related rights and duties (Brandth and Kvande, 2009).[15] A female member of the Norwegian Parliament presented the quota as a 'gentle push' (Håland, 2001) that sends a signal to men, but it works also as a moral support for men in negotiations with employers, colleagues or the mother of the child (Brandth and Kvande, 2003). A pivotal consequence of the quota in Norway is that it has become difficult and 'politically incorrect' to discuss care issues in the context of women's lives only. Furthermore, it has contributed to an understanding of child care as a social right of both parents. One could argue that the debates on men's role in child care initiated by women's movements have paved the way for men's own claims-making (Korsvik, 2011).

In contrast with the discourse of 'active fatherhood' that emerged in the Nordic countries in the 1990s (Lammi-Taskula, 2006), in the Czech Republic there was a discourse of 'active motherhood', expressing a conservative ideology of full-time motherhood and home care of children, and contributing to an explicit feminization of care (Hašková, Maříková and Uhde, 2009). Thus, although Czech feminist organizations argue that fathers should care for children on equal terms with mothers, they have not yet been lobbying extensively to reserve parental leave for fathers. Suggesting a father's quota is considered too radical in a society where emphasis has been on long periods of child-care leave, and where this arrangement is strongly appreciated by many women.

There are similarities in feminists' framing of care in the four countries. For example, attention paid to the 'costs of care' for women is identifiable in them all, albeit to different degrees and in different forms. In the two Nordic countries, men's role in child care and 'active fatherhood' are closely linked to this frame. Mothers, due to long periods of care leave, carry the costs of child care in working life, thus experiencing unequal career opportunities, lower salaries and pensions compared to men. A more equal sharing of parental leave is argued to alleviate these gender-biased consequences of parenthood. As we have illustrated above, in the Nordic context, and in Norway in particular, this is considered as a legitimate reason for the state to 'push' men on parental leave via the father's quota. This framing of care is emphasized much less in the Czech Republic and Spain than in the Nordic context.[16] Yet, it seems to us that for those women's movement actors that challenge traditional gender arrangements the core rationale of the frame is one and the same in all four countries – a change in women's lives requires a change in men's lives as well (see also Roseneil et al., this volume).

Our research shows that men's child-care responsibilities (and rights) are also framed by normative and moral arguments that emphasize the importance of active fatherhood. Such arguments articulate a child's right to parental care, and when encouraging men on parental leave, the focus is on their role as active parents. Emphasizing the father–child relationship is an important part of the politicizing of fatherhood (cf., Ellingsæter and Leira, 2006). The moral argument of parenthood opens up a positive discourse on 'care as a right', thus rearticulating care as something that should be in the interest of all – including men.

The division between traditional voices that argue for women's rights as 'mothers', claiming recognition for unpaid work, such as child care, and change-focused voices that see care as a shared responsibility of parents, is observable in all four countries. Despite the broad agreement that men's leave taking represents a *win-win* policy beneficial for women and children, as well as for men themselves, in all the countries claims are raised for long periods of maternity leave as a right for women. Such arguments, obviously, impair the strength of gender equality claims, where the allocation of care responsibilities between women and men is in focus. Voices emphasizing parental choice regarding the division of the leave can have a similar effect. Framing child care as a matter of 'free choice' is not necessarily intended as opposition to gender equality claims but can undermine the possibilities of policy intervention to change practices within families in a more gender-equal direction.

Finally, it is noteworthy that in all four countries, men's own voices have remained rather weak. Men's movement actors have mainly focused on men's rights in the context of post-divorce family life. Yet, the examples from the two Nordic countries, Norway in particular, suggest that men's voices are not irrelevant. In the state appointed committees that focused on men's social position and parenthood that preceded the father's quota arrangement, men did express their interest in more active fatherhood, which seems to have had a positive impact on the political acceptance of the new leave policy (Brandth and Kvande, 2009; Rantalaiho, 2003).

Care claims-making by minorities

The relationship between majority and minoritized women's organizations and groups has gained more attention since the outbreak of critique of cultural bias and hegemonic relations within women's movements in the 1980s (e.g. hooks, 2000/1984; Collins, 1991; Mohanty, 1986, 2003; Fraser, 1997; see also Nyhagen Predelli, Halsaa and Thun, and kennedy-macfoy, this volume; Nyhagen Predelli and Halsaa, 2012). In this context, we researched the relationship between majority organizations and Roma women's groups and organizations[17] as well as migrant women's groups and migrant-focused mixed-gender organizations.[18] The analysis that follows is based on interviews with women activists who are focused on migrant issues and Roma activists (see Uhde, 2009; Seikkula and Rantalaiho, 2010).

Specifically, we explored the realm of care claims-making in order to point to obstacles and potentialities associated with an inclusive transformative politics of care that does not only aim at improving the current situation but also wishes to change the logic on which it is built (e.g. the grounding of citizenship in paid employment). Our first insight is that the activities and claims-making of majority women's organizations and minoritized women's organizations are still disconnected from each other. On the one hand, the specific problems of migrant women and women from ethnic minority groups with regard to child care (with only minor exceptions) are not on the agenda of majority women's organizations. These organizations still predominantly focus on white middle-class women and the dominant interpretation of the work–life balance dilemma is articulated mainly from their point of view. On the other hand, discrimination against Roma women and migrant women on the basis of their minoritized status is seen by migrant-focused organizations and Roma women's organizations as the main problem. Thus, other power relations, such as gender relations, are not articulated as a pressing issue, even though migrant-focused organizations and Roma women's organizations emerged on the basis of Roma women's and (in some cases also) migrant women's shared gendered experiences and their interest in discussing these issues.

Organizations focusing on migrants acknowledge the issue of child care but do not define it as the most pressing or relevant issue, arguing that there are other more urgent problems, particularly the violation of employment rights. Organizations and women activists focusing on the Roma population put care of children to the forefront but do not challenge the gender specific division of labour and family model. Non-family care of the youngest children is not articulated as an issue for claims-making. Instead, home-based care by mothers is often preferred. Nevertheless, they do voice claims directed towards their community for gender-differentiated recognition which would take women's care work better into consideration. Indeed, neither migrant nor Roma women's organizations overlook care issues and their gendered aspect. It is true that in one form or another, problems related to the combination of paid work and family life and economically driven dependencies of carers are everyday issues in the lives of both migrant and Roma women.

However, in general Roma women's and migrant-focused organizations articulate care demands as second level claims. Minoritized groups and organizations generally formulate their claims on a more materially existential level that reflects the often severely constrained social and economic position of women migrants and Roma women. It holds true that the more existentially basic the level of one's deprivation, the more materially focused are struggles and claims.

Third country migrants' low status is conditioned by the fact that their residence status in most cases depends on their employment. Their primary claims are thus directed at the way both men and women migrants participate in the labour market, critically examining the precarious condition of most migrant workers, and demanding decent working conditions. Migrant-focused organizations criticize the dependency status of those – usually women – who enter the country on the family reunion visa and thus are in a more vulnerable position in case of partnership conflict. This is followed up by claims for equal access to health care and education for migrants, especially undocumented migrants. In the Czech Republic the issue of inclusion of younger migrant children through day-care services and education has become part of the agenda of migrant-focused organizations recently. The Czech Republic has the least developed integration policy with respect to immigrants compared with Spain, Finland and Norway (see *Migrant Integration Policy Index 2011* and Appendix II).

Roma women's marginal status is conditioned by their low levels of education, lack of access to economic resources and the marginal status of the whole community; thus their primary claims include access to education and the self-determination of the community, including recognition of the Roma language, which would simultaneously mean recognition of the community customs and Roma cultural traditions. In contrast to Spain and the Czech Republic, in Finland this has been an issue since the late 1980s and early 1990s.[19] Today, the care related claims of Roma women activists in Finland concern institutional and cultural recognition of different patterns of community and family life. They emphasize the historical importance of Roma women's economic activity for both Roma communities and the women themselves. This discursively resonates with the majority focus on employment as a source of self-realization in Nordic countries. Such discursive congruence between feminist and Roma women's groups' perception of women's economic activity is not present in the Czech Republic. Nevertheless, in Spain, Finland as well as in the Czech Republic, Roma women's groups claim access to the labour market for Roma women, though in separate gendered spheres. In fact, Roma women activists' work in larger Roma organizations was seen as a means for women to be engaged in paid employment in a non-discriminatory and safe environment and still fulfil expectations linked to women's role in their community.

There are points of intersection between the care claims-making of majority and minoritized women, and the reason for non-cooperation cannot be explained by a lack of concern about care issues by minoritized women. Rather it seems that majority organizations often do not pay sufficient attention to the more materially existential injustices experienced by members of minoritized groups. The different levels of claims-making may result in incompatible framing of their care claims. For example, in the Czech Republic migrant-focused organizations do not support claims for gender equality, which feminist organizations use to frame the claim for public day-care services; rather they use the framing of inclusion of women and children in society. Reframing this claim in terms of inclusion may provide more space for cooperation. Although their framing is different – gender equality vs. inclusion – majority and migrant-focused organizations might support each other's claims. However, it also depends on the wider social context. In Norway, the MiRa Centre supports claims for gender equality and prefers public day care over home-care allowances as vital to both gender equality and migrant women's inclusion into Norwegian society. In the Nordic countries both majority and minoritized organizations regard the significantly lower use of day-care services by Roma and migrant children as a problem.[20] Institutionalized respect for language differences and recognition of specific cultural needs and skills are seen as crucial in order to overcome assimilation pressure and discrimination against children from minoritized backgrounds. Of the countries in our study, Finland comes closest to these goals and the issue has been on the political agenda since the 1990s; Roma organizations there want more employees with a Roma background in day-care institutions as a means of combating racism.

Another example of incompatible framing is the claim for father's participation in child care. Roma women's organizations often do not support father's participation in child care in terms of gender equality. Rather they use the framing of a child's right to an active presence of men in the process of upbringing. In Finland the claim for a father's quota in the parental leave scheme thus potentially represents a contested issue between majority women's organizations and Roma women. Although the role of men is discussed in Roma women's organizations in Finland, Spain and the Czech Republic to some extent, they do not use it to question the mother's primary role in care.

Nevertheless, it seems legitimate to say that possibilities for remaking social citizenship also depend on the level of cooperation between diverse branches of the women's movement. What seems to be missing is a well-developed feminist politics of solidarity, which should, we suggest, be initiated by those who have relatively more power, that is majority women's organizations. Behind this lies a disturbing fact which is overlooked by the majority women's organizations – that the emancipation of some groups of women is made possible at the expense of others whose care responsibilities and needs are disregarded (cf. Le Feuvre et al., and Nyhagen Predelli et al., this volume; Uhde, 2012). In the context of increasingly neoliberal welfare states, with their emphasis on flexibility and the individualization of responsibility, the original emancipation project of the 1970s, and the ideal of financially self-sufficient employed women, stimulates a demand for the cheap care labour of other women, largely from marginalized and migrant backgrounds (see Ehrenreich and Hochschild, 2002; Zimmerman, Litt and Bose, 2006). Of the countries in our study, this is a widespread practice in Spain (Williams and Gavanas, 2008). Where care is performed as low-waged, precarious employment, often without access to basic social citizenship provisions, such as social security benefits, many middle-class women, who are themselves negatively affected by the prevailing gender order, participate in the reproduction of these very same structures. By reducing their individual burden they shift the problem elsewhere, to other groups. Until these issues are addressed by majority women's organizations, they will remain class- and culture-blind.

Conclusion: remaking social citizenship

In this chapter, we explored child care as a field of gender mobilization and an expression of women's collective agency. We showed that women's movements have defined child care as a social problem requiring political intervention and new policies. As a consequence, child care has become an issue that is seen to concern gendered relationships within the family, as well as the relationship between the state and the labour market, and between the state and the family. Women's movements – in all their diversity – have framed child care as an explicitly gendered issue. Some elements have regarded institutional or 'defamilialized' child care as a universal social right that can improve women's social status and living conditions, as well as those of children and families. Other sections have employed a maternal frame (today mostly presented in gender-neutral terms), claiming that home care of the youngest children should be recognized as a basis for social entitlements. Care-claiming has been strongly affected by these opposing arguments of feminist and traditional women's organizations that seem to run through the history of women's movements (e.g. Lister et al., 2007).

The framing of child-care claims by women's movements reflects political and socio-economic conditions as well as ideological-discursive changes, and thus it has shifted in our case countries over time. Although women's movements have formulated their demands using largely similar frames, the strength, timing and impact of the frames have differed. For example, living in a democratic regime is the condition facilitating the development of women's movements, and having progressive coalition partners in the formal political arena has a positive effect on fulfilling demands for institutional child care. In the Nordic countries, there has been a relatively high degree of trust in the state and support for state interventionism (e.g. Sümer, 2009). Public investment in child-care facilities was therefore considered legitimate, and women's movements directed their claims-making towards the state. Moreover, feminist actors played a major role in establishing the dual-earner family as the predominant model within of policy-making (e.g. Tyyskä, 1995; Bergman, 2004; Korsvik, 2011), and this has had path dependency effects on policy approaches to child care. Yet, demands for subsidized home-based care of the youngest children have also been influential in both Finland and Norway and 'parental choice' has become an important notion in care policies (e.g. Ellingsæter and Leira, 2006).

In the Czech Republic, the collapse of state socialism and the turn to the market-driven economy explain the current refamilializing model of organizing child care that disconnects mothers from the labour market.[21] The model is criticized by feminists whose impact in this policy area has been rather limited so far, due to the long absence of civil society and negative associations to feminism in society (e.g. Heinen, 2011; Ferge, 1997; Funk and Mueller, 1993; Heitlinger, 1996; Havelková, 1993).

In Spain we find yet another explanation for the child-care policy model: the popularity of domestic servants in middle-class homes – often migrant women – as well as a high reliance on the extended family for care partly explains why day-care services are scarce for the youngest children, and also why majority women's movements do not prioritize the issue (cf. Wall and Escobedo, 2009; Williams and Gavanas, 2008). Moreover, structural links between majority women being released from care and housework and minoritized women's precarious positioning in the labour market seem to establish barriers to the cooperation between majority and minoritized women's organizations as their claims in this setting appear to be contradictory.

Since the 1960s and 1970s, women's movements in Europe have sought to shift the framing of public and political discourses on child care from a politics of mothering to a politics of parenting. Yet, demands for institutional support for a more equal division of child care were not to the fore in every country in our study. In Finland and Norway the claim to support men's participation in care is strong, and there is broad agreement in society that only non-transferable paternity leave (father's quota) has real equality-promoting effects. This view is shared by organizations across the whole spectrum of the women's movement, as well as by state authorities and most political parties in Finland and Norway. In contrast, in the Czech Republic and Spain these claims have been only tentatively articulated by feminist organizations. In Spain the lack of support for these claims is related to the tradition of hired domestic workers that makes it possible for men not to engage in care and housework and for the state to define care as a private issue.

Differences between caring regimes and cultures in Europe, as well as in institutional settings, affect women's movements' discourses, politics and the strategic framing of child care. Yet, as our research shows, we also need to be sensitive to the variety of claims *within* countries. Women's movements attach different meanings to the same, or largely similar, policies and frame child-care demands in a range of ways. Their sometimes conflicting goals reflect multiple discursive, cultural and political interpretations of 'good child care', 'good motherhood', 'good fatherhood', and different ways of conceptualizing equality and feminism. Not all women's groups and organizations share the same goals and visions.

Our research reveals that women's movements do not only challenge or criticize established frames of child care and develop new ones, but they also employ *strategic framing* to make their claims resonate with the dominant discourse of national politics in their respective countries, or the dominant EU discourse. Examples of strategic framing include many women's organizations' active utilization of employment-centred frames concerning day care as a means of promoting women's labour force participation, and other organizations' use of the children's well-being or the integration frames in criticizing home-care allowances, as well as in advocating for public day-care services.

Claims around child care are taken up and framed by both majority and minoritized women's organizations. Yet, there is limited cooperation between minoritized and majority women's organizations. For example, Roma women's groups formulate their claims on a more materially existential level than (most) majority women's organizations, which reflects their experiences of discrimination and injustice. The experiences of minoritized women seriously question some of the classic arguments of women's movements across Europe. The situation of Roma women, for example, challenges feminist organizations' emphasis on employment-oriented child-care frames, and their lack of attention to minoritized women's problems in the labour market. However, claims around public support for home care of children raise questions about the idea of 'parental choice'. Feminist scholars have shown that parental choice is never free of structural and cultural dependency and is influenced by the dominant gender order in society and in the labour market. The idea of 'parental choice' is sometimes used to undermine claims to day care and often serves to reproduce gender inequality (e.g. Ellingsæter and Leira, 2006).

Despite the variety in child-care claims and frames, women's movements in all four countries have incorporated into their care claims-making demands related to *equality, social rights,* the *recognition of care needs* and the *redistribution of care responsibilities.* Large parts of the movements view institutional child care as a social citizenship right for children and their parents. Social justice for parents requires universal access to publicly subsidized, affordable and high-quality day care, as well as good parental leave arrangements. Unpaid care at home is in practice often in conflict with participation in paid employment that, across Europe, is regarded as one of the most important citizenship obligations. While this 'paid work paradigm' was supported and cherished by large parts of the women's movements in the countries in our study, others criticized discourses where paid work is seen as a citizenship obligation. As a consequence, public support for parental care of the youngest children was favoured by this part of the women's movement.

We suggest that institutional child care as a social right is not a sufficient demand in the feminist remaking of social citizenship. The redistribution principle needs to be complemented by the recognition of the diversity of claims and practices that exist amongst different cultural groups (cf. Fraser, 1997). So, alongside the promotion of universal access to high-quality nursery care, we should also recognize the variety of wishes and demands of women's movements concerning the organization of care, including respect for cultural and linguistic diversity. But we also have to pay attention to the different structural and cultural contexts that impact on the formation of these wishes and demands. Furthermore, the realization of these wishes is related to societal inequalities along the axes of gender, ethnicity, class and citizenship.

Traditionally, care has not been recognized as a citizenship issue, but since the 1980s, in the context of changes to the breadwinner/caregiver family, and thanks to feminist scholarship, care has increasingly been acknowledged as central to social citizenship. This cannot be understood without acknowledgement of the vibrancy and impact of the claims-making of women's movement around child care. Despite the widespread retrenchment in welfare services, and with some exceptions in parts of Central and Eastern Europe, child care appears to be one dimension of social citizenship that has been strengthened in many parts of Europe. In this context, we might claim that women's movements and feminist scholars have contributed significantly to the remaking of social citizenship, both in the sphere of policy-making and in the cultural-discursive practices of everyday life.

Notes

We are grateful to the editors of the volume for their comments and suggestions that have improved the chapter. Trine Rogg Korsvik from the University of Oslo was involved in research carried out in Norway. The authors of this chapter wish to thank her for her valuable contribution.

1. We emphasize the status of being denizen in contrast to being citizen to highlight the different legal status of those residing in the country but lacking formal citizenship.
2. We focus on these types of care claims since they have been of major importance for European women's movements. Other forms of work-care reconciliation policies that have been addressed by women's movements include flexible working time arrangements, six-hour working days, part-time work and after-school care.
3. In recent decades, traditional notions of family structure have been challenged by, for example, lone parenthood and same-sex parent families. Our case studies did not cover these families. There is a clear and growing demand for empirical research in Europe looking at how child-care and parental policies and politics respond to the needs of and claims of non-conventional families (cf. Roseneil et al., this volume).
4. Our focus is on women's movements as claims-makers. Other social movements, organizations and actors that have been central for child-care policies include political parties, trade unions, child psychologists, paediatricians, and educationalists/early years specialists, demographers, economists etc.
5. FEMCIT – Gendered Citizenship in Multicultural Europe: The Impact of Contemporary Women's Movements (2007–11; project no. 028746) was funded by the 6th Framework Programme of DG Research. For information about FEMCIT and its working papers and other publications, see www.femcit.org.
6. We focus on the demand on day-care services for children younger than three because most political controversies concern the issue whether nursery care should be aimed at for this age group or not. Older children under school-age are, in many parts of Europe, targeted by educational services and there is broad political agreement on the need to develop nursery care for them.
7. Legislation on day care was introduced in Finland in 1973, and a statutory right of all pre-school children to day care was introduced in 1990. In Norway, a similar right was established only in 2009 (Eydal and Rostgaard, 2011).
8. Yet, the attendance rates in day care have risen markedly in recent years, to 16 per cent of one-year-olds and 30 per cent of two-year-olds (Valiente, 2009).
9. Day-care services were recently provided to less than 7 per cent of children under the age of three (Hašková, Maříková and Uhde, 2009).
10. See also Esping-Andersen (2002) whose report had a significant influence on EU rhetoric on the issue.

11. Some regional governments in Spain have, however, introduced flat-rate allowances (Wall and Escobedo, 2009).
12. Such frames and arguments used in our interviews with representatives of organizations and groups that support home-care allowances and were also evident in the documents we analysed, for example the organizations' own statements, policy documents etc. (see Hašková, Uhde and Pulkrábková, 2011, Korsvik, Rantalaiho and Bergman, 2009; Rantalaiho, 2010).
13. For example, in the Czech Republic, Roma children have experienced discrimination in access to day care and school education. Given the shortfall in child-care services, nurseries must choose between those applying for day care. Often, the selection criterion of an employed mother is applied. Since most Roma mothers are unemployed or economically inactive, it is relatively easy to exclude Roma children from day care. Consequently, since many Roma children enter school without an experience of day care and since the Roma language is used in many Roma families, many of them end up in special schools because of language problems (see Pulkrábková, 2009).
14. However, recent studies demonstrate that paid domestic work – often performed by female migrants – is becoming more common even in the Nordic countries (Kvist and Peterson, 2010; Isaksen, 2010).
15. The non-transferable father's quota has gradually been increased, from 4 weeks (1993) to 12 weeks (2011) (BLD, 2011; see also Eydal and Rostgaard, 2011).
16. In the 1990s women's organizations in the Czech Republic openly argued for the need for women to become housewives if they so desired. This could, at least partly, explain the weak demands for men's more active role in child care in the Czech Republic. There is very marginal space for more radical changes. This is illustrated in the rejection that feminists received when suggesting a shortening of the parental leave to 18 months and reserving one-third for fathers (Kocourková, 2009).
17. Our research on Roma women's organizations focuses on Spain, the Czech Republic and Finland; Norway is not included as its Roma community is very small. We chose the Roma as one of our case-study groups because it is one of the major, and long established minoritized groups in three of the four countries in our study.
18. In the Czech Republic foreigners without citizenship status make up 3.8 per cent of the total population, in Spain 11.6 per cent, in Norway 5.7 per cent and in Finland 2.5 per cent (OECD, 2010).
19. Since the 1990s the Roma language is considered an official minority language in Finland that should be supported in pre-school and school education; nevertheless this depends on the municipality in question.
20. The crucial question is the age at which children supposed to attend public day care. Whereas for migrant-focused organizations this is often a pragmatic question if the mother needs to work to stay legally in the country, Roma women's organizations and groups prefer home-based care for children younger than three years of age but recognize the educational benefit of public day care for older children.
21. For a discussion of de- and refamilialization see for example Leitner, 2003; Saxonberg and Sirovátka, 2006; cf. Ellingsæter and Leira, 2006.

6
Remaking Bodily Citizenship in Multicultural Europe: The Struggle for Autonomy and Self-Determination

Joyce Outshoorn, Teresa Kulawik, Radka Dudová and Ana Prata

Introduction

Since the rise of the new wave of feminism in the 1960s, issues concerning the body have been at the heart of the challenge posed by women's movements. The female body has always been a contested site, subject to state policies regulating its procreative and sexual capacities, as well as its (in)violability. Violence against women was often condoned by state authorities as a family affair, and the control of women was generally delegated to private patriarchal authority. Women's bodies have been part of a broader imaginary about national vitality and served as markers of national belonging. They figure as 'materialization' of the imagined community of the nation and its borders (Yuval-Davis, 1998). Women's bodies were the cornerstone of their 'natural' otherness and exclusion from the rights of citizenship. It is, therefore, not surprising that women's movements across Europe (and elsewhere) had bodily integrity on the top of their agenda, leading to concrete demands on a whole range of body issues. The issue of bodily integrity lies at the core of the concept of bodily citizenship, which is concerned with guaranteeing that the individual is autonomous and free from external intervention in relation to decisions about her (or his) body.

The classic formulation of citizenship rights has not included bodily or sexual rights; in feminist scholarship on citizenship the concept of bodily citizenship is also underdeveloped (e.g. in Phillips, 1991a; Siim and Squires, 2008). Our research could therefore not depart from a fully developed theoretical framework, though there was some previous work from which we could proceed. In her examination of feminist conceptions of citizenship, Voet (1998:98–108) showed that the major strands of feminist thought used the liberal idea of self-determination and autonomy to make the case for bodily integrity. Lister (1997:126–8) made the case for including bodily integrity in citizenship, arguing that it is a precondition for the other citizenship rights. Shaver (1994) made a distinction between formal recognition of body rights in law, specifically the right to abortion, and abortion as a medical entitlement. The latter retains medical control over abortion, but in effect allows a liberal abortion practice by inviting less political contestation and more adequate public funding. Bacchi and Beasley (2002) make the distinction between those who are assumed to have control over their bodies – full citizens – and those who are regarded as being controlled by their bodies and can thus be deprived of their citizens' rights, an obviously gendered distinction. That there is little more conceptual work than this is surprising, given the centrality of bodies, both to feminist concerns and to a whole range of policies, particularly the pro- and anti-natalist measures, which have become increasingly significant with the re-emergence of bio-politics through bio-medicine and reproductive genetics over the past two decades.

This chapter sets out to examine how women's movements have contested state governance and dominant political discourses about the female body, and how they have changed problem definitions and policies impeding women's bodily self-determination in different political systems. It also discusses how the growth of multicultural societies in Europe and the process of Europeanization – 'the process in which domestic politics, policies and polities are changed through the engagement with the EU system' (Backe and George, 2006:57) – are impinging on political debates about the body, and possibly impacting upon attempts to enhance women's rights to bodily integrity.

Approach and methodology

Our research on women's movements and bodily citizenship took a historical and discursive institutionalist approach that stresses the importance of institutions and policy legacies in shaping current policies, alongside the central role of discourses in articulating policies (Kulawik, 2009; Schmidt, 2010). Such an approach draws attention to the importance of timing and sequencing, and its use in a comparative study enables the identification of key points of change, and the teasing out competing explanations of change. In analysing women's movements, our research draws on social movement theory, more specifically the political process approach (Kriesi, 2004; Tarrow, 2005) and framing theory (Ferree, 2003; Verloo and Lombardo, 2007). However, in this chapter, we have focused on the dominant discourses on our issues and the discourse and claims of women's movements and their possible incorporation in law and policy.

We carried out a comparative study of four country cases. As gender typologies of states have typically been based on social and economic arrangements, they were not helpful for selecting cases to study bodily issues. Nor were there regime typologies based on these issues that we could use for selection. We therefore opted for a 'most different system' research design, choosing four European states – the Czech Republic, the Netherlands,

Portugal and Sweden – from the four major regions of the current EU: the Nordic region, western Europe, central and eastern Europe and Southern Europe. This selection gave us both secular and religious countries, which we considered might be significant in terms of body politics. While the Czech Republic, Sweden and the Netherlands are largely secular, Portugal is still a solidly Catholic country (see Appendix II). Our selection also has a mix of old democracies (the Netherlands and Sweden) and countries with a recent transition to democratic rule (Portugal 1974–6; Czech Republic 1989). Consequently women's movements emerged in different decades, providing variation in the life cycle of women's movements and the (non)existence of feminist groups. Moreover, two of the four countries, the Netherlands and Portugal, have a colonial history, with a long tradition of migration from overseas to Europe, while Sweden and the Czech Republic have longstanding indigenous minorities, the Sami and Roma. All four countries are members of the European Union: the Netherlands is a founder member; Portugal joined in 1986, Sweden in 1995 and the Czech Republic in 2004.

We selected two 'body issues' for our analysis: abortion and prostitution. The legalization of abortion has been one of the top priorities of contemporary women's movements and it has been a pivotal issue in distinguishing feminist movements from women's movements. Legalization of abortion has followed very different time-paths in European countries and there is still considerable divergence in law across states. Prostitution has not been a high priority of women's movements, except in Sweden, but is an issue which raises contentious questions about sexuality, personal autonomy and the role of the state. In contrast to abortion, feminists are deeply divided about prostitution. Countries differ in their prostitution regimes:[1] regimes can be prohibitionist (making all prostitution illegal), abolitionist (making prostitution illegal but not criminalizing the prostitutes) or regulationist (with a degree of state control of prostitution). Interestingly, both of our issues are within the jurisdiction of the national state, and not of the EU. This makes both particularly suitable for the analysis of processes of Europeanization that are not directly related to EU regulation.

Our empirical work started by tracing the life cycle of our issues over recent decades, identifying the various public discourses and the major policy changes in respect of each. We then identified which women's organizations had been active on the issues, including those of minority women, how they framed their demands and to what extent their framings were adopted by governments and incorporated in the policy outcomes. We also looked across state boundaries to see if EU policies were influencing national policies and whether the rise of a supra-national arena was providing new opportunities for women's movements to achieve their demands. Finally, we analysed how discourses about these issues were affected by ongoing debates about migration and multicultural societies. The data we collected came from documents produced by the different groups in the debates, such as parliamentary records, government statements, party programmes, texts from women's movements, and reports from experts and interest groups. When information was lacking or contradictory, interviews were held with key actors in the debates – leaders of women's movement organizations, politicians and experts.

The abortion issue

Waves of reforms

Abortion had been forbidden since the late nineteenth century in all four countries, and was usually only allowed if a woman's life was endangered by the pregnancy. This criminalization was partly due to the rise of imperialist states and their interests in population policies, but can also be ascribed to the medical profession establishing its monopoly on reproduction, sidelining other health practitioners (Gordon, 1977; McLaren, 1978; Mohr, 1978). Only Russia, Sweden, Germany and Switzerland relaxed their restrictive laws before the Second World War. The Communist Central and Eastern European countries, usually prompted by concerns about the quality of the population, enacted more liberal laws in the 1950s. Eugenic arguments fed into the debates on the Swedish 1938 reform, and the 1957 Czechoslovakian reform was justified on medical grounds to make for a healthier motherhood (Dudová, 2010a). The eugenic legacy is still in evidence in the role of medical knowledge and professionals in debates about reproductive quality and quantity, and in contemporary debates about prenatal diagnostics and selection. Eugenics played little role in Portugal, although under the Salazar regime pro-natalist laws outlawed abortion. The Netherlands has no history of population policy due to conflicting moral positions on reproduction entrenched in the system of *Verzuiling* (pillarization – the strict organization of society along religious and class lines) and general opposition to state intervention in this area (Noordman, 1989:260–66).

In the 1960s a new wave of reform began. Sweden extended its law in 1946, adding a 'socio-medical' indication and including foetal damage as a ground for abortion in 1963 (Lindelöf, 2010). The prevailing discourse in the 1930s held that 'normal women' wanted abortions only because of poverty, a circumstance that could be prevented by social policy (Elgan, 1994). The adding of the socio-medical indication implied that after the Second World War abortion became conceived foremost as a psychological problem and approved in cases where women were defined as 'unstable' and 'worn out'. In the 1970s feminists framed abortion in terms of women's self-determination (Isaksson, 2007; Lennerhed, 2008:183) and in 1975 the law was adjusted accordingly. Abortion on demand was permitted until 12 weeks of pregnancy, and until 18 weeks after consultation with a social welfare officer. The latter requirement became optional in 1995. The Czech Republic granted a woman abortion on written demand during the first 12 weeks of pregnancy in 1987, on the basis of psychological arguments about the effects of being an unwanted child (Dytrych, Matějček and Schüller, 1975) and the development of better techniques for early abortion (Havránek, 1981). Attempts to restrict the abortion law after 1989 by anti-choice groups failed in 2004 and 2008; their pro-life framing could not dislodge the more permissive medical discourse or the strong secular tradition in Czech culture (Dudová, 2009).

In the Netherlands a more permissive interpretation of the law to allow for medical and psychiatric grounds developed in the 1960s, but as hospitals were reluctant to help, private abortion clinics jumped into the gap in the early 1970s, allowing women decision-making autonomy. These practices were more or less legalized by the 1981 Abortion Act which permits abortion if the woman is in an 'emergency situation' – to be judged by her and her doctor. There is a five-day waiting period to encourage 'conscientious' decision-making (and to stop 'abortion tourism') (Outshoorn, 1986). In Portugal debate on reform took off after the democratic transition of 1974. Law n.6/84 was enacted in 1984, permitting abortion on three grounds: the physical and mental health of the woman, foetal deformity and pregnancy due to rape. After a failed referendum in 1998 to extend the law, a second referendum paved the way for further reform in 2007 (Law n.16/2007). This decriminalized abortion up to 10 weeks of pregnancy on women's request in an authorized health-care centre. Public debate on both referenda centred on the need to end illegal abortion for reasons of public health (Prata, 2010a).

In all four countries there are still barriers to women's right to abortion, such as a term limit or an upper limit, usually related to the viability of the foetus outside the woman's body. Another barrier has been the requirement of residence to have an abortion in a country. Sweden allowed only non-resident women to have an abortion in 2008. The Czech Republic excluded them explicitly in 1973 in order to stop 'abortion tourism' (mainly from Austria) (Jiří Šráček, gynaecologist, interview 19 June 2009). During debates on health-care reform in 2008 the government used EU regulation to argue that allowing access to abortion for EU citizens was inevitable. The reform failed when the government fell, so that abortion is still not possible for non-resident women. In contrast, the Netherlands has allowed non-resident women to have an abortion since the early 1970s, with numbers decreasing from nearly 55,000 in 1977 to around 4300 in 2007 (Outshoorn, 2010a). The decline can be attributed to legalization in neighbouring countries, notably (West) Germany and Belgium. Portugal has never been a destination country for women from abroad seeking an abortion because of its strict legislation and late liberalization.

While abortion falls under the legislation of the nation-state, which generally precludes dissatisfied organizations (both women's and anti-abortion groups) taking their case to the supra-national level, the EU indirectly did play a role in abortion debates, as we saw in the Czech case. During the

Portuguese democratic transition, some of the framing of abortion by pro-choice activists highlighted how Portugal should emulate other democratic European nations by revising its outdated legislation. Women's organizations and MPs used the EU strategically to further their demands, such as the European Parliament's Report for Health and for Sexual and Reproductive Rights (2002) which recommends that abortion should be legalized, safe and accessible to all women. Comparison with other EU countries also plays a role in current debate to move the 10 week limit to abortion on demand to 12 weeks. In Sweden, accession to the EU in 1995 was accompanied by extensive debates about whether accession would endanger Sweden's liberal abortion regulations and other accomplishments of Swedish gender politics. Gender politics became a crucial 'boundary object' in redefining Sweden's identity and position in the New Europe after the end of the Cold War (Towns, 2002). The gender equality model and the new open borders helped remove the abortion barrier for non-resident women. In the Netherlands, the Abortion Act was partly legitimated by pointing out that it was not out of step with other European countries (HTK 1978/79, 15474, nr 3, *Memorie van Toelichting*, bijlage 1). In subsequent debates the low Dutch abortion rate (the lowest in the world till the mid-1990s, see Henshawe et al., 1999) became a source of national pride and a part of the self-image of the Netherlands as a morally progressive nation. It provided an effective weapon against opponents of the Act keen to reopen the political debates in later decades.

The claims and demands of women's and feminist movements

In our four countries, women's organizations already had a long history before the revival of feminism at the end of the 1960s. The contemporary movements emerged at different points in time and did not really develop in the Czech Republic. Here the democratic women's movements had been dismantled after the communist putsch in 1948 and the communist Výbor československých žen (Committee of Czechoslovak Women, later Český svaz žen – Czech Union of Women) became the only permitted women's movement until 1989 (see Bergman et al. this volume). It did convey some women's demands to the party leadership, but abortion reform was dominated by the experts. Even after the democratic turn, it is difficult to talk of a 'women's movement' in the Czech Republic, although there is a network of actors and activities supporting women's interests. Groups such as Gender studies o.p.s. the first post-communist organization (Forest, 2006:174), fought the conservative attempts to outlaw abortion in 2003–4. However, they did this by disputing the anti-abortion claims about the foetus's independent being, and on the grounds that women suffer from post-traumatic stress after an abortion, not by formulating a feminist claim to reproductive rights. No groups contested the limitation of access to abortion for non-resident women, although some of the feminist groups, such as the Multikulturní centrum Praha (Multicultural Centre Prague) or Evropská kontaktní skupina (European Contact Group), have taken on migrant women's problems about work and parenthood in recent years. Given that abortion was mainly framed in medical terms and not in terms of women's rights, it is hard to discuss abortion in terms of rights or citizenship for non-residents (Dudová, 2009).

Women's mobilization around abortion followed a different pattern in Sweden, which has a longstanding tradition of women's organizations both within and outside political parties (Florin and Kvarnström, 2001). Though bodily issues were integral to their agenda, both in the first and second wave of mobilization, within the framework of the social democratic welfare state, they figured as secondary to redistributive issues. So while Sweden was among the first movers in the repoliticization of gender inequality and the division of labour in the early 1960s, women's organizations were not at the forefront of abortion reform, which was led by left and liberal men. In the 'sex-role' debate of the early 1960s, reproductive rights were a non-issue (Lennerhed, 2008). During later debates women's organizations were in favour changing the law, but the scope of revision contested. This changed in the early 1970s. Then a new leading feminist organization Grupp 8 (Group 8), founded in 1968 mobilized against a bill that proposed an application procedure, arguing in terms of 'women's right to their bodies'. This helped change public opinion for the 1975 law granting abortion on demand (Isaksso, 2007; Eduards, 2007:15). The issue was then dormant till the EU accession debate in 1995 and later debates on sex selection.

In Portugal and the Netherlands, abortion was the central issue in the mobilization of women's movements. The feminist movement in the Netherlands was part of the broader democratization movement in society which was both cause and consequence of the breakdown of the *Verzuiling* in the 1960s. Abortion was the major demand of the new groups Man-Vrouw-Maatschappij (MVM – Man-Woman-Society) (founded in 1968) and Dolle Mina (Mad Mina) (1970). They framed the issue in terms of women's control over their bodies (*'baas in eigen buik'*), arguing that women are fully capable of taking their own decisions. In this way they challenged the dominant paternalistic and medical discourse and turned the issue into a lay matter, not to be left to the experts. In 1974 Dolle Mina set up Wij Vrouwen Eisen (WVE – We Women Demand), a coalition of autonomous feminist groups and women's organizations from political parties and trade unions, which led the legalization campaign. It succeeded in making its demands about decriminalization, self-determination and state funding of abortion the dominant discourse; the 1981 Act more or less met these demands. WVE still exists as a network and closely follows current debates about state funding of contraception and prenatal diagnostics. In recent years Women on Waves (WoW), founded by Dutch feminists in 1999, became involved in monitoring abortion politics. WoW was set up to fight for legalization in countries with prohibitive laws; its 'abortion boat' can help women outside the territorial waters of their country, as occurred in Portugal. Its licensing under Dutch law was contested until 2006, when it finally received the required permit (Outshoorn, 2009).

Portuguese women's groups employing feminist discourse were an intrinsic part of the democratic transition period, and they soon raised body issues, notably abortion reform. Once feminist and women's organizations, such as the Movimento de Libertação das Mulheres (Women's Liberation Movement), Movimento Democrático das Mulheres (MDM – Women's Democratic Movement), União Alternativa e Resposta (UMAR – United Women Alternative and Answer) and the Movimento pelo Aborto Livre e Gratuito (Movement for Free Contraception and Abortion), converged on the importance of decriminalizing abortion in the late 1970s, their demands became very similar. They demanded legal abortion reform in tandem with an overall contraception/sexuality law reform and sexual education agenda, framing the abortion issue predominantly in terms of social justice, women's rights, women's health rights and as a modernization issue for Portuguese society.

When abortion disappeared from the political agenda in the 1990s, only a few organizations continued working on further reform. The Movimento de Opinião pela Despenalização do Aborto em Portugal (MODAP – Opinion Movement for the Decriminalization of Abortion in Portugal)was created in 1990 as a platform uniting several organizations (Tavares, 2003). MODAP was an important part of the Yes for Tolerance movement during the first abortion referendum campaign, which employed framing about ending 'illegal and unsafe abortions' and 'public health'. In recent years it has functioned as a watchdog on the implementation process (Prata, 2010a.) Another time of heightened mobilization and activism occurred during the Women on Waves campaign, which kept the issue of abortion rights alive in the media and public opinion in the early 2000s (see also Roseneil, 2010a). The framings about unsafe abortion and public health were complemented by new frames about the inadequacy of the current law, the social injustice of the abortion trials and Portugal as a country with outdated legislation within the EU context.

Abortion and migration

The four countries have very different migration histories which have shaped the ethnic composition of its population. Despite this heterogeneity, ethnicity has generally not been the focal point in the abortion debate. In Portugal and Sweden, migrant and minority women were generally invisible in the abortion debates. In Portugal it might be argued that they were included indirectly in terms of their social status, but not in terms of race or ethnicity. The framing of 'desperate' women needing an abortion for socio-economic reasons did not single-out migrant or minority women.

In fact, the dominant Socialist/Marxist political culture led 'class' to be an overriding category, subsuming other categories, thus contributing to a discourse deprived of other diversities. In Sweden there was some concern in the 1980s about higher abortion rates in the resident migrant population, but these higher rates disappeared amongst the second generation (SOU, 1983:31). Ethnicity reappeared during the 2009 debate on the practice of sex selection. Some cases of sex selection by women with a migrant background were publicized and led to a lively debate, raising the question of whether women's decision-making autonomy should be suspended when it came to sex selection (Dagens Nyheter, 22, 25 February 2009). Sex selection is, unless when motivated by genetic diagnostics, a real taboo in Sweden. According to the recommendations of the National Board for Health and Welfare on maternal prenatal care, the sex of the foetus should preferably not be disclosed to the future parents. However, in May 2009 the Board upheld the decision-making autonomy of women, even in those cases when the abortion is induced by the sex of the foetus.

The debate about abortion in the Czech Republic became coloured by the controversy about forced sterilizations of Roma women in the mid-2000s and the debate on the extension of the right of abortion to non-residents in 2008. From the available sources it is obvious that between the 1960s to the 1980s, the Czechoslovak state put considerable effort into managing and influencing Roma reproductive behaviour in the attempt to assimilate and limit the Roma population (including preferential treatment by the abortion commissions when granting permission of abortion) (Motejl, 2005). Other instruments were financial subsidies to women who decided to undergo a sterilization, or even sterilization without the consent of the woman, or obtaining consent under threat and insufficient information. This issue remains controversial; the Czech government formally apologized to the victims in 2009 after five years of hesitation and inter-ministerial disagreements, but avoided discussions about financial compensation (Rovenský, 2009). Several influential actors never acknowledged Roma arguments to be true (e.g. Korbel, 2009).

In the Netherlands, despite a considerable migrant population from the former Dutch East Indies, and a large migration of Surinamese and 'guest workers' from the Mediterranean region, migration and migrant women rarely figured in the debates up to the 1981 Abortion Act. However, when it became evident in the 1980s that migrant women had a much higher abortion rate than 'native' Dutch women, this was deemed problematic as the dominant discourse sees abortion as an ultimate remedy, to be avoided by the use of contraception. The higher rates were explained in terms of failing or inadequate contraception, ascribed to the lack of information and sex education, and to 'cultural difference' which was held to impede adequate prevention. Successive cabinets expected that migrant women would 'catch up' with the white Dutch levels of abortion, but to date this has not happened. In 2005 the abortion rate (the number of abortions per 1000 women between 15 and 44 years of age) ranged from 4.5 for white Dutch women, to 13.6 for Turkish, 20.1 for Moroccan, 34.2 for Surinamese and 44.2 for Antillean women (Wijsen, Van Lee and Koolstra, 2007:31). Because of the high migrants' rate, the overall abortion rate increased and the Netherlands lost its first place in the international comparisons of abortion rates in 1997 (Sedgh et al., 2007). The problem definition in terms of inadequate contraception has not (yet?) been challenged in the recent anti-immigration and cultural nationalist mood. The policy response generally has been to continue funding prevention and sex education projects for 'groups at risk' (Outshoorn, 2010a).

As in Sweden, there was also a Dutch debate about selective abortion of the grounds of sex other than for medical reasons. Key in the public debate was the presumed preference for sons among migrants, an indication for abortion that the Abortion Act technically allows (the woman would have to plead an 'emergency situation'). The debate was sparked off by the Minister of Health who said that she could imagine a woman from a 'foreign culture' wanting an abortion if the foetus was female after already having borne several daughters (HTK, 1997–8, *Vragenuur*, TK 42:3386, 21 January 1997). She stated that 'we' should think thrice before wanting to lay down the law for all in 'our multicultural society' (Ibid:3388). The two major migrant women's organizations, AISA, a platform organization, and Tije, a black women's organization originating from the 1995 UN Women's conference in Beijing, protested against this 'cultural relativism' (Saharso, 2005:253). A year later a new cabinet decree prohibited sex selection by artificial reproductive technology for non-medical reasons (Staatsblad, 1998).

The prostitution issue

The waves of reform

All four countries have a history of regulating prostitution in the nineteenth century, but all moved towards an abolitionist position in the first decades of the twentieth century under the influence of social hygienist, feminist and religious movements. Abolitionism usually entails criminalizing all who profit from the earnings of prostitution (not always the prostitute herself) and outlawing brothels. In Sweden, prostitution was seen as anti-social behaviour and prostitutes became objects under surveillance of laws on vagrancy and contagious diseases (Svanström, 2006a). In the Netherlands, abolitionism was undermined by a pragmatic policy condoning prostitution unless it threatened public order. Until the 1970s prostitutes were socially accepted in the traditional red light districts and they were never criminalized. Under the Salazar regime, Portugal repressed prostitution as a hazard to public and moral health, but although prostitutes were criminalized, there was also some social acceptance of them. During communism in the Czech

Republic, prostitution officially did not exist, but prostitutes were seen as 'social parasites' who dodged 'decent' work. Authorities assumed that prostitution would disappear as socialism would end poverty and gender inequality, but by the 1950s this ideal had proved untenable. 'Social parasiting' (including prostitution) was added to the Penal Code and in 1969, and even 'part time' prostitutes (who also worked in legal employment) were criminalized (Vlček, 1985).

With the rise of a new global sex industry in the late 1970s (Outshoorn, 2004a), there occurred a second wave of changes in prostitution regimes. Portugal was the first of our countries to change its laws by decriminalizing the prostitute (but not pimping and brothels) in 1983 under the Social Democrat and Socialist governments. In public debate, prostitution was defined as a social problem, linked to criminality and deviant behaviour, and to be dealt with by prosecuting the profiteers and protecting the victims. A further revision occurred in 1995, altering article n.169 of the Criminal Code on trafficking. This now takes into account the exploitation a woman's situation of abandonment or need, alongside violence, threats and trickery in forcing her into prostitution. This recognized the need to protect individual rights and personal freedom, while in the 1970s and 1980s the legal view was that prostitution and trafficking were also offences to morality. In the 2000s public debate focused more on the links between trafficking and sexual exploitation, organized crime and migration than on prostitution itself. This can be illustrated by the First and Second National Plan Against Trafficking of Human Beings and by the CAIM project (Cooperation, Action, Investigation, World View), a public/private venture to fight women's trafficking and support its victims. Amendments to the law broadened the concept of trafficking and sexual exploitation (Law n. 99/2001and again in Law n.59/2007) to adapt to EU rulings and other supranational legal frameworks (Santos et al., 2008:575). This increased penalties, enabled the punishment of the client, and framed trafficking as slavery, instead of a crime against sexual freedom.

The next country to initiate change was the Czech Republic, which repealed the communist law in 1990, so that engaging in prostitution was no longer criminal. The 1990 repeal only prohibits sex businesses, pimping or procuring. But with more open borders the number of prostitutes began to grow (MCVR, 1999), causing local problems and leading to the promotion of a regulationist perspective by a number of local authorities. However, the fact that Czechoslovakia signed the International UN Convention for the Suppression of the Traffic in Persons and of the Exploitation of the Prostitution of Others (1949) in 1958 has made regulation impossible as it outlaws any form of profiteering from prostitution and registration of prostitutes. Its validity is guarded ferociously by those politicians opposed to regulation. The dominant discourse still regards prostitution as a major social issue or pathology, and with the AIDS epidemic the public hygiene framing made its come-back. The moral framing, pitting the 'decent' against 'indecent citizens', continues to construct the prostitutes as 'public order disturbers' and 'abusers' of the welfare system. The framing of prostitution as something external to Czech society is strengthened by the construction of prostitutes as minority or ethnically different women or migrants. When the Czech Republic joined the EU, it accepted the 2002 EU Framework on Human Trafficking and adapted its legislation. The imported trafficking discourse created a space for a new framing that not all prostitutes work voluntarily and that some are abused and lack rights. New feminist organizations offering support to women in the sex business and lobbying for their interests played a significant role in this discursive shift (Dudová, 2010b).

After protracted parliamentary debate, the Netherlands decriminalized prostitution in 2000 by lifting the ban on brothels. In the late 1970s local authorities could not deal with the new sex industry; as prostitution was forbidden by the Penal Code, attempts at regulation failed in the courts. Their lobby to legalize brothels led feminists to claim rights for prostitutes, such as the right to sexual self-determination, and to frame them as assertive, modern and professional sex workers. This framing was compatible with the dominant liberal discourse, and allowed for a discursive alliance of feminists, liberals and local authorities who wanted the ban removed (Outshoorn, 2001). A cornerstone of the new legislation is the distinction between voluntary and forced prostitution; the first is legal and recognized as sex work, the second, including trafficking, illegal. The Netherlands already had strict anti-trafficking laws since 1993; in 2005 these were adjusted in accordance with the UN Protocol. (Outshoorn, 2010b).

Regulating prostitution as sex work became part of the Netherlands' libertarian image abroad. Dutch feminists made full use of the EU (and UN) arena to set the issue of voluntary prostitution and sex work on their agendas and to define existing treaties as barriers to prostitutes' rights. Moreover, they helped to de-link prostitution from trafficking and to reframe forced prostitution as forced labour within the European policy arena. They also pioneered the establishment of cross-European NGOs to support victims of trafficking (Outshoorn, 2010b).

During the 2000s it became evident that the 2000 law was not effective in preventing trafficking, ridding the sex industry of crime or improving the position of sex workers (Outshoorn, 2010b). Public discourse reframed prostitutes as victims of human trafficking and organized crime and this became the cornerstone of new legislative proposals requiring registration of prostitutes and licensing of escort services (still to be passed by the Senate).

Sweden changed its prostitution regulation in 1998, but in a very different direction, by criminalizing the client. Historically prostitution had fallen under the Contagious Diseases Act and the Vagrancy law, which targeted 'anti-social behaviour' (Runcis, 1998; Dodillet, 2009; Baldwin, 1999) as part

of the coercive interventions which accompanied the welfare state formation. In 1971 the Criminal Code was adapted to allow for sex clubs (Dodillet
2009a:49). The 1981 report by the Prostitution Inquiry Committee, which
recommended tackling pimps and again banning sex clubs to fight prostitution (SOU, 1981: 71), was well received, but the understanding of sexual
services as a contractual relationship between equal individuals was heavily
critiqued. Women politicians of all parties, supported by feminist activists
and scholars, developed a new policy paradigm. Prostitution became defined
as obstructing the very goal of equal opportunities (*jämställdhet*) for women
and men. Simultaneously the reframing reversed the blame: prostitution
discourse had usually problematized the behaviour of women, seeing them
as victims as well as seducers, whereas the men as buyers were positioned
as 'victims' of their sexual instinct. In the new paradigm women and men
switched positions: the male buyers becoming problematized and women
positioned as weaker and later as victims (Svanström, 2006b; Dodillet,
2009a:342). The new 1990s hegemonic discourse aimed at changing men's
behaviour and abolishing prostitution altogether, culminating in the 1998
Prohibiting the Purchase of Sexual Services Act (SFS, 1998:408) as part of a
government bill (*Kvinnofrid* – peace for women) to combat violence against
women. Since then Sweden has been actively promoting its new policy
in the EU and elsewhere as part of its gender equality model. Its first EU
Commissioner, Anita Gradin, attempted to stop the general EU policy drift
to disconnect prostitution from trafficking in 1996. Surprisingly, Sweden
passed anti-trafficking laws only in 2002, a policy change long preceded
by other European countries. Overall, Swedish prostitution policy has to be
understood as both a new policy paradigm based on a certain interpretation
of gender as a power relation, and as path dependent, continuing the uto-
pian policy line of the Swedish model which aims to abolish social evils. A
recent evaluation (SOU 2010:49) concluded that the Act is effective in fight-
ing prostitution, but its research has been severely criticized and debated
(Lindeberg and Berg, 2010).

The claims and demands of women's and feminist movements

The movements in our four countries have taken very different positions
in the debates on prostitution law reform. In Sweden and the Netherlands,
feminists were able to change the dominant discourse in diametrically
opposed directions. Feminists in Sweden were divided over the issue of client criminalization, while in the Netherlands feminists in general see prostitution as sex work. In Portugal there is a division between the traditional
abolitionists, including both Catholic women and feminists, and an emerging minority moving towards the sex work position. In the Czech Republic
new feminist groups adopting the sex work position started to challenge
both the legal status quo and the regulationist discourse of many local

authorities. Prostitution was not a priority issue for women's movements, save for Sweden, where it became important to women parliamentarians in the 1990s.

Feminist activists, lawyers and academics in the Netherlands had already developed a sex work discourse early in the 1980s, formulating political demands, supporting victims of trafficking, lobbying authorities and creating academic expertise on the issue. The national women's policy agency picked up the new framing and funded the two major groups on the issue, the Rode Draad (Red Thread) (1986) and the Stichting tegen Vrouwenhandel (STV – Foundation Against Trafficking of Women) (1987) (Outshoorn, 2004b). The Red Thread started as a self-organization of prostitutes, supported by a small group of feminists. Their framing is in terms of sex workers' rights, autonomy and self-determination (Altink, 2000:23). STV, originating from the Working Group Against Sex Tourism which helped set trafficking on the political agenda in 1981, was a service organization for victims of trafficking. It has always embraced the sex work position, rejecting the idea that legal prostitution would increase trafficking. Both organizations supported the repeal of the brothel ban, demanded residence permits for trafficked women so that they could testify against their traffickers in court (in 1988 a first regulation allowing for this was adopted) and a more suitable definition of trafficking (achieved in 1993 with the passing of the Trafficking of Persons Act). STV then started to lobby for humanitarian asylum for victims of trafficking who have testified against their traffickers. This has not yet been achieved. Both organizations have always addressed migrant sex workers, who in turn participated in their activities, and supported the self-organization of migrant sex workers. There is little evidence, however, that the women's organizations from the large migrant communities have been active on the issue (Outshoorn, 2010b). The lack of interest is, along with having other priorities, partly due to the taboo nature of the issue among many migrants.

In Portugal only a few women's organizations have mobilized around the issues of prostitution and trafficking. The UMAR and the MDM organized several collective actions, including petitions, demonstrations and workshops. The MDM has collaborated with migrant organizations to raise awareness on how trafficking affects migrant women, and with the Association of Women Lawyers to change article n.215 of the 1982 Criminal Code on procuring. Another set of organizations highly involved with the issue of prostitution since democratization are Catholic women's organizations, such as O Ninho (The Nest) and Irmãs Oblatas (Sisters Oblatas), with an evangelizing mission launching programmes to rehabilitate and reintegrate prostitutes into the workforce (Prata, 2010b).

However, women's and feminist organizations have not taken any official stance on prostitution, although they have formulated political demands to protect and support victims of prostitution and trafficking. Most are either against the legalization of prostitution or avoid any public statement on the subject (Santos et al., 2008:206). Duarte contends that 'even within the feminist movement...there is still no serious discussion about prostitution' (2010:17). Therefore public debate has centred mostly on victimization and how prostitution represents violence towards women and their exploitation. In this discourse, migrant women are always the main group highlighted as particularly vulnerable to victimization. The high incidence of migrant prostitution and trafficking victims from the former colonies has contributed to the salience of migration in the overall debate. The dominant definition of women's exploitation is shared not only by the Catholic women's organizations, but also by women activists and feminists. Tavares (2006:7) argues that, 'at times, the moralist and conservative positions are intertwined with feminist abolitionist positions forming a political arch that reaches both the political right and some leftist sectors'. Only in recent years has there been an opening in this discourse towards sex work, due to the work of Ana Lopes, the founder of the first sex workers union in 2000, the IUSW (International Union of Sex Workers). She has been critical of the Portuguese feminist movement, arguing that it only sees sex workers as victims and treats prostitution as a Pandora's box (Oliveira, 2004). Recently some feminist organizations are moving to work jointly with sex workers and to open the debate on the legalization of prostitution and challenge the abolitionist perspective.

The discourse on prostitution and migration in Portugal has been mostly constructed without the participation of migrant, minority ethnic or anti-racist organizations, since these organizations have not focused much on women's issues. Likewise, the issues of migrant or minority ethnic women have only been addressed sporadically by women's organizations. Nonetheless, the national women's policy agency, the Comissão para a Igualdade e Direitos das Mulheres (CIDM – Commission for Equality and Women' Rights) has raised the issue of how prostitution and trafficking issues impact migrant women and has functioned as a bridge between migrant organizations and women's organizations, politicians and social scientists (Prata, 2010b).

In the Czech Republic two feminist organizations dealing with prostitution and trafficking emerged by the mid-1990s: Rozkoš bez rizika (Bliss Without Risk) and *LaStrada*. Both played the role of a third party in the public debates about prostitution during the 2000s, opposing the problem definitions of abolitionist MPs and Ministers not willing to change the legal situation, and local governments' representatives promoting the regulation of prostitution and the compulsory registration of prostitutes. The feminist organizations offered their own problem definition: a clear distinction between prostitution with and without consent; the notion of sex work instead of prostitution; and sex workers to be regarded as rational and fully fledged actors deserving protection and equal treatment (e.g. Malinová,

2008). The distinction was borrowed from a discursive framing used by some feminist groups as well as the majority of European Union institutions. It shifted the distinction of the 1990s between problematic (street and road prostitution) and unproblematic prostitution (indoor prostitution in apartments, erotic massage parlours and clubs) to one between voluntary and involuntary prostitution, or between prostitution and trafficking in the 2000s. While the few migrants' organizations that emerged in the early 2000s did not deal with prostitution, Bliss without Risks (focusing on support and health prevention to prostitutes) and LaStrada (focusing on the prevention of trafficking and offering support to its victims) included support and the lobbying for the interests of these groups in their programmes (Dudová, 2010b).

As already observed, Swedish women's movement organizations and women parliamentarians were able to make their discourse about prostitution the dominant one. This became possible when in the 1990s a new window of opportunity presented itself by the fall of the Wall with the ensuing ideological void, class loosing its position as major organizing principle in Swedish politics It opened the way for a third wave of feminist mobilization. Enabled by the Swedish policy process's heavy reliance on committees of inquiry, feminist experts redefined the gender political agenda, moving it beyond the redistributive equal opportunity frame. Gender relations came to be understood in terms of power: the term *könsmaktordning*, literally 'sex power system', expresses that gender relations are made up by structural relations of power (Eduards, 2002; Kulawik, 2007; Dodillet, 2009a:355). This discourse rapidly entered official policy documents. The National Federation of Women's Shelters, ROKS, founded in 1984, had a major impact on the reformulation of prostitution as a form of violence. Its expert knowledge had already been influential in the inquiry committee on Men's Violence against Women (*Kvinnofrid*), which strengthened the equation between prostitution and violence (SOU, 1996:60A). Violence became a priority issue, framed as major expression of a misogynist gender power structure. The difference between voluntary and forced prostitution became increasingly inconceivable, as was a woman who consents to sex for money. In the 1970s prostitutes had still had their own organization, the Sexual Power Front (Sexualpolitisk Front), which demanded rights and fought stigmatization, but today such mobilization is no longer thinkable. Migrant women's organizations generally agreed with the overall strategy of the women's movement, and were especially concerned with securing residence permits for the victims of trafficking (Dodillet, 2009b:23).

Prostitution and migration

In contrast to the abortion issue, migration has been at the centre of the debates on prostitution; it triggered the changes in prostitution regimes and dominated the debates over the past two decades in all four countries.

Migration already played an important role in the Czech Republic under communism, where demand was constructed as coming from abroad and supply was seen as motivated by the craving for luxurious Western goods. Prostitution by Roma women was part of this externalization: their ethnicity, their family relations and their (to the majority society incomprehensible) lifestyle influenced the understanding of prostitution as an affair of 'them', not 'us'. After 1989, the number of foreign women entering the country to work in the sex business grew, mainly because of the demand from German, Austrian and other western European men. The women came from Slovakia, Bulgaria, Vietnam and Ukraine, or were of Roma ethnicity, and sometimes both. Prostitution by Roma women and girls was not a new phenomenon, but with the introduction of the market economy, new forms of social exclusion and criminality have emerged that strongly affected the Roma minority. Moreover, pimping was organized often by international gangs or whole Roma families. In consequence, race and ethnicity started to play an important role in public debate. According to a governmental report (MVCR, 2000) the sex workers were rarely Czech citizens, and if they were, they were usually of Roma origin. Experts and politicians constructed the prostitutes, the pimps and the clients as foreigners, coming from abroad or ethnically different (Dudová, 2010b). This further polarized the distinction between the decent Czech citizen and the indecent non-citizen.

Prostitution and migration were also intertwined since the revival of the prostitution debates in the Netherlands when new evidence of the trafficking of women emerged in the late 1970s. The number of sex workers in the Netherlands was estimated to be around 7000 at that time, of which at least a quarter was from abroad; in 2000 the estimate was 20,000 to 25,000, of whom probably over 50 per cent came from abroad (Mensenhandel, 2002:83). Formerly sex workers came from Latin America, South East Asia and Africa, and after the fall of the Berlin Wall, mainly from Central and Eastern Europe. During the 1990s debates about new anti-trafficking legislation, the Christian Democrats developed a new discourse about the 'floods of illegal prostitutes'(Outshoorn, 2001:479); in subsequent debates victims of trafficking and illegal migrants became more and more indistinguishable. The post-2000 prostitution legislation constructed different categories of sex workers: legal Dutch and EU sex workers, sex workers from acceding EU states (only legal if they are independent workers – those in employment cannot obtain a working permit) and those from all non-EU countries (who do not get working permits and are thus illegal). This is also a racialized demarcation. Illegality creates bad working conditions for sex workers, but the concern about 'impoverished women' being trafficked stands in the way of granting work permits to non-EU sex workers which would improve the latter's lives. Pending legislation in parliament will further weaken the position of illegal migrant sex workers and encroach on the civil rights of sex workers by compulsory registration (Outshoorn, forthcoming).

As in the Netherlands, migration was an intrinsic part of the prostitution debate in Portugal. Early in the democratization process, the discourse on prostitution and trafficking was mostly connected to poverty, organized crime, and 'deviant behaviour'. With decolonization and accession to the EU, immigration increased considerably (particularly from Eastern Europe, Brazil and former African colonies), and public discourse on prostitution and trafficking changed accordingly. Academic research and the media have contributed to reinforcing this link. Both have stressed that the majority of women working in prostitution, or being trafficked, are migrants from countries outside the EU (many illegal) (Oliveira, 2004; Ribeiro et al., 2005; Peixoto, et al., 2005). The discourse about prostitutes and migration depicts migrant women as more vulnerable to prostitution and trafficking, and therefore to victimization. 'Migrant status', 'gender', and 'class' act jointly to determine a defenceless situation. In addition, there has also been considerable misrepresentation of migrant women in the media, which has contributed to negative stereotypes of specific migrant groups. Brazilian and Eastern European women, in particular, are the two main groups regularly portrayed as prostitutes, and such stereotypes pervade Portuguese society (Santos and Cunha, 2006).

In the debates about prostitution and trafficking in Sweden the imaginary about the 'East', the 'other part of Europe', plays a crucial role. In the mid-1990s restrictions of the Migration Act, which allows for withdrawing a residence permit if the 'foreigner does not live steadily and honestly', were motivated by the idea that the person who comes from the East may in fact be a prostitute (RD protocol, 1994/95:104) The Inquiry Committee on Sexual Crimes (SOU, 2001:14) assumed that most victims of trafficking come from Eastern Europe, and states that in Russia between 70 and 95 per cent of the women are unemployed (SOU, 2001:421). These figures are incorrect, which casts doubt over the expertise of Swedish Inquiry Committees. The policy narrative about prostitution and trafficking seeks to accomplish a kind of 'squaring the circle' argument. It proposes that the women should not be allowed to enter the country because they threaten the equality that characterizes Swedish gender relations. At the same time the women are portrayed as 'vulnerable' and weak, and one could expect that the very country that defines itself as a champion of human and women's rights would offer these women a place to stay. However, the argument is actually posed the other way round: women's vulnerability motivates why they should not be allowed to enter or stay. Allowing them to stay would mean, according to the Swedish policy narrative, encouraging unequal gender power relations (SOU, 2002:69; SOU, 2008:41).

Comparing change and gains

Abortion

Women's movements, including feminist movements, in our four countries did not employ the language of citizenship in claiming abortion rights (see also Nyhagen Predelli et al., and kennedy-macfoy, this volume). Their arguments took the specificity of the female body, its capacity to procreate, as their point of departure. They framed their claims predominantly in terms of autonomy, self-determination and the right to have an abortion, premised on the understanding that to decide about one's body is a fundamental precondition for full citizenship. But they also employed strategic framing, as for instance in Portugal, where women argued their case in terms of social justice and public health at a time when public debate fore-fronted class issues and illegal abortion.

It is evident that feminist movements have made a crucial difference in abortion debates: when there was no feminist movement, either due to timing or to the lack of democracy, limited reform was enacted, with control over access and availability remaining in the hands of the professionals, mainly medical doctors. This was the case with the early reform in Sweden in the 1960s, when there was not yet a feminist movement taking on body issues, and in the Czech Republic, where the Communist regime prevented the rise of an independent women's movement. Where feminist movements mobilized and developed a feminist discourse, as in the Netherlands, Portugal and in Sweden after 1970, laws incorporated, to varying degrees, a woman's right to decide. However, there are still significant barriers to abortion on demand, such as abortions after 10 or 12 weeks of pregnancy, and upper limits, usually concerning the viability of the foetus outside the woman's body. In our four countries, minority women generally were not visible in the abortion debates, and they also did not organize on the issue. Ethnicity came to the fore in sex-selection debates in Sweden and the Netherlands. Another exception is the debate about Czech state policy to encourage abortion and sterilization for Roma women in the Czech Republic. The lack of mobilization by minority women can be ascribed partly to the fact that majority women's movements framed their demands in universal terms: all women should have the right to an abortion. Sequence and timing are important too: minority women's groups were relatively late in forming their own organizations, and by that time found abortion more or less available. Their list of priorities was also different: work, education and immigration control (see kennedy-macfoy, this volume). Moreover, in none of the four countries are specific groups singled out for special treatment in the enacted legislation, therefore not inviting opposition on this point.

We also saw that our four cases do not allow for the neat distinction that Shaver (1994) found in the liberal welfare states that she studied: a distinction between abortion as a medical entitlement (Britain and Australia) and as a body right (the US and Canada). She came to the paradoxical conclusion that in the latter abortion rights were less secure because of the limitation of public funding and stronger political opposition, while in the former two 'medically mediated' abortion led to less contestation of abortion rights and more adequate public funding, making it a social right. Our cases each have different welfare state regimes, but the outcomes do not follow her distinction. Irrespective of the opposition (fierce and protracted in Portugal and the Netherlands) they all encompass public funding. As for 'body right', in Sweden and the Czech Republic the law states the right of women to choose (in the latter in the Memorandum to its law). In the Netherlands the law is ambiguous: the woman and the doctor *together* assess if there is an emergency situation justifying abortion – but if the doctor refuses he/she is obliged to refer the woman to another doctor. The Portuguese law does not formulate the right to choose, but a woman is free to choose her own health-care provider. Moreover the recent development in all countries of medicated abortion and internet commerce call the demarcation between legal and 'illegal' abortions into question, and further undoing Shaver's distinction.

Prostitution

Women's movements have also not framed their demands about prostitution in terms of citizenship. In the Netherlands the women's movement defined prostitution as sex work and sex workers as emancipated actors who have the right to sexual self-determination. Forced prostitution had to be criminalized. In the Czech Republic feminist organizations also made a distinction between prostitution with or without consent, framing sex workers as rational actors deserving equal treatment. This contradicted the dominant Czech discourse of prostitution as a social pathology, requiring regulation and the registration of prostitutes. Attempts at regulation failed because of the 1949 UN Trafficking Convention to which the Republic was a signatory. In Portugal most women's organizations are opposed to legalizing prostitution; there are strong Catholic-oriented organizations who frame prostitution as a social evil and sex workers as victims. However, in the 2000s feminists have started to criticize this dominant framing and to open the debate about sex work. In Sweden feminists framed the issue in terms of sex-power and gender equality, regarding prostitutes as victims and clients as oppressors, and marginalizing those feminists critical of this paradigm. Generally it is surprising that sexuality itself was barely addressed in the prostitution debates, save for references in the Netherlands about sexual self-determination and the need to 'educate' men about 'clean' sexuality in relationships in Sweden (Dodillet, 2009a).

In contrast to the abortion issue, migration has been a major focus of the prostitution debates in all countries. Historically prostitution and trafficking have been discursively linked, with the victim of trafficking as the primary figure of attention. The shift in prostitution regimes of the 1990s was prompted by the international revival of trafficking discourses, which can be linked to the concern about the mobility of women on a global scale. All four countries have encountered significant changes in the supply side of the sex market where migrant sex workers catch the eye as 'different'. In public debate the innocent and young victim of trafficking competes with the illegal female migrant profiting from the welfare state, while 'gangs of foreigners' run the international sex trade.

These shifts produce their own national framings in each of our four countries, but they have a common feature. Women's bodies serve as markers of national borders and what it means to be a decent citizen. The Czech Republic in the Communist era externalized prostitution as something 'Western'; after transition, it tended to depict sex workers as foreign (if not, they were Roma) and clients were western European men. This discourse polarized the issue along the lines of the decent tax-paying citizen – 'us' and the 'foreigners' – 'them' who abuse the health-care and social insurance system, showing the legacy of the prostitute as a social parasite. In the Netherlands the concern about victims of trafficking became intertwined with the fear of illegal migration, in evidence in the debates about 'floods' of illegal prostitutes. By its refusal of work permits for non-EU citizens, it creates its own problem of illegal workers. In Sweden the prostitute from the 'East' plays a central role in public discussions about trafficking and prostitution. While on the one hand she is portrayed as vulnerable and weak, on the other hand she is seen as threatening gender equality and should not be allowed into the country. In Portugal migrant sex workers are generally seen as more vulnerable to exploitation, while at the same time Brazilian and Eastern European women are often stereotyped as 'prostitutes'.

Prostitution policy is the prerogative of the national state, but trafficking is international, and subject to EU regulation and various UN Conventions. All countries have incorporated the European Council Framework on Human Trafficking (2001) and signed the UN Protocol on Trafficking (2000). Women's NGOs have been able to access the EU funding of anti-trafficking initiatives. These initiatives in turn have become contested as opponents of prostitution attempt to stop the funding of those that help victims of trafficking but do not 'help' women to exit sex work. The EU arena has provided women's movement actors with strategic opportunities to export their demands. In a process reversing the usual top–down approach, Dutch feminists placed human trafficking on the agenda of the European Parliament and the Council of Europe in the mid-1980s, delinking it from prostitution by distinguishing between voluntary and forced prostitution. This delinking has generally been adopted by various EU institutions in subsequent decades. In the mid-1990s Swedish feminists and their EU commissioner used the EU arena to export the Swedish 'model', but ran into the barrier of jurisdiction which designates prostitution to the national state.

Our research shows that sex workers in all four of our countries lack citizenship rights, albeit in varying degrees. They all lack bodily rights and protection against violence; in Portugal, the Czech Republic and Sweden they lack social and economic rights, in the Netherlands their civil rights threaten to be curtailed by compulsory registration. From an abolitionist point of view one might argue that, except for Sweden, the state does not protect women's rights, given that it allows prostitution. On the basis of our research, we contend that when states seek to protect women from prostitution, this generally leads to the curtailing of women's rights, more policing and exertion of 'soft' power by social work professionals over sex workers.

Our findings raise questions about the usefulness of the common vocabulary – such as abolitionism, prohibitionism or regulationist – employed to distinguish prostitution regimes (for the usage: Danna, 2001; Outshoorn, 2004a; Transcrime, 2005), which does not capture the wide range of prostitution activities or state attempts at control in our four countries. Moreover, our findings cast doubt on the relationship between prostitution and trafficking as abolitionists (e.g. Raymond, 2002) portray it. For them, prostitution leads to trafficking, so the best way to end trafficking is to eliminate prostitution. In all four countries, however, the majority of sex workers from abroad are not trafficked women, but women migrants who cross borders in order to make a living (Santos et al., 2008; Outshoorn, 2010b). Debates about prostitution have become intermingled with fear of migration and the purity of the nation, and prostitution policy has become boundary control, literally and symbolically, demarcating the nation from the foreign, the victims from the whores and decent citizens from footloose migrants.

Implications for bodily citizenship

In our introduction we observed that the classic formulation of citizenship rights did not include bodily rights; even in feminist scholarship on citizenship the concept of bodily citizenship is underdeveloped. Examination of the politics of women's movements has brought to the fore the concepts of autonomy and self-determination in arguing for abortion rights, which for them was the major issue of bodily integrity. These concepts are central to the project of remaking bodily citizenship. Women should be the ones to decide about an abortion, and not the state, the medical profession or the church.

But our findings about abortion also remind us that there are implications for social citizenship. The availability of contraception, abortion facilities and access to new reproductive technologies, as well their funding under a national health-care system, are part of social citizenship. Without these, reproductive rights remain formal rights. The debate about abortion rights for non-residents points to the need to relate bodily citizenship to the question of multicultural or transnational citizenship, so that state boundaries do not proscribe women's bodily citizenship.

Our findings also show that prostitution has been framed as an issue of bodily integrity, but has not generally constructed in public debates as being about sexuality. Many women's movement activists argued that prostitution is violence against women and that states should protect (female) bodies against violence. However, others have argued that prostitution can involve autonomy and (sexual) self-determination, and that it is best regarded as work. We agree that bodily citizenship should most definitely include freedom from violence, but that the most promising way to guarantee sex workers' rights is to consider it as an issue both of bodily citizenship and of economic citizenship. This takes into account the need to fight forced prostitution to maintain the bodily integrity of the sex worker, but also defends her right to work, doing away with barriers to selling sex and allowing for labour legislation and regulation. Social rights follow from defining prostitution as work, with rights to welfare state benefits and access to social insurance. Health care is also essential for sex workers' safety. Too often sex workers have had to undergo STD checks against their will under strict prostitution regulation. Full citizenship of sex workers requires access to medical care on a voluntary basis, with access to contraception and information about working safely. Sex workers' civil and political rights have often been curtailed. Moreover, the struggle for full citizenship should also take the existence of undocumented sex workers into account, as they run the risk of blackmail and exploitation. This would require accepting that many migrant women working in the sex business are not victims of human trafficking, but workers who want to earn money.

Prostitution is a prime example of how the dimensions of citizenship with which this book is concerned are fundamentally interrelated, demonstrating the necessity of seeing them holistically. It is an open question, though, whether allowing a woman to use her body for sexual services will allay the fear about wayward women, dangerous sexualities and chaos and social disorder engrained in public discourses about prostitution.

Finally, despite abortion law reform, there are still legal barriers to women's bodily citizenship, as well as problems of access to abortion facilities and contraception. Sex workers do not have full civil, social, economic and bodily rights. There is still much work to be done by women's and feminist movements in making and remaking bodily citizenship.

Notes

We would like to acknowledge the work of Susanne Dodillet and Karin Lindelöf for their reports on respectively prostitution and abortion in Sweden. We also thank Line Nyhagen Predelli and Ana Cristina Santos for their comments on the first draft of this chapter.
  1. Outshoorn defines prostitution regimes as 'sets of laws and practices governing prostitution that shape prostitution in their respective jurisdictions in distinctive ways, and make for more or less repression of the women selling sexual services and the possible prosecution of their involved parties, such as clients, entrepreneurs of sex work facilities or pimps' (Outshoorn, 2004a:6).

7
Remaking Political Citizenship in Multicultural Europe: Addressing Citizenship Deficits in the Formal Political Representation System

Monica Threlfall, Lenita Freidenvall, Małgorzata Fuszara and Drude Dahlerup

Introduction

Political citizenship is probably the dimension of citizenship with which readers are most familiar, at least in its conventional meaning of nationality, the right to vote and to stand for election. In fact, definitions of citizenship often conflate it with political citizenship. For instance, Leydet (2006), drawing on Cohen (1999), Kymlicka and Norman (2000), and Carens (2000), highlights three dimensions of citizenship, and these pertain to the political world: a person's citizenship, as a legal person free to act according to the law and to claim the law's protection; a person's right to act as a participant in political institutions (the above-mentioned voter and representative); and a person's membership of a political community (nation) that provides a source of identity (a nationality). However, the feminist critique has moved the discussion of citizenship beyond the rights granted by state authorities to the terrain of practices and identities chosen, constructed and performed by citizens and residents in their daily lives on intimate, social and political levels; in other words, moved it into the spheres of participation, identity and belonging, as understood by the FEMCIT project team.

Feminist critiques have also constructed models of political citizenship that see the proportionate presence of women in representative positions as crucial for women to enjoy effective political citizenship (e.g. Fraser, 2007; Krook, Lovenduski and Squires, 2009). Elective assemblies should arguably reflect the gendered make-up of society, so there should be gender-balanced participation in political decision-making. This notion has gained increased acceptance around the world (Dahlerup, 2006a), albeit in a patchy way, and constitutes this study's starting point.

Nonetheless we argue that full political citizenship for women remains incomplete. At a world level, despite recent gains in women's presence, just under 20 per cent of the world's parliamentarians are women (Inter Parliamentary Union-IPU, 2012). But crucially, women's increased participation in national legislatures as parliamentarians is not alone able to remedy the three separate but related 'deficits' that we believe need to be addressed in order to achieve fuller political citizenship for all citizens and residents. The first of these is the deficit in satisfaction with the representation system itself, from the citizens' perspective. Arguably, the election of local, regional and national representatives must be able to generate in citizens sufficient feelings of inclusion in, and satisfaction with, the representation system, and to incorporate the increased political expectations of women since the second wave of feminism and particularly of different collectives of women, such as Muslims and second and third generation ethnic minorities. We argue that the satisfaction deficit is partly due to a deficit in the way the relations of representation are conducted, not just a perception.

The second deficit that we identify is the 'ethnic representation deficit'. Even in very longstanding democracies, the political citizenship and representation needs of minorities remain underdeveloped or lacking. Remedying this deficit is additionally challenging, because of differences between minority women and minority men, and amongst ethnic minority women.

The third deficit in political citizenship is what we call the 'agency deficit' of women parliamentarians themselves. This refers to the unequal opportunities available to women parliamentarians to perform representation in their newly acquired positions. While the right to stand for election is regarded as the bedrock of political citizenship, the right to enjoy equal political room for manoeuvre once elected is not. Women should enjoy full freedom to build their own representative roles inside parliaments, rather than be there on sufferance. Elected women need full access to available channels to hold on to their positions as representatives in subsequent legislatures too. Standing for election will be a meagre right if there is any reduction in the agency of the elected representative. This is an underdeveloped notion in democratic thought: the fact of women being elected has consequences for practices inside parliaments, well beyond the moments of being selected and fielded.

The research on which this chapter draws targeted these three deficiencies of political citizenship for women. They constitute three fields in which representation systems fail to adequately fulfil the democratic concept of a modern polity – a state and a political society – that is able to offer political citizenship to women, as well as to men, and to ethnic minority women and men. Thus we interrogate some key dimensions of what is missing for the fulfilment of the ultimate goal of making elected assemblies perform in more inclusive ways in a Europe of gender and ethnic diversity. In this sense, the study's roots lie in the already successful claims-making of women's movements, and it takes the debate forward by discussing different kinds of women's representation rights, as expressed by ordinary citizens, law-makers and ethnic minority women's organizations.

The starting point: women's movements' demands for gender balance in elective assemblies

We accept McBride and Mazur et al.'s (2010:241) contention that 'in Western post-industrial democracies, women's movements have had remarkable success in achieving procedural access and policy response since the 1960s'. Our contribution to the project of understanding the 'remaking of citizenship' for women is embedded in the initial achievements of movements claiming political presence in elective office. These resulted in many new sets of party rules for candidate selection and in a marked increase in elected women to 42 per cent in the Nordic area and an average of 21 per cent across the rest of Europe (IPU, 2012).

In some Nordic countries, claims for women's political presence in representative assemblies are as old as the suffrage movement itself. Finnish women and men obtained the right to vote in 1906 and, with 10 per cent of women parliamentarians, it was for very long the world leader. Yet proportions of women hardly rose in Nordic countries until the 1970s, when four of the Nordic countries passed the 20 per cent threshold. This advance was due to the mobilizations of the autonomous women's movements together with women's groups inside political parties across the ideological spectrum, which demanded that parties introduce special measures such as targets, quotas and capacity-building for potential female candidates (Freidenvall, Dahlerup and Skjeie, 2006). It took place in an overall political climate supportive of equality as a matter of principle (Dahlerup and Freidenvall, 2005). Elsewhere in Europe the presence of women parliamentarians remained virtually stagnant at very low levels –around 4 per cent in Britain and France – until feminist pressure on the French Socialist party resulted in its acceptance of gender quotas: it fielded a high-profile 30 per cent of women in the 1979 European Parliament elections. With feminists active inside other Left and nascent Green parties around the world, concepts of political equality and representation were increasingly challenged to include attention to gender (see Lovenduski and Hills, 1981).

In the 1990s women's movement claims for women's political *presence* was reformulated in a more demanding way: gender parity (50–50 per cent) or gender balance (40–60 per cent) in all elective bodies. In France, *démocratie paritaire* (parity democracy) was claimed by feminist Deputy[1] Gisele Halimi on philosophical grounds (Halimi, 1994, Ramsay, 2003:66), and the idea travelled widely. Socialist International Women, the grouping of feminists in socialist and social-democratic parties, endorsed gender balance in the 1980s (see Threlfall, 2007) and countered male-centred arguments by publishing a statement of principle: achieving a balanced representation of the genders 'counted as a more important goal than pragmatic objections that suitable women were unavailable' (Socialist International Women, 1995). The *European Summit of Women in Power* organized by the European Commission in Athens in 1992 endorsed gender balance in terms of having no less than 40 per cent nor more than 60 per cent of candidates of either sex fielded for each party list. By the end of the year, the Party of European Socialists of the European Parliament had adopted gender-balance in its founding documents (Hix and Lesse, 2002).

The United Nations 4th World Conference on Women held in Beijing in 1995 finally obtained the member-states' endorsement of its longstanding goal of 'a full and equal share in political decision-making' for women (Beijing Declaration and Platform for Action, 1995). Attempting to get this implemented, the 2003 Congress of the Socialist International called for 'a higher quality of political decision-making', meaning that one-third of parliamentarians should be female (Socialist International, 2003, Jonas, 2005).

The discourse on gender parity representation and other equality measures encountered particular difficulties in European post-communist countries. The participation of women in the (virtually powerless) parliaments of Communist regimes in some countries even exceeded 30 per cent, partly due to an older form of quotas used by the single-party system, that relied on party appointments. But after the multiparty elections of the 1990s, women's presence plummeted to 5 per cent (Montgomery 2003:1, Fig. 1.1). The eastern European regimes had made abundant use of an official discourse of gender equality, and when they collapsed, the discourse became unpopular. From 2004, countries joining the EU became exposed to a different gender discourse and had to implement all the EU's equality laws. Women's organizations gained access to the campaigning European Women's Lobby, amongst other international bodies advocating equality and political empowerment. By 2010, around 15 Central and Eastern European parties had adopted some form of voluntary party quota, and five countries had passed legislation (calculated from The Quota Project database, 2010). In Poland and in Macedonia this achievement was the result of mobilization by grass-roots women's movements, both outside and inside the parties (Dimitrievska, 2004; Fuszara, 2006, 2008).

These claims for gender balance in political assemblies had mostly been made by women's movements *in the name of women as a single group* – a strategy that can be justified by speedy advances in countries such as Spain, Poland (see Fuszara, 2010) and Macedonia, and in many countries of the developing world. Globally, over one hundred parties in 67 countries had been convinced to adopt party rules and 52 countries had passed national legislation by 2011 (calculated from The Quota Project, 2011). The undifferentiated demand for 'more women' was based on the perception that all kinds of women were, and still are, excluded from legislatures simply because of their gender. Indeed, the unified approach fosters broad strategic coalitions between many different women's organizations, and forges a new 'strategic sisterhood' (see Nyhagen Predelli and Halsaa, 2012). Yet worldwide, women's political empowerment remains limited to a 20 per cent share of the legislative positions in Lower Houses (IPU at 31.08.2011). Put another way, men still occupy 80 per cent of parliamentary seats in the world and 78 per cent of those in Europe – clearly, worldwide political citizenship for women has not been achieved.

The conceptual background

Political citizenship and representation

The starting point of this three-part study of missing elements of political citizenship for women was an acceptance of the argument for 'descriptive' representation as theorized in feminist analyses: political assemblies should mirror the gendered proportions of the population. The reasons to some extent echo the old arguments for women's suffrage: it is a question of justice. The *justice argument* – women shall have half the seats because women are half the population – is the foundation of the political demand for parity outlined above. Women do not have to prove whether they are similar to, or different from, men, better or worse, nor that they will make a difference. Political scientist Anne Phillips shifts the burden of proof to men, asking: 'by what 'natural' superiority of talent or experience could men claim a right to dominate assemblies?' (1995:65). Nonetheless, demands for suffrage and for equal representation have also been based on two other arguments (Dahlerup, 1978, Hernes, 1982): the need for representation of women's life experiences, *the experience argument;* and *the interest argument*, based on the belief that a conflict of interests exists between men and women on a number of issues, which implies that men cannot represent women.

We also accept that the concept of a universal citizen is static, gender blind and hides inequalities: dominant (male, white) ideas and perspectives in society are left unquestioned. Carole Pateman (1989), for example, argues that women's struggles for civil, political and social rights have not followed along the same lines as the progression identified in Marshall's classic paradigm (1950:10–11), but this tends to be ignored, leaving women's claims and struggles outside of the domain of *political* citizenship (see the discussions by Strasser, this volume, and Nyhagen Predelli et al., this volume). Thus, universal citizenship conceals the fact we do not all have the *same needs* and interests, nor start from the same position in relation to power and resources.

In addition, we also see political citizenship as a *practice* that can be *performed* through the formal structures of political representation. For citizens standing both in the locus of *representee* and of *representor*, accessing and enjoying political citizenship is dependent on being represented and on performing the representative role. These notions of political citizenship build on Hanna Pitkin's (1967:209–11) dimensions of representation in which *formal* representation is complemented by *descriptive* representation (the resemblances between the representee-citizens and the representor-parliamentarians), leading to the demand for female parliamentarians in equal proportion to the female population. Her notion of *substantive* representation (the political outcome of representatives acting in the interest of the represented, in a manner responsive to them) is discussed in relation to women parliamentarians. The relation between women's descriptive representation and their substantive representation is a key field in contemporary research on gender and politics, though in fact research on the former is far more developed than research on the latter (Celis et al., 2008; Dahlerup, 2009; Wängnerud, 2009). Anne Phillips suggests that there is indeed a link between the *presence* of advocates and the substance of policy outcomes when she claims that 'when policies are worked out *for* rather than *with* a politically excluded constituency, they are unlikely to engage with all relevant concerns' (1995:13, emphasis added) and 'when those charged with making the political decisions are predominantly drawn from one of the two sexes or one of what may be numerous ethnic groups, this puts the others in the category of political minors' (1995:39). If descriptive representation helps to engender substantive representation, then a fuller and more inclusive political citizenship for women requires women parliamentarians to be allowed the capacity to act for women. We term any lack of freedom or inability in this regard the agency deficit – a missing domain of citizenship for women.

The following statement from Iris Marion Young (2000:134) neatly captures three aspects of representation, in effect framing our study:

> First, I feel represented when someone is looking after the interests I take as mine and share with some others. Secondly, it is important to me that the principles, values, and priorities that I think should guide political decisions are voiced in discussions. Finally, I feel represented when at least some of those discussing and voting on policies understand and express the kind of social experience I have because of my social group position and the history of social group relations.

In this extract one can find the subjective perception of a person who feels s/he is being represented at the institutional level by national or local representatives; then there is the element of *substantive* representation when values (such as gender equality and the interests of minority women) are voiced in political society and taken into account in the decision-making process; and then there is the stress placed on who the decision-makers are: some of them must be people with whom s/he shares a *descriptive* likeness so that 'the kind of social experience I have because of my social group' is reflected in legislation.

Thus, changing the meaning and practice of political citizenship implies and requires a more dynamic interaction between people, citizens' organizations and public institutions. It also involves marginalized groups defining their own needs and interests, bringing in voices that are usually silent, or silenced, and making relevant institutions more responsive to groups that are excluded from decision-making (see also kennedy-macfoy, this volume).

Representation and parliamentary studies

Two other literatures inspired the research on which this chapter is based. In relation to the question of the 'citizens' satisfaction deficit', the long-standing literature on parliamentarians' links to their electoral districts and its residents in single-member (one representative per electoral district) electoral systems was a starting point. The works of Bogdanor (1985) and Norton (2002) do much to de-mystify the nature of links between parliamentarian representors and the represented, while the notion of the 'personal vote' set out by Cain, Ferejohn and Fiorina (1987) is also relevant, in so far as it pays attention to the political attachment that voters may form with individual parliamentarians. Nonetheless our work in Sweden, Poland, Spain and Macedonia required us to rethink much that has been written, since these states use proportional representation systems with multimember constituencies, in which electors cannot focus their representational needs on one legislator, and the team of legislators has a very large area to represent.

The second literature taken on board – for the research on the agency gap – was that on women politicians. The older pre-feminist work focused on legislators' individual careers and achievements (e.g. Currell, 1974, Tinker, 1983, Prabhavathi, 1991, Rathke, 1992, Berman, 1994), while later studies looked at their effectiveness for advancing feminist policy goals, linking into theories of substantive representation (e.g. Jones and Jónasdottir, 1988/2008; Coote and Patullo, 1990; Skjeie, 1992; Inglehart and Norris, 2003; Childs, 2004, International Idea, 2005; Mateo Díaz, 2005; Lovenduski, 2005a).

Representation and ethnicity

Our three-pronged approach also sought to confront the challenge of incorporating perspectives on ethnicity and diversity. After a long post-war history of migrations from colonies and new states that saw the growth of settled, indigenous and naturalized ethnic minority populations, and after new twenty-first century migration patterns, what needs attention is the formal political representation of increasingly multicultural European electorates, as well as their voiced claims. Yuval-Davis (2008) pointed out that if the enjoyment of citizenship is the ability to have an input into decision-making at all levels, this cannot be limited only to the formal institutions of a *nation*-state: participation in informal networks and decision-making, such as women's organizations, should also be recognized. Taking ethnic diversity into account, she argues that political citizenship as membership of the nation-state at the national level may not be relevant for all, since people may feel membership of, and deploy power and decision-making in non-national arenas and networks (Yuval-Davis, 1997a, 2008), such as within ethnic minority communities or strongly single-ethnic neighbourhoods. Hence, gender awareness-raising, lobbying and campaigning by organizations composed of *minority* women's groups are examples of citizenship practices that can easily be overlooked, as if they were not part of the/a women's movement/s. Thus, a number of these were included.

It was also important to attend to diversity amongst minority women's groups: different nationalities and ethnic minority groups may not have a common women's movement history; and may enjoy, or lack, connections to women's advocacy organizations in their country of origin. Additionally, Hardy-Fanta (2006), who applied an intersectional approach to the political representation of African-American, Latino/a and Asian-American elected officials in the United States, demonstrated the importance of understanding the political agency of people of colour, particularly women of colour. She concluded that in order to understand the workings of political systems, the intersections of gender and ethnicity must be given particular attention and become separate empirical research questions.

Crucially, parallel to the trend towards the politicization of ethnicity in the sense of the emergence of ethnic minorities as political actors (Bird, Saalfeld and Wust, 2011:2) recent decades have witnessed the emergence of organizations of ethnic minority women in Europe, composed of newcomers and settled residents, constituting a new wing of civil society. Scholars focusing on women's political representation need to take this into account, particularly as it poses a new challenge of inclusion to parties in their gatekeeper roles vis-à-vis legislative arenas. Therefore we propose that feminist discussions of representation currently move along two separate tracks in Europe, a by now well-established 'gender track', and a separate, lightly trodden, 'ethnicity track'. Moreover we contend that the issue of representation for *minority women* remains poorly understood.

Thus, building on Nira Yuval-Davis's (2006) term *intersectionalizing citizenship*, this study advocates the need to *intersectionalize political representation* as well (see Freidenvall and Dahlerup, 2009 for a more detailed presentation of this view). An *intersectional lens* helps in the analysis of the ways in which structural patterns of inclusion and exclusion are shaped and affected by more than one factor and how these factors interact and often produce new effects. Thus our research asked the following questions: To what extent do individual citizens and representatives of minority women's organizations feel represented? How and by whom do they prefer to be represented? And, who do members of parliament perceive themselves as representing?

Approaches and methods

Seeking to develop a perspective which *intersectionalizes representation* meant involving a diversity of respondents in which ethnic minority respondents were over-represented in relation to their presence in the society of the countries studied. The fieldwork for the study deployed a mixed methods approach with discussion groups with ordinary citizens and denizens (non-national residents), and key informant interviews with individual parliamentarians and leaders of grass-roots ethnic minority organizations.[2] We carried out 20 taped discussion groups of two hours each, in order to address citizens' perspectives and the question of the 'satisfaction deficit', involving nearly 160 participants in 10 locations across four countries (Spain, Poland, Macedonia and UK). For the organizations' perspectives and the question of the 'representation deficit', we conducted over 60 interviews with spokespersons (whether leaders or organizers) from minority women's organizations in four countries (Spain, Poland, Macedonia, Sweden). For the parliamentarians' perspective and the question of their 'agency deficit', we interviewed with over 90 parliamentarians, both women and men, in five countries (Macedonia, Poland, Spain, Sweden and the UK).[3]

The rationale for the selection of countries was one of geographical spread: one country from the Nordic, western, southern, and eastern parts of the European Union, selected because each corresponded to the native language of at least one member of the research team; plus one non-EU state, chosen for its multiethnic party system. These countries included states with single-member and multimember electoral systems; with high and low levels of female representation, and with varying or no rules on gender quotas for candidates in elections. They included both 'old' and 'new' democracies, both ethnically relatively homogeneous and relatively diverse countries, and former colonial powers. However, the purpose was not to produce country comparisons, but to gather qualitative material from a wide range of European sources, in order to diagnose general problems (such as barriers to representation of women's interests), to pick out tendencies (such as who, in the opinion of minority group members, may represent them well), and to highlight solutions preferred by respondents (e.g. minority quotas) rather than pointing to inter-country differences.

The 'satisfaction deficit': citizens' perspectives on political inclusion

This part of our study looked at citizens' views about how they are represented. Conventional studies of the representational process focus on the orientations of *parliamentarians* rather than citizens, within the frame of the former's success and re-election. The citizens' view of descriptive representation and the need for resemblance or likeness in their representatives has not been researched in any detail. Bill Clinton announced on taking office, 'I want my government to look like America' (Morris, 2007). But would representation by resemblance make citizens feel represented and included? We also argue that part of the 'satisfaction deficit' is an insufficiency in the conventional form in which citizens are represented. In democracies, voters are asked to vote in order for parliaments to be filled with members from all the electoral districts and the Prime Minister to be selected, but district residents – constituents – do not, in practice, enjoy *the citizenship right to be politically represented* in ways that make them feel included in the political system, only to vote to choose their formal representatives. This is arguably a key deficit in a democratic society, particularly in one with participative structures and opportunities.

The participants in each country were groups of ethnic majority men from former shipyard cities (Glasgow, Bilbao, Gdansk) and landlocked Skopje; groups of ethnic majority capital city women (London, Madrid, Warsaw, Skopje); groups of Muslim women (Leicester, Barcelona, Bialystok, Skopje); and groups of ethnic minority men and women (London, Madrid, Warsaw, Skopje). Their oral statements and preferences expressed in a paper ranking exercise that was carried out at the end of the discussions were the basis for the analysis presented here.[4] Several ways were discovered in which the satisfaction deficit manifests itself.

Firstly, feelings of exclusion from the formal representation system were expressed in a homogeneously critical voice throughout the countries studied by both majority and minority citizens. Less than a handful reported feeling politically represented. The reasons given were similar: because all parties are the same, and politicians are motivated by personal ambition [... *they only care about their own interest. They don't care about the population* – Woman, Skopje], and they cannot be trusted to deliver on their promises [*We ordinary people should have benefited from his* (the Mayor's) *activities, but we don't see the final outcome* – Woman, Skopje]. Many declared they were unaware of having any representatives, or did not know the name of any for their electoral district, even when presented with a list for name recognition. Such critical voices suggested feelings of being politically abandoned, of being unable to control those they had voted for – let alone those they hadn't supported and don't want as their representatives – and sometimes even of being betrayed. This profiles a paradox: citizens can have the vote without experiencing a sense of political citizenship, even though the vote is a primary indication of it.

By contrast, a second collective voice was heard during the discussions, one that was more self-reflective and judicious and expressed interest in being politically included and represented. It emerged when discussions focused on actual relations between individual citizens and their representatives, when more fulfilling forms of citizenship through political representation were visualized and voiced. It was heard in discourses about wanting to have *more* contact with their representatives than at present, and more than they had ever imagined would be feasible. And when presented with four options of relations of representation, each one representing a type and level of intensity of contact with their representatives, the main preference of participants was for *periodic and regular contact* involving an exchange of views and of information by email or by post. A second possibility that would help them feel represented was to have *frequent contact* with their representatives, with these behaving as if they were the citizens' delegate to the parliament or assembly. Far fewer participants warmed to the option of having only *intermittent contact* with their representatives and fewer still preferred *disengagement* from the relationship of representation altogether. Although these findings are not representative for any of the countries, it is significant that in a deliberative situation, participants in discussions become mobilized towards engagement rather than towards disengagement.

In other words, in the citizen's imagination, feeling represented is associated with an ideal of an engaged political relationship with known individual(s) who are 'there' for them. Up to a point this can be associated with Pitkin's (1967:209) 'symbolic' representation and view of the function of representation as acting 'in a manner responsive' to the represented. Under majoritarian single-member systems, responsiveness has been understood by previous analysts to mean parliamentarians servicing constituents' individual problems as if they were 'errand-boys', as Dogan (2007) called them (see also Searing, 1994). In this study by contrast, the responsiveness that participants envisaged was mainly a public-issue or policy-oriented *interaction* with representatives, that is, a form of engagement. In addition, participants did not identify with what they perceived to be the current model of relations of representation in which representatives legislate as they think fit or along party lines without reporting back to the district that elected them. They associated this with fears about politicians not fulfilling their promises.

It is also significant that the two more interactive options of representational relationship mentioned above (labelled 'periodic' or 'frequent' contact) are not even on offer as a rule in the countries studied – not even in the UK despite its tradition of Members of Parliament (MPs) in the House of Commons playing an active role in the constituency. In fact, few UK MPs report back on their legislative activity, and few constituents ever use their MPs to communicate their views on policy matters. In this study, parliamentarians, local, regional and national, were perceived as not playing their role as *representatives* – appearing nameless, invisible, distant *legislators* or *party agents*, a perception that could be understood as a failure of symbolic representation. For citizens to feel represented, parliamentarians would have to *perform as representatives* as well as legislators in *inclusive, informative and transparent ways*. This profiles a notion of political citizenship as the enjoyment of active relations of representation, and articulates a latent demand. Both pose a considerable challenge to the current political class across Europe.

As to the question of *descriptive representation* for citizens in general, the discussion groups revealed some key issues. Participants were given the opportunity to rank how important it was for them to have a set of representatives who can each reflect their ethnic, religious or gendered identities (in contrast to displaying ideological affiliations, political skills or occupying the desired geographical tier of representation). The study found that resemblance *does* play a role in people's preferences of representatives, but it did not emerge as strongly as might have been expected given the deliberative setting, the characteristics of the discussion groups, and the campaigns to get more women into politics.

Across the four countries, the majority women were evenly divided between those preferring to be represented by a woman or a man, with only the London group clearly preferring a woman. Despite there being cases where embodied resemblance in a politician was appealing, it was not a dominant wish among any of the majority women, who primarily wished for very knowledgeable, well-trained and experienced people. In some cases, this in fact signified somebody educated and rational *like them* (another form of likeness not yet explored in the descriptive representation argument), and in others, it indicated someone with greater educational achievements and capacities than the women participants themselves. This suggests further research around what could be termed non-resemblance/non-likeness or distance preference.

Among majority men, feeling represented via an embodied likeness to the representative was present but not strong either. It was not essential for representatives to have the same background or to be someone who understood the lives of people like them. But majority *men* did prefer a *male* to a female representative, though not strongly so, and were not interested in the dual one man/one woman option, thus displaying some gendered preferences. There was also a relatively high preference (5th priority among 30 characteristics) for someone with *no* religion, which sometimes reflected the participant's own lack of belief. But for majority men also, knowledge, training and experience was the overall preferred characteristic of a representative that could make them to feel represented. These features were considered ideal in a representative by both men who manifested themselves as relatively *close* to possessing them themselves and by men who saw themselves as *far* from possessing them. This is significant for the current policy concern about the need for representatives to resemble (be close to) the population, since it appears to contradict it: both the 'distance' (non-resemblance) and the 'closeness' of representatives can generate feelings of being well-represented.

As to the mixed-gender groups of participants from the principal racialized ethnic minority in each country, they did display attachment to representation through resemblance/likeness, though in particular ways. There was a preference for *male* representatives among the Warsaw Vietnamese and the London African Caribbean groups, both of which contained women; and a preference for women, among the Skopje Roma group containing men. But in general the Roma specified they wanted to be represented by a Roma person. In general among ethnic minority groups an interesting preference was found, namely 'resemblance at one remove': to be represented by 'someone who understands the life of people like me', who is neither as close as 'like me' nor as different and distant as the very knowledgeable and experienced person.

In addition, representation by resemblance/closeness was crucial for the Muslim women's groups, who ranked being represented by a Muslim as their top priority, across the four countries. This went hand in hand with representation by ethnic likeness (Magrebi and Tatar) in Barcelona and Bialystok. But when it came to gender, the Muslim representative was preferably a *man* in Leicester (another case of non-resemblance) but could be a woman among the Macedonian Albanians. Muslim women also valued being represented by likeness-at-one-remove ('someone who understands the life of people like me') – though to a lesser extent than the ethnic minority groups. And in clear contrast to the majority men and majority women, Muslim women valued the knowledgeable and highly experienced representative to a far lesser extent than other women (though a bit more than the Glasgow men).

All in all, these qualitative findings show that there is a deficit of effective political representation for citizens, in so far as research participants in a deliberative setting of the discussion group perceive their views are not sufficiently taken into account, and even feel excluded despite having a vote. But the remedy appears not to be the introduction of straightforward descriptive representation for all. Having a likeness to, or a shared characteristic with, a representative does not constitute a prerequisite for majority men and women to feel represented, though is an important factor among ethnic and religious minorities. For most, feelings of inclusion in the representation system are more likely to be generated by contact and a dialogue with politicians who are (or appear to be) knowledgeable, well trained and experienced and are willing to provide feedback on their work and explain their views and policy-political decisions.

The 'ethnic representation deficit': minority women's organizations' perspectives on political inclusion

Given the spread of regional levels of representation to meet the claims of historic national minorities in the five countries studied, today those who suffer a more evident 'ethnic representation deficit' are primarily the Roma, post Second World War settled populations emanating from former colonies, their descendants and twenty-first century new residents from other European countries and developing nations. Furthermore, some groups who are national minorities in some states are also migrants in other states.

Nevertheless, nowhere do they enjoy direct representation in parliament by members of their communities in proportionate numbers, given their significant presence in the total population. These circumstances can, of course, be linked to the fact that supposedly homogeneous ethnic groups are often composed of people with different sub-group identities, histories and cultures (Phillips, 2007), so that the remedy via descriptive representation, unlike for women, is rarely used.

To gain insights into the nature of this democratic deficit with respect to the presence and concerns of ethnic minority women, our research on the ethnic representation deficit chose to focus on how ethnic minority leaders of intermediary organizations such as NGOs – mostly set up and run by and for ethnic minority women – perceive this deficit, and how they visualize their political representation. In the five countries covered for this part of our tripartite study, minority women have formed their own organizations, though in rather varied ways: either around policy issues (e.g. combating violence against women), or around national, ethnic, religious or regional background, or again, together with men or separately in women-only organizations (cf. chapters by Nyhagen Predelli et al. and kennedy-macfoy, this volume).

Firstly, what ideas on political inclusion do women who are organized in minority women's organizations profess? We asked spokespersons for the organizations (mostly leaders and organizers, often calling themselves 'coordinators') whether they prefer to be politically represented through likeness, by someone from the same or similar ethnic background or appearance (descriptive representation). And do they expect elected representatives with minority backgrounds to act in the interest of their ethnic group (i.e. substantive representation)? What are their most important criteria for representation? Many of the answers reflect the dilemmas faced by minority organizations in all the countries studied, illustrated by the following remark:

> Ha, ha! Difficult question! I think it should be a woman [meaning from my ethnic background]. But it probably has to be one with my feminist background. We are accustomed to being chameleons – and this may be a good thing. We go to church on Sundays, and then we go to our feminist meetings afterwards. (Representative of a Minority Women's Association, Poland)

The respondents were asked to choose between the following four alternatives. Would they prefer to be represented in political spheres by...:

1. A. a woman from *any minority* community.
2. B. a woman from their *own ethnic* group.
3. C. any *woman* (including from the majority community).
4. D. a *man* from their *own ethnic* group.

Firstly, it is revealing that leaders of women's organizations did not choose the possible option of supporting a male candidate from their *own* ethnic group (D). Asked to choose between a male candidate for elective office from her *own* community and a woman candidate from *any* community, a large proportion of the interviewees chose the woman 'because I am a feminist' – provided that she has a *minority* background. This position is illustrated in the following remarks:

> Question: By whom would you prefer to be represented in elected decision-making bodies?
> Answer: It is extremely important that there is somebody who understands how it is to be immigrant, but it does not have to be someone with the same ethnic background as me. But an immigrant woman. Preferably a woman with a background as an immigrant. A woman who understands the problems and difficulties we have and with whom you can have a talk.

> Question: Rather a minority woman than a man from your country of birth?
> Answer: Absolutely. I don't think it comes naturally to men to discuss questions about women's health, education, violence against women and the like. It is not given any priority [by the men – interviewer] (Representative of a minority women's association, Sweden).

> Question: Would you feel better represented by someone from your country of birth?
> Answer: No, no. On the contrary. I have a big problem with politicians from my country of birth! (laughing). I feel absolutely best represented by a person from another country [other than my home country – interviewer] someone who shares the experience of being an immigrant. (Representative of a minority association, Sweden).

Preference B, for a woman from one's own ethnic group, revealed itself to be complex. Many respondents argued that their specific group is severely underrepresented and must see an increase in the number of political representatives. But while advocating a better representation of their own ethnic group and of women, these leaders felt that not just any woman will do. Some expressed the view that they do not feel represented by certain specific women *in their own* group. A respondent from the secretariat of a Roma foundation in Spain claimed that she prefers a Roma *feminist* and criticized the existing Roma women politicians for not being sufficiently qualified. In other words, just *any minority* woman will not do. The leaders of the Kurdish, Iraqi, Moroccan and Afro-Swedish Women's Associations were part of the mainly non-European second wave of immigrants to Sweden. Most of these entered Sweden as refugees or asylum seekers in the 1980s and 1990s, in contrast to those who entered for employment purposes in the 1950s, 1960s and 1970s, who were mainly Finns and other Nordic citizens, Greeks, Italians, Turks, Poles and citizens of former Yugoslavia. The second wave leaders interviewed claimed that a white Finnish woman could not represent them, even if she was from a minority. Though Finnish immigrants also suffer from socio-economic disadvantages and language difficulties, they are not perceived as 'immigrants' because they are thought not to suffer from the same kind of discrimination as non-European immigrants. Thus, perceived discrimination seemed to be a basis for needing to be politically represented. These responses are comparable to those of ordinary citizens in the discussion groups in our study, who would ideally be represented *not* by someone very like them, but someone 'who understands the life of people like me even though their background is different', in other words, likeness 'at one remove'.

Key informant interviews thus revealed a specific set of preferences combining gender and ethnicity in significant ways. The most frequent preference (A), for being represented by any *minority* woman, underscores representation by likeness on two counts, gender and outsider/newcomer status, which trumped likeness on ethnic grounds. This is reminiscent of Pitkin's distinction between 'standing for' (which requires some *likeness*) rather than 'acting for' which does not. Interviewees also revealed a dual awareness of gender issues, intertwined with awareness of xenophobia against newcomers and discrimination against immigrant women in particular. It is significant that in this qualitative selection of key respondents, neither the narrowest, potentially sectarian form of representation (only my own ethnic group), nor the 'feminist unity' option (any woman, always) were prominent. Only close attention to intersections of ethnicity and gender revealed the preference for the nuanced option of feeling represented by a woman with a similar experience of exclusion as an outsider/newcomer.

While categories such as gender, ethnicity, sexual preference and class are not given 'once and for all' (hooks, 1982; Crenshaw, 1991a; Collins, 1991), empirical research on the interaction between them in relation to political representation is still required. This study of the organizational perspective of spokespeople served to confirm that, unquestionably, there remains a representation deficit for ethnic minorities, and that the gap cannot be bridged without attention to the intersection of gender and ethnicity. Current forms of representation are not inclusive enough to garner the approval of organized minority women and leaders, the most salient example being the Roma respondents:

> For ethnic minorities there is no representation. For the Gypsies' issue there is no representation in politics. (Woman, Roma women's organization, Spain)

Perhaps this very deficit led the same respondent to value cooperation with all women's groups in the new national Council of Women (Consejo de la Mujer), stating that

> We bear in mind that we are women and that unites us, it does not matter what culture we come from. (Woman, Roma women's organization, Spain)

As has been the case with most women's organizing throughout history, ambivalences and near-impossible strategic choices pose a challenge to women's agency. In their wish to work across cultural cleavages, some of the selected organizations even come close to what Nira Yuval-Davis (2008) labels 'transversal politics'. This implies combining standpoint epistemology – the world is seen differently from our different positions – with the idea that 'notions of difference should encompass, rather than replace, notions of equality' (Yuval-Davis, 2010). We found that many minority women's organizations use multiple strategies but also that these strategies are context-specific. However, in an Europeanized and globalized era, the context is almost never just the local or national setting, as Yuval-Davis reminds us (1997a). The Roma Women's Association in Spain was the most striking as it belonged to the state-run women's council's at the local, regional and national level, to the national Romany organization, and to the state-level Romany women's federation (CAMIRA), while planning a European level intervention as well. As the spokesperson said: '... well, we are collaborating wherever we can'. And most of the organizations interviewed in Spain were not averse to engaging with political parties in order to gain influence, perhaps because ethnic minority women's organizations feel they are not represented in Spanish politics. This engagement is illustrated by what was said by the coordinator for the mobilization of immigrants in the Spanish Socialist Party, who claimed that 10 years ago when immigrants came mostly from Latin America, newcomer women were usually leftists and socialists (perhaps because they were escaping repressive regimes as well as poverty and unemployment), but today, with new arrivals from Morocco and other North African countries, this has changed. Today, even the Conservative Party organizes immigrant associations, believing there are votes to be gained from those who have taken out Spanish nationality.

In general, women's organizations, both minority and majority, have always displayed ambivalences in their relation to elected women representatives, as reported in the next section on the women parliamentarians' perspective.

The 'agency deficit': parliamentarians' perspectives on their citizenship practice

The third citizenship deficit that prevents women from enjoying full political citizenship is what we have called the 'agency deficit' experienced by women parliamentarians after they become elected: they find themselves unable to choose how to fulfil their representational role, despite their political right to stand as candidates and take up office if elected. Little is known about the aspirations and preferences of women parliamentarians in Europe in the era of growing claims for gender parity representation, yet our research reveals that they feel they are the subject of a series of constrained choices regarding how and whom they wish to actively represent in the course of the lawmaking process.

Parliaments are key locations in terms of women's interest representation, yet ever since they won the right to stand for election, only a small number of women have managed to actually enter parliament. Their limited presence has dogged the progress of women-friendly (Hernes, 1987) policies through the legislature. Feminist political scientists argue that their experiences and viewpoints have limited purchase over parliamentary life, which is still dominated by a male political culture (Ford, 2010; Inglehart and Norris, 2003; Leyenaar, 2004, Lovenduski, 2005a; Diaz, 2005; Stevens, 2007). The idea in feminist research of the need to reach a *critical mass* of deputies – say 30 per cent – before substantive representation can come into effect through women-friendly policies has been challenged by the notion of *critical acts* (Dahlerup, 2006b:15) in which powerful individuals or even smaller groups of women politicians can achieve serious advances for women. Yet we found the need for a minimum mass was still expressed by women parliamentarians themselves, especially where there are indeed less than 30 per cent of them.

In order to investigate this 'agency deficit' suffered by women deputies with regard to their freedom to perform interest representation, interviews with female and male parliamentarians from different parties were conducted in the United Kingdom, Macedonia, Poland, Spain and Sweden. Women's presence in these countries' parliaments varied from the rather low figure of 20 per cent in Poland and 22 per cent in the UK, to 31 per cent in Macedonia, 37 per cent in Spain and 45 per cent in Sweden, the third highest in the world at the time (IPU at 31.08.11).

Despite their strikingly different situations and trajectories, interviewees in all five countries commented on the positive changes that had been occurring both in descriptive terms (proportionate presence) and in the substantive/policy-related representation of women, and were articulate regarding the barriers and constraints they faced. These consisted mainly of the difficulties encountered both in the process of becoming a Deputy in parliament, and in performing their roles as representatives. Deputies (mostly women, but men as well) claimed that it was more difficult for women to hold high public office. In each country, interviewees would pronounce an almost identical phrase 'a woman must be twice or three times better than a man to get an equal position to a man'.

In the context of the notion of the agency deficit, the study focused on women parliamentarians' agency to choose the focus of their representative role: Whom do the Deputies wish to represent? Who in parliament actually represents women? The majority of parliamentarians, both men and women, saw themselves as representatives of the whole society, of all inhabitants of the country, of their constituency and of the electorate in the constituency – despite the contradictions inherent to such a vision. And respondents of both genders stressed that they wanted all Deputies, male or female, to represent both women and men. At the same time, many Deputies claimed that in actual practice, women wished to represent women more often than men did. There were many reasons mentioned for this: male politicians are typically less interested in equality and women's issues; women's issues are under-appreciated; and men's and women's life experiences are different.

> We should all represent our common interests. However, while the society remains so chauvinist, it will be much easier for a woman than for a man to understand other women … . It is easier for me to understand what a girl can feel, who was basically kidnapped from her country to make her a prostitute here, on Plaza de España. I can understand her much easier than a man who is her client. (Woman Deputy, Spanish Congress (lower house of parliament), Socialist Party/PSOE)

Many women Deputies, when asked whether they feel they represent women and their interests, claimed to represent both men and women. They did not believe they represented women only, or women most of all. Among those who explained what 'being a representative of women' meant to them, three attitudes and interpretations of the role may be distinguished: (1) some Deputies described themselves just as a representative of women; (2) others knew that women considered them their representatives and they felt they could not betray their trust; (3) others emphasized the fact that they were advocates for women's rights. The last approach to representing women was employed not only by women, but also by men.

However, many women Deputies emphasized that the key issue was not for women's interests to be represented by women but for the political agenda to change due to women's presence and activities: in other words they did not want to be women's sole representatives, but rather they wanted women's interests to be a mainstream parliamentary responsibility. Some claimed that *who* represents women's interests was not important; what mattered was that without women's involvement, these interests and issues would never have become the subject of political debate:

> It is important that their [i.e. women's] interests are represented at all. And actually when you start to get a breakthrough, men start to get involved. (Woman MP, UK House of Commons, Labour Party)

A great many Deputies claim that women's interests can be represented both by men and by women. However, women Deputies in particular stress that this claim is more of an idealized notion than actual reality, because for reasons of similarity of life experiences, women make better advocates of women's interest. In fact, women's issues tend not to become a priority until they have found their way onto a woman parliamentarian's agenda. Moreover, many women deputies felt a certain obligation to represent women, especially when their roots lay in women's sections of political parties or in women NGOs. Even women parliamentarians with no such roots are approached by women's groups with requests for representation. In countries with a relatively long history of high levels of women in the main legislature, such as Sweden, male politicians have absorbed part of the equality agenda brought into the elected assemblies through a combined effort by the women's movements and female politicians. Many deputies explained how this descriptive representation was a precondition of later substantive representation. However, the respondents explained that this change in the political agenda was a long-term and difficult process, requiring constant efforts and relentless maintenance of interest in women's issues.

The study indicates that women's participation in the exercise of power – once in parliament – is on the increase in terms of Lukes's (2004) power dimension of *agenda control*. Those in power prevent issues that challenge their power from entering public debate. Women parliamentarians who thought of themselves as representatives of women wanted to focus on issues that are important for women, but found these absent or even eliminated from public discourse. Yet they succeeded in introducing them onto official agendas, thus effecting a shift in Lukes's power relations of agenda control, though the intensity of this shift varies from country to country. Women Deputies claimed to have initiated legislative debates on violence against women and the underrepresentation of women in politics, previously absent from public debate; and even on controversial questions such as reproductive rights in Poland and trafficking of women in Macedonia.

Lukes (2004) also discussed how those in power influence those subordinate to them to the extent that they accept the status quo as natural and optimal, even if their interests are clearly violated. This study found a number of women parliamentarians in every country, often from right-wing parties, who accept and enjoy their roles as mere support figures for their male leaders, and also found male parliamentarians who used the rhetoric of the 'natural' division of roles between the genders, the impossibility of a radical change in gender power relations due to the biological nature of women's maternal role. In contrast, all but two Swedish political parties call themselves 'feminist' in their programmatic documents, while women parliamentarians maintain a critical discourse against male dominance and women's marginalization in society – a reversal of the acceptance of subordination that Lukes typified.

The type of power relations that was discussed in the context of parliaments are also rampant inside political parties, where women strive to obtain agency and to secure outcomes favourable to them. The vast majority of women parliamentarians stressed that in practice they cannot act without party support. Asked if they ever felt conflict between being a women's representative and being a member of their political party, some recounted cases in which they had voted against the party line. Such a decision had been risky; it sometimes resulted in marginalization of the Deputy by her party and even in being removed from candidate lists. In the most difficult instances, the 'rebellious' Deputies were fined for their behaviour. In one extreme case, the woman in question left the party. It appears therefore that women alone are unable to effect change in areas of concern to them unless the interest of the political parties is first kindled and then prioritized. This was where their deficit of agency lay. Of course, male parliamentarians also have to tow the party line, but they are not in a comparable position, in so far as they are not seeking the agency to obtain the kind of conceptual and policy breakthroughs that deputies who see themselves as feminist are; and male deputies do not speak publicly about a moral duty to defend the interests of men. However, an ethnic minority, gay or disabled male Deputy might face a similar agency deficit as the women we interviewed.

Finally, the effectiveness of women parliamentarians, and their ability to exercise this form of citizenship practice – performing freely as representatives – was also constrained by a lack of clarity regarding what actually constitutes 'representing women's interests' in terms of the potential remedies offered to perceived problems. This led to a lack of unity of purpose among the women deputies. On the one hand, many respondents commented on how women are able to stand united in order to achieve shared goals such as measures against violence against women, and over placing an issue on the formal political agenda, for instance child care – even when they may in fact disagree on actual policy proposals such as the length of child-rearing leave. On the other, some women Deputies see long periods of paid leave as an indication of a respectful attitude to the role of mothers, while others think that long periods of leave reinforce the split between the private and public spheres and lead to women's continued exclusion from the job market (on this debate within feminism see Bergman et al., this volume). Defining 'women's interest' is an ongoing process, much of which is taking place outside parliament, in women's non-governmental organizations, the media and among specialists in universities and think-tanks. In this sense, the lack of a unified feminist agenda also constrains women deputies in their ability to perform forcefully as representatives of women.

Conclusion

This chapter investigated areas where political citizenship – in the sense of practices that citizens can engage in to take part in political society – remains deficient, identifying three political citizenship deficits. Firstly, the subjective experience of the deficit in citizens' satisfaction with political representation involved feeling marginal or even excluded from the relations of representation between elected parliamentarians and their constituents, as currently practiced, as well as perceiving their own lack of agency. It consisted of lack of knowledge, know-how, information and control over politics, politicians, and the performance of representatives. Yet it was found that for most citizens, symbolic inclusion in the representational order could be effected quite easily by their greater interaction with their representatives. Crucially, feeling represented could arise from the visibility of politicians who possessed the considerable knowledge, experience and training that citizens respect and see as necessary for conducting the complex business of governing and legislating. Citizens also understood that a situation of feeling well represented and satisfied with the system was unlikely to arise from representatives acting on their own, because these had to operate within party political frameworks. Nonetheless, they felt better represented if a politician kept a certain distance or independence from his/her party.

For the specific groups who felt more dissatisfied, overlooked or socially undervalued (such as Roma, Tartar and Muslim women), a sense of inclusion and representation would mainly come from a more visible political leadership composed of people who closely resembled them. By contrast, *majority* women did not generally perceive themselves as disenfranchised by the lack of resemblance with the *male* political establishment, only by the system as a whole. For instance, the Madrid majority women asserted that they did not believe any politician or government department, not even locally, would ever read any letter of complaint that they might write. The idea that they might influence a parliamentarian was applauded but impossible to believe in:

> ...that would be changing the concept, there is no chance of that, I don't see it... (Majority Woman, Madrid)

The question this raises is whether the arrival of more vocal women parliamentarians might serve to break through the public's sense of being condemned to a passive citizenship where others make the decisions without wanting to involve them, and might contribute to a stronger culture of greater interaction with representatives. Might women representatives play an effective role in reducing the general political satisfaction gap?

Secondly, and in contrast to the individual female voters or residents talking in focus groups, the main citizenship deficit experienced by *minority* women's *organizations* does not seem to be primarily one of inadequate agency nor lack of satisfaction, since the minority leaders and coordinators interviewed are organized in many ways, practicing political citizenship through lobbying and advocacy. Rather, it is an *ethnic representation deficit*. Leaders and coordinators do look to political parties, be they left or right, to keep organizations informed about up-coming elections, and invite political party spokespersons to meetings. Sometimes they even support female candidates. But their major focus (the reason for their existence) is necessarily the everyday problems that need to be solved, such as domestic burdens, work conditions and housing of the minority women they represent. These burdens, often involving discrimination, can often be specific to minority women and cause them to suffer from *both gendered and ethnic* forms of political exclusion when they are not addressed. The coordinators and leaders see parties both as gatekeepers of political inclusion and as an important potential collaborator, but as one that is not easy to access. Thus, for these organizations and the women for whom they act, the citizenship deficit is more one of insufficient political representation – a lack of agenda status – of their *concerns* as ethnic minority women and new residents.

As to how they would like to be represented, most of the minority women's organizations interviewed do not feel a need to be represented by someone from the *same* ethnic background, in contrast to the preferences of individual minority citizens and Muslim women. The leaders' preferences were (unwittingly) intersectional, namely for resemblance representation articulated through gender and ethnicity combined: they want to be represented by a woman (not a man), preferably by any *minority woman* who shares the experience of being marginalized.

Thirdly, there is a deficit of agency experienced by women parliamentarians. The opportunity provided by the interviews allowed them to give voice to their frustrations over the ongoing constraints on the performance of their chosen representational roles and on representing women's substantive interests in parliament. Thus we conclude that the original suffrage right – not just to vote but also to stand for election – in practice does not offer full political citizenship to women. Nor does it avoid the need to create equal access to positions of power for both sexes. Addressing this deficit requires a greater understanding and facilitation of the *citizenship practice of deciding how to represent*. Extensive sectors of women's movements demand that women's experiences and priorities should be on the legislative agenda and lead to policy change and implementation. But the legislatures do not offer the women who inhabit them a smooth ride. Parties, male Deputies, even female parliamentarians, continue to undervalue legislative interventions to foster women's full citizenship through substantive gender equality.

Overall, the study reveals how an intersectional approach to researching political representation – or *intersectionalizing representation* – highlights the political exclusion experienced by women. Without attention to the changing nature of intersecting axes of power, the experiences of a multitude of women who are positioned at the bottom of gender and racial/ethnic/ religious hierarchies risk being ignored. Similarly, without an intersectional perspective, gender-fair representation risks being a benefit for majority women only. In general, intersectionalizing representation implies opening up the political representation system to a greater diversity of citizens, not only those inhabiting the multiethnic and multicultural societies of which Europe is composed, but also those subject to other forms of discriminations, whether based on their sexuality, physical attributes and abilities, or travelling lifestyles.

The implication of this study's findings is that a broad debate is needed on the political and policy priorities of women and men, their differences and points of consensus. This could be informed by increased consultation with women's organizations, by the work of experts through parliamentary committees of enquiry and by the public practice of forms of deliberative democracy such as 'deliberative polling', 'citizens' juries' or 'consensus conferences'.[5] The latter involve the public in examining policy issues in considerable depth, calling in expert witnesses over a period of days, and can thereby include representatives of various social groups as participants. Together with increased outreach work by parliaments, explaining their work to the general public[6], and the setting up of interaction and feedback loops between representatives and their constituents, such initiatives could generate an elite and grass-roots consensus around prioritizing gender policies to achieve a fairer society. This could ultimately enliven and extend political citizenship for all.

Notes

1. 'Deputy/ies' is synonymous with member/s of parliament, except in the UK, where MP is used. Both are interchangeable with 'parliamentarian', 'legislator' and 'representative' except that the latter covers members of elected local and regional assemblies as well.
2. We want to thank those who assisted us with conducting and transcribing the interviews or focus groups: Maya Ernested, Jenny Hedström, Matilda Köhlmark, Ana Martínez, Anne Rudolph, Simonida Kacarska, Joanne Wilson, Magdalena Biejat, Joanna Fomina, Anna Konieczna, Marta Trembaczewska, Valentina Todorovska-Sokolowska, Marcin Sokolowski, the staff of Milward Brown SMG/KRC (Poland), THINKS Research (UK), BRIMA Gallup Intl.TNS (Macedonia), and Castelló Veintitrés, Salas de Argila SL, Salas Logismarket (Spain).
3. For further discussion of selection criteria, samples and methodology, see Threlfall (2009); Freidenvall and Dahlerup (2009); Fuszara (2010).
4. In the paper ranking exercise participants in the discussion group expressed preferences among 30 features of their ideal representatives by distributing 36 ranking points across 8 categories of features: (1) the number of representatives they have (electoral system); (2) the geographical level at which the representatives operate; (3) the kind and frequency of contact; (4) the ideas and policies of the ideal representative in relation to their party; (5) the kind of person they

would feel represented by in terms of likeness/closeness or distance from them; (6) the ethnic origin of the representative; (7) the religion of the representative; (8) the gender of the representative.

5. As advocated on the 'People and Participation' gateway. See http://www.people-andparticipation.net/display/Methods (accessed September 2011).

6. As carried out by the UK Parliament throughout 2010 and 2011: see UK Parliament, Parliamentary Outreach, http://www.parliament.uk/get-involved/outreach-and-training/

8
Remaking Citizenship from the Margins: Migrant and Minoritized Women's Organizations in Europe

madeleine kennedy-macfoy

Introduction

This chapter starts from the premise that an exploration of the contribution of migrant and minoritized women's organizations[1] is vital to any understanding of the processes of 'remaking citizenship' in contemporary Europe. It seeks to assess the role played by migrant and minoritized women's organizations by addressing three issues: firstly, the extent to which migrant and minoritized women's organizations in different national contexts use citizenship as a framework for their work; secondly, the organizations' perceptions of their relationship to wider women's and feminist movements; and thirdly, the particularities of migrant and minoritized women's efforts to mobilize on a platform of common needs, identities and interests, as distinct from those of majority women in European contexts.

The chapter is based on research that focused on migrant and minoritized women's organizations in three European countries: Belgium, England and Norway. Siim and Squires have argued that 'the emergence of diversity as a growing concern [in Europe] requires that comparative citizenship analyses develop ways of thinking about multiple inequalities and their intersections' (2007:404). Migrant and minoritized women's organizations are engaged in exactly this type of 'thinking' and 'doing'. Academic interest in migrant and minoritized women's organizations in different parts of Europe has grown slowly since the late 1990s (see for example Sudbury, 1998; Ouali, 2007; Ellerbe-Dueck, 2011). The FEMCIT project marks the first attempt to include such organizations within a framework that links women's citizenship to women's and feminist movements in European contexts (see Introduction, this volume, and Nyhagen Predelli et al., this volume). The research on which this chapter is based suggests that the collective interests addressed by migrant and minoritized women's organizations fall within the concerns of feminist citizenship scholarship of the past 20 years. Therefore, a focus on such organizations provides much-needed empirical evidence of the lived experiences of multiple and intersecting inequalities related to citizenship (see Yuval-Davis and Werbner, 1999a), and of the claims that arise from such experiences, in an age of multilevel governance (Siim and Squires, 2007).

'Mind the gap': between feminist theorizations and women's organizations' use of citizenship

Feminist theorizations: what does citizenship include/exclude?

Since the 1990s, feminist scholars have been actively engaging with the concept of citizenship, which re-emerged as a concept of interest during that decade amongst academics, politicians and journalists in Western democracies such as the UK (Phillips, 1993:75). Feminists sought to highlight the ways in which classical conceptualizations constrained access to the rights and privileges deriving from citizenship for women (see for example Dietz, 1987; Lister, 1997, 2003; Siim, 2000) and for other disadvantaged groups (Young, 1989; Yuval-Davis and Werbner, 1999a; Lewis, 2004b). There is, however, some considerable contestation amongst feminists over the usefulness of the concept: both in terms of the theorization of women's experiences and in terms of how women's organizations frame their claims and demands.

Ruth Lister is one of the strongest advocates for the usefulness of citizenship within feminism, arguing that it is pertinent for both theory and activism. Lister's starting point is the recognition that the process of *critically* reappropriating 'strategic concepts' such as citizenship is an important aspect of developing feminist political and social theory (1997:3). For Lister, citizenship is 'an invaluable strategic theoretical concept for the analysis of women's subordination and a potentially powerful political weapon in the struggle against it' (1997:195). Accordingly, feminists can use citizenship in three important ways: firstly, to show how women's exclusion has been central to the historical and traditional conceptualizations of liberal and republican approaches to citizenship (which have been most prevalent in European settings); secondly, to challenge the false universalism of the category 'woman' and to centralize the issue of difference; and thirdly, to address the tension between a gender analysis that is grounded in difference, and the inherent universalism of citizenship (1997:197). In terms of feminist praxis, Lister argues for an inclusive definition of political citizenship, through which 'women's 'accidental activism' in the interstices of the public and the private spheres, their active participation in a nascent global civil society and their contribution to the development of welfare citizenship come to be acknowledged and valued as acts of citizenship' (1997:199).

Other feminists view citizenship as being primarily about political participation. For example, Mary Dietz argues for a democratic conception of citizenship, since 'the power of democracy rests in its capacity to transform the individual...into a special sort of political being, a citizen among other citizens' (1987:14; see also Phillips, 1993:85). Proponents of this view accept the fundamental feminist argument the public/private dichotomy is a false one, and that 'the personal' is in fact deeply political. However, some, like Anne Phillips, are equally keen to stress that there is a 'qualitative' difference between the public and private spheres. Phillips calls this is a 'new language of citizenship', because it breaks from the discourses of the second wave feminist movement by accepting a fundamental difference between the public and the private, since that which is properly called 'politics' can only be practiced in the public space (1993:86). She argues further, that what makes citizenship valuable to feminism is precisely 'the way it restates the importance of political activity' (1993:87). In Dietz's view, feminists will be able to 'claim a truly liberatory politics of their own' only through a focus on the political potential of citizenship, rather than viewing the citizen as 'politically barren' and a 'bearer of rights alone' (1987:13–15).

An important difference between this type of feminist approach to citizenship and Lister's is the extent to which citizenship is viewed as covering a wide spectrum, or as limited to activities that can be labelled 'political', and how broadly the 'political' is defined. Phillips emphasizes that 'politics is a particular kind of activity, and not to be dissolved into everything else' (1993:86). However, for Lister (as for the authors this volume), political participation is only one of many important aspects of citizenship, and it should not be viewed as 'a measuring rod of citizenship' because many women would simply not 'measure up'. Instead, Lister proposes a distinction between *being* a citizen (status) and *acting* as a citizen (practice). To be a citizen is to enjoy the status of citizenship and the rights deriving from it, which enable social and political participation. To act as a citizen is to fulfil the potential that comes with being a citizen, but one does not stop being a citizen if one does not practice citizenship (Lister, 1997:41).

In this chapter, I suggest that women's activism within organizations is a key aspect of women's citizenship in two ways. Firstly, women's organizations stand out as important sites within which women enact[2] their political citizenship. Politics is conceived of broadly, in Held's terms, as being about power: 'that is about the *capacity* of social agents, agencies and institutions to maintain or transform their environment, social or physical' (cited in Lister, 1997:26, emphasis in the original). This broad conceptualization of politics is necessary if women's activism, which does not always take place through formal or public channels, but is no less political in its intent and effects, is to be recognized. Of course, not all of women's political actions can be labelled as acts of political citizenship. Phillips makes this point with the example of public campaigning for men to take on their equal share of domestic tasks: this clearly constitutes an act of citizenship, whereas privately working out the division of such tasks in one's own home does not (1993:86).[3] However, although we can identify a public sphere in which political citizenship is enacted, as Lister points out, 'it cannot be divorced from what happens in the private which shapes its contours and which can be the proper object of citizenship struggles' (1997:28).

Secondly, women's activism in organizations is related to citizenship because it is focused on issues that constitute 'the proper object of citizenship struggles' (Lister, 1997:28). Of course, activists may not explicitly use citizenship as their strategic/political framework, or even think or talk about their work in terms of citizenship (see Nyhagen Predelli et al., this volume). However, as discussed above, feminist theorists' critical reappropriation of this concept means that women's experiences can be included in the ever-burgeoning literature, research and policy-making within which citizenship is given top priority. Citizenship's substantive content is also made deeper and more nuanced through feminist theorization, which is in turn strengthened by empirical research. The FEMCIT project is a prime example of an effort to strengthen feminist theories of citizenship through new empirical research on the various ways in which women's movements across Europe have actively been remaking citizenship. One of the main contributions of the project has been to suggest that as well as thinking of citizenship in terms of rights, duties, participation and belonging, a gendered perspective highlights the many *dimensions* of citizenship. These include the widely recognized social, political and economic dimensions, and the more recently theorized bodily and intimate dimensions, as well as relating the issues of religion and ethnicity to citizenship (see Halsaa, Roseneil and Sümer, 2011).

What FEMCIT research has also shown, however, is that there can sometimes be a real schism between feminist theorists' attempts to strategically reappropriate the concept of citizenship, and activists' struggles to ensure that women's rights are recognized, protected and fully enjoyed by women (Nyhagen Predelli et al., this volume). In my research on migrant and minoritized women's organizations, I found that the extent to which the notion of citizenship is used explicitly by activists working in migrant and minoritized women's organizations depends very much on national context.

Is 'citizenship' a useful or relevant framework for your organization?

Starting in the late 1970s, and increasing rapidly during the 1980s and 1990s, migrant and minoritized women established (and in many cases, also disbanded) their own national, local or community-based organizations and networks in countries such as France (e.g. ACOFA, Association de Coopération des Femmes Africaines in 1993), Germany (MAISHA in 1996), the Netherlands (Tiye International in 1994), Norway (The Foreign Women's Group in 1979), and the UK (the Organisation of Women of Asian and African descent in 1978, and Southall Black Sisters in 1979). The research on which this chapter is based was a qualitative study comprising a period of ethnographic fieldwork and semi-structured interviews with activists within such organizations. The fieldwork was carried out over a period of four months in each country,[4] during which I worked as a volunteer in each organization and interviewed staff members.[5] The methods were chosen to enable a close understanding of how the organizations function, and to establish a good rapport with prospective interviewees. In Belgium, I conducted research with an organization that was established during the 1980s by a group of migrant and second generation women with parents from North Africa, Turkey and Italy. In England I researched two organizations: both were established during the mid-1980s by migrant women from different sub-Saharan African countries. The organization I researched in Norway was established at the start of the 2000s by group of migrant women from a number of sub-Saharan African countries.[6]

Although there were important differences between their answers to the question of whether and how a 'citizenship framework' was relevant to their work, all of the respondents indicated that the language of citizenship has permeated their work to a greater or lesser extent. In Belgium, one of the respondents expressed some ambivalence about the use of citizenship in the organization's work; she was both critical and embracing of the concept in her view of how the organization used it. Her criticism stemmed from what she perceived to be the ulterior motive of one of the funding bodies that support her organization's work, for insisting on a citizenship framework:

> Citizenship is a notion that comes both 'from the field' and from our funders' requirements, with all of its limitations. When it comes from the funders, then the requirement is for people who are living precariously to behave or lead their lives in a 'citizenly' way. I don't have the impression that this is something that is required of people who are not in a precarious position. In Brussels, there are a great number of people who earn very good wages and who come from mainly European countries, and I don't see any social cohesion programme relating to them.

Some of the work for which the organization is funded by this particular funder comes under the heading of 'social cohesion'. This is defined as: 'the entirety of the social processes through which individuals, or groups of individuals, irrespective of national or ethnic origin, cultural, religious or philosophical affiliation, social or socio-economic status, age, sexual orientation or health, enjoy equality of opportunity and of conditions in order to achieve economic, social and cultural well-being, and to actively participate, and be recognised in society' (COCOF, 2005:2, my translation). According to the basic principles of this conceptualization of social cohesion, the programmes run by organizations *must* take a 'citizenship approach, which will enable the target audience to learn about their rights and obligations, the rules for living together and about the notions of respect and diversity' (http://www.avcb-vsgb.be/fr/subsides.html?sub_id=338). Belgium is typical of many European countries, where discourses around multiculturalism (as an aspect of policy-making in the area of cultural and religious 'integration' or 'diversity management') has been replaced by a focus on 'social (or community) cohesion' (see Yuval-Davis et al., 2005 for a discussion of this in the UK context, and Koopmans, 2006 and Lentin, 2008 on Europe more generally). This is largely due to what has been seen as multiculturalism's 'failure' to address such issues as segregation, discrimination and marginalization, which purportedly goes hand in hand with the perception of ever increasing diversity in European contexts (see Strasser, this volume).

The organization's social cohesion programme consists of French language lessons, a daily homework school for young women in the evenings and a basic level of social support from a social worker. Most of the women who use the organization's services are immigrants – some newly arrived in Belgium/Brussels, others more established. The organization is located in one of the poorest boroughs (*communes*) of the Belgian capital, Brussels, with one of the highest percentages of immigrant and minoritized communities. In this respondent's view, the burden of ensuring that social cohesion takes place amongst the French-speaking population of Brussels,[7] rests more heavily on 'people who are living precariously'. In fact, in order to be eligible for the social cohesion funding, organizations must be located in boroughs that meet minimum criteria of socio-economic and social difficulties, which include, inter alia: high population density, a significant percentage of foreigners, a significant percentage of people receiving state benefits, and low rate housing (COCOF, 2005:3). Boroughs that have a significant percentage of foreigners (from other countries in Europe), but which are less socio-economically deprived, are not targeted for social cohesion activities. The respondent was critical of the funder's requirement of a citizenship framework for social cohesion work that is conducted exclusively in poor and highly diverse neighbourhoods. In her view, this showed that the funder actively contributes to making social cohesion a 'one way street', which those living the most precarious lives in Brussels are expected to travel.[8]

However, the same respondent also spoke positively of the citizenship framework, because, as she explained, the reasons for using it come 'from the field'. The organization's experiences of working with particular constituencies of migrant and minoritized women have shown that in some ways, a citizenship framework is both necessary and useful:

> In terms of the field, we also spur on the use of citizenship: getting the women interested in laws and in respecting laws, that is about citizenship; when there are elections; we talk to them about the elections and about the important issues related to the elections.

In this example from Belgium, we can see that the funder's requirements and the organization's experiences 'from the field' mutually reinforce the use of a citizenship framework. Also, the respondent's understanding of why the notion of citizenship is used by her organization, reflects, to some extent, both Phillips's and Dietz's focus on the political aspects of citizenship (discussed above).

In England, one of my respondents told me that citizenship was a framework that her organization had only recently started to include in their work. She gave the following explanation:

> We've been talking about working with women to have an approach to citizenship, [so they see that they are entitled] to a range of processes and entitlements *here*. A lot of times, women lose out because they do not engage with these processes; how do you access your rightful entitlements because you are a citizen in a particular context? And because people do not see themselves as citizens here, they actually adhere a lot to what is back home, and do not engage effectively. I think that in itself means that people lose out in terms of their voice, to be heard, their right to access services, their right to voting, and also their right to enjoy their lives as human beings within a country where they operate and exist.

This respondent focuses on the rights and entitlements aspects of citizenship, as a way of making the women that the organization works with aware of what differences being British citizens can make to their lives. The organization works with both minoritized and migrant women, some of whom are naturalized British citizens. Owing to the nature of the work they do, the organization is most interested in informing the women of the kinds of services (especially medical, but also social and legal) that they can access as citizens. However, as the respondent points out, a big part of the problem that the organization faces is the fact that, in her experience, many of the women that they work with do not consider themselves as citizens *here*, in the UK. In the respondent's view, the women tend to focus on what is happening in their 'home' countries, which means that they are not able to 'engage effectively', either by being politically active in the UK, through accessing much-needed services, or simply by 'enjoying life' in a country that is, to all intents and purposes (also) their home.

Over the last 10 to 15 years in the UK, the concept of citizenship has become a 'staple' of government and political discourses, especially in the area of education (see Osler and Starkey, 2001), and in relation to the 'integration' agenda (see Lewis, 2004b). It is, therefore, not so surprising to find that citizenship has also entered the discourses and work of civil society organizations, not least those focusing on migrant and minoritized communities.[9] What distinguishes this respondent's view from the way that citizenship is generally used in political discourse in the United Kingdom is her inclusion of the right to 'enjoy life as human beings' within citizenship. This indicates a more holistic conceptualization of citizenship that is more in line with Lister's broad view of citizenship than with Phillips's or Dietz's narrower approaches. The respondent suggests that her organization seeks to enhance migrant and minoritized women's lived experiences of citizenship, in terms of rights and participation, and in terms of self-fulfilment. This also contrasts with the example from Brussels, where citizenship was viewed somewhat more instrumentally as a means to the end of meeting a social cohesion agenda (the funder) or of encouraging migrant and minoritized women to become more politically engaged and active (the field).

When I asked my respondents in Norway whether the concept of citizenship was useful or relevant to the organization's work, I was told that it was neither.[10] One respondent explained that a key issue faced by the organization was the fact that for migrant and minoritized African/descent women in Norway, citizenship is experienced only at its most 'basic' level:

> I think citizenship for us, is very, very little. We're basically surviving for just basic rights. We haven't got to that stage, whereby we're thinking so high up, as citizens, [that]: these are our rights, these are what we have. No, we haven't got to that stage, we're still at the very basic stage; which is sad...the system is so racist; it is incredibly racist...as Norwegian citizens, there are certain things that we shouldn't do, and we have to abide by the law. In terms of abiding and toeing the line, we do; but taking it to that stage where we can actually stand in front of the Norwegian Parliament and say, 'As feminists and as minority women: this and this is what we demand!'
>
> I don't think we're there.

According to this respondent, for migrant and minoritized African/descent women in Norway, citizenship is currently reduced to 'basic rights'. This implies that a distinction can be made between a 'basic stage' of citizenship (surviving for basic rights) and a 'high up stage as citizens' (recognizing that one has rights and making demands according to one's needs). This closely resembles Lister's distinction between *being* a citizen (status) and *acting* as a citizen (practice). The respondent indicates that there are factors (such as systemic racism) that prevent people who are formal citizens, and who fulfil their citizenly duties (toeing the line and abiding by Norwegian laws), from practicing their citizenship. She goes so far as to rank citizenship according to status (basic) and practice (high), suggesting that even though migrant African/African descent women in Norway may formally be citizens, they have not yet reached the next stage of practicing citizenship. This higher stage of citizenship is linked to a politicized form of participation that would make it possible for migrant African/African descent women in Norway to stand outside of the Norwegian *Storting* (Parliament) and make demands 'as feminists and as minority women'. This is an example of what

Lister has called 'citizenship as the expression of agency [which] contributes to the recasting of women as actors on the political stage (1997:199).

The respondent from Oslo's view that citizenship was not a meaningful frame of reference because migrant African/African descent women in Norway are yet to enjoy more than a basic level of citizenship necessarily implies a third, 'mid-stage' (in addition to the 'basic' and 'high' stages) of citizenship. This is because, although she says that migrant African/African descent women are yet to practice their citizenship in political terms, the fact that the organization exists and is functioning, albeit in a limited capacity, indicates a degree of politicized activity, at least by some migrant African/African descent women in Norway. At the time that I did my research with this organization, they were not involved in any lobbying or advocacy activities, although they aspired to be. From my observations during my fieldwork, as well as from what my respondents told me during the interviews and in other conversations, the organization was limited by a lack of sufficient resources, both human and financial. The organization was able to secure funding for projects, but not the type of core funding that would enable them to have their own independent offices, employ full-time administrative and programmatic staff, and pursue a self-defined advocacy agenda. Cecilie Thun argues that one key effect of current funding structures for women's organizations in Norway is to force minoritized women's organizations into an 'implementation role', because they are seen as 'rational instruments for implementing public welfare aims' (see Thun, 2011). This leaves such organizations with little room for setting their own agendas. The findings from my research in Oslo support this argument.

The question of how the activists working in the organizations I researched perceived citizenship's relevance and usefulness to their work is inextricably linked to the specificities of context. In Brussels, requirements from funders (linked to a social cohesion agenda) and 'from the field' (linked to the need to inform migrant and minoritized women about laws and about political processes) mutually reinforced the organization's use of the citizenship framework. In London, one of the two organizations' experiences with naturalized migrant women motivated them to start using a citizenship framework, as a way of highlighting what new rights and entitlements are derived from the status of (British) citizen. In addition, the organization views citizenship holistically, as encompassing rights, participation and belonging. In Oslo, citizenship was not perceived to be a useful framework because migrant African/African descent women in Norway continue to face a level of racism that prevents them from practicing ('high') citizenship, in spite of their status as citizens ('basic' citizenship). It is my contention, however, that some migrant African/African descent women in Norway have reached what might be termed a 'mid-stage' of citizenship, since they have been able to mobilize and establish the organization with which I conducted my research. These examples are different from Nyhagen Predelli et al.'s finding, discussed in this volume that their interviewees did not tend to 'regard "citizenship" as a term that was relevant to their political activism'. Rather, they reinforce Birte Siim's (2000) argument that the use and understanding of citizenship is always contextual.

In the next section, the focus is on how the organizations I researched perceive their relationships to the wider women's movements in each context. This is also important in considering which groups of organized women view themselves, and are viewed, as contributors to the remaking of citizenship in Europe.

From the margins?

In 1984, bell hooks wrote: 'To be in the margin is to be part of the whole but outside the main body' (2000: xvi). hooks's statement was made critically in relation to the development of Western (especially North American) feminist theory. She argued, in line with earlier critiques from feminists of colour, lesbian and working class feminists (see Truth, 1851; Combahee River Collective, 1977), that 'feminist theory lacks wholeness, lacks the broad analysis that could encompass a variety of human experiences' (hooks, 2000:xvii). The same criticism has been made of the women's/feminist movements in European contexts such as the UK (see Carby, 1982; Bryan, Dadzie and Scafe, 1985; Grewal et al., 1988); Belgium (see Ouali, 2004, 2007; Plateau, 2009); and Norway (see Nyhagen Predelli and Halsaa, 2012). FEMCIT research supports the view that feminist scholarship tends to exclude much minoritized and migrant women's organizing from current definitions of the women's movement, or the feminist movement, because such women often organize outside of the 'usual spaces' of mainstream women's activism (see Halsaa, Roseneil and Sümer, 2011:80). Of course, the extent to which we can say that migrant and minoritized women's organizations have been or are part of the broader women's or feminist movements in European countries depends largely on how such 'movements' are defined, and on who is doing the defining.

The Research Network on Gender, Politics and the State (RNGS) advocates an understanding of feminist movements as 'a specific subset of the total population of women's movements' (Outshoorn, 2010c:145). However, it is quite usual to see women's/feminist movements used interchangeably. McBride and Mazur (2010) have pointed out that this is counterproductive, especially in comparative research, because what is considered 'feminist' is so highly contested. In Natasha Walter's view, the British movement/s is made up of 'a large collection of single-issue organisations that press for feminist aims in many different accents' (1998:44). This inclusive view makes it possible to situate the types of organizations founded by and for the benefit of migrant and minoritized women as an integral part of broader women's movements, since it recognizes that feminism can be 'spoken' in a variety of 'accents'.

Is your organization a feminist organization?

Recent empirical research does not show this potential inclusiveness to be the prevailing sentiment amongst organized migrant and minoritized women in some European countries. Representatives from migrant and minoritized women's organizations often argue that they are perceived, and perceive of themselves, as being marginal in relation to mainstream, majority women's and feminist movements (see Sudbury, 1998 on the UK context; Ouali, 2007 on Belgium; and Nyhagen Predelli and Halsaa, 2012 on Norway and the UK). This is especially so in contexts where they feel that the definition of a 'feminist' movement is one in which their needs and interests are perceived by organized majority women as 'different' (see Thun, 2011b for a discussion of the Norwegian context).[11]

However, this marginal position within feminist movements is also *voluntarily* taken up by migrant and minoritized women's organizations. In some contexts, migrant and minoritized women's organizations (and sometimes, also some majority women's organizations) have sought to distance themselves from prevailing definitions of feminism or feminist movements, which they view as harmful. One of my interviewees in London explained why her organization chose not to formerly 'label itself' a feminist organization:

> We tend not to label ourselves as feminist, because of the connotations of feminism in other fields, and working with women, particularly at the community level, once you put labels on yourself, women tend to be fearful, and not don't want to come close. But clearly, in terms of our principles and our approaches, clearly, we're a very feminist organization.

The organization avoids 'labelling' itself as feminist, not only because of the negative connotations to which the term 'feminist' gives rise, but also because it is strategic to do so, vis-à-vis the organization's constituency. Similarly, one of my interviewees in Oslo explained that: [The organization] is a feminist one, but not one that hates men, no.' The respondent draws attention to the negative mainstream definitions of feminism, often perpetuated in media accounts of feminist/women's activism, and according to which all feminists are '(bra-burning) man-haters'.[12] Although the speaker includes her organization within the category of 'feminist' organizations, she simultaneously excludes the organization from it because of the negative dominant view of feminism. Another interviewee in Oslo explained that whether the organization could be considered feminist depended on the way that feminism is defined. When I asked her whether she considered the organization to be a feminist organization, she replied:

> No...well, it depends on what your definition of feminism is. My definition of a feminist, of feminism is: a woman who is not afraid to say her

point of view, and does not hate men, of course. But then, is not afraid to stand up for what she believes in. If that is a feminist, then I am a feminist. I think that most of the members of [the organization] have the same views as I do, so if you define us as feminists, then it is a feminist organization; but without that misconception that feminists are women who fear men and have no respect for men. We just want equality, you know: what is good for the goose... you know?

In this statement, the respondent says that the organization's members consider themselves to be feminists (who do not hate, fear or lack respect for men). She also indicates, however, that there are people who would not view them as feminists, because the organization does not take a position which views men as 'the enemy'. She believes that the view that feminists hate, fear or lack respect for men is a 'misconception', because what her organization, as a feminist organization, wants, is simply for women to receive equal treatment with men ('what is good for the goose [is good for the gander]').

Racism within feminist circles has also been a strong deterrent to migrant and minoritized women, preventing them from aligning themselves with the various mainstream movements. At the end of the 1990s, Julia Sudbury found that: '[for black women activists] the term 'feminism' is associated with daily struggles against racist exclusion by white women's organizations' (1998:47). One example of such exclusion mentioned by Sudbury related to the issue of the competition between majority and minoritized/migrant women's organizations for funding; minoritized/migrant women's organizations tended to be the losers (1998:47). An interviewee in Oslo spoke of similar experiences:

They say: 'Oh, we all stand together.' But their projects are being funded; they are all in employment and none of the minority women. And all of the ideas come from us. So they use those ideas to promote themselves. We've always been left behind.

In this respondent's view, a rhetoric of 'all standing together' tends to be maintained by some organized majority women in Norway. However, when it comes to the crunch of securing the necessary funding for organizational activities, the speaker feels very much that minoritized/migrant women's ideas are taken over in the programmes of majority women's organizations, which ultimately turn out to be the main beneficiaries of scarce financial resources. This is somewhat in line with Nyhagen Predelli and Halsaa's finding that there are instances (or rhetorics) of 'strategic sisterhood' between minoritized and majority women's organizations in the Norwegian context (Nyhagen Predelli and Halsaa, 2012). However, on the whole, as the respondent above attests, there tend to be more instances of 'dissonance', and 'discourses of anger and irritation' (Nyhagen Predelli et al., 2008).

Empirical research conducted in Norway over the past three to four years shows that, specifically in the area of violence against women, migrant/ minoritized and majority women's organizations are unlikely to: (1) view each other as equals operating within the same movement/s; and (2) engage in much collaborative work (see Nyhagen Predelli and Halsaa, 2012). One key source of difficulty is the lack of intersectional thinking or activism by majority women's rights/feminist activists or organizations in Norway (see Thun, 2011b; Halsaa, Nyhagen Predelli and Thun, 2008). According to Thun, majority women activists from women's/feminist organizations in Norway speak about 'immigrant women's issues' as being distinct from and in conflict with 'feminist women's issues', and those (feminist) women are implicitly equated with 'white women'. Thun argues that this reflects an understanding of white Norwegian women as being 'real' women, with immigrant women juxtaposed as the 'deviant Other' (Thun, 2011b). Pristed Nielsen and Thun also argued: 'The underlying assumption [of organised majority Norwegian women] ... is that minority women organise primarily as 'ethnic minorities' and common interests as 'women' are downplayed' (2010:64).

With regards to the Belgian women's movement, Nouria Ouali has noted that migrant women (especially North African, Turkish and southern European women) in Belgium started to establish their own organizations only during the mid to late 1980s. This is in spite of the fact that there have been several waves of immigration to Belgium since the immediate post-war period (Martiniello and Rea, 2003), and there are now three generations of Belgian citizens who are descended from migrant parents or grandparents (Ouali, 2007:2).[13] Prior to the 1980s, migrant women were sometimes individual members of mainstream women's organizations, but most often, they were the beneficiaries of the services provided by civil society organizations in general; attending literacy classes, taking part in socio-cultural activities or receiving professional training (Ouali, 2007:2). In Ouali's view, the women's movement in Belgium has tended to include only minoritized women's issues when it has been politically expedient to do so (2004:38). In addition, migrant and minoritized women in Belgium have been demanding that the mainstream Belgian women's movements listen to their specific needs, and that mainstream women's rights/feminist activists change the infantilizing and maternalist attitudes that tend to characterize their interactions with migrant and minoritized women (Ouali, 2007:5).

Nadine Plateau argues that, internal political and theoretical differences notwithstanding, on the whole the French-speaking Belgian women's movement remained culturally and ethnically homogeneous, until the end of the 1990s, for a number of reasons. These include, firstly, the fact that the movement was dominated by, and reflected the interests and aspirations of, predominantly middle class (ethnically Belgian women). Secondly, the movement tended to focus on commonalities, whilst down-playing contestations linked to social and ethnic differences between members. Plateau also notes the tendency within feminist circles (as well as in other social movements on the political left and amongst the trade unions) to view migrants primarily as low status socio-economic groups, and not as cultural or ethnic groups. This meant that racism and discrimination went unacknowledged or were ignored (Plateau, 2009:80–1). This contrasts sharply with the Norwegian context, where, as Thun (2011b) argues, culture and ethnicity play a central role in how migrant and minoritized women's organizations are perceived, and excluded, by organized majority women.

According to the participants in my research, migrant and minoritized women's organizations have been located on the margins of the women's movements in at least these three European contexts, especially when such movements have explicitly self-identified as feminists. Narrow internal definitions of 'feminism' by majority activists were viewed as excluding the interests of migrant and minoritized women, who also distanced themselves from the mainstream negative portrayals of the terms 'feminist', and 'feminism'. When considering who has contributed to the remaking of citizenship, especially a feminist remaking, it is axiomatic that we take account of what has been happening 'on the (real and perceived) margins', whilst also bearing in mind, of course, that centres and margins are by no means fixed categories, shifting over time, across space, between and within groups and individuals. In the following section, I discuss the organizations' choice of positioning in each context. This is relevant to a consideration of the extent to which migrant and minoritized women's organizations can be said to be contributors to the remaking of citizenship in Europe because of the transnationality that characterizes both the experiences of such women, and the work of their organizations.

Identity and activism

Marginality is not the defining characteristic of migrant and minoritized women's organizations. They have been established to address specific needs, and as broadly political platforms for migrant and minoritized women to engage, on their own terms and 'in their own voices', in the ongoing struggles for women's (equal) rights in European contexts. Cassandra Ellerbe-Dueck's research suggests that minoritized women in Germany and Austria established their own organizations as a way of creating 'safe spaces'. Ellerbe-Dueck's theorization of 'safe spaces', 'takes into account the aspect of a 'virtual' reality ... [in Germany and Austria] where tangible 'Black spaces' are non-existent. 'Safe space' is crucial in the sustainment of advocacy work particularly in highly oppositional political times' (Ellerbe-Dueck, forthcoming, 2011).

Based on empirical research on women's organizing in Norway, Halsaa, Roseneil and Sümer (2011) have suggested that the establishment of minoritized and migrant women's organizations, and the activities they engage in, can be conceptualized as the performance of a specific type of 'recognition work'. The organizations are viewed as engaging in continuous and 'reflexive work' in order to be 'recognized as equal, reasonable, and rational citizens' in relation to both the wider Norwegian society and to the women's and feminist movements (see Halsaa, Roseneil and Sümer, 2011:81). This resonates with the much of what I was told by my research participants. However, as well as seeking recognition in the European contexts in which they were located, the organizations I researched also worked hard to maintain ties with, and sometimes engage in activism to effect change in various 'home countries'.

Transnational identities, transnational activism

In London, one of the organizations I researched was established as a space for migrant African/African descent women to organize autonomously, network with each other, share skills and expertise, identify issues of concern and publicly represent themselves.[14] This was considered to be essential, given their often highly precarious positions as migrants and refugees in the UK. One of my respondents echoed Ellerbe-Dueck's finding in Germany and Austria, when she explained to me that in founding the organization, the foremost objective had been: 'To create a safe space for African women to be able to speak autonomously and to set their own agenda.' She stated further, that the founding members had a clear idea of their identity, and of the group of women with whom they identified:

We saw ourselves as one, and not divorced from the African women on the continent. So maybe that was why we were able to infuse the programming with the passion, and with the *understanding* of the realities of African women on the ground.

This statement shows that the founders of this particular organization had a strong identification with 'African women on the continent'. The respondent attributes her own ability, and that of her colleagues, to be passionate about their work to this identification; and she emphasizes that this position gave them insight into the realities of the women on whose behalf the organization was established. From its inception, this organization did programmatic work with migrant African women and with minoritized African descent women living in the UK; they later extended their work to women living in countries across the African continent. The organization's founders clearly saw strong connections and continuities between the lives of African women living in African countries, African women who had migrated to the UK and minoritized women of African descent. Similarly, a respondent from the second organization in London spoke of the activists' working in the organization view of themselves as 'diaspora women;[15] and in Oslo, one respondent said that the organization was instrumental in encouraging women to develop their identity as 'pan-African women'.[16]

Linda Nicholson has argued that the nascent identity politics of the 1960s and 1970s provided a radical challenge to the underlying assumptions of liberal universalism (in Western democracies of the twentieth century) by altering the terms of inclusion through an insistence on the recognition of difference. For many people, at the time of its emergence and subsequently, identity politics represented a kind of nirvana for left-wing politics in general and more specifically, for political mobilization around the issues of 'race' and gender. This was because identity politics was believed to herald the dawning of 'a new day 'in terms of sex roles and race relations' (Nicholson, 2008:3; see also Sudbury, 1998). Sudbury's seminal research on black women's organizing between the 1970s and 1990s in the UK discusses the important role that a sense of shared identity played in their collective action (1998:93–141). This is reflected in my own research findings.

According to Ouali, migrant women from North Africa started to establish their own organizations in Belgium in order to address their needs, some of which were linked to their identities as Muslim women. Such needs were most often denied or derided by mainstream, majority Belgian women's organizations, which sought to impose a cultural conformity linked to their ideological, and ethnocentric versions of women's emancipation (2007:2). In addition, most of the organizations established in Belgium by and for immigrant populations (especially those from North Africa) did not take gendered differences into account; they tended not to include women, and those that did, offered limited activities (such as sewing or cooking). One of my respondents said that the founders of the Brussels organization were motivated to establish their own organization so that migrant women and their daughters would to be able to 'represent themselves, decide on their own activities and encourage other women to change their dependent attitudes'.

The founders of this organization migrated to Belgium from, or were descendents of parents from, a number of countries in southern Europe and Africa (including the Maghreb). This diversity is arguably why the issue of identity was not so prominent (as it was in London and Oslo) in explanations about why the organization had been established. That is not to say that there is no diversity amongst migrant women from sub-Saharan Africa or of sub-Saharan African descent in London and Oslo. However, as my respondents indicated, it was possible (and clearly also desirable) for the organization's members to share a collective identity/identification that linked women between African countries and to the African diaspora in European countries. In contrast, in Brussels, the need to organize on the basis of a shared identity came to light when a particular group of women (from the Maghreb countries of Africa) emerged as the majority users of the services provided by the organization. For example, during the early 2000s, the organization actively coached Moroccan women (both within and outside of the organization in Brussels, in partnership with organizations based in Morocco) to become advocates, lobbyists and demonstrators calling for the reform of the Moroccan Family Code (*la Moudawana*).[17]

Although many viewed identity politics positively, it has also faced a barrage of criticism: some critics pointed out that this type of politics places too much emphasis on the cultural realm and on recognition, and not enough focus on class-based differences or economic redistribution (see Kauffman, 1990). For other critics, identity politics is harmful to democracy because it encourages a focus on 'private' grievances, rather than on 'public' actions and consensus-building (e.g. Elshtain, 1993); yet others feel that it ultimately leads to the twin impasses of reductionism and essentialism (as in Modood, 1994). Critics have also highlighted the fact that identity politics have not been the sole preserve of progressive social movements, since political conservatives have also used a form of identity politics to great effect (see Pichardo, 1997). Lastly, critics pointed to identity politics' tendency to direct the focus towards what divides, rather than unites (see Gitlin, 1995). In their responses to these types of critiques, both Nicholson and Sudbury argue convincingly that although some of the criticism is accurate and deserved, much of it fails to recognize the political significance of identity politics. In Nicholson's words, identity politics 'forced us to recognize that since identity affects life possibilities, it needs to be addressed on a political level' (Nicholson, 2008:186). Sudbury points out that African and African Caribbean women's political activism within organizations in the UK 'reveals the hidden 'white male' behind the general usage of the term politics' (1998:96). By founding their own organizations and linking their identity to their activism, migrant and minoritized women take an overtly political stand: to exercise agency and determine their own agenda for social and political change. By becoming organized, such women enact what Nira Yuval-Davis (1999) has termed a multilayered citizenship, insofar as it is a gendered citizenship, which is racialized and mediated through cultural and religious differences, and in relation to transnational or diasporic affiliations.

The claims and demands that such organizations make, the services that they offer, as well as the specific ways in which they choose to position themselves in relation to various identities indicate the broad diversity between and within groups of migrant and minoritized women. This complexity calls for a nuanced approach, both in relation to the issue of combining identity positions and political activism, *and* how this is read through a citizenship frame. In reclaiming identity politics as central to social movements of equality relating to gender and 'race', Nicholson argues for a more complex understanding of identities. Using the analogy of a tapestry, Nicholson suggests: 'If we think of identity categories like threads in a tapestry that is the social whole, then the meaning of any identity category will change as it intersects with other identity category 'threads' as it changes across contexts and across time' (2008:186–7).

This is the process that is made visible within migrant and minoritized women's organizations. In addition, such organizations exemplify what Susan Hekman has referred to as a politics that moves beyond identity to identification, where 'political actors identify with particular political causes and mobilize to achieve particular political goals' (2000:304). What is promising about the move from identity to identification, as Hekman views it, is that although political actors' identifications 'are rooted in aspects of their identities', they do not depend on 'fixing the identity of a citizen in a particular location' (2000:304), and thus avoid some of the pitfalls of some forms of identity politics, discussed above. In all three research contexts, there was explicit recognition by the respondents of the diversity within the groups of women who founded the organizations, as well as those *for* whom the organizations were established. However, this did not preclude recognition of certain commonalities, relating to experiences (of migration), and of (marginal socio-economic) positionality in the respective contexts.

Conclusion

I have discussed three important considerations that need to be taken into account when assessing migrant and minoritized women's organizations' contributions to the remaking of citizenship. Firstly, there is the question of whether and how citizenship is used as a framework by the organizations. This depends on whether it is a framework that is chosen by the organization as a result of their experiences 'from the field', or one that comes 'from funders'. As the example from Belgium shows, there can be some ambivalence towards the use of the concept of citizenship, in cases where the organization chooses to frame its work in those terms, *and* their funders also require them to use a citizenship framework. The difficulty comes in trying to balance the needs of the migrant and minoritized women that the organization is working to meet, and the 'conditionalities' imposed by funders, who may have a radically different agenda from the organizations they fund. This shows how claims around citizenship can be instrumentalized in different ways. The tension here was between the organization's attempts to centralize the experiences and needs of migrant and minoritized women, versus the funder's focus on a perceived wider societal need for social cohesion, especially targeted at 'precarious' communities. The notion of citizenship thus clearly had a role to play in Brussels.

This was equally true in London, where one of the organizations had begun to use the notion as a tool for fostering a sense of permanent presence and belonging that they hoped would in turn lead to a greater awareness of their rights and entitlements as citizens amongst migrant and minoritized women. In contrast, in Oslo, despite the awareness of such rights and entitlements as Norwegian citizens, according to my respondents, migrant and minoritized African/descent women have yet to assert their political agency. A distinction was made between a 'basic' and 'high' stage of citizenship: the former is limited to the formal rights deriving from legal citizenship; the latter includes both a sense of being the holder of such former rights *and* having the opportunity to take a public and political stand to defend those rights. The respondent felt that because of 'a racist system', migrant and minoritized African/descent women in Norway are currently at only the 'basic stage' of citizenship. This means they can engage only in a 'diminished form of politics' (Fisher, 2002:134), since they lack the ability to be present and vocal in the public sphere, and make their demands 'as feminists and minority women'. In addition, I argued that the fact that the organization exists and functions, albeit with limited resources, suggests a 'mid-stage' of constrained citizenship, consisting of the process of becoming organized and making claims for full citizenship.

The second issue discussed in the chapter was the respondents' perceptions of their organizations as marginal to the main women's movements in the three contexts, particularly when those movements are explicitly labelled feminist. We find some ambivalence again, this time in relation to the term 'feminist'. The organizations' willingness to identify explicitly as feminist was limited by the negative mainstream view of feminists and feminism as 'man-hating' and/ or dominated by lesbians. The respondents also expressed the feeling that there was no place for their organizations within the mainstream women's and feminist movements in each context, since the experiences of migrant and minoritized women were either ignored or excluded.[18]

The final section of the chapter showed that insofar as migrant and minoritized women's organizations were established on the basis of shared identities or identifications, and they carry out work that reflects the multilayered and differentiated lived experiences of migrant and minoritized women, their contribution to the remaking of citizenship is indispensable to a contemporary feminist politics of citizenship. This is a politics which must 'synthesise equality and difference in the construction of women's...citizenship' (Lister, 1997:167). One central implication of the work done by the migrant and minoritized women's organizations that were the subjects of this research is that attempts within feminist scholarship to expose the inherent gender bias of classical approaches to citizenship must go hand in hand with an exposure of its equally inherent racialized and cultural biases. The establishment of migrant and minoritized women's organizations, and gradually increasing academic efforts to engage with the work of such organizations, are important steps in the right direction.

Notes

I would like to thank all three editors of this volume for their close reading of, and fruitful comments and suggestions for, this chapter.

1. In this chapter, 'migrant' refers to women who have recently migrated to the country under discussion, and 'minoritized' refers to women from settled 'minority' communities. I use the term 'minoritized' rather than '(ethnic) minority' in line with Yasmin Gunaratnam's argument that the former term gives a 'sense

of the active process of racialization that are at work in designating certain attributes of groups in particular contexts as being in a 'minority" (2003:17).

2. According to Engin Işın, the 'enactment of citizenship implies an understanding of political participation beyond a narrowly defined political realm and beyond the canons of electoral politics' (http://www.enacting-citizenship.eu/index.php/sections/blog_post/53/, accessed August 2011).

3. From a more expansive approach to citizenship, this is an example of intimate citizenship (see Roseneil et al., this volume).

4. The field work for this study was conducted in England between June and October 2009; in Belgium between April and August 2010; and in Norway between September and December 2010.

5. My research participants agreed to take part in my research on the condition that the information they shared with me remained anonymous. I will, therefore, not use the organizations' or the participants' names.

6. Given the wide variety and large numbers of such organizations, and the constraints of my research time and funding, I had to make some strategic choices about how to focus the research. I decided to research organizations established by and for sub-Saharan African women/women of sub-Saharan African descent. However, I was only able to find one functioning organization in Norway that fit this profile, and one in Belgium that was established by and for a group of migrant women.

7. Belgium now holds the world record for being without a government for the longest period – over a year at the time of writing – as a result of the failure to form a coalition government after elections in June 2010. This is due to the deep seated divisions between the French and Dutch speaking parts of the country. Belgium is a federal state composed of three regions (Flanders, Wallonia and Brussels-Capital region) and three communities (Flemish-speaking, French-speaking and German-speaking). Each community and region has its own elected council and government. The Flemish region and community have merged, unlike the others. Brussels-Capital was established as an independent region (equal to Wallonia and Flanders) by the constitutional structure of the new federal Belgium established in 1988–9 and the state reforms of 1993. The majority of *Bruxellois* people speak French, although Brussels-Capital is officially bilingual (French/Flemish). In reality, the ratio of French to Flemish speakers is approximately 5:1 (Florence and Martiniello, 2005). All of the discussion relating to Belgium in this chapter is restricted to the general French-speaking region or more specifically to the bilingual city/region of Brussels where the organization I researched is located. It is beyond the scope of the chapter (as it was of the research) to include perspectives from either Flanders or the German-speaking community in the east of Belgium.

8. The citizenship framing of social cohesion programmes can also be seen as part of a concerted effort by the local authorities in Belgium to address the 'fall out' resulting from the rise of the far right in Flanders in the late 1980s, and a wave of 'riots' in some of the 'immigrant neighbourhoods' of Brussels in 1991 (see Grégoire, 2010). This was later mirrored in England, in the policy recommendations for 'community cohesion' that were made in the Cantle Report, which looked into the causes of the 'riots' that took place between (mainly) young men of south Asian descent and the police in three towns in the north of England in 2001 (see Yuval-Davis et al., 2005; Worley, 2005).

9. See Assies (2005) for an interesting discussion of how the State, civil society and the market are intertwined in the 'political economy of citizenship'.

10. It is important to note that 'citizenship' in Norwegian, *statsborgerskap*, refers to the legal aspect of citizenship. The way that 'citizenship' is used in academic literatures, including this chapter, and in political discourses, translates to *medborgerskap* or *samfunnsborgerskap*. Neither of these is commonly used in Norwegian, they are almost exclusive to academic texts (see Brochmann, 2002:56–60). I do not think that this has influenced the Norwegian findings, however, since the interviews were conducted in English with people who came to Norway from countries where the concept of citizenship, in its 'thicker' sense, is used more generally and has more policy and political resonance than is the currently the case in Norway.

11. Of course, this is a highly contested issue between minoritized and majority feminists (see Nyhagen Predelli and Halsaa, 2012). Contextual specificities are key: so, in a country with a small population such as Norway, the number of national majority women's organizations are small in comparison to the UK, for example, and the number of national organizations (as opposed to local community groups or networks) run by and for migrant and minoritized even smaller. In addition, my findings (as well as those of Thun, 2011a and Nyhagen Predelli and Halsaa, 2012) are based on the *perceptions* of our respondents, which may or may not reflect the reality of such important factors as: which organizations receive state funding, or which organizations are invited to consultation proceedings, inter alia (see Thun, 2011a).

12. This finding is also reflected in Christina Scharff's research on young women's reasons for not identifying with feminism in Germany and the UK. These include the perception that feminists are man-haters, and tacitly also lesbians and unfeminine (see Scharff, 2011).

13. Immigration to the three countries that were the focus of this research has, of course, been vastly different in terms of the provenance of immigrants, the reasons for immigration, and the immigration 'regimes' adopted by each state.

14. This was similarly true for majority women organizing in countries such as the UK and the United States of America during the 1960s (see Hanisch, 1969).

15. 'Diaspora' is used here in reference to Africa, and refers to people of 'African descent' living outside of Africa (in Europe, in this specific instance). It is important to note that 'African descent' can be construed both narrowly and broadly: in the former sense, it refers exclusively to people whose parents or grandparents were born in or came from Africa; in the latter sense, it refers to all peoples, across the world, who have any connection to the African continent, going back to the earliest encounters between Africa and the rest of the world. It was meant in its narrower sense by the respondent.

16. Use of the term 'pan-African' dates back to the early twentieth century, when it was used by leaders such as Marcus Garvey (from Jamaica), to galvanize African Caribbean peoples in the Caribbean, in the UK and in the US to join a movement of return to Africa; and scholar activists such as Trinidadian Claudia Jones, and African-American scholar and activist W. E. B Dubois, who was one of the organizers of a series of Pan-African Congresses in Europe and the United States between 1900 and 1945. In the post-war period, which saw the rapid growth of anti-imperialist and nationalist liberation struggles in many colonies in Africa, the term was also used by African nationalist leaders (all of whom went on to become inaugural presidents of their respective independent nations) such as Kwame Nkrumah of Ghana, Sekou Touré of Guinea, Julius Nyerere of Tanzania, Jomo Kenyatta of Kenya, Nnamdi Azikiwe of Nigeria and Patrice Lumumba of Zaire (now the

Democratic Republic of Congo). A pan-African vision is one which seeks to transcend the divisions created by the national boundaries imposed on the continent by the colonial European powers (Britain, France, Germany, Belgium, Spain and Portugal), as well as ethnic divisions within and between nations. In the context of an African diasporic community in Europe, pan-Africanism takes on a further connotation of promoting a collective voice of resistance to racism/racialization and stigmatization, poverty and marginalization.

17. Such activism complemented the unprecedented efforts of Moroccan women's movements in Morocco, which led to the 2004 Reform of the *Moudawana*. This reform fundamentally altered women's rights in Morocco by, inter alia, making divorce easier; increasing the age of consent for marriage to 18 years; and giving women the ability to pass citizenship on to their children (see http://www. telquel-online.com/133/sujet2.shtml, accessed September 2011).

18. See Nyhagen Predelli and Halsaa (2012) for a more in-depth discussion of the relationships between activists in minoritized and majority women's organizations in Norway, the UK and Spain, and publications from the UK research project 'Sisterhood and After: the women's liberation oral history', http://www.sussex. ac.uk/cce/research/current/sisterhoodandafter (accessed September 2011).

9
'Citizenship Is Not a Word I Use': How Women's Movement Activists Understand Citizenship

Line Nyhagen Predelli, Beatrice Halsaa and Cecilie Thun

Introduction[1]

Citizenship has become a core concept in feminist theory. Yet, the phrase 'citizenship is not a word I use' summarizes a central finding from our research with women's movement activists in Norway, Spain and the United Kingdom (UK). Our interviewees tended not to regard 'citizenship' as a term that was relevant to their political activism – a finding that contrasts with citizenship's status as a central notion in feminist scholarship. Citizenship is, however, also a highly contested term in feminist theory. The interviewees' rejections may reflect concerns based on experiences of inequalities related to citizenship, which in the language of feminist theory appear as barriers to lived citizenship, and in this respect our findings support efforts to expand the notion of citizenship. This book's concern with the role of women's movements in remaking citizenship in multicultural Europe is addressed in this chapter through the following questions: How is the term citizenship understood by contemporary women's movement activists? Is citizenship a concept used normatively by movement activists – does the term have political relevance for women's movement claims? What reflections and experiences do activists report in relation to lived citizenship? And, finally, does 'citizenship' as a concept have a positive potential for future women's movement activism?

Lister and colleagues argue that there is 'remarkably little empirical analysis of lived citizenship in comparison with the volume of theorizing about citizenship in individual member states of the European Union (EU), never mind cross-nationally. This is particularly the case with regard to citizens' own understanding of citizenship's meaning' (Lister et al., 2007:168; see also Kabeer, 2005:1). Our study of women's movement activists and citizenship in Norway, Spain and the UK seeks to fill some of this gap in current scholarship.

The first section of our chapter traces relevant developments in scholarly discussions of citizenship, and in the following section the research methods and contexts for our research are presented. We then move on to examine how the women's movement activists whom we interviewed understand the term 'citizenship', and to explore their reflections on and experiences of exclusion and inclusion in lived citizenship, and whether they use the citizenship frame and how useful they think it is in their activism – do they embrace it or reject it? Moreover, we look at the alternative frames (Benford and Snow, 2000; Ferree and Merrill, 2000) – equality, social justice and human rights frames – that are being used by the activists whom we interviewed, before a concluding section that summarizes our findings and addresses the usefulness of 'citizenship' as a concept that can bridge feminist theory and women's movement activism.

Remaking the concept of citizenship

'Citizenship' refers to a status of equality within bounded political communities (Benhabib, 2004). The emphasis on equality has made citizenship a revolutionary notion and a tool 'for marginalized groups struggling for social justice' (Lister, 2007:49). The seeming simplicity of the term conceals complex issues, however, such as who are supposed to carry the status of equals, what counts as equality and where should any boundaries be drawn? Feminists have revealed how citizenship is inherently gendered (e.g. the phrase 'all men are equal'), and how the term has been applied in a state-oriented way, focusing primarily on political-legal issues of rights and responsibilities. They have engaged intensively in grappling with citizenship both normatively and empirically to make the term more inclusive (Lister, 1997; Friedman, 2005; Kabeer, 2005; Squires, 1999; Tastsoglou and Dobrowolsky, 2006). Gender-related issues such as care work and unpaid work (Lister, 1997) are being discussed in relation to social and economic dimensions of citizenship (Bergman et al., and Le Feuvre et al., both this volume). Further dimensions of citizenship have also been introduced, including multicultural (Lister et al., 2007; Siim, 2007; Siim and Squires, 2007; Yuval-Davis, 1997a, 2008), bodily (Outshoorn et al., this volume), sexual (Bell and Binnie, 2000) and intimate citizenship (Roseneil, 2010b; Roseneil et al., this volume) citizenship. In the broad feminist view of citizenship, civil society is a dynamic space in which citizenship is lived, contested and negotiated. The non-state arenas of social movements and civil society organizations, and the horizontal citizen-to-citizen relations, constitute important sites of citizenship practice.

The value of any conferred citizenship status is context-dependent, as rights and obligations vary across different bounded political communities (Joppke, 2010:154). Moreover, the state is no longer necessarily the appropriate unit of justice when citizenship rights are disaggregated from the territorial state (Young, 2000:250; Benhabib, 2004; Fraser, 2008:13). A growing concern with the 'exclusionary dynamics of the nationally bound citizenship'

(Tambakaki, 2010:21) has inspired discussions of post-national, cosmopolitan and global citizenship alternatives (Sassen, 2002; Hutchings, 1999; Carter, 2001; Strasser, this volume). The growth of transnational political structures and 'the rise of a global human rights culture after World War II' (Soysal, 2004, as cited in Joppke, 2010:21; see also Reilly, 2009) have contributed to such discussions. Furthermore, increasing migration across national borders and socio-economic globalization processes have inspired innovative feminist discussions of a politics of belonging, and of the relationship between human rights and citizenship (Benhabib, 2004; Tambakaki, 2010; Yuval-Davis, 2008; Roseneil, forthcoming). New forms of belonging and membership have emerged, and there is a growing concern with dilemmas between the practice of exclusive membership in nation-states and ideas of universal human rights (Benhabib, 2004:17).

It has been argued that citizenship has become a momentum concept with 'egalitarian and anti-hierarchical potential' (Hoffman, 2004:138). Struggles for rights, recognition, participation and inclusion can be described as citizenship struggles (see for example Lister, 1997; Kabeer, 2005; Tastsoglou and Dobrowolsky, 2006) irrespective of whether 'citizenship' is a term used by the parties involved. At the same time, 'citizenship' is also an inevitably exclusive concept, as it confirms a particular 'insider' status and a set of rights and obligations for a group of people within the bounded political community, and sets the 'insiders' apart from those defined as 'other', strangers, aliens and outsiders (Işın, 2005:377). The claim that citizenship is 'internally inclusive' and 'externally exclusive' (Brubaker,1992) is, however, too simplistic, as it exaggerates and fixes a distinction between 'included citizens' and 'excluded aliens', rather than seeing the relationship between inclusion and exclusion as both fluid and contested (Benhabib, 2004:19). Feminists have a solid tradition of addressing the internally excluding notions and practices of citizenship, or the production of hierarchies and inequalities within the privileged 'citizen group' (Hernes, 1988; Pateman, 1989; Siim, 1991). Women are still in many ways excluded from the status of citizen and are struggling to obtain both legal and actual rights to equality. Feminists and other academics have argued for a wider interpretation of social dynamics to include state–family relations in addition to state–market relations, that is 'the personal is political' (Phillips, 1991), and for a recognition of actors beyond those that are class based. Political, economic, social and cultural rights should be gender-sensitive and address issues related to the personal, sexual and intimate.

Feminist scholarship has also contested the limitation of citizenship to issues of status, rights and duties, and has launched a broader understanding of citizenship which encompasses participation and belonging. Feminist contributions have highlighted citizenship as lived practice – as social relations and participatory practices within all spheres of life, be they political, economic, social, cultural, religious, bodily, domestic or intimate (Halsaa, Roseneil and Sümer, 2011). The concept of lived citizenship captures citizenship as practice: it is about 'the meaning that citizenship actually has in people's lives and the ways in which people's social and cultural backgrounds and material circumstances affect their lives as citizens' (Hall and Williamson, 1999:2, as cited in Lister et al., 2007:168). Moreover, lived citizenship 'is about how individuals understand and negotiate the three key elements of citizenship: rights and responsibilities, belonging and participation' (Lister et al., 2007:168). As lived practice, citizenship is not a fixed status or the attribute of a particular group of individuals included in a given polity, but rather involves dynamic processes of negotiation and struggle taking place within a variety of contexts at local, national and transnational levels of interaction.

During recent years there has been growing focus on citizenship in relation to the challenges of increasingly multicultural societies, in particular indigenous, national and ethnic minority claims to a special status with concomitant rights, as well claims of recognition, participation and belonging. The notion of multicultural citizenship (Kymlicka, 2010) foregrounds issues of marginalization, discrimination and inequalities related to people's nationality, race and ethnicity. The claims of ethnic minority groups, indigenous peoples and national minorities have at times been framed as group citizenship rights, and have generated extensive debates on the extent to which societies based on individual citizenship rights can and should accommodate group citizenship rights (see Vertovec and Wessendorf, 2010). Following Okin's (1999) question about whether multiculturalism is bad for women, there has been an intense and heated international debate about the paradox that political efforts to remedy wrongs done to ethnic minorities may increase the problems of women within those minorities (Al-Hibri, 1999; Nussbaum, 1999; Shachar, 2001). This dilemma highlights the need for multicultural policies designed to respond to citizenship struggles by minority groups and to take gender into account.

Combining feminist ideas about how citizenship struggles are gendered with notions of how citizenship struggles are rooted in racial and ethnic inequalities and discrimination reveals intersectional tensions between inclusionary ideals and exclusionary practices. Scholars are increasingly addressing the issue of how 'citizenship analyses must negotiate equality in the context of diversity' (Siim and Squires, 2007:414; see also Siim, 2007). In other words, the concept of citizenship must be intersectionalized, as suggested by Yuval-Davis (2008).

Due to 'how relentlessly the idea of inclusion produces exclusion' (Işın, 2005:381), the concept of citizenship also poses a dilemma for both feminist scholarship and women's movement activism: should it be used normatively to frame struggles for equality and justice? If so, what opportunities and limitations does such usage bring? The question about the extent to which the term 'citizenship' is considered useful in struggles for justice and equality is open to debate and empirical research, and scholarly investigations must pay particular attention to place, space and scale (Desforges, Jones and Woods, 2005). Women's movements and their claims-making at local, regional, national, transnational and global levels constitute important sites for such investigations. Our research, which examines how women's movement activists in three European countries understand and talk about citizenship, is a contribution to this effort.

Research methods

Our discussion of how women's movement activists understand the term 'citizenship' is based on qualitative, in-depth, face-to-face interviews with 30 women's movement activists; 10 in Spain, 10 in Norway, and 10 in the UK.[2] These three rather different countries were chosen to obtain a variety of circumstances and contexts in which women's movements have mobilized to claim women's political interests. With a small number of interviewees, our study is not representative of women's movement activists in the three countries. However, the interviews highlight important viewpoints, reflections and experiences that are likely to indicate salient cross-national differences, as well as being indicative of broader issues within women's movements in Europe. The activists we interviewed are from a variety of ethnic backgrounds, with roughly half from ethnic majority and half from ethnic minority backgrounds. Those from ethnic majority backgrounds were born in the respective countries in which they live but their experiences are of course varied in other respects. Those from ethnic minority backgrounds also represent varied experiences and are either from a national minority group, first generation immigrants, refugees or asylum seekers, or born to immigrant parents. All the interviewees were recruited from organizations that seek to advance women's interests and to influence public policy. Organizations were selected on the basis of existing academic literature, web sites that offer comprehensive listings of current women's organizations, and activist recommendations. Our main aim was to recruit activists from women's organizations with explicit feminist aims and identities, but we have also included women's organizations that do not necessarily describe themselves as feminist. They do, however, view themselves as part of the broader women's movement. The names and organizational affiliations of our research participants are kept confidential.

Topic guides were developed to structure the interviews along similar dimensions in each country. The guides were used as flexible research tools, providing the key issues to be discussed while also allowing some context-based variations and follow-up questions. For example, interviewees in the UK were asked about specific policy initiatives meant to speed up the naturalization process for immigrants who partake in voluntary work. The analysis is based on an inductive approach, grounded in the interview data, and inspired by the as yet underdeveloped comparative discourse analysis approach (Kantola, 2007), which attempts to bridge the gaps between historical institutional analysis, comparative analysis and feminist discourse analysis (Mazur and McBride, 2010).

Historical and socio-political contexts

Concerns about citizenship issues have, as discussed above, emerged for a number of reasons. Colonial and post-colonial legacies, transitions from authoritarian to democratic regimes, experiences of civil and other wars, changing patterns of migration, the institutionalization of human rights, the growth of women's policy agencies, and the development and enlargement of the European Community[3] have deeply but differently affected contemporary European countries. Crucial events in the political histories of Norway, Spain and the UK have impacted women's movements in terms of claims-making, political opportunities and outcomes (Mazur and McBride, 2010; Kulawik, 2009). Without going into much historical detail, some important issues nevertheless should be mentioned.

While the allied struggle against Hitler's regime (1939–45) strengthened political relations between Norway and the UK, Spain followed a very different political trajectory. The Spanish fascists, who won the Civil War (1936–9), sided with the German regime, and in effect isolated Spain from western Europe.[4] The death of Franco and the end of the fascist regime in 1975, together with the period of transition culminating in the democratic Constitution of 1978, are defining moments in Spanish history.

Norway does not have a colonial history like Spain and the UK, but cannot deny 'colonial complicity' (Vuorela, 2009:19). Since the 1970s, Norway has experienced increasing migration from non-Western countries, but a ban on labour immigration was implemented in 1975. Spain and the UK have both been heavily influenced by their respective and different colonial histories. Spain has only recently become a country of net immigration, while the influx of residents from former colonies to the UK during the 1960s led to the restrictive 1968 Commonwealth Immigration Act.

In Norway, the first significant anti-racist movement emerged in the 1980s (Nydal, 2007), but the existence of racism was acknowledged relatively late by the Norwegian state and by Norwegian society at large. Due to a combination of recent increase in immigration and new EU initiatives, debates on political rights for immigrants and Roma people have intensified in Spain. Unlike Norway and Spain, the UK has had a strong anti-racist movement since the 1960s, and the state introduced anti-discrimination laws and policies as early as the 1960s, resulting in anti-racist policies setting the standard for gender equality policies. On the Migrant Integration Policy Index (MIPEX), which in 2010 ranked Sweden as the overall top country for migrant integration, Norway, Spain and the UK were all grouped as states considered 'partially favourable for promoting integration'.[5] Spain, however, scored low on migrants' political participation, on their access to nationality, as well as on anti-discrimination policies. Norway scored very high on migrants' political integration but low on their access to nationality, and was given a medium score on anti-discrimination policies. UK scored 'half-way to best practice' on immigrants' political participation, 'slightly favourable' on access to nationality, and high on anti-discrimination policies (also see country profile tables in the Appendix II).

A strong mobilization of feminism took place from the late 1960s in Norway and the UK, where gender equality policies were institutionalized during the 1970s.[6] These processes were implemented later in Spain (Valiente, 2003b:41), where during the fascist regime (1939–75) only the Falangist organization for women was legally sanctioned by the state, and other women's associations operated as clandestine (Threlfall, 1996). The fascist regime, supported by the Catholic Church, was characterized by gender hierarchy, promoted a strict division of gender roles, and celebrated motherhood as the only decent and proper role for women.

The state–society partnership, or 'institutional symbiosis' (Hernes, 1988:189), of the public and private in Norway, explains the greater inclination among feminists there (compared to other countries) to regard the state as a 'friend' and as a tool to be used strategically (Siim, 1991:178). Gender equality policies in Norway and Spain emerged earlier than anti-racist policies, in contrast with the UK where anti-racist policies preceded gender equality policies.[7] In the context of periods of Social Democratic government (1982–96 and 2004–11), as well as new EU initiatives, the institutionalization of gender equality in Spain has accelerated, and Spain has moved from being a 'dictatorship and a latecomer in gender equality policies to being one of the European pioneers' (Lombardo, 2009:4). In sum, differences in timing and sequence have affected the ways in which gender, race, ethnicity and migration intersect and are articulated (or not) within women's movements and state policies in Norway, Spain and the UK.

Importantly, the term 'citizenship' has different connotations in the three countries of our study. Norway does not have an ordinary or proper Norwegian word for 'citizenship', but sociologist Grete Brochmann (2002:56–60) has introduced *samfunnsborgerskap* to broadly cover the English term 'citizenship'. She uses *statsborgerskap* about the legal aspects and *medborgerskap* about the social aspects (identity, loyalty, belonging, trust, and participation). The term *medborgerskap* has increasingly been used in Norwegian politics to denote participation and belonging within democratic institutions and civil society. In Spanish society, citizenship (*ciudadanía*) appears generally to be understood in a more limited and specific way and is mainly associated with nationality and long-term residency within the territory of the Spanish state (Medrano, 2005). However, according to Medrano (2005), Spaniards tend to associate the notion of rights with actual residents in Spain rather than with formal citizens of Spain.

In the UK, an understanding of 'citizenship' which covers all of the dimensions of citizenship (status, rights, duties, loyalty, belonging and active participation) is being promoted through government documents and citizenship education in schools (see Kiwan, 2007). Moreover, the term 'active citizenship' has been used in British politics to mobilize voluntary work and community participation (Lister, 1997; Yuval-Davis, 1997a).

Women's movement activists' understandings of citizenship

In the next three sections we examine how women's movement activists in Norway, Spain and the UK understand the concept of citizenship. They were all asked to respond to a general question worded either as 'When I say the word citizenship, what do you think about?' or as 'When I say the word citizenship, what does it mean to you?'

Norway: citizenship as responsibilities and participation in society

The wider Norwegian context, with its history of a social-democratic, inclusive, consensus-oriented and 'women-friendly' (Hernes, 1987) welfare state, provides the background for how citizenship was talked about among the interviewed activists in Norway. Generally, 'citizenship' is not a term that the activists in Norway use in any of its meanings. When we asked what the term 'citizenship' (*medborgerskap* or *samfunnsborgerskap*) means to them, some interviewees said they were entirely unfamiliar with it. Others felt unsure, but did make some suggestions about the possible meaning of the word. For example, one activist associated it with 'inhabitants', and said that 'all those who are being born, they must, they do belong in a society, and then they are citizens' (*medborgere*). Similarly, another activist stated that 'it does not [mean] anything more than that we all are [citizens]'. A third activist in Norway asserted that although 'citizenship' is not part of her vocabulary, it means that 'you are a part of society; you have a voice'. Another interviewee associated 'citizenship' with academic language and suggested that it is a political buzzword. She understood 'citizenship' to mean a person who is part of the society as an individual with responsibility towards others, and as someone who is contributing in a positive way; one who tries to influence the everyday life he or she is a part of in a positive direction.

As interviewers we did not use the Norwegian term *statsborgerskap* ('state citizenship'), which might have led more participants to reflect on legal issues such as being or becoming a naturalized citizen; having or obtaining a passport. However, one majority and two minority activists quickly associated the term '*medborgerskap*' with being a citizen of Norway (*statsborger*), a term which refers explicitly to the vertical relation between individuals and the state (in the form of rights and obligations). The other activists instead reflected on citizenship as *medborgerskap*, which signals more of the horizontal dimension of citizenship; that is, relations between citizens and citizens' participation and belonging in society.

Activists in Norway also offered some brief but interesting comments when we asked them to reflect on the meaning of a 'good citizen', a follow-up question which was also asked in Spain and the UK and solicited similar responses. One activist in Norway, who did not associate the term 'citizenship' with anything in particular, thought a 'good citizen' is someone who respects the law, does not cause any problems for others, and contributes to society on the basis of his or her capabilities. Similarly, another interviewee associated good citizenship with taking responsibility for herself as well as for the society. To the extent that the activists in Norway associated anything with the term 'citizenship' it was in the sense of being a responsible, decent person who takes care of others, rather than it being a matter of individuals' rights in terms of any legal claims on the state. Among those who offered more substantial comments, the concept of citizenship was related to values of caring for others and for society as such, and to participatory activities, including having a voice, being actively involved and trying to influence society in a positive direction. For several minority activists, this also meant learning the Norwegian language, understanding cultural codes and participating in the labour market (economic citizenship). A focus on political citizenship was almost absent among the interviewees in Norway, contrary to Spain, probably because voting rights, quotas and women's presence in politics are taken for granted in Norway. The activists in Norway, just like the activists in Spain and the UK, do take advantage of their voting rights, and most of them confirmed that they take part in political activities such as demonstrations and petitions. Since 1983, immigrants who have resided in Norway for a minimum of three years have the right to vote in local and regional elections, and Norway does not discriminate on the basis of country of origin in granting immigrants the right to vote. Hence the issue of voting is not politicized. The issue of 'ordinary' or formal political participation was not talked about by activists in Norway without them being prompted. Some of the activists did, however, talk about their engagement in politics related to conditions in their country of origin. They felt restricted in voicing their protest against oppressive regimes from which they had fled, and feared being identified by embassy employees, as well as not being granted visitor rights to their country of origin.

In contrast to the UK, the activists in Norway made very few direct or indirect references to state power, except in relation to restrictions on home return for activists with refugee status. Instead, the interviewees talked about feelings of belonging (or not) in Norwegian society. This can be understood in relation to the generally positive view of the state as a 'friend' or potential ally both of people generally and of voluntary organizations in Norway. The representation of Norwegian citizens as responsible and caring in the interviews is also related to the discourse of state–society partnership, a discourse which is reflected among both majority and minority activists. Minority activists were quite clear, however, that they can never become '100 per cent Norwegian'. In various ways, they experienced being viewed by others as temporary 'guests' in Norway. Norwegian is a new language for migrants arriving in Norway (except for those originating from other Nordic countries), which contrasts with the experience of many migrants from former colonies to Spain and the UK. Moreover, those who had fled their country of origin expressed a desire to return, should it become possible. The fact that they are often involved in struggles related to their country of origin adds weight to their ambivalent feelings of belonging.

Spain: political citizenship and individual rights

The wider Spanish context, with its history of empire, civil war, a fascist regime and the transition to a democratic regime in the second half of the 1970s, provides the background for how citizenship was talked about among the activists in Spain. For example, the historical legacy of the Franco regime was noted by one interviewee as having hindered the development of the notion of citizen participation in Spain, as well as excluding women from the notion of citizenship.

Many of the activists in Spain focused immediately on citizenship as embodying a set of rights for individuals living within a particular nation-state or polity. Such rights were most often talked about in terms of 'equal rights' or 'human rights', extending to a number of dimensions including the political, social and economic, and being in possession of such rights was seen as a measure of inclusion in society. Concomitantly, the absence of rights was seen as a measure of exclusion. Citizenship was also viewed by activists in Spain as encompassing a number of duties or obligations, such as respect towards other individuals, caring about the place in which you live, and respect for the law. The quotes below illustrate the links made by activists in Spain between citizenship and rights:

> Full rights, for any person – to me this would summarize the meaning of the word citizenship. These rights would include all manner of civil, political, social and economic rights that every person should have access to – that's what I call citizenship.
>
> Citizenship means that a person has the right to develop socially in all spheres. Through access to voting, to political participation, both formal and informal, access to social services, to education, to employment. In other words, citizenship should be universal for everybody, regardless of where they are, without any kind of constraints arising from the place you were born.

In Spain, contrary to Norway and the UK, political citizenship in terms of the right to vote and to participate in policy-making processes was talked about as a fundamental aspect of inclusionary citizenship practice. A few contextual issues have probably contributed to this focus. In Spain, claims concerning migrants' right to vote have recently been forwarded in the public sphere 'from immigrant associations, left-wing political parties and other social actors' (Zapata-Barrero, 2010:397; see also Hellgren, 2007). While EU citizens who are living in another EU member state are eligible to vote or stand as a candidate in local and European elections, the issue of non-EU immigrants' right to vote in Spain has only recently been addressed by the state. During the past few years, reciprocal agreements have been made with a number of Latin American countries and also with Norway and other countries, giving immigrants officially residing in Spain for five years whose origin is from one of these countries the right to vote in municipal elections from 2011. In practice, however, the condition of the existence of a reciprocal agreement 'results in far-reaching restrictions [on political citizenship] or de facto nonexistence of voting rights' (Groenendijk, 2008:5) for individuals who do not happen to originate from a country with a reciprocal agreement. Moreover, gender quotas were a hot topic in Spain during the period of our interviews. Parity provisions, introduced in the March 2007 Equality Law, were taken to the Spanish Constitutional Court by the Popular Party with accusations of unconstitutionality (Lombardo, 2009).[8]

In this context, it is not surprising that voting rights was a significant issue among the activists we interviewed. One ethnic minority activist, for example, emphasized the demand by immigrants 'to be able to vote at least in the regional and local elections'. She was also concerned about how rules on acquiring Spanish nationality differ by country of origin, thus referring to discriminatory legacies from Spain's colonial past. Another ethnic minority activist also emphasized what she saw as a fundamental right for all residents to vote, and the injustice she perceived in some immigrants having to wait 10 years to obtain citizenship with full voting rights.

These findings demonstrate how activists in Spain focused on the rights to political citizenship, as well as on the notion that such rights should be equal for everyone. In Spain, the concept of rights was a central element in the 1975–78 transition to democracy, and continues to play an important role in political claims-making related to gendered, regional, ethnic and language-based groups and identities.

The UK: citizenship as welfare rights, and patterns of exclusion and discrimination

The wider UK context, with its history of empire, post-colonial immigration, a liberal welfare regime with high levels of inequality and lower spending on social protection relative to other European welfare regimes (Fenger, 2007), and an active anti-racist movement combating well-documented racist practices, provides the background for how citizenship was talked about among the UK activists. Their views centred on issues of inclusion and exclusion in relation to nationality, participation and belonging. Moreover, they referred to racism and discrimination as barriers to inclusive citizenship for ethnic minorities. Access to welfare rights, rather than political rights, was also emphasized. The notion that the UK has different tiers of citizenship for different groups of people depending on their ethnic minority status was, for example, mentioned by an ethnic minority activist who framed citizenship in terms of individual rights and freedom from racism: 'Citizenship is about being an individual who has rights, the same rights as everybody else. And due to the level of racism and institutional racism...they have several different tiers of citizenship.' This activist was also very critical of the system in which immigrants are required to gain their passport through different routes,[9] while the same level of involvement (in paid and voluntary work) is not required of British born citizens. Some UK activists talked critically about the government's policy of encouraging immigrants to volunteer in order to integrate in society and as a means to speed up their naturalization. An ethnic minority activist was sceptical about the government's expectation that all immigrants should be able to volunteer, and stated that the marginalized position of refugees and asylum seekers may prevent them from participating in the voluntary sector.

One UK interviewee, a majority activist, stated that she does not think much about citizenship as an issue, because she herself is 'a person with the right to vote and whose name is on the electoral register and with a national insurance number. But it never occurs to me that it applies to me.' Instead, she associates citizenship with women refugees and asylum seekers who have been trafficked or are escaping violence in their homeland. The only UK interviewee who does not participate in political elections is an asylum seeker who has applied for citizenship. She was concerned with her lack of freedom of movement due to not having a British passport. She clearly identified citizenship with status, and saw the holding of a passport as imbuing a person with power – the power to travel and to freely leave and enter the country one resides in. Having been a resident without papers in the UK for many years, she was frustrated with the length of time it has taken for her claim to asylum to be processed: 'If citizenship goes with power, then I need a passport to gain the power. So how long is it going to take me to work for that power to come? So if it is going to take me centuries, at the end I will be dead.'

The association of citizenship with state power was also highlighted by another UK ethnic minority activist, who found citizenship to be 'a very problematic term.... Because it suggests borders; it suggests boundaries, it suggests limitations and it suggests ways in which the state can penetrate and surveillance communities and individuals.'

A lack of freedom of movement was also mentioned by UK activists who are full citizens or have permanent residency in the country. These interviewees highlighted how people from ethnic and religious minority backgrounds are often targeted by police and by immigration officials.[10] For example, one activist stated that her freedom of movement is constrained by her race: '... you can't go in and out of the country without being asked many, many questions, depending on your race'. Similarly, another British-born activist stated:

> The notion of citizenship is that...you have access, free access as a citizen to travel and to be part of this global community'.... But I don't feel, me

being an Indian woman, an Asian woman, black feminist, lesbian and all that, single parent, or a parent with somebody. It doesn't give me the same rights of movement and the same rights of access to a voice, or access to services, or the freedom of just movement.

In the UK, a large section of the immigrant population has enjoyed voting rights due to their origin in a Commonwealth Country (totalling 55 countries including Australia, Canada, New Zealand, Bangladesh, India and Pakistan). The issue of voting rights has therefore not been highly politicized in the UK context, despite the fact that the state discriminates on the basis of country of origin in granting the right to vote only to immigrants of certain nationalities. One interviewee recounted her discovery that being a citizen of a Commonwealth country entitles her to vote, but despite being a legal resident and tax payer in the UK, she also emphasized that she is 'a woman with no recourse' and that she is 'not entitled to any benefits from the public purse', including child benefit if she and her partner were to have a baby. Stressing that she doesn't mind paying taxes and that doing so is part of being a citizen, she felt her lack of access to social or welfare rights is discriminatory as she is not entitled to the same rights as other UK tax payers. The UK has imposed similar rules for Bulgarian and Romanian immigrants to the UK, despite their status as EU citizens.[11] All other EU and EEA citizens are entitled to child benefit, other welfare benefits and tax credits while residing in the UK. The unequal rules applied to different groups of residents in the UK is an example of discriminatory practices which in effect create different tiers of citizenship.

In comparison with the activists in Norway, the UK activists demonstrated a far less benign view of the state. This is in line with British radical and Marxist feminist traditions of scepticism towards a centralized state which has provided women with less political access and representation than alternative arenas located within civil society and sub-national politics (Siim, 2000:101). Moreover, Asian and Black women, as well as the broader anti-racist movement in the UK, have been highly critical of the state's racist practices. Therefore, rather than seeing the state as a 'friend' or potential ally, UK activists emphasize how the state can be implicated in racist and discriminatory practices which marginalize black and ethnic minority communities. Similar to our findings from Norway, however, activists in the UK are less concerned with political citizenship in terms of voting rights and more with issues of participation and belonging, probably because voting rights are taken for granted, while issues of participation and belonging are still fraught with tension.

In Norway and Spain, activists' responses revealed that they do not use the term 'citizenship' in political claims-making. In the UK, the activists we interviewed were also presented with the FEMCIT project's multidimensional understanding of citizenship along the political, economic, social, multicultural and religious, bodily and intimate dimensions, and were asked specifically about the extent to which they currently use, or would consider it a good idea to use, a citizenship frame in their claims-making. The overwhelming finding was that UK activists, like the activists in Norway and in Spain, do not currently use the term citizenship in their mobilization and claims-making: several interviewees said, 'Citizenship is not a word I use', and there was also an inclination to describe it as an academic, abstract term. The preference for a human rights frame, an equality frame or a social justice frame, rather than a citizenship frame, was clearly expressed. Although activists appreciated the multidimensionality of FEMCIT's understanding of citizenship, they did not consider it useful to women's movement activism. For example, one activist stated that she does not envisage using the term in her activism: 'But as a feminist doing the work I do, it wouldn't be the language I would use. It is a secondary concern to me as a way forward.' Even though she finds the concept to be 'hugely modelled on patriarchal notions' and therefore of limited use to women, she did not close the door entirely on using the concept of citizenship: 'I think we women are extremely clever at taking the concept which is current at the time and using it to our own ends. And if citizenship can be used that way, go for it. If it is going to get in the way, drop it.' In other words, if those with political power are using the concept, then women's movements should consider using it strategically to further their own ends.

Lived citizenship: experiences of exclusion and inclusion

We turn now to the issue of lived citizenship, and explore the activists' reflections on the possibility of practising full citizenship. Although 'citizenship' was not a term used, the activists did have a lot to say about their own experiences of inclusion and exclusion. What scholars analytically call 'lived citizenship', or 'everyday life citizenship', was filled with meaning. The activists are all 'active citizens', in that they engage in political activities related to women's everyday life, participate in independent women's movement organizations outside the formal political system and work towards women's integration in political institutions (Siim, 2000:5). As women's movement activists, they are eager to contribute and to influence society in ways they consider to be positive. They participate in formal politics in various ways, including political elections. The minority activists in our study speak fluent Norwegian, Spanish or English; they are either in work or in education – and in those respects they might be seen as objectively 'well integrated'. However, each individual's effort to be an 'active citizen' is only half the picture; the discriminatory and exclusionary structures and processes that they encounter must also be addressed.

We asked about 'lived citizenship', or about experiences of exclusion and inclusion along the citizenship elements of rights and duties, participation and belonging, and found that there are hindrances to women's ability to exercise full citizenship in all three countries. Sometimes these are easily identifiable, such as direct forms of street racism or institutional racism. At other times they are more difficult to identify; discrimination often works exactly because we do not see it, or because we consider it to be 'normal', as one of the Norwegian majority activists put it. The activists' experiences give useful information about how gender, race, ethnicity, religion and class intersect and affect everyday lived citizenship.

Lived citizenship in Norway

The activists in Norway were concerned with what they saw as their duty to contribute to creating a better society, rather than with the duties of the state and society towards the individual. This finding is related to the strong tradition in Norway of participation in voluntary community work ('*dugnadsarbeid*'), which is perceived as a civic duty for all inhabitants (Lorentzen and Dugstad, 2011). Another finding is that activists thought that women in Norway are privileged compared to women in other countries, and they also viewed majoritized women as privileged compared to minoritized women in Norway.[12] Research participants saw gender equality as a societal goal and agreed that it has yet to be realized. They also stated that minority women experience barriers related to a lack of language skills, professional and private networks, and, most of all, job experience. A lack of self-earned income was viewed as contributing to minority women's dependence on men and as impacting negatively on their lived citizenship.

When barriers to economic citizenship were discussed by majority women in Norway, they addressed them in class terms and related to socialization processes. According to one majority activist, she has never met any 'physical hindrance' or experienced that anyone has told her not to do certain things because she is a woman. In her opinion, the real barriers are due to her upbringing and gender socialization, which have led to a lack of self-confidence. As a girl she felt that it was expected of her to care for family members and others. When she grew up, she felt that if she took care only of herself, she was being egoistic. As an adult, she has become aware of this; however, she thinks it is very difficult to get rid of that feeling of being egoistic. This feeling, she said, is a result of her experience of growing up with certain expectations to her as a girl and internalizing these gender specific norms.

These experiences resonate with studies of working class women in Norway (Skilbrei, 2005) and the UK (Skeggs, 1997). They show how the interaction of gender and class shape limitations for working class women, who have to relate to strict ideals of motherhood, responsibility and sexuality (Skeggs, 1997, as cited in Skilbrei, 2005:52). The 'decent thing to do' for a working class woman is to take care of her children and husband, as well as other relatives.

For women in Norway, family life or aspects of social and intimate citizenship (see Bergman et al., and Roseneil et al., both this volume) – the uneven distribution of child-care responsibilities between women and men – were experienced as barriers to full citizenship. For example, women in Norway are still expected to take the main responsibility for child care. One majority activist outlined what she regarded as an 'underlying expectation' that when women become mothers, 'they should stay at home as much as possible and not prioritize other issues, at least when children are young'. Another majority participant also talked about the need for an increase in the availability and acceptance of individually tailored solutions for women, in contrast to a more rigid understanding of gender equality which prescribes that women must take on paid employment, work 'like men', and place their children in nurseries. A more flexible attitude towards women's choices would also give more space for minority women's preferences, she suggested. This majority activist is well educated, and her middle class upbringing taught her that she had many options before her. However, the reality of combining motherhood with a career and feminist principles was experienced as challenging, and she chose to take unpaid leave for some time to care for her child. Her experience convinced her that there is more than one way to be a 'good feminist'. The story indicates that expectations surrounding motherhood do not only affect working class or minority women; however, the ideal of combining motherhood and a career is perhaps stronger in the middle class – and this ideal is difficult to live up to.

The Norwegian activists stated that, from a legal and formal perspective, women and men in Norway enjoy equal rights; however, they perceived women to have fewer opportunities than men in practice. Nevertheless, to focus explicitly on gender discrimination may be difficult because some of it is hard to put a finger on. Gender discrimination is often invisible because it seems 'normal' to us or it constitutes 'the sum of little things', as one of the interviewees phrased it. They can seem like minor issues, like one activist's experience of not always being taken seriously due to being soft-spoken. Moreover, to voice critiques of discrimination of women, and to address inequality as such in Norwegian society, was experienced as difficult by interviewees. The discursive space for such interventions was found to be limited due to a general discourse of gender equality having been achieved in Norway – and perhaps also because of a lack of consideration of class differences.

A problem for minority activists in Norway, in contrast with majority activists, is a lack of recognition; an issue that runs like a scarlet thread through the minority women's stories. The interviews displayed various 'accommodation strategies' used by minority women in order to cope with numerous forms of everyday discrimination, and also the necessity to counter prejudice and prove themselves to be 'worthy' of living in Norway. They talked about their lived experience in terms of overcoming barriers related to language skills, networking, access to work and educational qualifications, but unlike the UK participants they did not frame their experiences much in terms of 'racism'. This was not surprising, because the word 'racism' is difficult to use in everyday Norwegian, despite an active anti-racist movement in Norway (Nydal, 2007). 'Racism' is a taboo concept as well as an insult to Norwegians who see themselves as beyond racist behaviour (Gullestad, 2006). The interviewees could therefore have hesitated even mentioning the term, let alone talk about racism in any depth with researchers of ethnic majority backgrounds. When minority activists in Norway mentioned the term 'racism', it was very briefly or in passing, and mainly in relation to Muslims' experience of being labelled as terrorist, or headscarf wearing Muslim women being viewed as 'dumb' and being discriminated against in the labour market. Although racism was not talked about much in our interviews in Norway, the importance of race, religion and ethnicity was indicated by the inclination of minority women activists to associate our questions of inclusion and exclusion with their own minoritized backgrounds, while the majority activists never made that connection when outlining their own lived citizenship. Instead, majority activists associated dynamics of inclusion and exclusion more specifically with gender issues. Race and ethnicity remained silenced issues among them, a finding in line with the taboo surrounding race-talk in Norway generally.

Lived citizenship in Spain

As in Norway, among the activists in Spain there was not much talk about racism and discrimination in everyday life; rather, as stated previously, the main focus was on issues of inclusion and exclusion in the polity and on political, social and economic rights. As in the UK and in Norway, however, activists in Spain talked about how cultural and religious practices within ethnic minority communities can hinder women's citizenship, and how gender-based violence provide barriers to citizenship for all women. At the centre of their discourse in this regard was the concept of human rights, which was presented as taking precedence over any cultural or religious practices that may be deemed as contrary to human rights.[13] Some majority interviewees in Spain also saw the wearing of the Muslim headscarf as problematic, as they perceived it as a sign of women's submission, echoing Spanish-born women's tradition of wearing a headscarf in a more patriarchal past. When asked about the barriers she perceived for minority women to be included in Spanish society, one minority activist replied that even though these women have rights, they are largely unable to make use of them owing to a lack of knowledge. She continued:

> and sometimes they are also unaware of their duties and the social norms prevalent in this country. And this disorientation is what gives rise to vulnerability. These women's dependency on their husbands, their lack of financial independence, their lack of freedom of residency, since their right to stay in their country is conditional upon their husband's, so really, these women are subject to a lot of constraints....

The interviewee perceived a lack of awareness of women's rights among immigrant women as a big problem, and suggested that learning about rights is the most important step forward. She went on to suggest that immigrant women, rather than being dependent on men and having their residency permit processed through their partners, should be 'entitled to be granted a residence permit and, if it expires, to be able to renew it without depending on the man'. Her views were echoed by other activists who saw women's dependency on men's residence status as highly problematic in relation to safeguarding their rights to freedom from gender-based violence. For example, one interviewee stated that 'for immigrant women, the foremost fear is that if they report their husbands they will get thrown out of the country'. However, her solution to such problems was not to forward claims regarding citizenship, but to frame policy demands as issues of human rights and women's rights. She emphasized that women who suffer from violence should be entitled to protection regardless of their citizen status, as human rights are universal and therefore must apply also to women with insecure immigrant status.[14] Such views were echoed by another activist in Spain who also framed human rights as a priority concern over and above the citizenship status of individuals: 'We work from the standpoint of rights…. What we defend is that in Spain, safeguarding human rights is something that takes precedence over any kind of immigration policy.'

Activists in Spain, Norway and the UK alike were concerned with issues of gender-based violence within immigrant communities and with misleading stereotypes about ethnic minority communities and individuals. Activists in Spain and the UK noted that immigrant women without legal documents who experience domestic violence are in a particularly vulnerable position, since they may be financially dependent on their partners and avoid reporting violence due to fears of deportation. As noted earlier, activists in the UK referred to the 'no recourse to public funds' rule which prevents women with insecure immigration status who experience partner violence from accessing public funds.[15] Rather than framing this as a citizenship issue, however, activists in both the UK and in Spain framed the support for immigrant women experiencing violence as first and foremost a human rights issue: 'Yes, that seems to be a basic bloody human right, let alone a citizenship issue, to not have to choose between violence and homelessness and destitution.'

Only a couple of minority activists in Spain focused specifically on direct experiences of racism and discrimination in their interviews. An activist working for a Roma (Gypsy)[16] women's organization gave the example of Roma women who are widowed with no legal right to draw a pension due to having married only via 'Gypsy rituals': 'This constitutes an example of an unacknowledged cultural difference which involves discrimination'. Another interviewee claimed that governmental institutions do not discriminate, 'when you go there they pay attention to you even if you are not a naturalized citizen with voting rights'. Rather, she identified racism as a phenomenon she has experienced 'in the street by someone who says 'nigger, go back to Africa' and through immigrants with professional qualifications being by-passed for employment by lesser qualified Spanish-born individuals. A third activist, on the other hand, said she had felt discrimination at the institutional level more strongly than at the personal level. The example she gave was that of a recent policy proposal for immigrants to sign an 'integration contract'. She identified this type of discourse as discriminatory and racist.

A majority activist in Spain working for an organization promoting the interests of Roma women also noted the existence of negative stereotypes: 'they [Roma women] are thought to be submissive, prone to abuse and more male chauvinism than other women'. Her organization denies these stereotypes, 'because patriarchal male chauvinism is present in all cultures and is not more pronounced in the Gypsy culture even though that perception unfortunately still persists'. She was also concerned about stereotypes regarding Muslim women. She refuted the idea that some religions are more discriminatory against women than others, as well as the notion that all Muslim women are oppressed.

Activists in Spain also identified the lack of affordable child-care facilities as a barrier to women's participation in politics and in paid work, while at the same time noting that this issue is now on the government's political agenda. In this regard, interviewees also noted the difficulty of reconciling immigrant women's work in domestic services with its long hours and low pay with child-care responsibilities.

Lived citizenship in the UK

In the UK, several of the activists associated the term 'citizenship' with the term 'British' – not in the sense of having a British passport, but in the sense of wanting to be accepted or included as an equal citizen without having to experience racism and discrimination in public spheres such as politics, employment, or on the street. Race and ethnicity and also to some extent religion (Islam) were clearly felt as negative markers and as barriers to full citizenship by all of the interviewees in the UK. Unlike Norway, majoritized interviewees in the UK also emphasized the continued prevalence of racialized discrimination. One minority activist explained that she finds it difficult to 'buy into' the notion of 'global citizenship or European citizenship' as long as black and ethnic minority people in the UK do not have the same rights and the same access to services as ethnic majority people in the UK.

The UK activists expressed a broad range of concerns about exclusionary, marginalizing and discriminatory practices that prevent minority women from experiencing equal citizenship. Some interviewees mentioned the current citizenship test which has to be passed by those seeking formal citizenship in the UK. Many referred to additional hurdles that were also mentioned by activists in Norway and Spain, such as restricted access to paid work, as well as barriers related to voluntary work, language skills and educational qualifications. At the same time, people of racial and ethnic minority backgrounds born in the UK, as well as immigrants, refugees and asylum seekers, experience a number of constraints and barriers to equal citizenship due to their skin colour, culture or religious beliefs. These findings echo those of the Parekh Report on multiethnic Britain, which highlighted experiences of racism and discrimination based on skin colour, culture and religion (The Runnymede Trust, 2000). For example, a minority activist born in the UK talked about citizenship as a term that signifies belonging. Yet, she does not feel that she belongs to the society in which she lives, and does not feel a connection with the word 'citizenship'. When asked why, she replied that her childhood experiences of racism in shops and of being the only black person at school, as well as her adult experience that contemporary society is 'very racist' and does not take seriously the issues that affect black people, make her feel that she is not fully accepted: 'We are still facing those kinds of issues every day so that is why I cannot embrace the word citizenship because I don't feel like a citizen.' The interviewee went on to suggest that due to such experiences, people might choose to remain within their own communities and families, rather than taking an active part in the broader community, and that they might not want to get involved in anything 'for fear of reprisals, for fear of being told that you do not belong here'. Her story illustrates how citizenship as lived, everyday practice can be experienced in terms of exclusion, just as strongly as experiences of exclusion that are related to citizenship as status and rights.

While UK activists generally focused on exclusionary practices within various arenas of the majority society as barriers to citizenship, some UK activists (as well as activists in Spain and in Norway) also talked about obstacles found within immigrant communities, such as patriarchal practices which hinder women's participation. For example, a British citizen of ethnic minority background recounted how she does not feel included or accepted as a citizen, and that she has experienced 'loads' of barriers and limitations 'on the grounds of my colour, my gender, my sexuality'. She did not think that minority women can fully exercise citizenship in the UK society. Yet, she pointed to immigrant communities themselves as posing the strongest barriers to minority women's participation. Due to what she perceives as the 'patriarchal nature of those communities' she regards it as difficult for black women to speak out about issues of oppression originating within minority communities.

Several of the minority activists interviewed in Norway, Spain and the UK were directly involved in working against issues such as forced marriage, honour-based violence, female genital mutilation and other forms of gender-based violence within their own communities. Some majority women activists also spoke specifically about 'culture' as a barrier to citizenship, and argued that cultural practices which contradict human rights should not be tolerated.

In addition to emphasizing barriers to participation originating within immigrant communities, however, some UK activists were also concerned with stereotypes about such communities in general, and about women from ethnic minority backgrounds in particular. For example, Muslim women were mentioned as a group that is frequently associated with negative stereotypes. One interviewee reflected on the issue of passing a citizenship test, and how that in itself does not guarantee the equal treatment of a new citizen in terms of her religion, race and ethnicity. She mentioned that Muslim women, in particular those who wear a burqa or a hijab, might be taunted on the street and suffer from a lack of access to citizen rights due to racism and discrimination.

Another UK-born interviewee stated that her race is more salient than her gender in everyday life. When something happens to her, she reflects on whether it is due to her being black or being a woman. More often than not, she finds that her skin colour explains more than her gender. Differences related to race, ethnicity, gender and religion were thus identified as the basis of different forms of exclusion from full lived citizenship.

In sum, activists in all three countries talked about barriers to full citizenship experienced by women, in particular barriers related to inclusion, participation and belonging. They mentioned difficulties in accessing work and affordable, quality child care, and the importance of being able to balance work and family duties. Additional barriers experienced by minoritized women were related to their lack of language skills, educational qualifications and networking, as well as to oppressive practices within ethnic minority communities and discriminatory practices within the majority society related to gender, race, ethnicity and religion.

Conclusion: a gap between feminist scholarship and movement activism

We have examined how the concept of citizenship is understood by women's movement activists, the extent to which they use a citizenship frame in their political claims-making, and the experiences they talk about in relation to citizenship as lived practice. Our findings demonstrate the importance of considering the specific historical and socio-political contexts in which social movement activism is situated in order to understand why the interviewed women's movement activists in Norway, Spain and the UK understand the term 'citizenship' differently.

In Norway, the term 'citizenship' was unfamiliar to most of the interviewees, but when asked to freely associate around it, several activists emphasized people's responsibility to play an active part in society, to contribute positively to it, and to care about the well-being of others. The women we interviewed in Norway mainly talked about the responsibilities and duties of individuals to society – the horizontal dimension of citizenship – when they talked about citizenship as an abstract term. They talked a lot about the need to be recognized, but they did not talk much about individual rights or about the state. This indicates that such rights are taken for granted in the Norwegian welfare state, and that the state is viewed as a rather benign entity.

In Spain, activists focused first and foremost on the rights of the individual – on political rights, on women's right to equality (in the labour market and through public provision of child care), and on freedom from gender-based violence. They talked about citizenship in terms of the inclusion or exclusion of ethnic minority groups in the polity, and on the different access to nationality, naturalization and voting that are accorded different immigrant groups in Spain. The vertical state–citizen discourse foregrounds citizenship as rights, and is related to the expectations that the democratic state should remedy previous discrimination of women, that Spain only recently became a country of net immigration and has yet to grant many immigrant groups the right to vote, and that racism and discrimination have only recently begun to be seriously addressed by policy-makers.

Women's movement activists in the UK, however, associated the term 'citizenship' more with issues of national identity, participation and belonging, and with racist and discriminatory practices by the state and in society at large that exclude and marginalize ethnic minority communities in general and ethnic minority women in particular. The vertical aspect of citizenship in the UK is not primarily about rights, as in Spain, but about criticism of the state. These views can be understood in reference to the UK context, where colonial and post-colonial legacies continue to play an important role in relations between majoritized and minoritized groups. Although the UK state has been at the forefront of developing legislation to prevent racism and discrimination, racist and discriminatory practices are still abundant (Pitcher, 2009).

Although the term 'citizenship' was not applied by the activists themselves, we have profited from using 'citizenship' as an analytical concept when interpreting our findings. In particular, the concept of 'lived citizenship' – how individuals understand and negotiate rights and responsibilities, belonging and participation (Lister et al., 2007:168) – has been useful. Through a focus on the lived experiences of women's movement activists, we have identified a broad set of barriers to women's full political, economic, social, multicultural and intimate citizenship. In this respect, activists in Norway, Spain and the UK are concerned with similar issues.

We found that very few of the women's movement activists whom we interviewed explicitly made a link between conceptions of citizenship as an active participatory practice and as a struggle for a set of rights (Lister, 2007:52). They did not talk about their own mobilization as a 'citizenship practice', but rather as a struggle for the realization of human rights, equality and justice.

Through our analysis of how women's movement activists' talk, and do not talk, about citizenship, we have identified a divergence between the feminist scholarly focus on an inclusionary normative notion of citizenship as lived practice – as social relations and participatory practices within all spheres of life, be they political, economic, social, cultural, religious, bodily or intimate (Halsaa, Roseneil and Sümer, 2011) – and the ways in which activists understand and use the notion of citizenship. Although a complex, multidimensional and multilevel notion of citizenship corresponds empirically with the activists' agendas, the activists do not apply the concept normatively. The activists do associate citizenship with issues such as status, rights, participation and belonging, but they emphasize its fundamentally exclusionary aspects, and tend to see it as an abstract term which is not very useful in everyday movement practise. Consequently, the analysis of interviews with women's movements activists in Norway, Spain and the UK show limited evidence of 'citizenship' being used as a term to frame political demands. The notion appears to have little political purchase or relevance in enabling women's movement activists to mobilize politically. Only in specific contexts, such as those addressing issues of racism and discrimination experienced by ethnic minority women in general and by women with insecure or dependent citizenship status in particular, does the term appear to be of any relevance to movement activism. However, activists who work on issues related to women's insecure immigration status, especially in relation to domestic violence, stated a clear preference for a human rights frame for their claims-making. Overall, normative frames other than that of citizenship, in particular the human and women's rights frames, and also the (gender) equality and social justice frames, are preferred by activists addressing inequalities and discriminatory practices across national and political contexts.

Our findings thus indicate a gap between grassroots women's movement activists and feminist scholarship in relation to citizenship as a normative concept, and substantiate the claim that 'citizenship' has an ambiguous status in relation to feminism. However, we also found agreement regarding the empirical descriptions of barriers and limitations to full citizenship. The partial mismatch we have found between theory and activism, and between normative conceptualizations and empirical descriptions, is evidence of different discourses among academic feminists and grassroots women's movement activists. This does not necessarily imply, however, that the 'citizenship' concept should be discarded; rather, both the concept and practice of lived citizenship should be 'remade' to promote inclusion, participation, justice and equality. Due to the importance of citizenship as a political–institutional concept at local, national and global levels, feminist citizenship scholarship has the potential to serve as a useful bridge between grass-root feminism and more formal, institutional politics, if it succeeds in producing knowledge of lived citizenship that translates to feminist activist communities as well as to institutional politics. Only then can the 'remaking of citizenship' become an accepted, as well as strategic, frame in women's movement discourse and policy demands.

Notes

1. Our research was supported by a grant from the European Commission's 6th framework programme for the project FEMCIT: Gendered Citizenship in a Multicultural Europe: The Impact of Women's Movements. The authors wish to thank Sasha Roseneil, Sevil Sümer, Joyce Outshoorn, madeleine kennedy-macfoy, Monica Threlfall and other FEMCIT colleagues for valuable comments on previous drafts.

2. The authors wish to thank Adriana Sandu for conducting the interviews in Spain, and Hannah Helseth for conducting five interviews in Norway. The remaining interviews in Norway were conducted by Cecilie Thun. All interviews in the UK were by Line Nyhagen Predelli. Twenty-eight interviews were conducted in the period May 2007–June 2008, and two in 2009. Interviews were conducted in Norwegian, Spanish and English and transcribed. The Spanish ones were translated into English.

3. The UK became an EU member state in 1973; Spain in 1986. Norway is not an EU member, but complies with EU legislation via the European Economic Area agreement (with some exceptions).

4. For example, Spain was not granted UN membership until 1955.

5. MIPEX measures policies to integrate migrants in 25 EU Member States and three non-EU countries via 140 policy indicators (http://www.mipex.eu/ [accessed 20 June 2011]).

6. Norway: the Equal Pay Council (1959); the Gender Equality Council (1972); the Gender Equality Ombud (1979); the Gender Equality Act (1979). Spain: the Institute of Women (1983). UK: the Equal Pay Act (1970); the Sex Discrimination Act (1975); the Equal Opportunities Commission (1975)

7. Both Norway's recent anti-discrimination legislation and Spain's National Observatory against Racism and Xenophobia were introduced in 2005.

8. In January 2008, the Constitutional Court rejected this claim, and gave its approval to the parity provision of the Spanish Equality Law (Lombardo, 2009).

9. In the UK, citizenship can be acquired through descent, declaration, marriage, or adoption. The 2009 Borders, Citizenship and Immigration Act made further distinctions between different routes to citizenship for immigrants.

10. For documentation of the discriminatory stop and search practices, see the Equality and Human Rights Commission (EHRC, 2010).

11. Romanian and Bulgarian nationals are not allowed to become 'an unreasonable burden on public funds'; see http://www.ukba.homeoffice.gov.uk/eucitizens/bulgarianandromaniannationals/ [accessed 21 June 2011].

12. We use the terms (ethnic) 'majority' and (ethnic) 'minority', as well as 'minoritized' (Gunaratnam, 2003) and 'majoritized', when talking about different feminist and women's movement actors. Our approach is inspired by Yasmin Gunaratnam (2003), who applies a social constructivist perspective to the terms 'minority' and 'minority'. She employs the term 'ethnic minority' not in a descriptive sense, but sees the label and its connotations as socially constructed and therefore uses the term in quotation marks. Gunaratnam prefers the term 'minoritized', as it signals 'the active processes of racialisation that are at work in designating certain attributes of groups in particular contexts as being in a 'minority'' (2003:17). In our own writing, for the sake of readability we have not consistently used quotation marks around the terms 'majority' and 'minority'. Moreover, we use these terms interchangeably with 'minoritized' (as suggested

by Gunaratnam), and 'majoritized'. The term 'majoritized' signals that 'the majority is constituted as a majority by virtue of its power to, simultaneously, define the rules, be a fellow player and act as judges' (Gullestad, 2002: 100; our translation). This 'majority-inclusive perspective' takes seriously the fact that majorities and minorities are constituted in relation to each other, and that the very categories that are being constituted are a result of differences in material as well as discursive forms of power: '[t]here are differences of power and of being marked and unmarked, privileged and non-privileged, powerful and non-powerful' (Staunæs, 2003:105; see also Staunæs and Søndergaard, 2006; Frankenberg,1993; Brah, 1996:186). In other words, the labelling of people as 'majority' or 'minority' is in large part determined by existing power relations and power differentials between different groups. Minoritization and majoritization processes occur through social relations that are shaped by power, resources, interests, language and discourse. The distinction between race and ethnicity, which used to refer to alleged biological versus cultural and/or religious differences, is blurred. Theories of race are discredited by scholars, but 'race talk' in everyday life is very much alive (Taylor, 2003) and we therefore apply the term.

13. Female genital mutilation and domestic abuse among minority women were talked about as religious and cultural practices, rather than as practices rooted in gender inequality.

14. In Spain, immigrant women who are victims of domestic violence or sexual exploitation obtained a concession for independent residence in Organic Law 4/2000, which granted them a one year permit with access to social benefits but no right to work (Protection of Migrants, 2007:11; Amnesty International, 2008).

15. The immigration regulation 'no recourse to public funds' affects non-British nationals and Bulgarian and Romanian nationals (other EU and EEA nationals are exempt from the rule). The regulation denies state support and welfare benefits to those with insecure immigration status, and has therefore made immigrant women who experience domestic violence particularly vulnerable (see Amnesty International and Southall Black Sisters, 2008).

16. The interviewed activists in Spain used the term 'Gypsy'. We have retained this usage when quoting interviewees, but our preferred term is 'Roma'. For a conceptual discussion see Hancock (2002).

Appendix I: The FEMCIT Project: Research Design and Methodology

In 2005 a multidisciplinary group of feminist social researchers – gender studies researchers, sociologists, political scientists, historians, and ethnologists/anthropologists – from across Europe came together to respond to a call by the European Commission for social scientific research on 'citizens and governance'.[1] From various positions of engagement with feminist scholarship and activism, we saw this as an opportunity to do a large scale piece of cross-national research on the difference that women's movements have made, politically, socially and culturally. Strategically mobilizing, and simultaneously problematizing and interrogating, the language of citizenship that has been so central to the European project of governance in recent years, we constructed a research project to explore the ways in which women's movements, in all their variety and complexity, might, and might not, have contributed to the transformation of citizenship over the past 40 years, in the changing multicultural contexts of Europe.

The 'Gendered Citizenship in Multicultural Europe: impact of contemporary women's movements' project – FEMCIT – was funded from 2007 to 2011. It asked a big, macro-level question about *the impact of women's movements:* how have post-1960s women's movements remade citizenship, in an increasingly multicultural and diverse Europe? We sought to answer this question through a series of case studies that addressed gendered citizenship in terms of state practice, at national and transnational level, and in terms of collective action within civil society (above all in women's organizations and groups), and everyday life and cultures. FEMCIT worked with an expanded, feminist-inspired conceptualization of citizenship that incorporated the central fields of struggle of women's movements over the past 40 years, investigating six interrelated 'dimensions' of citizenship – political, social, economic, multicultural, bodily and intimate citizenship (see Figure I.1).

As shown in Figure I.1, each dimension of citizenship was addressed by a 'work package' that addressed particular issues that have been the subject of women's movement claims-making.

213

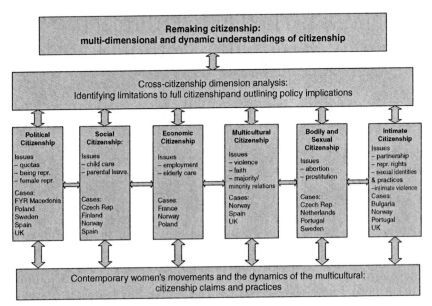

Figure I.1   The Overall Structure of the FEMCIT Project

So, the *political citizenship* work package addressed the question of the formal political representation of women and members of minoritized groups, with sub-projects on gender and ethnic quotas, on gendered and racialized experiences of 'being represented' (or not), and on the experience of being a woman member of an elective assembly.

The *social citizenship* work package focused on women's movements' claims around child care – including the tension within women's movements between those advocating the public provision of day care and those seeking home care allowances – and claims around parental leave, and the issue of men's involvement in raising children.

The *economic citizenship* work package explored the influence of second wave women's movements on normative assumptions, practices and policies related to women's employment, and included a mapping of women's movement journals and an analysis of employment opportunities and policies in the (highly gendered and racialized) growing sector of elder care, which is a highly gendered and racialized sphere of employment.

The *multicultural citizenship* work package was concerned with the relationship between feminism, ethnic identity and religion. It had three sub-projects: one that examined the relations between majoritized and minoritized organizations within contemporary women's movements, focusing particularly on those that are working around violence against women; another that explored the citizenship experiences and practices of

Christian and Muslim women, and their relationship with feminism; and a third sub-project that researched the meanings of 'citizenship' for women's movement activists.

The work package on *bodily and sexual citizenship* addressed the question of feminist body politics through case studies of the issues of abortion and prostitution, tracing feminist interventions and debates around these issues and their impact on policy and the political process.

The *intimate citizenship* work package addressed the impact of women's movements on intimate citizenship and personal life, mapping first the claims and demands of women's movements, and other movements for gender and sexual equality, around intimate life, then analysing changes in intimate citizenship law and policy over the past 40 years, and finally researching everyday experiences of intimate citizenship, with a particular focus on partnership, reproductive rights and parenting, sexual identities and practices and intimate violence.

In the seventh work package we carried out our integrative work, bringing together the findings from the six citizenship dimensions to try to develop an overarching understanding of the impacts and legacies of contemporary women's movements for gendered citizenship, and conducting a number of further cross-citizenship dimension research projects on, for example, minoritized and immigrant women's organizations, and gender mainstreaming.

Each of FEMCIT's work packages focused on a selection of countries, mostly chosen according to a 'most different' comparative research design, based on their differing welfare and gender regimes, or political/religious histories, but also selected pragmatically, according to the national location, expertise and linguistic competence of key partners in the project. In all we carried out research in 13 countries: Belgium, Bulgaria, Czech Republic, Finland, France, FYR Macedonia, Netherlands, Norway, Poland, Portugal, Spain, Sweden and the UK.[2]

The work packages used a variety of research methods, including biographical-narrative interviews, individual and focus group interviews with activists, experts and key informants, survey questionnaires, participant observation, policy mapping, primary analysis of policy and movement texts, and secondary analysis of statistical data. In total, we carried out approximately 520 face-to-face individual interviews, 20 focus group interviews with 160 participants and two small scale surveys.

We also carried out a number of 'memory work' exercises within the FEMCIT research group as a methodological tool for self-reflexivity with respect to majoritizing and minoritizing processes (Berg, 2009; Gunaratnam, 2003), and in order to think self-critically about power relations within the research group. We were motivated to do this in the context of the contradiction between our research focus on the multicultural, and on processes of racialization and minoritization, and the predominantly white composition of the research group. Our use of memory work focused primarily on issues of whiteness, ethnicity, and processes of racialization.

Alongside the empirical and theoretical exploration of the relationships between women's movements, gendered citizenship and the multicultural, FEMCIT has had a normative and political agenda: to engage in a process of imaging what full, gender-fair, liberatory citizenship in Europe might be, and to channel our ideas into the policy process through engagement with women's organizations, and European and national level policy-makers. One outcome of this agenda was the production of *The FEMCIT Manifesto for Multi-Dimensional Citizenship*, a collectively written document in which we present some of the most pressing claims and demands of women's movements in Europe across our six dimensions of citizenship.[3] We hope that the FEMCIT Manifesto will inspire debate within women's movements, in political groups and parties, amongst policy-makers and practitioners, within groups of friends, and between researchers.

Notes

1. FEMCIT was an FP 6 Integrated Project (Project No. 028746) that ran from 2007–2011. See www.femcit.org and the FEMCIT Final Report for more information about the project, its findings and a full list of FEMCIT related publications (Halsaa, Roseneil and Sümer, 2011).
2. With the benefit of hindsight, the project might have been better designed had the partners been brought together with regard to their national expertise and linguistic competence, in order to produce a systematically comparative project using the same countries across all the work packages. Researchers live and learn!
3. See http://www.femcit.org/files/femcit_manifesto.pdf (accessed 29 January 2012) and Appendix IV.

Appendix II: Profiles of the FEMCIT Countries

Table II.1 Overviews of FEMCIT countries

	Belgium	Bulgaria	Czech Republic	Finland	France	FYROM (Macedonia)	Netherlands	Norway	Poland	Portugal	Spain	Sweden	UK
Population[1] (mil) [2011]	10.9	7.5	10.5	5.4	65.0	2.1	16.7	4.9	38.2	10.6	46.2	9.4	62.4
GDP per capita[2] [2010]	119.0	44.0	82.0	116.0	107.0	35.0	133.0	179.0	62.0	81.0	101.0	123.0	114.0
Human Development Index rank[3] [2010]	18.0	58.0	28.0	16.0	14.0	71.0	7.0	1.0	41.0	40.0	20.0	9.0	26.0
Gender Inequality Index rank[4] [2008]	6.0	36.0	27.0	8.0	11.0	...	1.0	5.0	26.0	21.0	14.0	3.0	32.0

Table II.2   Aspects of multicultural citizenship in the FEMCIT countries

	Belgium	Bulgaria	Czech Republic	Finland	France	FYROM (Macedonia)
Main minority groups [5] %	Flemings 57, Walloons 32, Italians 2, French 1, Dutch 1, Moroccans 1[6]	Turks 9, Roma 5, Bulgarian-speaking Muslims or Pomaks 2–3[7]	Moravians 4, Slovaks 2, Polish 0.5[8]	Swedish-speakers 5.5, Russian-speakers 1, Roma/Gypsies 0.2, Sami 0.1[9]	Occitan-speakers 5–10, Alsatians 2, North Africans 5, Portuguese 1, Roma/Gypsies 1[10]	Albanians 25, Turks 4, Roma 3[11]
Religious demography[19] %	Roman Catholicism 47, Islam 4, Protestantism 1[20]	Orthodox Christianity 85, Islam 13, Catholicism 1[21]	Roman Catholicism 27, Protestantism together 3, Czech Hussite Church 1[22]	Evangelical Lutheran Christianity 83, Finnish Orthodox Church 1, Pentecostal Church 1[23]	Roman Catholicism 51, Islam 8–10, Protestantism 3[24]	Orthodox Christianity 65, Islam 32[25]
Migration Integration Policy Index (MIPEX) overall rank[33] [2010] overall rank	6.	26.	19.	4.	15.	...
MIPEX Anti-discrimination rank[34]	7.	6.	25.	8.	9.	...
MIPEX Political participation rank[35]	10.	28.	29.	2.	16.	...
MIPEX Family reunion for third-country nationals rank[36]	8.	23.	13.	7.	22.	...

Netherlands	Norway	Poland	Portugal	Spain	Sweden	UK
Frisians 4, Turks 2, Surinamese 2, Moroccans 2, Indonesians 2[12]	Sami 1, Polish 1, Swedes 0.6, Pakistanis 0.6[13]	Germans 0.4, Kashub-Speakers 0.1, Belarusian 0.1[14]	Azoreans 3, Madeirans 3, Cape Verdeans 0.5, Roma/Gypsies 0.4[15]	Catalans 16, Galicians 6, Basques 3, Roma/Gypsies 2, Ecuadoreans 1, Moroccans 1[16]	Finns 5, Roma 0.5, Jews 0.3, Sami 0.2[17]	Indians 2, African/Caribbean 1.7, Pakistanis 1, Turks 0.4–0.5[18]
Roman Catholicism 30, Dutch Reformist 15, Calvinist Reformist 7[26]	Evangelical Lutheran Christianity 82, Protestant Christian denominations 4, Islam 2[27]	Roman Catholicism 94, Polish Orthodox Church 1, Jehovah's Witnesses 0.3[28]	Roman Catholicism 70, other Christian denominations 2, Islam 0.1[29]	Roman Catholicism 76, Evangelical Christians and other Protestants 3, Islam 2[30]	Evangelical Lutheran Christianity 75, Islam 5, other Protestant groups 4[31]	Anglicanism 29, Protestant Churches 14, Catholicism 10, Islam 3[32]
5.	7.	24.	2.	8.	1.	12.
12.	16.	27.	5.	21.	3.	4.
3.	1.	29.	7.	12.	6.	13.
19.	8.	10.	1.	3.	4.	20.

Table II.3   Aspects of bodily and intimate citizenship in the FEMCIT countries

	Belgium	Bulgaria	Czech Republic	Finland	France	FYROM (Macedonia)
Fertility rates[37] [2010]	1.8[38]	1.5	1.5	1.9	2.0[39]	1.6
Access to abortion[42]	1990 on request	1956 on request; 1968, 1973 restrictions introduced; 1990 on request	1950 first legalized; 1986 on request	1950s first legalized; 1970 indications broadened	1975 on request	1977 on request
Same-sex relationship recognition[45]	2000 legal cohabitation, same-sex and opposite sex[46]; 2003: same-sex marriage[47]	Not recognized	2006 registered partnership	2002 registered partnership[48]	1999 Pacte civil de solidarité (PACS), same-sex and opposite sex	Not recognized

Table II.4   Aspects of economic citizenship in the FEMCIT countries

	Belgium	Bulgaria	Czech Republic	Finland	France	FYROM (Macedonia)
Gender pay gap[51] % [2009]	9[52]	15	26	20	16[53]	...
Female/ male employment rate[54] % [2010]	57/ 67	56/ 63	56/ 74	67/ 69	60/ 68	34/ 53
Female/ male part-time employment[55] % [2010]	42/ 9	3/ 2	10/ 3	20/ 10	30/ 7	7/ 5

Netherlands	Norway	Poland	Portugal	Spain	Sweden	UK
1.8	2.0	1.4	1.3[40]	1.4	2.0	2.0[41]
1984 on request	1964 indications broadened; 1978 on request	1932 restricted access; 1993 restrictions furthered	1984 restricted access; 2007 on request	1985 restricted access; 2010 on request[43]	1938 first legalized; 1975 on request	1967 restricted access[44]
1998 registered partnership; 2001: civil marriage	1993 registered partnership; 2009: same-sex marriage[49]	Not recognized	2001 unregistered partnership; 2010: same-sex marriage	1998 registered cohabitation; 2005: same-sex marriage	1995 registered partnership; 2009: same-sex marriage	2004 civil partnership; 2010: civil partnership on religious premises[50]

Netherlands	Norway	Poland	Portugal	Spain	Sweden	UK
19	17	10	10	17	16	20
69/ 80	73/ 77	53/ 66	61/ 70	52/ 65	70/ 75	64/ 75
77/ 25	43/ 15	12/ 6	16/ 8	23/ 5	40/ 14	43/ 13

Table II.5   Aspects of social citizenship in the FEMCIT countries

	Belgium	Bulgaria	Czech Republic	Finland	France	FYROM (Macedonia)
Couples' paid leave[56] [2008]	18.0	...	...	33.0	23.4	...
Maternity leave, maximum[57] [2008]	13.9	...	...	29.0	21.4	...
Paternity leave, maximum[58] [2008]	4.1	...	...	21.3	7.4	...
Children under three in formal care or pre-school[59] % [2010]	42.0	31.0	3.0	26.0	43.0	...
Women's share in tertiary education[60] % [2008]	55.0	55.0	56.0	54.0	55.0	53.0

Netherlands	Norway	Poland	Portugal	Spain	Sweden	UK
16.4	44.0	...	24.8	26.7	46.8	12.4
16.0	38.0	...	23.8	19.3	39.8	12.0
0.4	35.0	...	20.8	17.4	28.6	0.4
54.0	42.0	9.0	44.0	34.0	45.0	40.0
52.0	61.0	58.0	54.0	54.0	60.0	57.0

Table II.6 Aspects of political citizenship in the FEMCIT countries

	Belgium	Bulgaria	Czech Republic	Finland	France	FYROM (Macedonia)
Date of women's full enfranchise-ment[61]	1948	1944	1920	1906	1944	1945
Electoral system[62]	Proportional repre-sentation with party lists	Proportional repre-sentation with party lists	Proportional repre-sentation with party lists	Proportional repre-sentation with party lists	Two-round single member plurality	Proportional repre-sentation with party lists
Seats in Lower Chamber[63] [2010]	150	240	200	200	577	123
Voter turnout rates[64] [Parliamentary elections in 2000s] %	81–91	62–72	58–64	65–67	59–60	55–74
Women in parliament[65] % [2010]	39	21	22	43	19	31
Women in local politics[66] % [2008] 1) Municipal council members 2) Mayors	1) 33 2) 10	1) 30[67] 2) 10	1) 25 2) 18	1) 36[68] 2) 15[69]	1) 35 2) 14	1) 22 2) 4

Netherlands	Norway	Poland	Portugal	Spain	Sweden	UK
1919	1913	1918	1976	1931	1921	1928
Proportional repres-entation with party list (single district)	Proportional repre-sentation with party lists	Proportional repre-sentation with party lists	Proportional repre-sentation with party lists	Proportional repre-sentation with party lists	Proportional repre-sentation with party lists	Single member plurality ('first past the post')
150	169	460	230	350	349	650
75–80	75–77	40–54	58–64	68–76	80–84	59–65
39	40	24	27	36	45	22
1) 26	1) 38	1) 21	1) N/A	1) 46	1) 42	1) 29
2) 20	2) 23	2) 8	2) 6	2) 15	2) 30[70]	2) 2[71]

Notes

1. Retrieved from: http://epp.eurostat.ec.europa.eu/tgm/table.do?tab=table&init =1&language=en&pcode=tps00001&plugin=1, provisional values (accessed 11 September 2011).
2. Retrieved from: http://epp.eurostat.ec.europa.eu/tgm/table.do?tab=table&init= 1&plugin=1&language=en&pcode=tsieb010 (accessed 9 March 2011).
3. The *Human Development Index* (HDI) is a composite national measure of health, education and income. Retrieved from: http://hdr.undp.org/en/media/PR3-HDR10-HD1-E-rev4.pdf (accessed 10 October 2011). This year's HDI should not be compared to the HDI appearing in previous editions of the Human Development Report due to its use of different indicators and calculations.
4. The Gender Inequality Index (GII) was introduced in the Human Development Report 2010 as a new measure of gender inequality. 'A measure that captures the loss in achievements due to gender disparities in the dimensions of reproductive health, empowerment and labour force participation.' (HDR 2010:26) Retrieved from: http://hdr.undp.org/en/media/HDR_2010_EN_Complete_reprint.pdf (accessed 24 April 2011).
5. Approximate percentage of total population. Minority Rights Group International. Retrieved from: http://www.minorityrights.org/directory (accessed 13 April 2011).
6. 2006
7. 2001
8. 2001
9. 2006
10. 2005
11. 2002
12. 2005
13. Retrieved from: http://www.ssb.no/english/subjects/02/01/10/innvbef_en/tab-2011–04-28–01-en.html (accessed 18 May 2011).
14. 2002
15. 2005
16. 2005
17. 2005
18. Retrieved from: http://www.turkishweekly.net/news/29895/population-of-turk-ish-diaspora.html (accessed 18 May 2011).
19. Minority Rights Group International. Retrieved from: http://www.minorit-yrights.org/directory (accessed 13 April 2011). Supplemented with http://2001–2009.state.gov/g/drl/rls/irf/2008/index.htm (accessed 4 May 2011), and http://www.unhcr.org/refworld/country,,,,CZE,,4cf2d0a32,0.html (accessed 4 May 2011).
20. 2001
21. 2008
22. 2001
23. 2008; Pentecostal church communities registered as associations have an estimated 45,000 members. Only a fraction of Pentecostal churches are registered, however, and the actual number of worshippers is higher.
24. 2008
25. 2008
26. 2002

27. 2008
28. 2007
29. Estimated numbers.
30. 2008; estimated numbers.
31. 2008; estimated numbers.
32. 2003
33. *The Migrant Integration Policy Index (MIPEX)* measures and compares integration policies across European and North American countries. Policy indicators include: labour market mobility, family reunion, education, political participation, long term residence, access to nationality, anti-discrimination. Retrieved from: http://www.mipex.eu.
34. *The Migrant Integration Policy Index (MIPEX)* measures and compares integration policies across European and North American countries. Policy indicators include: labour market mobility, family reunion, education, political participation, long term residence, access to nationality, anti-discrimination. Retrieved from: http://www.mipex.eu.
35. *The Migrant Integration Policy Index (MIPEX)* measures and compares integration policies across European and North American countries. Policy indicators include: labour market mobility, family reunion, education, political participation, long term residence, access to nationality, anti-discrimination. Retrieved from: http://www.mipex.eu.
36. *Migrant Integration Policy Index (MIPEX)* measures and compares integration policies across European and North American countries. Policy indicators include: labour market mobility, family reunion, education, political participation, long term residence, access to nationality, anti-discrimination. Retrieved from: http://www.mipex.eu.
37. *Total fertility rate* refers to the 'mean number of children that would be born alive to a woman during her lifetime if she were to pass through her childbearing years conforming to the fertility rates by age of a given year.' Eurostat (2010) Retrieved from: http://epp.eurostat.ec.europa.eu/tgm/table.do?tab=table&init=1&language=en&pcode=tsdde220&plugin=1 (accessed 5 April 2011).
38. 2009
39. 2009
40. 2009
41. 2009
42. Retrieved from: http://www.un.org/esa/population/publications/abortion/profiles.htm (accessed 11 May 2011). See also International Planned Parenthood Federation, European Network (2007) Retrieved from: http://www.ippfen.org/NR/rdonlyres/2EB28750-BA71-43F8-AE2A-8B55A275F86C/0/Abortion_legislation_Europe_Jan2007.pdf (accessed 13 April 2011).
43. Retrieved from: http://www.guttmacher.org/media/inthenews/2010/03/03/index.html (accessed 10 October 2011).
44. The Abortion Act of 1967 does not apply to Northern Ireland.
45. Registered partnerships or civil partnerships refer to legally recognized same-sex partnerships which resemble marriage. Terminologies and contents may be different among countries. Data retrieved from: http://law-library.rutgers.edu/SSM.html, http://www1.umn.edu/humanrts/edumat/hreduseries/TB3/act6/a6h3.htm, and http://ilga-europe.org/home/guide/country_by_country (accessed 13 April 2011).
46. Not limited to couples.

47. Legal cohabitation recognizes two persons as legal cohabitants who form a household and are not bound by a marriage or by another legal cohabitation.
48. Finnish authorities are discussing the introduction of a gender-neutral marriage legislation at the time of writing.
49. See also: www.gender.no (accessed 10 October 2011).
50. 2004: Civil Partnership Act 2010: Section 202 of Equality Act implemented. Retrieved from: http://homeoffice.gov.uk/equalities/lgbt/ (accessed 10 October 2011).
51. The Gender Pay Gap (GPG) 'represents the difference between average gross hourly earnings of male paid employees and of female paid employees as a percentage of average gross hourly earnings of male paid employees.' Retrieved from http://epp.eurostat.ec.europa.eu/tgm/table.do?tab=table&init=1&language=en&pcode=tsiem040&plugin=1 (accessed 11 October 2011).
52. 2008
53. Provisional value.
54. Retrieved from: http://epp.eurostat.ec.europa.eu/tgm/refreshMapView.do?tab=map&plugin=1&init=1&toolbox=data&pcode=tsiem010&language=en (accessed 13 April 2011).
55. Retrieved from: http://epp.eurostat.ec.europa.eu/tgm/refreshMapView.do?tab=map&plugin=1&init=1&toolbox=types&pcode=tps00159&language=en# (accessed 11 May 2011).
56. Full-time employment, in weeks. Sum of various combinations of leave taken by the two parents. In countries where the total entitlement is 'affected by the distribution between parents, the shortest entitlement has been assumed'. Ray, R., Gornick, J. C., Schmitt, J (2008) *Parental Leave Policies in 21 Countries. Assessing Generosity and Gender Equality*. Washington: Center for Economic and Policy Research. Retrieved from: http://www.scribd.com/doc/5427460/Parental-Leave-Policies-in-21-Countries-Assessing-Generosity-and-Gender-Equality (accessed 18 September 2011).
57. Full-time employment, in weeks. Ray, R., Gornick, J. C., Schmitt, J (2008) *Parental leave policies in 21 countries. Assessing generosity and gender equality*. Washington: Center for Economic and Policy Research. Retrieved from: http://www.scribd.com/doc/5427460/Parental-Leave-Policies-in-21-Countries-Assessing-Generosity-and-Gender-Equality (accessed 18 September 2011).
58. Full-time employment, in weeks. Ray, R., Gornick, J. C., Schmitt, J (2008) *Parental leave policies in 21 countries. Assessing generosity and gender equality*. Washington: Center for Economic and Policy Research. Retrieved from: http://www.scribd.com/doc/5427460/Parental-Leave-Policies-in-21-Countries-Assessing-Generosity-and-Gender-Equality (accessed 18 September 2011).
59. Eurostat (2010) *The World's Women*. Retrieved from http://unstats.un.org/unsd/demographic/products/Worldswomen/WW_full%20report_BW.pdf (accessed 5 April 2011).
60. Women's share of tertiary enrolment 'refers to the percentage of students enrolled in tertiary education who are female. This indicator helps assess gender disparity with regard to participation in tertiary education. When the indicator approaches 50% it reflects a good level of gender parity.' Retrieved from http://epp.eurostat.ec.europa.eu/cache/ITY_OFFPUB/KS-QA-10–037/EN/KS-QA-10–037-EN.PDF (accessed 13 April 2011). See also http://unstats.un.org/unsd/demographic/products/indwm/tab4d.htm (accessed 13 April 2011).

61. Retrieved from: http://www.iwdc.org/resources/suffrage.htm (accessed 6 April 2011).
62. ACE Electoral Knowledge Network. Retrieved from: http://aceproject.org/ace-en/comparative-data/CDTable?question=ES001&view=country&set_language=en, and International IDEA (Institute for Democracy and Electoral Assistance) http://www.idea.int/esd/world.cfm (accessed 21 September 2011).
63. Inter-Parliamentary Union (IPU) Database on Women in National Parliaments, situation as of 30 November 2011. Retrieved from: http://www.ipu.org/wmn-e/classif.htm (accessed 10 January 2012).
64. ACE Electoral Knowledge Network. Retrieved from: http://aceproject.org/ace-en/comparative-data/CDMap?question=ES and International IDEA (Institute for Democracy and Electoral Assistance) http://www.idea.int/vt/ (accessed 21 September 2011).
65. Inter-Parliamentary Union (IPU) Database on Women in National Parliaments, situation as of 30 November 2011. Retrieved from: http://www.ipu.org/wmn-e/classif.htm (accessed 10 January 2012).
66. Council of European Municipalities and Regions (CEMR) (2008) *Women in Local Politics in Europe*. Retrieved from: http://www.ccre.org/docs/pisa_women_in_local_politics_figures.pdf (accessed 25 April 2011).
67. 2003
68. 2007
69. 2006
70. 2002
71. Retrieved from: http://www.cfwd.org.uk/uploads/pdfs/Leaders09Final.pdf (accessed 12 October 2011).

Appendix III: FEMCIT Working Papers

All available online at: http://femcit.org/publications.xpl

Political Citizenship

1. Freidenvall, L. (2010) Intersectionalizing Representation: Ethnicity, Gender and Political Representation in Multicultural Europe, WP1, Working Paper No.1 (27 pages)
2. Dahlerup, D. (2010) What Constitutes Successful Substantive Representation of Women? Theoretical and Methodological Problems in the Study of Women's Substantive Representation, WP1, Working Paper No. 2 (18 pages)
3. Threlfall, M. (2011) Equal Opportunities or Barriers? Women in the Parliaments of Poland and Macedonia, WP1, Working Paper No. 3 (24 pages)
4. Threlfall, M. (2011) Citizens' Preferences for their Political Representation: a Qualitative Study of the UK, Spain, Poland and Macedonia, WP1, Working Paper No.4 (36 pages)

Social Citizenship

5. Rogg Korsvik, T., Rantalaiho, M. and Bergman, S. (2009) Research on Political Actions and Claims by Women's Movements and Other NGOs in Childcare and Parental Leave Issues in Norway and Finland Since the 1960s, WP2, Working Paper No. 1 (83 pages)
6. Uhde, Z. (ed.) (2009) Report on the Activities and Political Claims of Majority Women's NGOs and Minoritized women's and Gender-Based NGOs or Groups on Care, and Specifically on Childcare in the Czech Republic Since the End of the Second World War, WP2, Working Paper No. 2 (80 pages)

Economic Citizenship

7. Le Feuvre, N. and Metso, M., Stene-Kristiansen, T., Krajewska, A. (2009) Mapping the Labour Market Experiences of 'Majority' and 'Minority' Women in France, Norway and Poland, Working Paper No. 1, WP3 (88 pages)
8. Metso, M. and Le Feuvre, N. (ed.) (2009) Mapping Economic Citizenship Issues from Women's Movement Publications in Finland, France, Norway, Poland and the UK, Working Paper No.2, WP3 (242 pages)

Multicultural Citizenship

9. Eggebø, H. (2007) Register of Organizations and Networks with a Gender Profile in Norway 1990–2008 (in Norwegian), Working Paper No.1, WP4 (124 pages)
10. Nyhagen Predelli, L., Perren, K., Halsaa, B., Thun, C. and Manful, E. (2008) Women's Movements: Constructions of Sisterhood, Dispute and Resonance: The Case of The United Kingdom, Working Paper No. 2, WP4 (306 pages)
11. Sandu, A., Nyhagen Predelli, L., Halsaa, B., Thun, C. and Manful, E. (2009) Women's Movements: Constructions of Sisterhood, Dispute and Resonance: The Case of Spain, Working Paper No. 3, WP4 (180 pages)
12. Halsaa, B., Thun, C. and Nyhagen Predelli, L. (2008) Women's Movements: Constructions of Sisterhood, Dispute and Resonance: The Case of Norway, Working Paper No. 4, WP4 (407 pages)
13. Nyhagen Predelli, L. (2010) Religion, Gender, Feminism and Citizenship, Working Paper No. 5, WP4 (29 pages)
14. Nyhagen Predelli, L., Manful, E., Halsaa, B., Thun, C. and Quintero, E. (2010) Christian and Muslim Women in Norway, Spain and The United Kingdom: A Qualitative Study of Religion, Gender and Citizenship (Summary of Key Findings), Working Paper No. 6, WP4 (7 pages)
15. Halsaa, B., Thun, C. and Nyhagen Predelli, L. (2010) Religion, Gender and Citizenship: A Case Study of Christian and Muslim Women in Norway, Working Paper No. 7, WP4 (203 pages)
16. Nyhagen Predelli, L. and Manful, E. (2010) Religion, Gender and Citizenship: A Case Study of Christian and Muslim Women in the UK, Working Paper No. 8, WP4 (212 pages)
17. Quintero, E. and Nyhagen Predelli, L. (2010) Religion, Gender and Citizenship: A Case Study of Christian and Muslim Women in Spain, Working Paper No. 9, WP4 (179 pages)
18. Nyhagen Predelli, L., Halsaa, B., Manful, E., Thun, C. and Quintero, E. (2010) Christian and Muslim Women in Norway, Spain and the UK: A Qualitative Study of Religion, Gender and Citizenship, Working Paper No. 10, WP4 (272 pages)

Sexual and Bodily Citizenship

19. Outshoorn, J. (2008) Women's Movements and Bodily Integrity: Towards a Dynamic Institutionalist Approach, Working Paper No. 1, WP5 (30 pages)
20. Outshoorn, J. (2010) Abortion, Multiculturalism and Europeanization, Working Paper No. 2, WP5 (27 pages)
21. Dudová, R. (2009) Abortion in Czechoslovakia/the Czech Republic from 1959 until Today, Working Paper No. 3, WP5 (138 pages)
22. Dudová, R. (2010) Prostitution and Trafficking in Czechoslovakia/the Czech Republic from 1959 until Today, Working Paper No. 4, WP5 (122 pages)
23. Outshoorn, J. (2010b) Prostitution, Migration and Europeanization , Working Paper No. 5, WP5 (30 pages)

Intimate Citizenship

24. Roseneil, S., Crowhurst, I., Hellesund, T., Santos, A. C. and Stoilova, M. (2008) Policy Contexts and Responses to Changes in Intimate Life, Working Paper No. 1, WP6 (Revised, October 2009) (394 pages)

25. Roseneil, S. (ed.) (2009) Changing Cultural Discourses about Intimate Life: The Demands and Actions of Women's Movements and Other Movements for Gender and Sexual Equality and Change, Working Paper No. 2, WP6 (398 pages)
26. Roseneil, S., Crowhurst, I., Hellesund, T., Santos, A. C. and Stoilova, M. (2010) Intimate Citizenship: Statistical and Contextual Background, Working Paper No.3, WP6 (66 pages)

Integrative Analysis

27. Halsaa, B. (2008) Draft Report on Design and Methodology, Working Paper No. 1, WP7 (25 pages)
28. Strasser, S. (2008) Multicultural Tensions and Integrative Reflections, Working Paper No. 2, WP7 (39 pages)
29. Halsaa, B. (2009) The Impact of women's Movements and the Architecture of Gender-Fair Citizenship – Conceptual Discussions, Working Paper No. 3, WP7 (34 pages)
30. Rømer Christensen, H. and Breengaard, M. H. (2011) Mainstreaming Gender, Diversity and Citizenship: Concepts and Methodologies, Working Paper No. 4, WP7 (142 pages)
31. Halsaa, B., Roseneil, S. and Sümer, S. (2011) FEMCIT: Gendered Citizenship in Multicultural Europe: the Impact of Contemporary Women's Movements, Final Report, Working paper No. 5, WP7 (133 pages).

THE FEMCIT MANIFESTO FOR

MULTI-DIMENSIONAL CITIZENSHIP

TOWARDS FULL, GENDER-FAIR,
LIBERATORY CITIZENSHIP
IN EUROPE

MANIFESTO SIGNATORIES
THE FEMCIT RESEARCH PROJECT

Solveig Bergman
Michala Hvidt Breengaard
Hilda Rømer Christensen
Isabel Crowhurst
Susanne Dodillet
Radka Dudova
Helga Eggebø
Lenita Freidenvall
Mireille Garcia
Berit Gullikstad
Beatrice Halsaa
Hana Haskova
Tone Hellesund
madeleine kennedy-macfoy
Trine Rogg Korsvik
Teresa Kulawik
Nicky Le Feuvre
Karin S. Lindelöf
Esmeranda Manful
Milka Metso
Line Nyhagen-Predelli
Joyce Outshoorn
Esther Quintero
Minna Rantalaiho
Sasha Roseneil
Adriana Sandu
Ana Cristina Santos
Sabine Strasser
Mariya Stoilova
Sevil Sümer
Monica Threlfall
Cecilie Thun
Anna Wilroth

FULL, GENDER-FAIR, LIBERATORY CITIZENSHIP IN EUROPE MEANS

- Ending discrimination and inequality on the grounds of gender, sexuality, 'race'/ethnicity, class, religion, nationality, age and disability

- Recognising the cultural complexity and diversity of contemporary Europe

- Respecting the individuality, autonomy and relationships of all who live in Europe, not just European nationals

- Accepting that the peoples of Europe and the world are interdependent

- Promoting social and environmental sustainability

- Striving for equality and justice for all across all dimensions of citizenship

FEMCIT IS A RESEARCH PROJECT FUNDED BY THE SIXTH FRAMEWORK OF THE EUROPEAN COMMISSION. WE ARE AN INTERDISCIPLINARY TEAM OF OVER 40 RESEARCHERS BASED IN 11 COUNTRIES.

We believe that citizenship for women in Europe is incomplete. To be gender-fair, understandings of citizenship need to be extended. Our research shows how important it is to perceive citizenship as composed of at least six dimensions – political, economic, social, multicultural & religious, bodily & sexual, and intimate.

This Manifesto presents some of the most pressing claims and demands of women's movements and feminist researchers in Europe today across these six dimensions of citizenship.

We hope that the FEMCIT Manifesto for Multi-Dimensional Citizenship will inspire debate in political groups and parties, amongst policy-makers and practitioners, within groups of friends, and between researchers.

For further information about FEMCIT, see *www.femcit.org*

Political citizenship
- Constitutional gender equality
- Voting rights for all residents
- Gender parity in political assemblies
- Strengthen democracy at all levels
- Increase the inclusion of diverse populations in political institutions

Economic citizenship
- Equality in pay, wealth and ownership and a living wage for all
- Develop alternative and sustainable economies
- Gender budgeting and analysis of gendered impacts of all economic policies
- Recognition of the work-life balance needs of all
- Fairer alternatives to informal and undeclared work

Social citizenship
- Recognise and value unpaid and paid care work
- Affordable and high quality child and elder care
- Paid care-leave for all carers
- Promote men's involvement in care
- Full social rights for migrants and minority groups

Multicultural and religious citizenship
- Prioritize tackling all forms of racism and ethnic discrimination
- Equal state treatment of all forms of faith and belief, including non-belief
- No public ban on headscarves
- Include the voices of all women in policy-making
- No detention of asylum seekers

Bodily and sexual citizenship
- Sexual self-determination for all
- Better services for women suffering from violence
- Acknowledge violence against women as issues of women's and human rights
- Free contraception and abortion
- Extend the granting of asylum on the grounds of sexuality

Intimate citizenship
- Legal and social recognition of the multiplicity of forms of intimate life
- Equality for single people – an end to couple privilege
- Equal access to assisted conception for all women
- Acknowledge the complex individuality of every human being
- Recognition of trans-rights and an end to transphobia

References

Abraham, M., Chow, E. N., Maratou-Alipranti, L. and Tastsoglou, E. (2010) 'Rethinking Citizenship with Women in Focus' in M. Abraham, E. N. Chow, L. Maratou-Alipranti and E. Tastsoglou (eds) *Contours of Citizenship. Women, Diversity and Practices of Citizenship* (Farnham: Ashgate), pp. 1–22.

Acker, J. (2009) 'From Glass Ceiling to Inequality Regimes', *Sociologie du Travail*, vol. 51, no. 2, 199–217.

Ahmed, S. (1998) *Differences That Matter: Feminist Theory and Postmodernism* (Cambridge: Cambridge University Press).

Al-Ali, N. and Koser, K. (eds) (2002) *New Approaches to Migration? Transnational Communities and the Transformation of 'Home'* (London and New York: Routledge).

Alcoff, L. M. (2005) *Visible Identities: Race, Gender and the Self* (Oxford and New York: Oxford University Press).

Al-Hibri, A. Y. (1999) 'Is Western Patriarchal Feminism Good for Third World/Minority Women?' in S. M. Okin (ed.) *Is Multiculturalism Bad for Women?* (Princeton: Princeton University Press), pp. 41–6.

Álvarez, L. et al. (1968) 'El Trabajo del Ama de Casa' [The Work of the Housewife] *ABC 24*, February, 40.

Amnesty International (2008) *Amnesty International Report 2008 – Spain*, http://www.unhcr.org/refworld/docid/483e27b155.html, date accessed 21 June 2011.

Amnesty International and Southall Black Sisters (2008) *No Recourse No Safety: The Government's Failure to Protect Women from Violence* (London: Amnesty International UK and Southall Black Sisters).

Anderson, B. (1998) *Long Distance Nationalism. World Capitalism and the Rise of Identity Politics* (Amsterdam: CASA).

Anttonen, A. and Sipilä, J. (1996) 'European Social Care Services: Is It Possible to Identify Models?', *Journal of European Social Policy*, vol. 6, 87–100.

Appadurai, A. (2003) 'Sovereignty without Territoriality: Notes for a Postnational Geography' in S. M. Low and D. Lawrence-Zuniga (eds) *The Anthropology of Space and Place. Locating Culture* (Malden and Oxford: Blackwell Publishing), pp. 337–49.

Armbruster, H. (2003) 'Homes in Crisis: Syrian Orthodox Christians in Turkey and Germany' in N. Al-Ali and K. Koser (eds) *New Approaches to Migration: Transnational Communities and the Transformation of Home* (London and New York: Taylor and Francis), pp. 17–33.

Armbruster, H. (2008) 'Introduction: The Ethics of Taking Sides' in H. Armbruster and A. Lærke (eds) *Taking Sides. Ethnics, Politics, and Fieldwork in Anthropology* (New York and Oxford: Berghahn Books), pp. 1–22.

Armbruster, H. and Lærke, A. (2008) *Taking Sides. Ethnics, Politics, and Fieldwork in Anthropology* (New York, Oxford: Berghahn Books).

Assies, W. (2005) 'Some Notes on Citizenship, Civil Society and Social Movements' in W. Assies, M. A. Calderon and T. Salman (eds) *Citizenship, Political Culture and State Transformation in Latin America* (Amsterdam: Dutch University Press).

Ateş, S. (2007) *Der Multikulti-Irrtum. Wie wir in Deutschland besser zusammenleben können* [The Multicultural Error: How We Can Live Better Together in Germany] (Berlin: Uhlstein Verlag).

Bacchi, C. (1999) *Women, Policy and Politics: The Construction of Policy Problems* (London: Sage).

Bacchi, C. and Beasley, C. (2002) 'Citizen Bodies: Is Embodied Citizenship a Contradiction in Terms?', *Critical Social Policy*, vol. 22, 324–52.

Backe, I. and George, S. (2006) *Politics in the European Union* (Oxford: Oxford University Press).

Baldwin, P. (1999) *Contagion and the State in Europe, 1830–1930* (Cambridge: Cambridge University Press).

Bambra, C. (2007) 'Defamilisation and Welfare State Regimes: A Cluster Analysis', *International Journal of Social Welfare*, vol. 16, no. 4, 326–38.

Banaszak, L. A., Beckwith K. and Rucht, D. (2003) *Women's Movements Facing the Reconfigured State* (Cambridge: Cambridge University Press).

Bauböck, R. (1994) *Transnational Citizenship: Membership and Rights in International Migration* (Aldershot: Edward Elgar).

Bauböck, R. (2001) 'Recombinant Citizenship' in M. Kohli and A. Woodward (eds) *Inclusions and Exclusions in European Societies* (London and New York: Routledge), pp. 38–57.

Baumann, G. (1996) *Contesting Culture. Discourses of Identity in a Multicultural Europe* (Cambridge: Cambridge University Press).

Baumann, G. (1999) *The Multicultural Riddle: Rethinking National, Ethnic and Religious Identities* (London and New York: Routledge).

Beck, U. (2000) *The Brave New World of Work* (Cambridge: Polity Press).

Beck, U. and Beck-Gernsheim, E. (1995) *The Normal Chaos of Love* (Cambridge: Polity Press).

Beck, U. and Beck-Gernsheim, E. (2002) *Individualization* (London: Sage).

Beck, U. and Sznaider, N. (2010) 'Unpacking Cosmopolitanism for the Social Sciences: A Research Agenda', *British Journal of Sociology*, vol. 61 (supplement), 381–403.

Bell, D. and Binnie, J. (2000) *The Sexual Citizen: Queer Politics and Beyond* (Cambridge: Polity Press).

Bell, M. (2002) *Anti-Discrimination Law and the European Union* (Oxford: Oxford University Press).

Benford, R. D. and Snow, D. A. (2000) 'Framing Processes and Social Movements: An Overview and Assessment', *Annual Review of Sociology*, vol. 26, 611–39.

Benhabib, S. (1998) 'Democracy and Identity: In Search of the Civic Polity', *Philosophy and Social Criticism*, vol. 24, no. 2–3, 85–100.

Benhabib, S. (2002) *The Claims of Culture. Equality and Diversity in the Global Era* (Princeton: Princeton University Press).

Benhabib, S. (2004) *The Rights of Others: Aliens, Residents and Citizens* (Cambridge: Cambridge University Press).

Benhabib, S. with Waldron, J., Honig, B. and Kymlicka, W. (2006) *Another Cosmopolitanism* (Oxford and New York: Oxford University Press).

Berg, A-J. (2009) 'Silence and Articulation: Whiteness, Racialization and Feminist Memory work', *NORA – Nordic Journal of Feminist and Gender Research*, vol.16, no. 4, 213–27.

Bergman, S. (2004) 'Collective Organizing and Claim Making on Child Care in Norden: Blurring the Boundaries between the Inside and the Outside', *Social Politics: International Studies in Gender, State & Society*, vol. 11, 217–46.

Bergman, S. and Rantalaiho, M. (2011) *Childcare as a Field of Claims-making and Political Mobilisation by Women's Movements in Finland and Norway*. FEMCIT Deliverable to the European Commission. Work Package 2, Social Citizenship. Oslo: Nordic Gender Institute, NIKK.

Bergqvist, C., Kuusipalo, J. and Styrkarsdóttir, A. (1999) 'Family Policy in the Nordic Welfare States' in C. Bergqvist et al. (eds) *Equal Democracies? Gender and Politics in the Nordic Countries* (Oslo: Scandinavian University Press).

Berlant, L. (1997) *The Queen of America Goes to Washington City. Essays on Sex and Citizenship* (Durham and London: Duke University Press).

Berman, M. (1994) *The Only Boobs in the House Are Men: A Veteran Woman Legislator Lifts the Lid on Politics Macho Style* (Royal Oak: Momentum Books LLC).

Bertone, C. (2003) 'Claims for Child Care as Struggles over Needs: Comparing Italian and Danish Women's Organizations', *Social Politics: International Studies in Gender, State & Society*, vol. 10, 229–55.

Bhavnani, K. K. (ed.) (2001) *Feminism and 'Race': A Reader* (Oxford: Oxford University Press).

Bird, K., Saalfeld, T. and Wust, A. (2011) *The Political Representation of Immigrants and Minorities. Voters, Parties and Parliamentarians in Liberal Democracies* (London and New York: Routledge).

BLD (2011) *Endringar i kontantstøtta [Changes in Cash-for-care Benefit]*. Press release, 6 October 2011, Barne-, likestillings- og inkluderingsdepartementet [Norwegian Ministry of Children, Equality and Social Inclusion]. http://www.regjeringen. no/nb/dep/bld/pressesenter/pressemeldinger/2011/endringar-i-kontantstotta. html?id=659583, date accessed 7 October 2011.

Bleijenbergh, I. and Roggeband, C. (2007) 'Equality Machineries Matter: The Impact of Women's Political Pressure on European Social-care Policies', *Social Politics: International Studies in Gender, State & Society*, vol. 14, 437–59.

Bogdanor, V. (ed.) (1985) *Representatives of the People? Parliamentarians and Constituents in Western Democracies* (London: Gower).

Brah, A. (1996) *Cartographies of Diaspora: Contesting Identities* (Hoboken: Taylor & Francis).

Brandth, B. and Kvande, E. (2003) *Fleksible fedre: maskulinitet, arbeid, velferdsstat [Flexible Fathers: Masculinity, Work, Welfare State]* (Oslo: Universitetsforlaget).

Brandth, B. and Kvande, E. (2009) 'Norway: the Making of the Father's Quota' in S. B. Kamerman and P. Moss (eds) *The Politics of Parental Leave: Children, Parenting, Gender and the Labour Market* (Bristol: Policy Press).

Bredal, A. and Skjerven, L. S. (2007) *Summary of Report on Forced Marriage Cases Dealt with by Public Support Services. Incidence and Challenges*, http://www.regjeringen.no/ nn/dep/bld/Tema/Vald-og-overgrepi-nare-relasjonar/tvangsekteskap/summary-of- report-on-forced-marriage-cas.html?id=476205, date accessed 16 October 2009.

Breines, W. (2006) *The Trouble Between Us. An Uneasy History of White and Black Women in the Feminist Movement* (Oxford and New York: Oxford University Press).

British Council and Migration Policy Group (2011) *Migrant Integration Policy Index*, http://www.mipex.eu, date accessed 13 January 2012.

Brochmann, G. (2002) 'Statsborgerskap, medborgerskap og tilhørighet' [Nationality, Citizenship and Belonging] in G. Brochmann, J. Rogstad and T. Borchgrevink (eds) *Sand i maskineriet. Makt og demokrati i det flerkulturelle Norge [Sand in the Machinery. Power and Democracy in Multicultural Norway]* Makt- og demokratiutredningen (Oslo: Gyldendal Akademisk), pp. 56–84.

Brubaker, R. (1992) *Citizenship and Nationhood in France and Germany* (Cambridge, MA: Harvard University Press).

Brubaker, R. (2001) 'The Return of Assimilation? Changing Perspectives on Immigration and its Sequels in France, Germany, and the United States' in C. Joppke and E. Morawska (eds) *Toward Assimilation and Citizenship: Immigrants in Liberal Nation-States* (Basingstoke: Palgrave Macmillan), pp. 39–58.

Brunnbauer, U. (2008) 'Making Bulgarians Socialist: The Fatherland Front in Communist Bulgaria (1944–1989)', *East European Politics and Societies*, vol. 22, 44–79.

Bryan, B., Dadzie, S. and Scafe, S. (1985) *The Heart of the Race. Black Women's Lives in Britain* (London: Virago).

Bryceson, D. and Vuorela, U. (2002) *The Transnational Family: New European Frontiers and Global Networks* (Oxford: Berg).

Buscatto, M. and Marry, C. (2009) 'Le plafond de verre dans tous ses éclats: La féminisation des professions supérieures au XXe siècle' [The Glass Ceiling in Shards: The Feminisation of Professions in the Twentieth Century], *Sociologie du travail*, vol. 51, no. 2, 170–82.

Cain, B., Ferejohn, J. and Fiorina, M. (1987) *The Personal Vote* (Cambridge, MA: Harvard University Press).

Čákiová, J. (2005) *Český svaz žen a jeho úloha v letech 1967–1970 [Czech Union of Women and its Role in the Years 1967–1970]*. Diploma Thesis. Charles University, Prague.

Carby, H. (1982) 'White Women Listen! Black Feminism and the Boundaries of Sisterhood', in Centre for Contemporary Cultural Studies (ed.) *The Empire Strikes Back: Race and Racism in '70s Britain* (London: Hutchinson).

Carens, J. H. (2000) *Culture, Citizenship, and Community. A Contextual Exploration of Justice as Evenhandedness* (Oxford: Oxford University Press).

Carter, A. (2001) *The Political Theory of Global Citizenship* (London: Routledge).

Castel, R. (1995) *Les métamorphoses de la question sociale: Une chronique du salariat [Metamorphoses of the Social Question: A Chronicle of the Workforce]* (Paris: Fayard).

Castel, R. (2003) *L'Insécurité sociale. Qu'est-ce qu'être protégé? [Social Insecurity. What Is to Be Protected?]*, La République des idées (Paris: Seuil).

Castells, M. (1997) *The Power of Identity* (Oxford: Blackwell Publishers).

Celis, K., Childs, S., Kantola, J. and Krook, M. L. (2008) 'Rethinking Women's Substantive Representation', *Representation*, vol. 44, no. 2, 99–110.

Charles, N. (2000) *Feminism, the State and Social Policy* (London: Macmillan Press).

Childs, S. (2004) *New Labour's Women MPs: Women Representing Women* (Abingdon: Routledge).

Cohen, J. (1999) 'Changing Paradigms of Citizenship and the Exclusiveness of the Demos', *International Sociology*, vol. 14, no. 3, 245–68.

Collins, P. H. (1991) *Black Feminist Thought. Knowledge, Consciousness, and the Politics of Empowerment* (London and New York: Routledge).

Combahee River Collective (1977) *The Combahee River Collective Statement: Black Feminist Organizing in the Seventies and Eighties*, http://afrospear.com/2008/01/31/black-feminism-combahee-river-collective-statement/, date accessed 5 December 2011.

Cooke, L. P. and Baxter, J. (2010) '"Families" in International Context: Comparing Institutional Effects Across Western Societies', *Journal of Marriage and Family*, vol. 72, no. 3, 516–36.

Coote, A. and Patullo, P. (1990) *Power and Prejudice* (London: Weidenfeld & Nicholson).

Council Directive 1996/34/EC of 3 June 1996 on the Framework Agreement on Parental Leave concluded by UNICE, CEEP and the ETUC. *Official Journal* L 14, 19/06/1996.

Council Directive 2010/18/EU of 8 March 2010 implementing the revised Framework Agreement on Parental Leave concluded by BUSINESSEUROPE, UEAPME, CEEP and ETUC and repealing Directive 96/34/EC. *Official Journal* L 68/13, 18/03/2010.

Crenshaw, K. W. (1991a) 'Demarginalizing the Intersection of Race and Sex: A Black Feminist Critique of Antidiscrimination Doctrine, Feminist Theory and Antiracist

Politics' in K. Bartlett and R. Kennedy (eds) *New Perspectives on Law, Culture and Society* (Boulder: Westview).

Crenshaw, K. W. (1991b) 'Mapping the Margins: Intersectionality, Identity Politics and Violence Against Women', *Stanford Law Review*, vol. 43, 1241–98.

Crompton, R. (ed.) (1999) *Restructuring Gender Relations and Employment: The Decline of the Male Breadwinner* (Oxford: Oxford University Press).

Crompton, R. (2006) *Employment and the Family. The Reconfiguration of Work and Family Life in Contemporary Societies* (Cambridge: Cambridge University Press).

Crompton, R. and Lyonette, C. (2006) 'Work-Life "Balance" in Europe', *Acta Sociologica*, vol. 49, no. 4, 379–93.

Crompton, R., Lewis, S. and Lyonette, C. (eds) (2007) *Women, Men, Work and Family in Europe* (London: Palgrave).

Currell, M. (1974) *Political Woman* (London: Croom Helm).

Czech EU presidency (2009) *Dvanáct bodů k snahám českého předsednictví otevřít debatu o barcelonských cílech [Twelve Arguments by the Czech EU Presidency in Order to Open the Debate on Barcelona Targets]*, http://www.vlada.cz/cz/media-centrum/aktualne/reakce-ceskeho-predsednictvi-na-prohlaseni-evropske-socialisticke-strany-53174/, date accessed 18 March 2011.

Dahlerup, D. (1978) 'Women's Entry into Politics: The Experience of the Danish Local and General Elections 1908–20', *Scandinavian Political Studies*, vol. 1, no. 2–3, 139–60.

Dahlerup, D. (2006a) 'The Story of the Theory of Critical Mass', *Politics and Gender*, vol. 2, no. 4, 511–22.

Dahlerup, D. (ed.) (2006b) *Women, Quotas and Politics* (London and New York: Routledge).

Dahlerup, D. (2009) *What Constitutes Successful Substantive Representation of Women? Theoretical and Methodological Problems in the Study of 'Women's Substantive Representation'.* Paper presented at the World Congress of the International Political Science Association, Santiago de Chile, 11–16 July 2009. FEMCIT Deliverable to the European Commission. Work Package 1, Political Citizenship. Stockholm: University of Stockholm.

Dahlerup, D. and Freidenvall, L. (2005) 'Quotas as a "Fast Track" to Equal Representation of Women: Why Scandinavia Is No Longer the Model', *International Feminist Journal of Politics*, vol. 7, no. 1, 26–48.

Daly, M. and Rake, K. (2003) *Gender and the Welfare State: Care, Work and Welfare in Europe and the USA* (London: Polity).

Danna, D. (2001) *Policies about Prostitution in the EU in the Nineties.* PhD Thesis. University of Trento.

Daskalova, K. (1999) 'Феминизъм и равенство в Българския XX век' [Feminism and Equality in Twentieth Century Bulgaria] in R. Muharska (ed.) *Майки и дъщери. Поколения и посоки в българския феминизъм [Mothers and Daughters. Generations and Directions in Bulgarian Feminism]* (Sofia: Polis).

Décret Relatif à la Cohésion Sociale (COCOF) (2005) Bruxelles: Commission Communautaire Française.

Della Costa, M. and James, S. (1973) *The Power of Women and the Subversion of the Community* (Bristol: Falling Wall Press).

Desforges, L., Jones, R. and Woods, M. (2005) 'New Geographies of Citizenship', *Citizenship Studies*, vol. 9, no. 5, 439–51.

Dettmeijer-Vermeulen, C. E. et al. (2002) *Mensenhandel. Eerste rapportage van de Nationaal Rapporteur [Human Trafficking. First report of the National Rapporteur]* (Den Haag: Bureau NRM).

Díaz, M. M. (2005) *Representing Women? Female Legislators in West European Parliaments* (Colchester: ECPR Press).

Dietz, M. (1987) 'Context Is All: Feminism and Theories of Citizenship', *Daedalus*, vol. 116, no. 4, 1–24.

Dimitrievska, D. (2004) *Quotas: The Case of Macedonia*, IDEA Publications. http://www.quotaproject.org, date accessed 16 February 2012.

Dobrowolsky, A. and Jenson, J. (2004) 'Shifting Representations of Citizenship: Canadian Politics of "Women" and "Children"', *Social Politics: International Studies in Gender, State and Society*, vol. 11, no. 2, 154–80.

Dodillet, S. (2009a) *Är sex arbete?[Is Sex Work?]* (Stockholm: Vertigo).

Dodillet, S. (2009b) *The Discovery of Trafficking in Sweden – The Impact Women's Movements*. FEMCIT Deliverable to the European Commission. Work Package 5, Sexual & Bodily Citizenship. Stockholm/Huddinge: Södertörn University.

Doezema, J. (2010) *Sex Slaves and Discourse Masters. The Construction of Trafficking* (London and New York: Zed Books).

Dogan, M. (2007) 'Parliamentarians as Errand Boys in France, Britain and the United States', *Comparative Sociology*, vol. 6, no. 4, 430–63.

Dorlin, E. (ed.) (2008) *Black Feminism. Anthologie du féminisme africain-américain, 1975–2000 [Black feminism. Anthology of African-American Feminism, 1975–2000]*, Bibliothèque du féminisme (Paris: l'Harmattan).

Duarte, M. (2010) *Prostitution Policies in Portugal*. Exploratory Workshop on Exploring and Comparing Prostitution Policy Regimes in Europe, University of Birkbeck, London, UK, 15–17 September 2010.

Dudová, R. (2009) *Abortion in Czechoslovakia /the Czech Republic from 1950 until Today*. FEMCIT Working Paper No. 3, Work Package 5, Sexual & Bodily Citizenship. Leiden: Leiden University. http://www.femcit.org/files/WP5_WorkingpaperNo3.pdf, date accessed 3 October 2011.

Dudová, R. (2010a) *Prostitution and Trafficking in the Czechoslovakia /Czech Republic from 1950 until Today*. FEMCIT Working Paper No. 4, Work Package 5, Sexual & Bodily Citizenship. Leiden: Leiden University. http://www.femcit.org/files/WP5_WorkingpaperNo4.pdf, date accessed 2 April 2011.

Dudová, R. (2010b) 'The Framing of Abortion in the Czech Republic: How the Continuity of Discourse Prevents Institutional Change', *Sociologický časopis [Czech Sociological Review]*, vol. 44, no. 6, 945–75.

Dussuet, A. (2005) *Travaux de femmes: Enquêtes sur les services à domicile [Women's Work: Survey on Domestic Work]*, Le travail du social (Paris: l'Harmattan).

Dustin, M. (2006) *Gender Equality, Cultural Diversity: European Comparisons and Lessons*. London: Gender Institute, London School of Economics and Political Science. http://www.lse.ac.uk/collections/genderInstitute/NuffieldReport_final.pdf, date accessed 20 February 2011.

Dvořáková, Z. (2008) 'Lidovci nepustí další díl Julínkovy reformy ani do vlády' [Christian Democrats Will Not Let the Next Part of the Reform Proposed by Julínek to the Government Session Pass], *Týden.cz*, 11 November 2008. http://www.tyden.cz/rubriky/domaci/pat-kolem-julinka-co-vadi-zelenym-a-lidovcum_90199.html, date accessed 13 December 2011.

Dytrych, Z. et al. (1975) 'Children Born to Women Denied Abortion', *Family Planning Perspectives*, vol. 7, 165–71.

Eduards, M. (2002) *Förbjuden handling. Om kvinnors organisering och feministisk teori [Forbidden Action. About Women's Organising and Feminist Theory]* (Malmö: Liber).

Eduards, M. (2007) *Kroppspolitik [Body Politics]* (Stockholm: Atlas).

Eerste Kamer (1997–2011) *Handelingen [Official Reports from the First Chamber of the Dutch Parliament]*.

EHRC (2010). *Stop and Think: A Critical Review of the Use of Stop and Search Powers in England and Wales*. Equality and Human Rights Commission.

Ehrenreich, B. and Hochschild, A. R. (eds) (2002) *Global Woman. Nannies, Maids, and Sex Workers in the New Economy* (New York: A Metropolitan/OWL Book).

Einhorn, B. (1993) *Cinderella Goes to Market. Citizenship, Gender and Women's Movements in East Central Europe* (London: Verso).

Ellerbe-Dueck, C. (2011) 'Networks and "Safe Spaces" of Black European Women in Germany and Austria' in H. Armbruster and U. H. Meinhof (eds) *Negotiating Multicultural Europe: Borders, Networks, Neighbourhoods* (Basingstoke: Palgrave Macmillan).

Ellingsæter, A. L. and Gulbrandsen, L. (2001) 'Kontantstøtten: stor reform med små virkninger' [Cash-for-care: A Major Reform with Minor Effects], *Søkelys på arbeidsmarkedet*, vol. 18, no. 1, 15–25.

Ellingsæter, A. L. and Leira, A. (2006a) 'Epilogue: Scandinavian Policies of Parent hood – A success story?' in A. L. Ellingsæter and A. Leira (eds) *Politicising Parent hood in Scandinavia. Gender Relations in Welfare States* (Bristol: Policy Press).

Ellingsæter, A. L. and Leira, A. (eds) (2006b) *Politicising Parenthood in Scandinavia. Gender Relations in Welfare States* (Bristol: Policy Press).

Ellingsæter, A. L. and Gulbrandsen, L. (2007) 'Closing the Child Care Gap: the Interaction of Childcare Provision and Mothers' Agency in Norway', *Journal of Social Policy*, vol. 36, no. 4, 649–69.

Elshtain, J. B. (1981) *Public Man, Private Woman. Women in Social and Political Thought* (Princeton: Princeton University Press).

Elshtain, J. B. (1993). *Democracy on Trial*. cbc Massey Lecture Series (Toronto, ON: House of Anansi Press Ltd).

Erel, U. (2009) *Migrant Women Transforming Citizenship. Life-Stories from Britain and Germany* (Farnham: Ashgate).

Eriksen, T. H. (2007) 'Complexity in Social and Cultural Integration: Some Analytical Dimensions', *Ethnic and Racial Studies*, vol. 30, no. 6, 1055–69.

Erk, J. (2005) 'Sub-state Nationalism and the Left–right Divide: Critical Junctures in the Formation of Nationalist Labour Movements in Belgium', *Nations and Nationalism*, vol. 11, no. 4, 551–70.

Ervik, R. (2010) *Elderly Care and Economic Citizenship in Norway: Traditional and Emerging Forms of Employment in the Elderly Care Sector and Their Impact on Majoritized and Minoritized carers*. FEMCIT Deliverable to the European Commission. Work Package 3, Economic Citizenship. Bergen: Uni Research/Uni Rokkan Centre.

Esping-Andersen, G. (1990) *The Three Worlds of Welfare Capitalism* (Cambridge: Polity Press).

Esping-Andersen, G. (ed.) (1996) *Welfare States in Transition. National Adaptations in Global Economies* (London: Sage).

Esping-Andersen, G. with Gallie, D., Hemerijck, A. and Myles, J. (2002) *Why We Need a New Welfare State* (Oxford: Oxford University Press).

Estanque, E. (1999) 'Acção Colectiva, Comunidade e Movimentos Sociais' [Collective Action, Community and Social Movements], *Revista Critica de Ciências Sociais*, vol. 55, 85–111.

European Commission (2010a), *EU Citizenship Report 2010: Dismantling the Obstacles to EU Citizens' rights*, http://ec.europa.eu/justice/policies/citizenship/docs/com_2010_603_en.pdf, date accessed 21 April 2011.

European Commission (2010b) *European Union Citizenship Analytical Report*, Flash Eurobarometer, http://ec.europa.eu/public_opinion/flash/fl_294_en.pdf, date accessed 1 April 2011.

European Council (2002) *Barcelona Council Conclusions*, http://www.consilium. europa.eu/uedocs/cms_data/docs/pressdata/en/ec/71025.pdf, date accessed 12 December 2011.

Evans, D.T. (1993) *Sexual Citizenship: the Material Construction of Sexuality* (London: Routledge).

Eydal, G. B. and Rostgaard, T. (2011) 'Gender Equality Revisited – Changes in Nordic Childcare Policies in the 2000s', *Social Policy & Administration*, vol. 45, no. 2, 161–79.

Ezekiel, J. (2002) *Feminism in the Heartland* (Dayton: Ohio State University Press).

Fauré, C. (ed.) (1997) *Encyclopédie politique et historique des femmes [Political and Historical Encyclopedia of Women]* (Paris: Presses Universitaires de France).

Fenger, H. J. M. (2007) 'Welfare Regimes in Central and Eastern Europe: Incorporating Post-Communist Countries in a Welfare Regime Typology', *Contemporary Issues and Ideas in Social Sciences*, vol. 3, no. 2, http://journal.ciiss.net/index.php/ciiss/article/view/45/37, date accessed 12 December 2011.

Ferge, Z. (1997) 'Women and Social Transformation in Central-Eastern Europe', *Czech Sociological Review*, vol. 33, no. 2, 159–78.

Ferree, M. M. (2003) 'Resonance and Radicalism: Feminist Framing in the Abortion Debates of the United States and Germany', *American Journal of Sociology*, vol. 109, no. 2, 304–44.

Ferree, M. M. and Martin, P. Y. (eds) (1995) *Feminist Organizations: Harvest of the New Women's Movement* (Philadelphia: Temple University Press).

Ferree, M. M. and Merrill, D. A. (2000) 'Hot Movements, Cold Cognition: Thinking about Social Movements in Gendered Frames', *Contemporary Sociology*, vol. 29, no. 3, 454–62.

Ferree, M. M. and Tripp, A. (eds) (2006) *Global Feminism: Transnational Women's Activism, Organizing, and Human Rights* (New York: New York University Press).

Fisher, T. (2002) 'Black Women, Politics, Nationalism and Community in London', *Small Axe*, vol. 6, no. 1, 133–50.

Florence, E. and Martiniello, M. (2005) 'Social Science Research and Public Policies: The Case of Immigration in Belgium', *International Journal on Multicultural Studies*, vol. 7, no. 1, 49–67.

Florin, C. and Kvarnström, L. (eds) (2001) *Kvinnor på gränsen till medborgarskap: genus, politik och offentlighet 1800–1950 [Women on the Borders of Citizenship: Gender, Politics and the Public 1800–1950]* (Stockholm: Atlas Akademi).

Fog-Olwig, K. (1998) 'Epilogue: Contested Homes: Home-making and the Making of Anthropology' in N. Rapport and A. Dawson (eds) *Migrants of Identity. Perceptions of 'Home' in a World of Movement* (Oxford and New York: Berg), pp. 225–36.

Forest, M. (2006) 'Emerging Gender Interest Groups in the New Member States: The Case of the Czech Republic', *Perspectives on European Politics and Society*, vol. 7, 170–84.

Forgeau, F. (2007) 'Idéal ou culture politique? Un examen du modèle norvégien d'égalité des sexes' [Ideal or Political culture? A Review of the Norwegian Model of Gender Equality], *Nordiques*, vol. 14, 31–46.

Fougeyrollas, D. (2005) 'Controverses et anathèmes au sein du féminisme français des années 1970' [Controversies and Anathemas within French Feminism of the 1970s], *Cahiers du genre*, vol. 39, 13–26.

Fox, J. (2005) 'Unpacking Transnational Citizenship', *Annual Review of Political Science*, vol. 8, 171–201.

Fraisse, G. (2009) *Service ou servitude. Essai sur les femmes toutes mains* [Service or Servitude. An Essay on Domestic Service] (Paris: Le Bord de l'eau éditions).

Franco, A. (2007) 'La concentration des hommes et des femmes dans les différents secteurs d'activité' [The Concentration of Men and Women in Different Spheres of Activity], *Eurostat – Statistiques en bref*, no. 53, 1–8.

Frankenberg, F. (1993*) White Women, Race Matters: The Social Construction of Whiteness* (London: Routledge).

Fraser, N. (1994) 'After the Family Wage: Gender Equity and the Welfare state', *Political Theory*, vol. 22, no. 4, 591–618.

Fraser, N. (1995) 'From Redistribution to Recognition? Dilemmas of Justice in a "Post-Socialist" Age', *New Left Review*, vol. 212, 68–93.

Fraser, N. (1997) *Justice Interruptus: Critical Reflexions on the 'Postsocialist' Condition* (New York: Routledge).

Fraser, N. (2000) 'After the Family Wage: A Postindustrial Thought Experiment' in Barbara Hobson (ed.) *Gender and Citizenship in Transition* (Basingstoke: Macmillan), pp. 1–32.

Fraser N. (2007a) 'Reframing Justice in a Globalizing World' in T. Lovell (ed.) *(Mis)recognition, Social Inequality and Social Justice. Nancy Fraser and Pierre Bourdieu* (London and New York: Routledge), pp.17–35.

Fraser, N. (2007b) 'Transnationalizing the Public Sphere: On the Legitimacy and Efficacy of Public Opinion in a Post-Westphalian World' in S. Benhabib, I. Shapiro and D. Petranovics (eds) *Identities, Affiliations, and Allegiances* (Cambridge: Cambridge University Press).

Fraser, N. (2008). *Scales of Justice: Reimagining Political Space in a Globalizing World* (Cambridge: Cambridge University Press).

Freidenvall, L., Dahlerup, D. and Skjeie, H. (2006) 'The Nordic Countries. An Incremental Model' in D. Dahlerup (ed.) *Women, Quotas and Politics* (London and New York: Palgrave).

Freidenvall, L. and Dahlerup, D. (2009) *Minority Women's Organisations and Diverse Claims for Representation: Intersections of Gender and Ethnicity*. ECPR General Conference in Potsdam, Germany, 10–12 September 2009.

Friedman, J. (2002) 'From Roots to Routes. Tropes for Trippers', *Anthropological Theory*, vol. 2, no. 1, 21–36.

Friedman, M. (2005) *Women and Citizenship* (Oxford: Oxford University Press).

Ford, L. E. (2010) *Women & Politics. The Pursuit of Equality* (Boston: Wadsworth Publishing Co Inc).

Funk, N. and Mueller, M. (eds) (1993) *Gender Politics and Post-Communism: Reflections from Eastern Europe and the former Soviet Union* (New York and London: Routledge).

Furedi, F. (2004) *Therapeutic Culture: Cultivating Vulnerability in an Uncertain Age* (London: Routledge).

Fusulier, B. (2009) 'The European Directive: Making Supra-national Parental Leave?' in S. Kamerman and P. Moss (eds) *The Politics of Parental Leave: Children, Parenting, Gender and the Labour Market* (Bristol: Policy Press).

Fuszara, M. (2006) *Kobiety w polityce [Women in Politics]* (Warszawa: TRIO).

Fuszara, M. (2008) 'One Step Forward, One Step Back: Polish Dance Around Quota System' in D. Dahlerup and L. Freidenvall, in cooperation with International IDEA, *Electoral Gender Quota Systems and Their Implementation in Europe* (Brussels: European Parliament).

Fuszara, M. (2010) 'Citizenship, Representation and Gender', *Polish Sociological Review*, vol. 4, no. 172, 367–89.

Gershuny, J. and Sullivan, O. (2003) 'Time Use, Gender and Public Policy Regimes', *Social Politics: International Studies in Gender, State and Society*, vol. 10, no. 2, 205–28.

Giddens, A. (1992) *The Transformation of Intimacy: Sexuality, Love and Eroticism in Modern Societies* (Cambridge: Polity Press).

Gilroy, P. (2004) *After Empire. Multiculture or Postcolonial Melancholia* (London and New York: Routledge).

Gitlin, T. (1995) *The Twilight of Common Dreams: Why America Is Wracked by Culture Wars* (New York: Henry Holt & Co.).

Glazer, N. (1997) *We Are All Multiculturalists Now* (Cambridge, MA: Harvard University Press).

Glenn, E. N. (2000) 'Citizenship and Inequality: Historical and Global Perspectives', *Social Problems*, vol. 47, no. 1, 1–20.

Glick Schiller, N., Basch, L. and Szanton-Blanc, C. (1992) *Towards a Transnational Perspective on Migration: Race, Class, Ethnicity, and Nationalism Reconsidered* (New York: New York Academy of Sciences).

Glick Schiller, N., Basch, L. and Szanton-Blanc, C. (1995) 'From Immigrant to Transmigrant. Theorizing Transnational Migration', *Anthropological Quarterly*, vol. 68, no. 1, 48–63.

Gordon, L. (1977) *Women's Body, Women's Rights: A Social History of Birth Control in America*, 2nd edn (Harmondsworth: Penguin).

Grégoire, N (2010) 'Identity Politics, Social Movement and the State: "Pan-African" Associations and the Making of an "African community" in Belgium', African Diaspora, vol. 3, 160–82.

Grewal, S. et al. (eds) (1988) *Charting the Journey: Writings by Black and Third World Women* (London: Sheba Feminist Press).

Griffin, G. (1995) *Feminist Activism in the 1990s* (London: Taylor and Francis).

Griffin, G. (ed.) (2004) *Employment, Equal Opportunities and Women's Studies. Women's Experiences in Seven European Countries* (Königstein: Helmer Verlag).

Grillo, R. (2003) 'Cultural Essentialism and Cultural Anxiety', *Anthropological Theory*, vol. 3, no. 2, 157–73.

Grillo, R. (2007) 'An Excess of Alterity? Debating Difference in a Multicultural Society', *Ethnic and Racial Studies*, vol. 30, no. 6, 979–98.

Grillo, R. (2008) *The Family in Question: Immigrant and Ethnic Minorities in Multicultural Europe* (Amsterdam: Amsterdam University Press).

Groenendijk, K. (2008) *Local Voting Rights for Non-nationals in Europe: What We Know and What We Need to Learn*. The Migration Policy Institute: Transatlantic Council on Migration. http://www.migrationpolicy.org/transatlantic/docs/Groenendijk-FINAL.pdf, date accessed 21 June 2011.

Groenendijk, K. et al. (2007) *The Family Reunification Directive in EU Member States: The First Year of Implementation* (Nijmegen: Wolf Legal Publisher).

Guillaumin, C. (1992) *Sexe, race et pratique du pouvoir: l'idée de Nature [Sex, Race and the Exercise of Power: The Idea of Nature]* (Paris: Côté-Femmes).

Gullestad, M. (2002) *Det norske sett med nye øyne. Kritisk analyse av norsk innvandringsdebatt [The Norwegian Seen with New Eyes. A Critical Analysis of the Norwegian Immigration Debate]* (Oslo: Universitetsforlaget).

Gullestad, M. (2006) *Plausible Prejudice: Everyday Experiences and Social Images of Nation, Culture and Place* (Oslo: Universitetsforlaget).

Gullikstad, B. (2009) *Norwegian Policies for Gender Equality and Ethnic Integration.* FEMCIT Deliverable to the European Commission. Work Package 3, Economic Citizenship. Bodø: Nordland Research Institute.

Gunaratnam, Y. (2003) *Researching 'Race' and Ethnicity – Methods, Knowledge and Power* (London: Sage).

Håland, K. (2001) *Kontantstøtten – et veiskille i norsk familiepolitikk? En sammenligning av kontantstøtten til småbarnsforeldre og fødselspermisjonsordningene [Cash-for-care – A Divide in Norwegian Family Policy? A Comparison of Cash-for-care for Parents of Small Children and the Parental Leave Scheme].* Masters' Thesis. NTNU, Trondheim.

Halimi, G. (1994) *Femmes, Moitié de la terre, moitié du pouvoir: Plaidoyer pour une Démocratie Paritaire [Women, Half of the Earth, Half of the Power: A Case for a Parity Democracy]* (Paris: Gallimard).

Hall, S. and D. Held (1989) 'Citizen and Citizenship' in S. Hall and M. Jacques (eds) *New Times: The Changing Face of Politics in the 1990s* (London: Lawrence and Wishart), pp. 173–88.

Hall, T. and Williamson, H. (1999) *Citizenship and Community* (Leicester: Youth Work Press).

Halsaa, B., Nyhagen Predelli, L. and Thun, C. (2008) *Women's Movements: Constructions of Sisterhood, Dispute and Resonance: The Case of Norway.* FEMCIT Working Paper No. 4, Work Package 4, Multicultural Citizenship. Oslo and Loughborough: University of Oslo. http://www.femcit.org/files/WP4_WorkingpaperNo4.pdf, date accessed 5 September 2011.

Halsaa, B., Roseneil, S. and Sümer, S. (eds) (2011) *FEMCIT: Gendered Citizenship in Multicultural Europe. The Impact of Contemporary Women's Movements.* FEMCIT Final Report submitted to the European Commission. Working Paper No. 5, Work Package 7, Integrative Analysis. Bergen: University of Bergen/Uni Rokkan Centre. http://www.femcit.org/files/FEMCIT%20Final%20Report%20Published.pdf, date accessed 6 June 2011.

Hammar, T. (1990) *Democracy and the Nation State: Aliens, Denizens and Citizens in a World of International Migration* (Aldershot: Avebury).

Hancock, I. (2002) *We are the Romani People* (Hatfield: University of Hertfordshire Press).

Hanisch, C. (1969) *The Personal Is Political*, http://www.carolhanisch.org/CHwritings/PIP.html, date accessed 24 October 2011.

Hannerz, U. (1992) *Cultural Complexity: Studies in the Social Organization of Meaning* (New York: Columbia University Press).

Hardy-Fanta, C. (ed.) (2006) *Intersectionality and Politics* (Binghamton: Haworth Press).

Hašková, H. (2005) 'Czech Women's Civic Organising under the State Socialist Regime, Socio-economic Transformation and the EU Accession Period', *Sociologický časopis [Czech Sociological Review]*, vol. 41, no. 6, 1077–110.

Hašková, H. (2009) *Fenomén bezdětnosti [The Phenomenon of Childlessness]* (Prague: SLON).

Hašková, H. and Klenner, C. (2010) 'Why Did Distinct Types of Dual Earner Models in Czech, Slovak and East German Societies Develop and Persist?', *Zeitschrift für Familienforschung [Journal of Family Research]*, vol. 22, no. 3, 266–88.

Hašková, H., Maříková, H. and Uhde, Z. (2009) 'Leaves, Allowances, and Facilities: Childcare Past and Present' in H. Hašková and Z. Uhde (eds) *Women and Social Citizenship in Czech Society: Continuity and Change* (Prague: Institute of Sociology, Academy of Sciences of the Czech Republic).

246 *References*

Hašková, H., Uhde, Z. and Pulkrábková, K. (2011) 'The Framing of Care Claims by Czech Women's Groups in a Post-socialist Context' in M. Hrženjak (ed.) *Politics of Care* (Ljubljana: Peace Institute).

Haug, F. et al. (1987) *Female Sexualization: A Collective Work of Memory* (London: Verso).

Hausmann, M. and Sauer, B. (eds) (2007) *Gendering the State in the Age of Globalization: Women's Movements and State Feminism in Postindustrial Democracies* (Lanham and Plymouth: Rowman & Littlefield Publishers).

Havelková, H. (1993) 'Patriarchy in Czech Society', *Hypatia*, vol. 8, no. 4, 89–96.

Havránek, F. (1981) 'Význam mini-interrupce (regulace menstruace) jako metody regulace porodnosti' [The Significance of Mini-Abortion (Menstrual Regulation) as a Method of Birth Regulation], *Československá Gynekologie*, vol. 46, no. 6, 481–5.

Heinen, J. (2011) 'From Equality to Difference? Comparing Gendered Family Policies in post-1945 Eastern Europe' in K. Hagemann, K. H. Jarausch and C. Allemann-Ghionda (eds) *Children, Families and States: Time Policies of Childcare, Preschool, and Primary Education in Europe* (New York and Oxford: Berghahn Books).

Heinen, J. and Portet, S. (eds) (2004) 'Egalité des sexes en Europe centrale et orientale: Entre espoirs et déconvenus' [Sexual Equality in Central and Eastern Europe: Between Hopes and Disappointments], *Transitions*, vol. 44, no. 1.

Heitlinger, A. (1996) 'Framing Feminism in Post-Communist Czech Republic', *Communist and Post-Communist Studies*, vol. 29, no. 1, 77–93.

Hekman, S. (2000) 'Beyond Identity: Feminism, Identity and Identity Politics', *Feminist Theory*, vol. 1, no. 3, 289–308.

Hellgren, Z. (2007) '(De)constructing European Citizenship: Political Mobilization and Collective Identity Formation among Immigrants in Sweden and Spain', http://aa.ecn.cz/img_upload/3bfc4ddc48d13ae0415c78ceae108bf5/ZHellgren_DeconstructingEuropeancitizenship.pdf, date accessed 21 June 2011.

Hernes, H. M. (1982) *Staten – Kvinner ingen adgang? [The State – No Access for Women?]* (Oslo and Bergen: Tromsø Universitetsforlag).

Hernes, H. M. (1987) *Welfare State and Woman Power. Essays in State Feminism* (Oslo: Norwegian University Press).

Hernes, H. M. (1988) 'The Welfare State Citizenship of Scandinavian Women' in K. B. Jones and A. G. Jonasdottir (eds) *The Political Interests of Gender* (London: Sage), pp. 187–213.

Hix, S. and Lesse, U. (2002) *Shaping a Vision: A History of the Party of European Socialists 1957–2002* (Brussels: Party of European Socialists).

Hobson, B. (2000a) 'Economic Citizenship: Reflections through the European Policy Mirror' in B. Hobson (ed.) *Gender and Citizenship in transition* (Basingstoke: Macmillan), pp. 89–117.

Hobson, B. (ed.) (2000b) *Gender and Citizenship in Transition* (Basingstoke: Macmillan).

Hobson, B. and Lister, R. (2002) 'Citizenship' in B. Hobson, J. Lewis and B. Siim (eds) *Contested Concepts in Gender and Social Politics* (Cheltenham: Edward Elgar).

Hochschild, A. (1997) *The Time Bind: When Work Becomes Home and Home Becomes Work* (New York: Metropolitan Books).

Hochschild, A. (2000) 'Global Care Chains and Emotional Surplus Value' in A. Giddens and W. Hutton (eds) *On the Edge: Globalization and the New Millennium* (London: Sage Publishers), pp. 130–46.

Hoffman, J. (2004) *Citizenship beyond the State* (London: Sage).

hooks, b. (1982) *Ain't I a Woman: Black Women and Feminism* (London: Pluto).

hooks, b. (2000) *Feminist Theory: From Margin to Center*, 2nd edn (London: Pluto Press).

Hutchings, K. (1999) 'Feminist Politics and Cosmopolitan Citizenship' in K. Hutchings and R. Dannreuther (eds) *Cosmopolitan Citizenship* (Basingstoke: Macmillan, pp. 120–42.

İlkkaracan, P. (1998) 'Doğu Anadolu'da Kadın ve Aile' [Woman and Family in East Anatolia] in A. B. Hacimirzaoglu (ed.) *75 Yılda Kadınlar ve Erkekler [Women and Men in 75 Years (of the Turkish Republic)]* (Istanbul: Tarih Vakfi) pp. 173–92.

İlkkaracan, P. (ed.) (2000) *Women and Sexuality in Muslim Societies* (Istanbul: Women for Women's Human Rights – New Ways)

Inglehart, R. and Norris, P. (2003) *Rising Tide. Gender Equality and Cultural Change around the World* (Cambridge: Cambridge University Press).

Isaksson E. (2007) *Kvinnokamp [Women's Struggle]* (Stockholm: Atlas).

Isaksen, L. W. (ed.) (2010) *Global Care Work: Gender and Migration in Nordic Societies* (Lund: Nordic Academic Press).

Işın, E. F. (2005) 'Engaging, Being, Political', *Political Geography*, vol. 24, 373–87.

Işın, E. F. and Turner, B. S. (eds) (2002) *Handbook of Citizenship Studies* (London: Sage).

IPU (Inter-Parliamentary Union) (2012) *Women in National Parliaments*, http://www.ipu.org/wmn-e/world.htm, date accessed 31 May 2011.

Jany-Catrice, F. (2010) 'La construction sociale du "secteur" des services à la personne: une banalisation programmée?' [The Social Construction of the Home Care Services "Sector": A Planned Trivialisation?, *Sociologie du travail*, vol. 52, no. 4, 521–37.

Jenson, J. (2008) 'Writing Women Out, Folding Gender In: The European Union "Modernises" Social Policy', *Social Politics: International Studies in Gender, State and Society*, vol. 15, no. 2, 131–53.

Jenson, J. (2009) 'Lost in Translation: The Social Investment Perspective and Gender Equality', *Social Politics: International Studies in Gender, State and Society*, vol. 16, no. 4, 446–83.

Jonas, M. (2005) Personal communication.

Jonasdottir, A. and Jones, K. (2008) *The Political Interests of Gender Revisited: Redoing Theory and Research with a Feminist Face* (Manchester: Manchester University Press).

Jones, K. and Jonasdottir, A. (1988) *The Political Interests of Gender: Developing Theory and Research with a Feminist Face* (London: Sage)

Joppke, C. (2003) 'The Retreat of Multiculturalism in the Liberal State: Theory and Practice', *The British Journal of Sociology*, vol. 55, 237–57.

Joppke, C. (2010) *Citizenship and Immigration* (Cambridge: Polity Press).

Kabeer, N. (ed.) (2005) *Inclusive Citizenship. Meanings and Expressions* (London: Zed Books).

Kantola, J. (2007) *Feminists Theorize the State* (London: Palgrave).

Kauffman, L.A. (1990) 'The Anti-Politics of Identity', *Socialist Review*, vol. 21, 67–80.

Kelek, N. (2005) *Die fremde Braut. Ein Bericht aus dem Inneren des türkischen Lebens in Deutschland [The Foreign Bride: A Report from Inside Turkish Life in Germany]* (Cologne: Kiepenhauer und Witsch).

Kessler-Harris, A. (1996) 'Gender Identity, Rights to Work and the Idea of Economic Citizenship', *Schweizerische Zeitschrift für Geschichte*, vol. 46, 411–26.

Kessler-Harris, A. (2001) *In Pursuit of Equity: Women, Men and the Quest for Economic Citizenship in Twentieth Century America* (New York: Oxford University Press).

Kessler-Harris, A. (2003) 'In Pursuit of Economic Citizenship', *Social Politics*, vol. 10, no. 2, 157–75.

Kiwan, D. (2007) 'Citizenship Education in England at the Cross-roads? Four Models of Citizenship and Their Implications for Ethnic and Religious Diversity', *Oxford Review of Education*, vol. 34, no. 1, 39–58.

Kocourková, J. (2009) 'Czech Republic: Normative or Choice Oriented System?' in S. B. Kamerman and P. Moss (eds) *The Politics of Parental Leave: Children, Parenting, Gender and the Labour Market* (Bristol: Policy Press).

Kooiman, J. (2003) *Governing as Governance* (London: Sage).

Koopmans, R. (2006) *Tradeoffs Between Equality and Difference – The Crisis of Dutch Multiculturalism in Cross-national Perspective*, Free University Amsterdam.

Koopmans, R. (2010) 'Tradeoffs between Equality and Difference: Immigrant Integration, Multiculturalism and the Welfare State in Cross-National Perspective', *Ethnic and Migration Studies*, vol. 36, no. 1, pp. 1–26.

Koopmans, R. and Statham, P. (2000) *Challenging Immigration and Ethnic Relations Politics: Comparative European Perspectives* (Oxford and New York: Oxford University Press).

Korbel, J. (2009) 'Sterilizace Romek pokračuje, vláda se neomluví' [Sterilization of Roma Women Continues, the Government Will Not Apologize], *Deník.cz*, 30 July 2009. http://www.denik.cz/z_domova/sterilizace-romek-pokracuje20090730.html, date accessed 2 April 2011.

Korsvik, T. R. (2011) 'Childcare Policy since the 1970s in the "Most Gender Equal Country in the World": A Field of Controversy and Grassroots Activism', *European Journal of Women's Studies*, vol. 18, no. 2, 135–53.

Korsvik, T. R., Rantalaiho, M. and Bergman, S. (2009) *Research on Political Actions and Claims by Women's Movements and Other NGOs in Childcare and Parental Leave Issues in Norway and Finland since the 1960s*. FEMCIT Working Paper No. 1, Work Package 2, Social Citizenship. Oslo: Nordic Gender Institute, NIKK. http://www.femcit.org/publications.xpl?page=FEMCITpapers#SC, date accessed 17 November 2011.

Krajewska, A. (2010) *Institutionalised elderly care in Poland: Legal frameworks and real-life practice*. FEMCIT Deliverable to the European Commission. Work Package 3, Economic Citizenship. Warsaw: Warsaw University.

Krajewska, A. and Orłowska, D. (2009) *Migration Policies and Practices in Poland*. FEMCIT Deliverable to the European Commission. Work Package 3, Economic Citizenship. Warsaw: Warsaw University.

Kremer, M. (2007) *How Welfare States Care: Culture, Gender and Citizenship in Europe* (Amsterdam: Amsterdam University Press).

Kriesi, H. (1989) 'New Social Movements and the New Class in the Netherlands' *American Journal of Sociology*, vol. 94, no. 5, 1078–116.

Kriesi, H. (2004) 'Political Context and Opportunity' in D. A. Snow, S. Soule and H. Kriesi (eds) *The Blackwell Companion to Social Movements* (Oxford: Blackwell Publishing), pp. 67–91.

Krook, M. L., Lovenduski, J. and Squires, J. (2009) 'Gender Quotas and Models of Political Citizenship', *British Journal of Political Science*, vol. 39, 781–803.

Kuchařová, V. and Svobodová, K. (2006) *Síť zařízení denní péče o děti předškolního věku v ČR [Network of Childcare Services for Pre-school Children in the Czech Republic]* (Praha: VÚPSV).

Kulawik, T. (2007) 'Von der Geschlechtsneutralität zum Kampf um Geschlechtermacht? Zur Entstehung einer Feministischen Partei in Schweden' [From Gender Neutrality to Struggle for Gender Power? About the Emergence of a Feminist Party in Sweden], *Femina Politica. Zeitschrift für Feministische Politikwissenschaft*, vol. 16, no. 1, 9–22.

Kulawik, T. (2009) 'Staking the Frame of a Feminist Discursive Institutionalism', *Politics and Gender*, vol. 5, no. 2, 262–71.

Kuntsman, A. and Miyake, E. (eds) (2008) *Out of Place: Interrogating Silences in Queerness/Raciality* (York: Raw Nerve Books).

Kvist, E. and Peterson, E. (2010) 'What Has Gender Equality to Do with It? An Analysis of Policy Debates Surrounding Domestic Services in the Welfare States of Spain and Sweden', *NORA: Nordic Journal of Feminist and Gender Research*, vol. 18, no. 3, 185–203.

Kymlicka, W. (1995) *Multicultural Citizenship: A Liberal Theory of Minority Rights* (Oxford: Oxford University Press).

Kymlicka, W. (2000) 'Citizenship in Culturally Diverse Societies: Issues, Contexts, Concepts' in W. Kymlicka and W. Norman (eds) *Citizenship in Diverse Societies* (Oxford: Oxford University Press), pp. 1–41.

Kymlicka, W. (2010) 'The Rise and the Fall of Multiculturalism? New Debates on Inclusion and Accommodation in Diverse Societies' in S. Vertovec and S. Wessendorf (eds) *The Multiculturalism Backlash. European Discourses, Policies and Practices* (Abingdon and New York: Routledge), pp. 32–49.

Kymlicka, W. and Norman, W. (1994) 'Return of the Citizen: A Survey of Recent Work on Citizenship Theory', *Ethics*, vol. 104, no. 2, 352–81.

Lammi-Taskula, J. (2006) 'Nordic Men on Parental Leave: Can the Welfare State Change Gender Relations?' in A. L. Ellingsæter and A. Leira (eds) *Politicising Parenthood in Scandinavia. Gender Relations in Welfare States* (Bristol: Policy Press).

Lammi-Taskula, J. and Takala, P. (2009) 'Finland: Negotiating Tripartite Compromises' in S. B. Kamerman and P. Moss (eds) *The Politics of Parental Leave: Children, Parenting, Gender and the Labour Market* (Bristol: Policy Press).

Landolt, P. (2001) 'Salvadoran Economic Transnationalism: Embedded Strategies for Household Maintenance, Immigrant Incorporation, and Entrepreneurial Expansion', *Global Networks*, vol. 1, no. 3, 217–41.

Latcheva, R., Edthofer, J., Goisauf, M. and Obermann, J. (2006) *Situationsbericht und Empfehlungskatalog: Zwangsverheiratung und arrangierte Ehen in Österreich mit besonderer Berücksichtigung Wiens [Situation Report and Catalogue of Recommendations: Forced Marriage and Arranged Marriages in Austria, with Particular Reference to Vienna* (Wien: Magistrat 57- Frauenförderung und Koordinierung von Frauenangelegenheiten).

Le Feuvre, N. and Lapeyre, N. (2005) 'Les "scripts sexués" de carrière dans les professions juridiques en France' [The "Sexual Scripts" of Careers in Legal Professions in France], *Knowledge, Work and Society*, vol. 3, no. 1, 101–26.

Le Feuvre, N. and Martin, J. (2001) 'Les services de proximité aux ménages: de la solidarité à la précarité de l'emploi féminin' [Domestic Services for Households: From Solidarity to Job Insecurity for Women], *Némésis, Numéro spécial 'économie plurielle, économie solidaire: l'emploi en question'*, vol. 3, 299–332.

Le Feuvre, N. and Roseneil, S. (2011) *Entanglements of Economic and Intimate Citizenship at the Cutting Edge of European Social Change*. European Sociological Association Conference, Geneva, Switzerland, 7–10 September 2011.

Le Feuvre, N., Metso, M. and Chaker, S. (2010) *The Economic Citizenship Experiences of Minoritized and Majoritized Women in Elderly Care in France*. FEMCIT Deliverable to the European Commission. Work Package 3, Economic Citizenship. Toulouse: University of Toulouse-Le Mirail.

Le Feuvre, N. et al. (2009) *Mapping the Labour Market Experiences of 'Majority' and 'Minority' Women in France, Norway and Poland*. FEMCIT Working Paper No.1, Work Package 3, Economic Citizenship. Toulouse: University of Toulouse-Le Mirail.

Leira, A. (2006) 'Parenthood Change and Policy Reform in Scandinavia, 1970s–2000s' in A. L. Ellingsæter and A. Leira (eds) *Politicising Parenthood in Scandinavia. Gender Relations in Welfare States* (Bristol: Policy Press).

Leira, A. and Saraceno, C. (2002) 'Care: Actors, Relationships and Contexts' in J. Lewis, B. Hobson and B. Siim (eds) *Contested Concepts in Gender and Social Politics* (Cheltenham: Edward Elgar).

Leitner, S. (2003) 'Varieties of Familialism. The Caring Function of the Family in Comparative Perspective', *European Societies*, vol. 5, no. 4, 353–75.

Lennerhed, L. (2008) *Historier om ett brott: illegala aborter i Sverige på 1900-talet* [*Histories about a Crime: Illegal Abortions in Sweden in the 20th Century*] (Stockholm: Atlas).

Lentin, A. (2008) 'Europe and the Silence about Race', *European Journal of Social Theory*, vol. 11, no. 4, 487–503.

Lewis, G. (2004a) *Citizenship: Personal Lives and Social Policy* (Bristol: Policy Press in Association with the Open University).

Lewis, G. (2004b) ' "Do Not Go Gently…": Terrains of Citizenship and Landscapes of the Personal' in G. Lewis (ed.) *Citizenship: Personal Lives and Social Policy* (Bristol: Policy Press in Association with the Open University).

Lewis, J. (1992) 'Gender and the Development of Welfare Regimes', *Journal of European Social Policy*, vol. 2, no. 3, 159–73.

Lewis, J. (ed.) (1993) *Women and Social Policies in Europe* (Hampshire: Edward Elgar).

Lewis, J. (1997) 'Gender and Welfare Regimes: Further Thoughts', *Social Politics: International Studies in Gender, State & Society*, vol. 4, 160–77.

Lewis, J. (ed.) (1998) *Gender, Social Care and Welfare State Restructuring in Europe* (Aldershot: Ashgate).

Lewis, J. (2002) 'Gender and Welfare State Change', *European Societies*, vol. 4, no. 4, 331–57.

Lewis, J. (2003) 'Economic Citizenship: A comment', *Social Politics*, vol. 10, no. 2, 176–85.

Lewis, J. (2007) 'Gender, Ageing and the "New Social Settlement": The Importance of Developing a Holistic Approach to Care Policies', *Current Sociology*, vol. 55, no. 2, 271–86.

Lewis, J. and Giullari, S. (2005) 'The Adult Worker Model Family, Gender Equality and Care: The Search for New Policy Principles and the Possibilities and Problems of the Capabilities Approach', *Economy and Society*, vol. 34, no. 1, 76–104.

Leydet, D. (2006) Citizenship in E. N. Zalta (ed.) *The Stanford Encyclopedia of Philosophy*, http://plato.stanford.edu/entries/citizenship, date accessed 12 January 2012.

Leyenaar, M. (2004) *The Political Empowerment of Women: The Netherlands and Other Countries* (Leiden and Boston: Martinus Nijhoff Publishers).

Lindeberg, C. and Berg, M. (2010) *Skrota sexköpslagen för kvinnornas skull* [*Scrap the Legislation of Purchase of Sexual Services for the Sake of Women*], http://www.expressen.se/debatt/1.2071323/debatt-skrota-sexkopslagen-for-kvinnornas-skull, date accessed 28 April 2011.

Lindelöf, K. S. (2010) *Report on Bodily and Sexual Citizenship and the Impact of Women's Movements on the Abortion Issue in Sweden (1964–2009).* FEMCIT Deliverable to the European Commission. Work Package 5, Sexual & Bodily Citizenship. Stockholm/Huddinge: Södertörn University.

Lister, R. (1989) *The Female Citizen* (Liverpool, Liverpool University Press).

Lister, R. (1997) *Citizenship: Feminist Perspectives* (Basingstoke and New York: Palgrave Macmillan).

Lister, R. (2003) *Citizenship: Feminist Perspectives* (2nd ed.) (Basingstoke: Palgrave Macmillan).

Lister, R. (2004) 'Citizenship and Gender' in K. Nash and A. Scott (eds) *The Blackwell Companion To Political Sociology* (Oxford and Malden, MA: Blackwell Publishers), pp.323–32.

Lister, R. (2007) 'Inclusive Citizenship: Realizing the Potential', *Citizenship Studies*, vol. 11, no. 1, 49–61.

Lister, R. et al. (2007) *Gendering Citizenship in Western Europe. New Challenges for Citizenship Research in a Cross-national Context* (Bristol: The Policy Press).

Lombardo, E. (2009) *Spanish Policy on Gender Equality: Relevant Current Legislation and Policies*. Report to the European Parliament. Directorate General for Internal Policies.

Lombardo, E., Meier, P. and Verloo, M. (2009) *The Discursive Politics of Gender Equality Stretching, Bending and Policy-Making* (London and New York: Routledge).

Lord Morris of Handsworth (2007) *House of Lords Debate*, 7 June, 12.42pm. http://www.publications.parliament.uk/pa/ld200607/ldhansrd/text/70607–0004.htm, date accessed 13 December 2011.

Lorentzen, H. and Dugstad, L. (2011) *Den norske dugnaden [The Norwegian Community Work]* (Oslo: Høyskoleforlaget).

Lovenduski, J. (2005a) *Feminizing Politics* (Cambridge and Malden, MA: Polity Press).

Lovenduski, J. (ed.) (2005b) *State Feminism and Political Representation* (Cambridge: Cambridge University Press).

Lovenduski, J. and Hills, J. (eds) (1981) *The Politics of the Second Electorate* (London: Routledge & Kegan Paul).

Lukes, S. (2004) *Power. A Radical View*, 2nd edn (London: Palgrave Macmillan).

Lutz, H. (ed.) (2008) *Migration and Domestic Work: A European Perspective on a Global Theme* (Aldershot and Burlington: Ashgate).

Lykke, N. (2004) 'Between Particularism, Universalism and Transversalism. Reflections on the Politics of Location of Three European Feminist Journals', *NORA*, vol. 12, no. 2, 72–82.

Lyon, D. (2010) 'Intersections and Boundaries of Work and Non-work. The Case of Eldercare in Comparative European Perspective', *European Societies*, vol. 12, no. 2, 163–85.

Lyon, D. and Glucksmann, M. (2008) 'Comparative Configurations of Care Work Across Europe', *Sociology*, vol. 41, no. 1, 101–18.

Lyon, D. and Woodward, A. E. (2004) 'Gender and Time at the Top: Cultural Constructions of Time in High-Level Careers and Homes, *European Journal of Women's Studies*, vol. 11, no. 2, 205–22.

Mackay, F. (2008) 'The State of Women's Movements in Britain. Ambiguity, Complexity and Challenges from the Periphery' in S. Grey and M. Sawer (eds) *Women's Movements: Flourishing or in Abeyance?* (London: Routledge), pp. 17–32.

Makkai, T. (1997) 'Social Policy and Gender in Eastern Europe' in D. Sainsbury (ed.), *Gendering Welfare States* (London: Sage), pp. 188–205.

Malinová, H. (2008) *Sex a Prostitute [Sex and Prostitution]*, http://www.rozkosbezrizika.cz/01_htm/021_ZAKON.htm, date accessed 22 June 2010.

Malos, E. (ed.) (1980) *The Politics of Housework* (London: Allison & Busby).

Maříková, H. (2008) 'Caring Fathers and Gender (In)Equality?' *Polish Sociological Review*, vol. 162, no. 2, 135–52.

Marshall, T. H. (1950) *Citizenship and Social Class and Other Essays* (Cambridge: Cambridge University Press).

Marshall, T. H. (1963) *Class, Citizenship, and Social Development* (New York: Anker Books).

Martiniello, M. and Rea, A. (2003) *Belgium's Immigration Policy brings Renewal and Challenges*, Migration Policy Institute. http://www.migrationinformation.org/Profiles/display.cfm?ID=164, date accessed 2 May 2011.

Mason, J. (2004) 'Managing Kinship over Long Distances: the Significance of "the Visit"' *Social Policy and Society*, vol. 3, no. 4, 421–9.

Mazur, A. G. (2002) *Theorizing Feminist Policy* (New York: Oxford University Press).

Mazur, A. G. and McBride, D. E. (2010) 'Gendering New Institutionalism' in D. McBride and A. G. Mazur (eds) *The Politics of State Feminism. Innovation in Comparative Research* (Philadelphia: Temple University Press).

McBride Stetson, D. (1997) 'Gender and European Politics: The Limits of Integration', *Political Science and Politics*, vol. 30, no. 2, 195–7.

McBride Stetson, D. (2001) *Abortion Politics, Women's Movements, and the Democratic State: A Comparative Study of State Feminism* (Oxford and New York: Oxford University Press).

McBride, D. E. and Mazur, A. G. (eds) (2010) *The Politics of State Feminism: Innovation in Comparative Research* (Philadelphia: The Temple University Press). This should be Temple University Press, not The Temple etc

McLaren, A. (1978) *Birth Control in Nineteenth Century England* (London: Croom Helm).

Méda, D. and Périvier, H. (2007) *Le deuxième âge de l'émancipation. La société, les femmes et l'emploi [The Second Age of Emancipation. Society, Women and Employment]*, La République des idées (Paris: Seuil).

Medrano, J. D. (2005) 'Nation, Citizenship and Immigration in Contemporary Spain', *International Journal on Multicultural Societies*, vol. 7, no. 2, 133–56.

Mercer, C. H. et al. (2004) 'Increasing Prevalence of Male Homosexual Partnerships and Practices in Britain 1990–2000: Evidence from National Probability Surveys' *AIDS*, vol. 18, no. 10, 1453–8.

Metso, M. and Le Feuvre, N. (2009) *Equal Opportunity and Diversity Policies & Practices in France*. FEMCIT Deliverable to the European Commission. Work Package 3, Economic Citizenship. Toulouse: University of Toulouse-Le Mirail.

Metso, M. et al. (2009) *Mapping Economic Citizenship Issues from Women's Movement Publications in Finland, France, Norway, Poland and the UK*. FEMCIT Working Paper No. 2, Work Package 3, Economic Citizenship. Toulouse: University of Toulouse-Le Mirail. http://www.femcit.org/files/WP3_WorkingpaperNo2.pdf, date accessed 13 January 2012.

Meurs, D. and Pailhé, A. (2010) 'Position sur le marché du travail des descendants directs d'immigrés en France: Les femmes doublement désavantagées?' [Opinion on the Labour Market for Direct Descendants of Immigrants in France: Doubly Disadvantaged Women?], *Economie et statistique*, no. 431–2, 129–51.

Mirza, H. (ed.) (1997) *Black British Feminism – A Reader* (London: Routledge).

Modood, T. (1994) 'Political Blackness and British Asians', *Sociology* vol. 28, 859–876.

Modood, T. (2005) *Multicultural Politics: Racism, Ethnicity and Muslims in Britain* (Edinburgh: University of Edinburgh Press).

Mohanty, C. T. (1986) 'Under Western Eyes: Feminist Scholarship and Colonial Discourses', *Boundary 2*, vol. 12, no. 3, 333–58.

Mohanty, C. T. (2003) 'Under Western Eyes Revisited: Feminist Solidarity Through Anticapitalist Struggle', *Signs*, vol. 28, no. 2, 499–537.

Mohr, J. (1978) *Abortion in America. The Origins and Evolution of National Policy 1800–1900* (New York: Oxford University Press).

Montgomery, K. (2003) 'Introduction' in R. E. Matland and K. A. Montgomery (eds) *Women's Access to Political Power in Post-communist Europe* (Oxford: Oxford University Press), pp. 1–18.

Moraga, C. and Anzaldúa, G. (eds) (1983) *This Bridge Called My Back: Writings by Radical Women of Color* (New York: Kitchen Table).

Moss, P. (ed.) (2010) *International Review of Leave Policies and Related Research 2010.* Employment relations research series no. 115. London: The Department for Business, Innovation and Skills. http://www.leavenetwork.org/fileadmin/Leavenetwork/Annual_reviews/2010_annual_review.pdf, date accessed 30 November 2010.

Motejl, O. (2005) *Závěrečné stanovisko veřejného ochránce práv ve věci sterilizací prováděných v rozporu s právem a návrhy opatření k nápravě [Final Statement of the Public Defender of Rights in the Matter of Sterilisations Performed in Contravention of the Law and Proposed Remedial Measures]* (Brno: Public Defender of Rights).

Mouffe, C. (1992) 'Feminism, Citizenship and Radical Democratic Politics' in J. Butler and J. Scott (eds) *Feminists Theorize the Political* (London: Routledge).

MVČR (1999) *Rozbor problému souvisejících s prostitucí a vymezení podmínek jejich systémového řešení [Analysis of Prostitution Related Problems and Demarcation of Conditions for Systemic Solutions]* (Prague: Ministry of the Interior of the Czech Republic).

Myant, M. (1989) *The Czechoslovak Economy 1948–1988: The Battle for Economic Reform* (New York: Cambridge University Press).

Narayan, U. (1997) *Dislocating Cultures: Identities, Traditions, and Third World Feminism* (New York and London: Routledge).

Narayan, U. and Harding, S. (eds) (2000) *Decentering the Center. Philosophy for a Multicultural, Postcolonial, and Feminist World* (Bloomington: Indiana University Press).

Navaro-Yashin, Y. (2002) *Faces of the State. Secularism and Public Life in Turkey* (Princeton: Princeton University Press).

Newman, J. and Clarke, J. (2009) *Publics, Politics and Power: Remaking the Public in Public Services* (London: Sage).

Nicholson, L. (2008) *Identity Before Identity Politics.* (Cambridge; New York: Cambridge University Press).

Nicole-Drancourt, C. (2009) 'Un impensé des résistances à l'égalité des sexes: Le régime temporel' [An Unthought Resistance to Gender Equality: The Temporal Régime], *Temporalités: Revue de sciences sociales et humaines,* no. 9, 1–18.

Noordman, J. (1989) *Om de kwaliteit van het nageslacht. Eugenetica in Nederland 1900–1950 [On the Quality of Offspring. Eugenics in the Netherlands 1900–1950]* (Nijmegen: SUN).

Nordic Statistical Yearbook (2010) *Nord 2010: 001* (Copenhagen: Nordic Council of Ministers).

Norris, P. (1994) *Political Recruitment: Gender, Race and Class in the British Parliament* (Cambridge, New York and Melbourne: Cambridge University Press).

Norton, P. (ed.) (2002) *Parliaments and Citizens in Western Europe* (London: Frank Cass).

Nussbaum, M. C. (1999) 'A Plea for Difficulty' in S. M. Okin (ed.) *Is Multiculturalism Bad for Women?* (Princeton: Princeton University Press), pp. 105–14.

Nydal, K. (2007) '*Sosialmoralsk engasjement og politisk aktivisme. Fremveksten av en antirasistisk bevegelse i Norge 1975–1988' [Social-moral Engagement and Political Activism. The Emergence of an Antiracist Movement in Norway 1975–1988],* PhD Thesis. Det humanistiske fakultet, Universitetet i Oslo.

Nyhagen Predelli, L. et al. (2008) *Women's Movements: Constructions of Sisterhood, Dispute and Resonance: The Case of the United Kingdom.* FEMCIT Working Paper

No. 2, Work Package 4, Multicultural Citizenship. Loughborough: University of Loughborough. http://www.femcit.org/files/WP4_WorkingpaperNo2.pdf, date accessed 8 September 2011.

Nyhagen Predelli, L. and Halsaa, B. with Cecilie Thun, Adriana Sandu and Kim Perren (2012) *Majority-Minority Relations in Contemporary Women's Movements: Strategic Sisterhood* (Basingstoke: Palgrave Macmillan).

OECD (Organisation for Economic Co-operation and Development) (2006) *Men and Women in OECD Countries* (Paris: OECD).

OECD (Organisation for Economic Co-operation and Development) (2010) *OECD Factbook (2010)*, http://www.oecd-ilibrary.org/economics/oecd-factbook-2010_factbook-2010-en, date accessed 30 January 2011

Offen, K. (2000) *European Feminisms 1700–1950. A Political History* (Stanford: Stanford University Press).

Okin. S. (2005) 'Multiculturalism and Feminism: No Simple Question, No Simple Answers' in A. Eisenberg and J. Spinner-Halev (eds) *Minorities within Minorities. Equality, Rights and Diversity* (Cambridge: Cambridge University Press), pp. 67–89.

Okin, S. M. (1999) *Is Multiculturalism Bad for Women?* (Princeton: Princeton University Press).

Oláh, L. S. (2011) 'Family Policies and Birth Rates in Postwar Europe' in K. Hagemann, K. H. Jarausch and C. Allemann-Ghionda (eds) *Children, Families and States: Time Policies of Childcare, Preschool, and Primary Education in Europe* (New York and Oxford: Berghahn Books).

Oliveira, A. (2004) *AsVvendedoras deIilusões: Estudos sobre Prostituição, Alterne e Striptease [Illusion Sellers: Studies About Prostitution and Striptease]* (Lisbon: Editorial de Notícias).

Ong, A. (1999) *Flexible Citizenship. The Cultural Logics of Transnationality* (Durham: Duke University Press).

Ongan, G. (2008) 'Zuschreiben oder ernsthaftes Bekämpfen: Zwangsverheiratung aus der Perspektive der Bildungs-, Beratungs- und Therapieeinrichtung Peregrina' [To Blame or to Fight: Forced Marriage from the Perspective of the Education, Counselling and Treatment Centre in Peregrina] in B. Sauer and S. Strasser (eds) *Zwangsfreiheiten. Feminismus und Multikulturalismus [Forced Freedoms. Feminism and Multiculturalism]* (Vienna: Promedia).

Orloff, A. S. (1993) 'Gender and the Social Rights of Citizenship: The Comparative Analysis of Gender Relations and Welfare States', *American Sociological Review*, vol. 58, 303–38.

Orloff, A. S. (1996) 'Gender in the Welfare State', *Annual Review of Sociology*, vol. 22, no. 1, 51–78.

Orloff, A. S. and Palier, B. (2009) 'The Power of Gender Perspectives: Feminist Influence on Policy Paradigms, Social Science and Social Politics', *Social Politics: International Studies in Gender, State and Society*, vol. 16, no. 4, 405–12.

Osler, A. and Starkey, H. (2001) 'Citizenship Education and National Identities in England and France: Inclusive or Exclusive?', *Oxford Review of Education*, vol. 27, no. 2, 287–305.

Østergaard-Nielsen, E. (2003) *Transnational Politics. Turks and Kurds in Germany* (London, New York: Routledge).

Ouali, N. (2004) 'Etudes sur les Migrations: l'intérêt d'une approche en terme de genre' [Migration Studies: The Significance of a Gendered Approach], *Sophia*, vol. 39, 38–40.

Ouali, N. (2007) 'Femmes immigrées en Belgique: les enjeux pour le mouvement des femmes' [Immigrant Women in Belgium: Challenges for the Women's Movement], *Dossier societé, Fédération des Amis de la Morale Laïque asbl*.

http://www.faml.be/dossier-societe/item/49-femmes-immigr%C3%A9es-en-belgique-les-enjeux-pour-le-mouvement-des-femmes, date accessed 2 May 2011.

Outshoorn, J. (1986) *De politieke strijd rondom de abortuswetgeving 1964–1984 [The Political Dispute about Abortion Legislation 1964–1984]* (Den Haag: VUGA).

Outshoorn, J. (1996) 'The Stability of Compromise. Abortion Politics in Western Europe' in M. Githens and D. M. Stetson (eds) *Abortion Politics. Public Policy in Cross-Comparative Perspective* (New York and London: Routledge), pp. 145–65.

Outshoorn, J. (2001) 'Debating Prostitution in Parliament. A Feminist Analysis', *European Journal of Women's Studies*, vol. 8, no. 4, 473–92.

Outshoorn, J. (2004a) 'Introduction: Prostitution, Women's Movements and Democratic Politics', in J. Outshoorn (ed.) *The Politics of Prostitution. Women's Movements, Democratic States and the Globalization of Sex Commerce* (Cambridge: Cambridge University Press).

Outshoorn, J. (2004b) 'Voluntary and forced prostitution: the 'realistic approach' of the Netherlands in J. Outshoorn (ed.) *The Politics of Prostitution. Women's Movements, Democratic States and the Globalization of Sex Commerce* (Cambridge: Cambridge University Press), pp.185–205.

Outshoorn, J. (2009) *A Return to Morality Politics? Framing, Policies and Party Alignments in the Netherlands.* ECPR First Politics and Gender Conference, Belfast, Northern Ireland, 21–23 January 2009.

Outshoorn, J. (2010a) *Abortion, Migration and Europeanization. Report on the Netherlands, Leiden.* FEMCIT Working Paper No. 2, Work Package 5, Sexual & Bodily Citizenship. Leiden: Leiden University. http://www.femcit.org/files/WP5_WorkingpaperNo2.pdf, date accessed 13 January 2012.

Outshoorn, Joyce (2010b) *Prostitution, Migration and Europeanization. Report on the Netherlands, Leiden.* FEMCIT Deliverable to the European Commission. Work Package 5, Sexual & Bodily Citizenship. Leiden: Leiden University.

Outshoorn, J. (2010c) 'Social Movements and Women's Movements' in D. E. McBride and A. G. Mazur (eds) *The Politics of State Feminism: Innovation in Comparative Research* (Philadelphia: The Temple University Press), pp.143–64.

Outshoorn, J. (forthcoming) 'The Return of the Victim: Changes in Dutch Prostitution Policy'.

Outshoorn, J. and Kantola, J. (eds) (2007) *Changing State Feminism* (New York: Palgrave Macmillan)

Özbilgin, M. F. and Woodward, D. (2004) ' "Belonging" and "Otherness": Sex Equality in Banking in Turkey and Britain', *Gender, Work and Organisations*, vol. 11, no. 6, 668–88.

Parekh, B. (2000) *Rethinking Multiculturalism. Cultural Diversity and Political Theory* (Basingstoke: Macmillan).

Parreñas, R. (2001) 'Mothering from a Distance. Emotions, Gender, and Intergenerational Relations in Filipino Transnational Families', *Feminist Studies*, vol. 27, no. 2, pp. 361–90.

Pateman, C. (1988) *The Sexual Contract* (Cambridge: Polity Press).

Pateman, C. (1989) *The Disorder of Women: Democracy, Feminism and Political Theory* (Cambridge: Polity Press).

Peixoto, J. et al. (2005) *O Tráfico de Migrantes em Portugal: Perspectivas Sociológicas, Jurídicas e Políticas [Migrant Trafficking in Portugal: Sociological, Juridical and Political Perspectives]* (Lisbon: ACIME).

People and Participation.net (n.d.) *Methods Pages*, http://www.peopleandparticipation.net/display/Methods, date accessed 13 December 2011.

Pfau-Effinger, B. (1998) 'Gender Cultures and the Gender Arrangement – A Theoretical Framework for Cross-national Comparisons on Gender', *Innovation: the European Journal of Social Sciences. The Spatiality of Gender*, vol. 11, no. 2, 147–66.

Pfau-Effinger, B. (2004) *Development of Culture, Welfare States and Women's Employment in Europe* (Aldershot: Ashgate).

Pfau-Effinger, B. and Geissler, B. (eds) (2005) *Care Arrangements and Social Integration in European Societies* (Berlin: Policy Press).

Phillips, A. (1991a) 'Citizenship and Feminist Theory' in G. Andrews (ed.) *Citizenship* (London: Lawrence and Wishart), pp. 76–88.

Phillips, A. (1991b) *Engendering Democracy* (Cambridge: Polity Press).

Phillips, A. (1993) 'Citizenship and Feminist Theory' in A. Phillips *Democracy and Difference* (Cambridge: Polity Press).

Phillips, A. (1995) *The Politics of Presence* (Oxford: Clarendon Press).

Phillips, A. (1999) *Which Equality Matters?* (Cambridge and Oxford: Polity Press).

Phillips, A. (2007) *Multiculturalism without Culture* (Princeton: Princeton University Press).

Phillips, A. (2010) 'Einwilligung, Autonomie und Zwang: Erfahrungen in Großbritannien' [Consent, Autonomy and Coercion: Experiences in the UK] in S. Strasser and E. Holzleithner (eds) *Multikulturalismus queer gelesen. Zwangsheirat und gleichgeschlechtliche Ehe in pluralen Gesellschaften [Multiculturalism Read Queer. Forced Marriage and Same-sex Marriage in Plural Societies]* (Frankfurt am Main: Campus), pp. 182–201.

Phillips, A. and Saharso, S. (2008) 'Guest Editorial: The Rights of Women and the Crises of Multiculturalism', *Ethnicities*, vol. 8, no. 3, 291–301.

Phoenix, A. and Brah, A. (2004) 'Ain't I a Woman? Sojourner's "Truth"', *Journal of International Women's Studies*, vol. 5, no. 5, 75–85.

Pichardo, N.A. (1997) 'New Social Movements: A Critical Review', *Annual Review of Sociology*, vol. 23, 411–30.

Picq, F. (1993) *Libération des femmes: les années mouvement [Women's Liberation: The Movement Years]* (Paris: Seuil).

Pitcher, B. (2009) *The Politics of Multiculturalism: Race and Racism in Contemporary Britain* (Basingstoke: Palgrave Macmillan).

Pitkin, H. (1967) *The Concept of Representation* (Berkeley: University of California Press).

Plateau, N. (2009) 'The Women's Movement and the Challenge of Interculturality: The Case of French-speaking Belgium' in M. Franken, A. Woodward, A. Cabo and B. M. Bagilhole (eds) *Teaching Intersectionality: Putting Gender at the Centre* (Budapest and Stockholm: Central European University Press with Stockholm University), pp. 79–88.

Plummer, K. (1995) *Telling Sexual Stories: Power, Change and Social Worlds* (London: Routledge).

Plummer, K. (2003) *Intimate Citizenship: Private Discussions and Public Dialogues* (Seattle and London: University of Washington Press).

Pollart, A. (2003) 'Women, Work and Equal Opportunities in Post-Communist Transition', *Work, Employment & Society*, vol. 17, no. 2, 331–57.

Portet, S. (2004) 'Le temps partiel en Pologne: Un trompe-l'oeil de la segmentation sexuée du marché du travail' [Part-time Work in Poland: A Sham of Sexual Segmentation of the Labour Market], *Travail, genre et sociétés*, vol. 12, no. 2, 127–44.

Prabhavathi, V. (1991) *Perceptions, Motivations and Performance of Women A.P. State Legislators, 1956–83* (Columbia: South Asia Books).

Prata, A. (2010a) *Abortion in Portugal. Report on Portugal.* FEMCIT Deliverable to the European Commission. Work Package 5, Sexual & Bodily Citizenship. Leiden: Leiden University.

Prata, A. (2010b) *Prostitution and Trafficking in Portugal. Report on Portugal.* FEMCIT Deliverable to the European Commission. Work Package 5, Sexual & Bodily Citizenship. Leiden: Leiden University.

Prins B. and Saharso S. (2010) 'From Toleration to Repression: The Dutch Backlash against Multiculturalism' in S. Vertovec and S. Wessendorf (eds) *The Multiculturalism Backlash: European Discourses, Policies and Practices* (London and New York: Routledge) pp. 72–91.

Pristed Nielsen, H. and Thun, C. (2010) 'Inclusive Women's Organisations in Denmark and Norway?' *Kvinder, Køn og Forskning,* vol. 2, no. 3, 62–71.

Puar, J. K. (2007) *Terrorist Assemblages: Homonationalism in Queer Times* (Durham: Duke University Press).

Pulkrábková, K. (2009) 'The Roma Minority: Changing Definitions of Their Status' in H. Hašková and Z. Uhde (eds) *Women and Social Citizenship in Czech Society: Continuity and Change* (Prague: ISASCR).

Quota Project (2011) *Global Database of Quotas for Women,* http://www.quotaproject.org/, date accessed 16 February 2012.

Ramsay, R. (2003) *French Women in Politics* (London and New York: Berghahn).

Rantalaiho, M. (2003) 'Pohjoismaisen isyyspolitiikan isäkuva' [The Image of the Father in Nordic Fathers' Politics] in H. Forsberg and R. Nätkin (eds) *Perhe murroksessa. Kriittisen perhetutkimuksen jäljillä* (Helsinki: Gaudeamus).

Rantalaiho, M. (2010) 'Rationalities of Cash for Childcare: The Nordic Case' in J. Sipilä, K. Repo and T. Rissanen (eds) *Cash-For-Childcare: The Consequences for Caring Mothers* (Cheltenham: Edward Elgar).

Rathke, A. M. (1992) *Lady, If You Go into Politics: North Dakota's Women Legislators, 1923–1989* (N. Dakota: Sweetgrass Communications).

Raymond, J. G. (2002) 'The New UN Trafficking Protocol', *Women's Studies International Forum,* vol. 25, no. 5, 491–502.

Razack, S. (2004) 'Imperilled Muslim Women, Dangerous Muslim Men and Civilized Europeans: Legal and Social Responses to Forced Marriages', *Feminist Legal Studies,* vol. 12, no. 2, 129–74.

RD protocol (1994/95: 104) *Minutes Swedish Parliament.*

Reilly, N. (2009) *Women's Human Rights. Seeking Gender Justice in a Globalizing Age* (Cambridge: Polity Press).

Ribeiro, F. B., Ribeiro, M., Sacramento, O. and Silva, C. (2005) *Prostituição Abrigada em Clubes (Zonas fronteiriças do Minho e Trás-os-Montes) [Prostitution in Clubs (Border Areas in Minho and Trás-os Montes)]* (Lisbon: CIDM Colecção Estudos de Género).

Richardson, D. (2000) 'Constructing Sexual Citizenship: Theorizing Sexual Rights', *Critical Social Policy,* vol. 20, no.1, 105–35.

Rodrigues, E. (1995) 'Os novos movimentos sociais e o associativismo ambientalista em Portugal' [The New Social Movements and Environmental Activism in Portugal] *Oficina do CES,* vol. 60.

Rose, N. (2007) *The Politics of Life Itself. Biomedicine, Power and Subjectivity in the Twenty-First Century* (Princeton and Oxford: Princeton University Press).

Rose, N. and Miller, P. (1992) 'Political Power beyond the State: Problematics of Government', *British Journal of Sociology,* vol. 42, no. 2, 173–205.

Roseneil, S. (2000) 'Queer Frameworks and Queer Tendencies: Towards an Understanding of Postmodern Transformations of Sexuality', *Sociological Research*

Online, vol. 5. http://www.socresonline.org.uk/5/3/roseneil.html, date accessed 24 October 2011.

Roseneil, S. (ed.) (2010a) *Changing Cultural Discourses about Intimate Life: The Demands and Actions of Women's Movements and Other Movements for Gender and Sexual Equality and Change*. FEMCIT Working Paper No. 2, Work Package 6, Intimate Citizenship. London: Birkbeck, University of London. http://www.femcit.org/files/WP6_WorkingpaperNo2, date accessed 26 March 2010.

Roseneil, S. (2010b) 'Intimate Citizenship: A Pragmatic, Yet Radical, Proposal for a Politics of Personal Life', *European Journal of Women's Studies*, vol. 17, no. 1, 77–82.

Roseneil, S. (2012) 'Doing Feminist Social Research after the Cultural Turn: Research with Practical Intention' in S. Roseneil and S. Frosh (eds) *Social Research after the Cultural Turn* (Basingstoke: Palgrave Macmillan).

Roseneil, S. (ed) (forthcoming) *Beyond Citizenship: Feminism and the Transformation of Belonging* (Basingstoke: Palgrave Macmillan).

Roseneil, S. et al. (2008) *Policy Contexts and Responses to Changes in Intimate Life*. FEMCIT Working Paper No. 1, Work Package 6, Intimate Citizenship. London: Birkbeck, University of London. http://www.femcit.org/files/WP6_WorkingpaperNo1Revised.pdf, date accessed 24 October 2011.

Roseneil, S. et al. (2011) 'Intimate Citizenship and Gendered Well-being: the Claims and Interventions of Women's Movements in Europe' in J.-M. Bonvin, M. Renom and A. E. Woodward (eds) *Transforming Gendered Well-Being in Europe: the Role of Social Movements* (Farnham: Ashgate).

Roseneil, S. and Budgeon, S. (2004) 'Cultures of Intimacy and Care Beyond "the Family": Personal Life and Social Change in the Early 21st Century', *Current Sociology*, vol. 52, no. 2, 135–59.

Roseneil, S. and Stoilova, M. (2011) 'Heteronormativity and the Regulation of Intimate Citizenship in Bulgaria' in R. Kulpa and J. Mizielinska (eds) *De-Centring Western Sexualities: Central and Eastern European Perspectives* (London: Ashgate), pp. 167–90.

Roth, S. (2004) 'One Step Forwards, One Step Backwards, One Step Forwards. The Impact of EU Policy on Gender Relations in Central and Eastern Europe', *Transitions*, vol. 44, no. 1, 15–28.

Rouse, R. (1991) 'Mexican Migration and the Social Space of Postmodernism', *Diaspora: A Journal of Transnational Studies*, vol. 1, no. 1, 8–23.

Rovenský, J. (2009) 'Vláda lituje protiprávních sterilizací Romek' [The Government Regrets Illegal Sterilizations of Roma Women], *Právo*, 23 November 2009. http://www.novinky.cz/domaci/185092-vlada-lituje-protipravnich-sterilizaci-romek.html, date accessed 2 April 2011.

Runcis, M. (1998) *Steriliseringar i Folkhemmet [Sterilisations in "People's Home"]* (Stockholm: Ordfront).

Safi, M. (2008) 'The Immigrant Integration Process in France: Inequalities and Segmentation', *Revue française de sociologie*, vol. 49 (English language supplement), 3–44.

Saharso, S. (2003) 'Feminist Ethics, Autonomy and the Politics of Multiculturalism', *Feminist Theory*, vol. 4, no. 2, 199–215.

Saharso, S. (2005) 'Sex-selective Abortion: Gender, Culture and Dutch Public Policy', *Ethnicities*, vol. 5, no. 2, 248–81.

Sainsbury, D. (ed.) (1994) *Gendering Welfare States* (London: Sage).

Sainsbury, D. (ed.) (1999) *Gender and Welfare State Regimes* (Oxford: Oxford University Press).

Samad, Y. and Eade, J. (2002) *Community Perceptions of Forced Marriage* (London: Foreign and Commonwealth Office. Community Liaison Unit).

Santos, A. C. (2008) *Enacting Activism: Political, Legal and Social Impacts of LGBT Activism in Portugal*. PhD Thesis. University of Leeds.

Santos, B. S. (1992) *O Estado e a Sociedade em Portugal (1974 – 1988) [State and Society in Portugal (1974–1988)]* (Porto: Afrontamento).

Santos, B. S., Gomes, C., Duarte, M. and Baganha, M. (2008) *Tráfico de mulheres em Portugal para fins de exploração sexual [Trafficking Women in Portugal for Sexual Exploitation]* (Porto: CIG Colecção Estudos de Género).

Santos, C. A. and Cunha, I. F. (2006) 'Media, Immigration and Ethnic Minorities II', *Immigration Observatory* 19, High Commission for Immigration and Ethnic Minorities (Lisbon: ACIME), pp. 19–108.

Saraceno, C. and Keck, W. (2010) 'Can We Identify Intergenerational Policy Regimes in Europe?', *European Societies*, vol. 12, no. 5, 675–96.

Sassen, S. (2002) 'Towards Post-National and Denationalized Citizenship' in E. F. Işın and B. S. Turner (eds) *Citizenship Studies* (London: Sage), pp. 277–92.

Sawer, M. and S. Grey (eds) (2008) *Women's Movements: Flourishing Or in Abeyance?* London and New York: Routledge.

Saxonberg, S. and Sirovátka, T. (2006) 'Failing Family Policy in Post-Communist Central Europe', *Journal of Comparative Policy Analysis: Research and Practice*, vol. 8, no. 2, 185–202.

Scheffer, P. (2001) 'Das Multikulturelle Drama' [The Multicultural Drama] in *Frankfurter Allgemeine Zeitung*, 21 Juli, 1–2 (first published as *Het multiculturele drama* in NRC Handelsblad, 29.1.2000).

Scharff, C. (2011) 'It Is a Colour Thing and a Status Thing, Rather Than a Gender Thing, Negotiating Difference in Talk about Feminism', *Feminism & Psychology* 21(4): 458–76.

Schiller, M. (2010) 'Zwangsverheiratung im Fokus: Ein Vergleich von Auftragsstudien in europäischen Ländern' [Forced Marriage in Focus: A Comparison of Commissioned Studies in European Countries] in S. Strasser and E. Holzleithner (eds) *Multikulturalismus queer gelesen. Zwangsheirat und gleichgeschlechtliche Ehe in pluralen Gesellschaften [Multiculturalism Read Queer. Forced Marriage and Same-sex Marriage in Plural Societies]* (Frankfurt am Main: Campus), pp. 47–70.

Schmidt, V. (2010) 'Taking Ideas Seriously: Explaining Change through Discursive Institutionalism as the fourth New Institutionalism', *European Political Science Review*, vol. 2, no. 1, 1–25.

Searing, D. D. (1994) *Westminster's World* (Cambridge, MA: Harvard University Press).

Sedgh, G. et al. (2007) 'Legal Abortion Worldwide: Incidence and Recent Trends', *International Family Planning Perspectives*, vol. 33, no. 3, 106–16.

Seikkula, M. and Rantalaiho, M. (2010) *Childcare Arrangements among the Roma in Finland*. FEMCIT Deliverable to the European Commission. Work Package 2, Social Citizenship. Oslo: Nordic Gender Institute, NIKK.

Sevenhuijsen, S. (1998) *Citizenship and the Ethics of Care: Feminist Considerations on Justice, Morality and Politics* (London and New York: Routledge).

Sevenhuijsen, S. (2003) 'The Place of Care: The Relevance of the Feminist Ethic of Care for Social Policy', *Feminist Theory*, vol. 4, no. 2, 179–97.

Shachar, A. (2000) 'On Citizenship and Multicultural Vulnerability', *Political Theory*, vol. 28, 64–89.

Shachar, A. (2001) *Multicultural Jurisdictions. Cultural Differences and Women's Rights* (Cambridge: Cambridge University Press).

Shaver, S. (1994) 'Body Rights, Social Rights and the Liberal Welfare State', *Critical Social Policy*, vol. 39, 66–93.

Siim, B. (1991) 'Welfare State, Gender Politics and Equality Policies: Women's Citizenship in the Scandinavian Welfare States' in E. Meehan and S. Sevenhuijsen (eds) *Equality Politics and Gender* (London: Sage).

Siim, B. (2000) *Gender and Citizenship. Politics and Agency in France, Britain and Denmark* (Cambridge: Cambridge University Press).

Siim, B. (2003) *Medborgerskabets Udfordringer: Etniske Minotritetskvinders Politiske Myndiggørelse [The Challenges of Citizenship: Political Maturity of Ethnic Minority Women]* (Aarhus: Magtudredningen).

Siim, B. (2007) 'The Challenge of Recognizing Diversity from the Perspective of Gender Equality: Dilemmas in Danish Citizenship', *Critical Review of International Social and Political Philosophy*, vol. 10, no. 4, 491–511.

Siim, B. and Squires, J. (2007) 'Contesting Citizenship: Comparative Analyses', *Critical Review of International Social and Political Philosophy*, vol. 10, no. 4, 403–16.

Siim, B. and Squires, J. (eds) (2008) *Contesting Citizenship* (London and New York: Routledge).

Silberman, R. and Fournier, I. (2008) 'Second Generations on the Job Market in France: A Persistent Ethnic Penalty', *Revue française de sociologie*, vol. 49, 45–94.

Simonazzi, A. (2008) 'Care Regimes and National Employment Models', *Cambridge Journal of Economics*, vol. 10, 1–22.

Skeggs, B. (1997) *Formations of Gender and Class* (London: Sage).

Skilbrei, M.-L. (2005) 'Klasse, etnisitet og kjønn som erfaringer: om å være vanlig, arbeidsom og anstendig' [Class, Ethnicity and Gender as Experience: On Being Normal, Hard-working and Decent], *Sosiologi i dag*, vol. 4, 50–68.

Smart, C. and Shipman, B. (2004) 'Visions in Monochrome: Families, Marriage and the Individualization Thesis', *British Journal of Sociology*, vol. 55, no. 4, 491–509.

Smith, B. G. (2000) *Global Feminisms since 1945: Rewriting Histories* (London: Routledge).

Smith, R. M. (2002) 'Modern Citizenship' in E. F. Işın and B. S. Turner (eds) *Handbook of Citizenship Studies* (London: Sage), pp. 105–16.

SOU (1981) *Prostitution i Sverige. Bakgrund och Åtgärder* (Stockholm: Liberförlag).

Soysal, Y. (1994) *Limits of Citizenship: Migrants and Postnational Membership in Europe* (Chicago: University of Chicago Press).

Sparks, H. (1997) 'Dissident Citizenship: Democratic Theory, Political Courage, and Activist Women', *Hypatia*, vol. 12, no. 4, 74–110

Spinner-Halev, J. (2005) 'Autonomy, association and pluralism', in A. Eisenberg and J. Spinner-Halev (eds) *Minorities within Minorities: Equality, Rights and Diversity*, (Cambridge: Cambridge University Press), pp. 157–71.

Squires, J. (1999) *Gender in Political Theory* (Cambridge: Polity Press).

Squires, J. (2007) *The New Politics of Gender Equality* (Basingstoke: Palgrave Macmillan).

Srivastava, S. (2005) 'You're Calling Me a Racist? The Moral and Emotional Regulation of Anti-Racism and Feminism', *Signs: Journal of Women and Culture in Society*, vol. 31, no. 1, 29–62.

Staatsblad (1998). Nr 336, Besluit van 26 mei 1998, houdende een verbod op geslachtskeuze om niet-medische redenen (Besluit verbod geslachtskeuze om niet-medische redenen).

Staatsblad (2009) *Besluit van 18 mei 2009, houdende wijziging van het Besluit afbreking zwangerschap (vaststelling zwangerschapsduur)[Decree of 18 May 2009, Change of*

Resolution about Termination of Pregnancy (Determining the Duration of Pregnancy)], no. 230, 9 June.

Statens offentliga utredningar (SOU) [Swedish Government Official Reports] (1983) *Familjeplanering och abort: erfarenheter av ny lagstiftning [Family Planning and Abortion: Experiences of New Law Implementations]*, no. 31 (Stockholm: Liber/Allmänna förlaget).

Statens offentliga utredningar (SOU) [Swedish Government Official Reports] (1996) *Kvinnofrid [Women's Peace]*, no. 60A.

Statens offentliga utredningar (SOU) [Swedish Government Official Reports] (2001) *Sexualbrotten. Ett ökat skydd för den sexuella integriteten och angränsande frågor [Sexual Crime. An Increased Protection for Sexual Integrity and Relating Questions]*, no. 14.

Statens offentliga utredningar (SOU) [Swedish Government Official Reports] (2002) *Människosmuggling och offer för människohandel [Human Trafficking and Victims of Human Trafficking]*, no. 69.

Statens offentliga utredningar (SOU) [Swedish Government Official Reports] (2008) *Människohandel och barnäktenskap – ett förstärkt straffrättsligt skydd [Human Trafficking and Child Marriage – a Strengthened Penal Protection]*, no. 41.

Statens offentliga utredningar (SOU) [Swedish Government Official Reports] (2010) *Förbud mot köp av sexuell tjänst. En utvärdering 1999–2008 [Prohibition of the Buying of Sexual Services. An Evaluation 1999–2008]*, no. 49. http://www.sweden.gov.se /content/1/c6/11/98/61/2ac7d62b.pdf, date accessed 11 December 2011.

Staunæs, D. (2003) 'Where Have All the Subjects Gone? Bringing Together the Concepts of Intersectionality and Subjectification', *NORA: Nordic Journal of Women's Studies*, vol. 11, no. 2, 101–10.

Staunæs, D. and Søndergaard, D. M. (2006) 'Intersektionalitet – Udsat for Teoretisk Justering' [Intersectionality – Exposed to Theoretical Adjustment], *Kvinder, Køn & Forskning [Women, Gender and Research]*, vol. 15, no. 2–3, 43–56.

Stevens, A. (2007) *Women, Power and Politics* (Basingstoke: Palgrave).

Stevens, J. (1999) *Reproducing the State* (Princeton, NJ: Princeton University Press).

Stocking G. W. (1968) *Race, Culture, and Evolution: Essays in the History of Anthropology* (Basingstoke: Macmillan).

Stoltz, P. (2000) *About Being (T)here and Making a Difference: Black Women and the Paradox of Visibility* (Lund: Department of Political Science, Lund University).

Strasser, S. (2008) 'Ist doch Kultur an allem Schuld? Ehre und kulturelles Unbehagen in den Debatten um Gleichheit und Diversität' [Is Culture to Blame After All? Honour and Cultural Discomfort in Debates about Equality and Diversity] in B. Sauer and S. Strasser (eds) *Zwangsfreiheiten. Feminismus und Multikulturalismus [Forced Freedoms. Feminism and Multiculturalism]* (Vienna: Promedia), pp. 63–77.

Strasser, S. (2009) *Bewegte Zugehörigkeiten. Nationale Spannungen, transnationale Praktiken und transversale Politik [Moving Affiliations. National Tensions, Transnational Practices and Transversal Politics]* (Vienna: Turia & Kant).

Strasser, S. (2010) 'Ist der Multikulturalismus noch zu retten?' [Can Multiculturalism Still be Saved?] in S. Strasser and E. Holzleithner (eds) *Multikulturalismus queer gelesen. Zwangsheirat und gleichgeschlechtliche Ehe in pluralen Gesellschaften [Multiculturalism Read Queer. Forced Marriage and Same-Sex Marriage in Plural Societies]* (Frankfurt am Main: Campus), pp. 342–66.

Strasser, S. and Markom C. (2010) 'Kulturelles Unbehagen: eine kleine Stadt und ihre große Sorgen' [Cultural Discomfort: A Small Town and Its Big Worries] in Strasser, S. and Holzleithner, E. (eds) *Multikulturalismus queer gelesen. Zwangsheirat und gleichgeschlechtliche Ehe in pluralen Gesellschaften [Multiculturalism Read Queer. Forced*

Marriage and Same-sex Marriage in Plural Societies] (Frankfurt am Main: Campus), pp. 71–119.

Stratigaki, M. (2004) 'The Cooptation of Gender Concepts in EU Policies: The Case of "Reconciliation of Work and Family"', *Social Politics: International Studies in Gender, State and Society,* vol. 11, no. 1, 30–56.

Stratigaki, M. (2005) 'Gender Mainstreaming vs Positive Action', *European Journal of Women's Studies,* vol. 12, no. 2, 165–86.

Sudbury, J. (1998) *Other Kinds of Dreams: Black Women's Organisations and the Politics of Transformation* (London: Routledge).

Sümer, S. (2009) *European Gender Regimes and Policies: Comparative Perspectives* (Farnham: Ashgate).

Svanström, Y. (2006a) *Offentliga Kvinnor: Prostitution i Sverige 1812–1918 [Public Women: Prostitution in Sweden 1812–1918]* (Stockholm: Ordfront).

Svanström, Y. (2006b) 'Prostitution in Sweden: Debates and Policies 1980–2004' in G. Gangoli and N. Westmarland (eds) *International Approaches to Prostitution, Law and Policy in Europe and Asia* (Bristol: The Policy Press), pp. 67–90.

Szikra, D. (2010) 'Eastern European Faces of Familialism: Hungarian and Polish Family Policies from a Historical Perspective' in Á. Scharle (ed.) *Manka Goes to Work. Public Childcare in the Visegrad Countries 1989–2009* (Budapest: Budapest Institute for Policy Analysis). http://www.budapestinstitute.eu/uploads/manka_goes_to_work_2010.pdf, date accessed 5 December 2011.

Tahon, M.-B. (2004) *Sociologie des rapports de sexe [Sociology of Gender Relations]* (Rennes and Ottawa: Presses universitaires de Rennes/Presses de l'université d'Ottawa).

Tambakaki, P. (2009) *Human Rights, or Citizenship?* (Abingdon and New York: Birkbeck Law Press).

Tarrow, S. (2005) *The New Transnational Activism* (New York: Cambridge University Press).

Tastsoglou, E. and Dobrowolsky, A. (eds) (2006) *Women, Migration and Citizenship* (Aldershot: Ashgate).

Tavares, M. (2003) *Aborto e Contracepção em Portugal [Abortion and Contraception in Portugal]* (Lisbon: Livros Horizonte).

Tavares, M. (2006) *Prostituição. Diferentes posicionamentos no movimento feminista [Prostitution. Different Perspectives on the Feminist Movement],* http://www.umarfeminismos.org/images/stories/pdf/prostituicaomantavares.pdf, date accessed 2 November 2010.

Taylor, C. (1996) *Multiculturalism and 'The Politics of Recognition'* (Princeton: Princeton University Press).

Taylor, P. C. (2004) *Race: A Philosophical Introduction* (Cambridge: Polity Press).

Taylor-Gooby, P. (2008) 'The New Welfare State Settlement in Europe', *European Societies,* vol. 10, no. 1, 3–24.

The Runnymede Trust (2000) *The Future of Multi-Ethnic Britain. The Parekh Report.* Commission on the Future of Multi-Ethnic Britain and the Runnymede Trust. (London: Profile Books).

Therborn, G. (2004) *Between Sex and Power: Family in the World, 1900–2000* (London: Routledge).

Thomas C. (2009) *Forced and Early Marriage: A Focus on Central and Eastern Europe and Former Soviet Union Countries,* http://www.un.org/womenwatch/daw/egm/vaw_legislation_2009/Expert%20Paper%20EGMGPLHP%20_Cheryl%20Thomas%20revised_.pdf, date accessed 10 October 2011.

Threlfall, M. (1996) 'Feminist Politics and Social Change in Spain' in M. Threlfall (ed.) *Mapping the Women's Movement* (London: Verso), pp. 115–51.

Threlfall, M. (2004) 'Towards Parity Representation in Party Politics' in M. Threlfall, with C. Cousins and C. Valiente *Gendering Spanish Democracy* (London: Routledge), pp.125–62.

Threlfall, M. (2007) 'Explaining Gender Parity Representation in Spain: The Internal Dynamics of Parties', *West European Politics*, vol. 30, no. 5, 1068–95.

Threlfall, M. (2009) *Feeling Represented: Diverse Women's Needs and Preferences for their Political Representation in a Multiethnic Europe*. ECPR General Conference, Potsdam, Germany, 10–12 September 2009.

Thun, C. (2011) ' "Norwegian Women got Gender Equality through their Mother's Milk, but Anti-racism is another Story". An Analysis of Power and Resistance in the Norwegian Feminist Discourse', forthcoming in *NORA – Nordic Journal of Feminist and Gender Research*.

Thun, C. (forthcoming) *Women-Friendly Funding? Conditions for Women's Organizations' Critical Advocacy in Norway.*

Tinker, I. (1983) *Women in Washington* (Beverley Hills and London: Sage).

Towns, A. (2002) 'Paradoxes of (In)Equality. Something is Rotten in the Gender Equal State of Sweden', *Cooperation and Conflict*, vol. 2, 157–79.

Transcrime (2005) *Study on National Legislation on Prostitution and the Trafficking in Women and Children*. European Parliament, Policy Department C. Citizens' Rights and Constitutional Affairs, Universitá degli Studi di Trento/Università Cattolica del Sacro Cuore. http://transcrime.cs.unitn.it/tc/412.php, date accessed 30 September 2009.

Tweede Kamer (1997–2011) *Handelingen [Official Reports from the Second Chamber of the Dutch Parliament]*

Tyyskä, V. (1995) *The Politics of Caring and the Welfare State. The Impact of the Women's Movement on Child Care Policy in Canada and Finland, 1960–1990*, Suomalaisen tie-deakatamien toimituksia, Sarja-ser. B: 277 (Helsinki: Suomalainen tiedeakatemia).

Uhde, Z. (forthcoming) 'Autoritářství trhu: kritická diagnóza deformované eman-cipace žen' [The Market Authoritarianism: Critical Diagnosis of Distorted Emancipation of Women] *Filosofický časopis*, vol. 60, no. 1.

Uhde, Z., Dudová, R., Pulkrábková, K. and Soudková, S. (eds) (2009) *Report on the Activities and Political Claims of Majority Women's NGOs and Minoritised Women's and Gender-based NGOs or Groups on Care, and Specifically on Childcare in the Czech Republic Since the End of the Second World War*. FEMCIT Working paper No. 2, Work Package 2, Social Citizenship. Praha: Academy of Science of the Czech Republic. http://www. femcit.org/files/WP2_WorkingpaperNo2.pdf, date accessed 10 May 2010.

UN General Assembly (2007) *Protection of Migrants: Report of the Secretary General*, 62nd Session, A/62/299, 24 August 2007.

UN Women (1995) *Beijing Declaration and Platform for Action, ch.1, §1*. 4th World Conference on Women. http://www.un.org/womenwatch/daw/beijing/platform/, date accessed 16 February 2012.

Ungerson, C. (2003) 'Commodified Care Work in European Labour Markets', *European Societies*, vol. 5, no. 4, 377–96.

Valiente, C. (2002) 'The Value of an Educational Emphasis: Child Care and Restructuring in Spain since 1975' in S. Michel and R. Mahon (eds) *Child Care Policy at the Crossroads: Gender and Welfare State Restructuring* (New York: Routledge).

Valiente, C. (2003a) 'Central State Child Care Policies in Postauthoritarian Spain: Implications for Gender and Carework arrangements', *Gender & Society*, vol. 17, no. 2, 287–92.

Valiente, C. (2003b) 'The Feminist Movement and the Reconfigured State in Spain (1979s-2000)' in L. A. Banaszak, K. Beckwith and D. Rucht (eds) *Women's Movements Facing the Reconfigured State* (Cambridge: Cambridge University Press), pp. 30–47.

Valiente, C. (2009) 'Child Care in Spain after 1975: The Educational Rationale, the Catholic Church, and Women in Civil society' in K. Schelwe and H. Willeken (eds) *Child Care and Preschool Development in Europe: Institutional Perspectives* (Basingstoke and New York: Palgrave Macmillan).

Valiente, C. (2011) '(Pre)school Is Not Childcare: Preschool and Primary School Education Policies in Spain since the 1930s' in K. Hagemann, K. H. Jarausch, and C. Allemann-Ghionda (eds) *Children, Families, and States: Time Policies of Childcare, Preschool and Primary Education in Europe* (New York and Oxford: Berghahn).

van Houdt, F., Suvarieol, S. and Schinkel, W. (2011) 'Neoliberal Communitarian Citizenship – Current Trends Towards "Earned Citizenship" in the United Kingdom, France and the Netherlands', *International Sociology*, vol. 26, no. 4, 408–32.

Verloo, M. and Lombardo, E. (2007) 'Contested Gender Equality and Policy Variety in Europe: Introducing a Critical Frame Analysis Approach' in M. Verloo (ed.) *Multiple Meanings of Gender Equality. A Critical Frame Analysis of Gender Policies in Europe* (Budapest: CPS Books), pp. 21–50.

Vertovec, S. (1999) 'Conceiving and Researching Transnationalism', *Ethnic and Racial Studies*, vol. 22, no. 2, 447–62.

Vertovec, S. (2007) 'Super-diversity and Its Implications', *Ethnic and Racial Studies*, vol. 29, no. 6, 1024–54.

Vertovec, S. and Wessendorf, S. (eds) (2010) *The Multicultural Backlash. European Discourses, Policies and Practices* (London: Routledge).

Viegas, J. M. L. (2004) 'Implicações democráticas das associações voluntárias: O caso português numa perspectiva comparativa europeia' [Democratic Implications of Voluntary Organizations: The Portuguese Case in a Comparative European Perspective], *Sociologia, Problemas e Práticas*, vol. 46, 33–50.

Vláda České Republiky (2009) *Dvanáct bodů k snahám českého předsednictví otevřít debatu o barcelonských cílech [Twelve Arguments by the Czech EU Presidency in order to open the Debate on Barcelona Targets]*, http://www.vlada.cz/cz/media-centrum/aktualne/reakce-ceskeho-predsednictvi-na-prohlaseni-evropske-socialisticke-strany-53174/, date accessed 5 December 2011.

Vlček, M. (1985) *Příživnictví v československém trestním právu [Parasitism in Czechoslovak Criminal Law]* (Prague: Academia).

Voet, R. (1998) *Feminism and Citizenship* (London: Sage).

Vuorela, U. (2009) 'Colonial Complicity: The "Postcolonial" in a Nordic Context' in S. Keskinen, S. Tuori, S. Imi and D. Mulinari (eds) *Complying with Colonialism: Gender, Race and Ethnicity in the Nordic Region* (Farnham: Ashgate).

Walby, S. (1994) 'Is Citizenship Gendered?', *Sociology*, vol. 28, no. 2, 379–96.

Walby, S. (2004) 'The European Union and Gender Equality: Emergent Varieties of Gender Regime', *Social Politics: International Studies in Gender, State & Society*, vol. 11, no. 1, 4–29.

Walby, S. (2009) *Globalization & Inequalities: Complexity and Contested Modernities* (London: Sage).

Wall, K. and Escobedo, A. (2009) 'Portugal and Spain: Two Pathways in Southern Europe' in S. B. Kamerman and P. Moss (eds) *The Politics of Parental Leave: Children, Parenting, Gender and the Labour Market* (Bristol: Policy Press).

Walter, N. (1998) *The New Feminism* (London: Little Brown).

Wängnerud, L. (2009) 'Women in Parliaments: Descriptive and Substantive Representation', *Annual Review of Political Science*, vol. 12, 51–69.

Weeks, J. (2007) *The World We Have Won: the Remaking of Erotic and Intimate Life* (London and New York: Routledge).

Wengraf, T. (2007) *Guide to BNIM Biographic-Narrative Interpretative Method: Interviewing for Life-Histories, Lived Situations and Ongoing Personal Experiencing*, tom@tomwengraf.com. Version 7.11e.

Werbner, P. and Yuval-Davis, N. (1999) 'Introduction: Women and the New Discourse of Citizenship' in N. Yuval-Davis and P. Werbner *Women, Citizenship and Difference* (London and New York: Zed Press).

Wijsen, C., Lee, L. v. and Koolstra, H. (2007) *Abortus in Nederland 2001–2005 [Abortion in the Netherlands 2001–2005]* (Delft: Eburon).

Wikan, U. (2002) *Generous Betrayal: Politics of Culture in the New Europe* (Chicago: University of Chicago Press).

Williams, F. (2009) *Claims and Frames in the Making of Care Policies in Europe: Recognition, Rights and Redistribution*. Paper submitted to RC19 meeting Social Policies: Local Experiments, Travelling Ideas, Université de Montréal, Canada, 20–22 August 2009.

Williams, F. and Gavanas, A. (2008) 'The Intersection of Childcare Regimes and Migration Regimes: A Three Country Study' in H. Lutz (ed.) *Migration and Domestic Work: A European Perspective on a Global Theme* (Aldershot and Burlington: Ashgate).

Williams, J. C. (2000) *Unbending Gender: Why Family and Work Conflict and What To Do About It* (Oxford: Oxford University Press).

Wimmer A. and Glick Schiller, N. (2002) 'Methodological Nationalism and Beyond: Nation–state Building, Migration and the Social Sciences', *Global Networks*, vol. 2, no. 4, 301–34.

Worley, C. (2005) ' "It's not about Race. It's about Community": New Labour and "Community Cohesion" ', *Critical Social Policy*, vol. 25, no. 4, 483–96.

Young, I. M. (1989) 'Polity and Group Difference: A Critique of the Ideal of Universal Citizenship', *Ethics*, vol. 99, 250–74.

Young, I. M. (1990) *Justice and the Politics of Difference* (Princeton: Princeton University Press).

Young, I. M. (2000) *Inclusion and Democracy* (Oxford: Oxford University Press).

Yuval-Davis, N. (1997a) 'Women, Citizenship and Difference', *Feminist Review*, vol. 57, 4–27.

Yuval-Davis, N. (1997b) *Gender and Nation* (London: Sage).

Yuval-Davis, N. (1999a) 'The "Multi-Layered Citizen": Citizenship in the Age of "Glocalization" ', *International Feminist Journal of Politics*, vol. 1, no. 1, 119–37.

Yuval-Davis, N. (1999b) 'What is "Transversal Politics"?', *Soundings*, vol. 12, 94–98.

Yuval-Davis, N. (2006) 'Intersectionality and Feminist Politics', *European Journal of Women Studies*, vol. 13, no. 3, 193–209.

Yuval-Davis, N. (2008) 'Intersectionality, Citizenship and Contemporary Politics of Belonging' in B. Siim and J. Squires (eds) *Contesting Citizenship* (London: Routledge), pp. 159–72.

Yuval-Davis, N. (2010) '*What is "Transversal Politics?"*' Geopolitical Everyday (blog) March 14, http://geopoliticaleveryday.wordpress.com/2010/03/14/what-is-transversal-politics-nira-yuval-davis/, date accessed 13 January 2012.

Yuval-Davis, N., Anthias, F. and Kofman, E. (2005) 'Secure Borders and Safe Haven and the Gendered Politics of Belonging: Beyond Social Cohesion', *Ethnic and Racial Studies*, vol. 28, no. 3, 513–35.

Yuval-Davis, N. and Werbner, P. (1999a) 'Introduction: Women and the New Discourse of Citizenship', in N. Yuval-Davis and P. Werbner (eds) *Women, Citizenship and Difference* (London: Zed Books).

Yuval-Davis, N. and Werbner, P. (eds) (1999b) *Women, Citizenship and Difference* (London and New York: Zed Books).

Zajíček, K. (1973) 'Přes sto tisíc zmařených životů. Jaké změny v povolování interrupcí?' [Over One Hundred Thousand Destroyed Lives. What Changes in Permission of Abortions?], *Vlasta*, vol. 29, no. 19, 20.

Zapata-Barrero, R. (2010) 'Managing Diversity in Spanish Society: A Practical Approach', *Journal of Intercultural Studies*, vol. 31, no. 4, 383–402.

Zaretsky, E. (2005) *Secrets of the Soul: A Social and Cultural History of Psychoanalysis* (New York, Vintage Books).

Zimmerman, M. K., Litt, J. S. and Bose, C. E. (eds) (2006) *Global Dimensions of Gender and Care* (Stanford: Stanford University Press).

Zontini, E. (2007) *Transnational Families*, Sloane Families Research Network. http://wfnetwork.bc.edu/encyclopedia_entry.php?id=6361&area=All, date accessed 22 September 2011.

Index

abolitionism, 127, 130, 132, 138, 139
  see also prostitution
abortion, 5, 14, 46, 48, 119–27, 133,
    135–7, 139–40, 214–15, 220, 227
  1981 Abortion Act, 122, 123, 126
  as a bodily right, 119, 136–7
  criminalization of, 121, 137
  decriminalization of, 122,
    124, 125
  on demand, 121, 123–4, 136
  limitation of access to, 123
  as a medical entitlement, 119, 136
  tourism, 122
  see also sex selection
'active fatherhood', 107–9
'active motherhood', 108
activism, 17, 25, 38, 46–7, 84, 125,
    167–9, 175–6, 178–80, 182, 187–9,
    191, 201, 208, 210–11
  see also feminist activists;
    transnational activism; women's
    movement activists
adult citizen worker, 11–12, 71, 76, 80–1,
    83–4, 86, 88, 90–2
agency, 3, 5, 12, 15, 25, 41–3, 64–5,
    68, 94, 97, 99, 112, 131–2, 142, 148,
    174, 182–3
  deficit, 15, 142, 146–9, 157–8, 161–3
anti-racist
  movement, 7, 132, 193–4, 198, 200,
    204
  policies, 198, 200
anti-trafficking legislation, 129–30,
    134, 138
Armbruster, Heidi, 22, 30, 37
assimilationism, 26, 28
autonomy, 5, 9, 14, 20, 23, 25–6, 36–8,
    41, 49, 63, 83–4, 88, 92, 118, 120,
    122, 126, 131, 136, 139–40
  economic, 26, 83–4, 88, 100
  sexual, 28–9, 38, 55
  see also self-determination

Bacchi, Carol, 98, 119
Bambra, Clare, 70, 73, 89

Barcelona Agreement, 101
Beasley, Chris, 119
Beck, Ulrich, 7, 23, 43, 81, 84
Beijing, *see* United Nations 4th World
    Conference on Women
Belgium, 6, 16, 19, 40, 122, 166, 170–1,
    175, 178, 181, 183, 185, 187, 215,
    217–18, 220, 222, 224
  see also Brussels
belonging, 1, 3, 8, 9, 16–17, 21, 25,
    30–3, 36–7, 41, 59, 65, 69, 118, 141,
    169, 174, 183, 190–1, 194–8, 200–1,
    207–10
Benhabib, Seyla, 22–3, 27, 36, 97,
    189–90
Bergman, Solveig, 12, 19, 32, 71, 74, 78,
    94–117, 123, 161, 189, 202
Berlant, Lauren, 42, 68
biographical-narrative interpretative
    method, 6, 10, 44, 215
bodily citizenship, 4, 13–14, 19, 42,
    118–19, 124, 135–40, 189, 214–15,
    220
bodily integrity, 13, 46, 65–6, 118–19,
    139–40
Brubaker, Rogers, 26, 28, 190
Brussels, 170–1, 173–4, 181–3, 185
Bulgaria, 6, 10, 19, 44, 46–7, 49–51,
    53, 56, 58–63, 68–9, 134, 200,
    211–12, 214–15, 217–18, 220,
    222, 224

capitalism, 12, 79, 81, 84, 93,
    235, 241
care, 12–13, 25, 32, 39, 70, 72–4, 80–1,
    92, 95–6, 109–10, 116
  'care work paradox', 91
  child-, 5, 12–13, 19, 32, 46, 48–50, 71,
    72, 78, 83, 94–108, 109–17, 161,
    214, 222
  collectivization of, 83
  commodification of, 12, 70–2, 80–1,
    85, 92
  day-, 12–13, 19
  domestic, 78, 81, 86, 91